Michael Joe Okpalanozie

Christianity, Islam and African Traditional Religion in Nigeria

Conflicts and Challenges to Peaceful Co-existence

THEOLOGISCHE REIHE, BAND 095

Michael Joe Okpalanozie

Christianity, Islam and African Traditional Religion in Nigeria

Conflicts and Challenges to Peaceful Co-existence

eos

First impression 2011
ISBN 978-3-8306-7500-6

A catalogue record for this book is available from the German Library
http://dnb.ddb.de

EOS – Editions of Sankt Ottilien
www.eos-verlag.de | mail@eos-verlag.de
Printed in Germany

This book is dedicated
to my late Parents
Mr/Mrs Edmund/Caroline Okpalanozie
and my Friend,
late Msgr. Martin Okpala

TABLE OF CONTENTS

CHAPTER TWO
ISLAM IN NIGERIA:
SPREAD, ORGANISATIONS AND SECTS

CHAPTER THREE
PROBLEMS AND CONFLICTS

CHAPTER FOUR
KATHOLIC CHURCH DOCUMENTATIONS
ON CALLS FOR PEACE IN NIGERIA

CHAPTER FIVE
THE EFFORTS OF THE MOSLEMS AND THE ADHERENTS
OF AFRICAN TRADITIONAL RELIGION
FOR PEACE IN NIGERIA

CHAPTER SIX
AREAS OF COLLABORATION BETWEEN CHRISTIANITY,
ISLAM AND AFRICAN TRADITIONAL RELIGION
IN A FUTURE NIGERIA

CHAPTER SEVEN
EVALUATION AND CONCLUSION

ACKNOWLEDGEMENT

A work of this magnitude could never have seen the light of day if I were to do it all alone. That it has come to this level is as a result of contributions of many well wishers and supporters. It is on this note that I wish to sincerely appreciate the efforts of many who contributed in making this work, 'a dream come true', taking note of course the impossibility of mentioning by name all who contributed to this success story.

My gratitude goes, first of all, to God Almighty who, through his love and gracious ubiquitous presence, granted me the desired health and energy throughout the period of the studies. I remember and appreciate in a very special way, my beloved late Parents, Mr/Mrs Edmund and Caroline Okpalanozie, who were the very first tender and loving teachers of my life. May you be peacefully rested in the Lord. I am grateful to Late Very Rev. Msgr. Martin Okpala, who made it possible for me to ever start this academic pursuit overseas. Unfortunately, he could not live to see its conclusion. He is an admirable mentor who positively touched so many souls. Though deceased, he lives on in his good works. May he find eternal rest in the bosom of Our Lord Jesus Christ.

Prof. Dr. Günter Riße is a professor per excellence. His friendly and brotherly disposition and approach to the moderation of this work is second to none. He offered me the highest desired decorum for a research work. The way he helped in sourcing for work materials and posting them to me beat my imagination. The devotion and thunder-like promptness with which he read my work and gave immediate suggestions cannot but be described as "Super". Remain ever blessed as I will remain ever grateful. Prof. Dr. Vellguth Klaus, is worthy of my gratitude. His articles on Nigerian situations speak volumes of his interest in anything Nigeria. I benefited from them too. I thank him for gladly accepting to be the second moderator of this work.

I extend my gratitude to my Bishop Emeritus, Most Rev. Dr. S. A. Okafor with whose permission this academic journey was undertaken. My appreciation goes also to my incumbent - His Lordship, Most Rev. Dr. P. C. Ezeokafor, under whose administration this work was completed. I appreciate the magnanimity of the Diocese of Trier for offering me a place to stay and help in pastoral duties as I studied. In line with this, I thank Rev. Fr. Martin Röhrig for allowing the use of one of the Fathers' houses under his care. I thank also the Parishioners of Alken/Löf 'Seelsorgeeinheit' for their good will and support. May God grant them health of mind and body.

I appreciate immensely the brotherliness and friendliness of Prof. Dr. Johannes Rütsche who I always refer to as brother in foreign land (Nwanne di na mba). His piety, humility and dedication to his apostolate which speak for themselves constitute also a challenge to me. Also worthy of thanks is Very Rev. Fr. Rüsche Friedhelm. His joviality, openness and readiness to help is worthy of emulation. He is really an amiable Pastor. I remain grateful to Rev. Fr. Dr. Anthony Onyekwelu who, on my visit to America made it possible for me to have access to Fordham University Library. Apart from the "fruit-ful- friendly merciless wickedness" with which he critically read through and corrected the whole manuscript, he made enriching useful suggestions that will ever be appreciated. In the same vein, I thank Rev. Fr. Dr. Augustine Okochi, who also read through the whole work to make the final corrections. My unalloyed gratitude goes to Very Rev. Dr. Msgr. Dennis Isizoh who not only allowed me free access to Vatican Library but also gave out some pertinent books at no cost. The books recommended by Very Rev. Msgr. M. Kukah, his brotherly advice and encouragement were very contributive and therefore appreciated. The patience exhibited by the workers at the African Department of the Missiological Institute Library in Aachen, Germany, when I visited them in the course of my research is commendably appreciated.

I remain ever grateful to Mrs. Weyler Helene, Mrs. Rosalia Fogt, Mr/Mrs. Rudi and Helga Schaaf, Mr/Mrs. Hermann-Josef and Anneliese Schütz. Others are the families of Mr/Mrs. Rudolf and Christa Hüber-Allemann, Mr/Mrs. Jurgen and Karin Braun, Mr/Mrs. Theo and Marlene Gleis, Mr/Mrs. Karl-Josef and Ingeborg Lürwer, Miss Marianne Vogelsang, Mr/Mrs. Robert and Rita Siepe and Mr/Mrs Hans Wolf. For making this work easier through suggestions and companionship, I unalloyedly appreciate the inestimable motivation provided by my dear brother priests: Msgr. G. Onuora, Goddy Okeke, Peter Okeke, Patrick Chukwuma, Martin Ibeh, Ferdinand Ezekwonna, Tony Ejeziem, Innocent Izunwanne, Poly Obikwelu, Livy Mmaduadichie, Jerry Ikegbusi, Hyacinth Nwankwo, and Charles Okoye. I will not forget the Rev. Srs who through their good wishes and prayers contributed immensely to the success of this journey. May our Mother Mary and her Son, Jesus Christ, stand ever beside them. The secret hands of brotherly and sisterly good wishes and love coming from my immediate family members are inexplicable. They have surely continued to propel me on. In particular, Bar. Tony Okpalanozie was ever ready to buy and send me the necessary books from Nigeria. May they all experience the Divine Assistance. As said before, an attempt to mention by name all who contributed in no small measures to bringing this work to its conclusion would require my writing volumes. Therefore may HE who knows the best and sees the secrets of our hearts reward your contributions with ultimate appreciation that will supersede and beat your imaginations.

GENERAL INTRODUCTION

I. Introduction

The claim that Nigerians are a religious people seems to have become a curse rather than a blessing. Religion has become a divisive rather than a unifying force in Nigeria. It is now readily and sentimentally misused and wrongly applied against peaceful co-existence of the citizenry, rather than offer hope and answers to the problems and questions of the citizenry. In the words of the Fathers of the Second Vatican Council in Nostra Aetate:

> Men look to their different religions for an answer to the unsolved riddles of human existence. The problems that weigh heavily on the hearts of men are the same today as in the ages past. What is man? What is the meaning and purpose of life? What is upright behaviour and what is sinful? Where does suffering originate, and what end does it serve? How can genuine happiness be found? What happens at death? What is judgment? What reward follows death? And finally, what is the ultimate mystery, beyond human explanation, which embraces our entire existence, from which we take our origin and towards which we tend? Throughout history even to the present day, there is found among different peoples a certain awareness of a hidden power, which lies behind the course of nature and the events of human life. At times there is present even the recognition of a supreme being, or still more of a Father. This awareness and recognition results in a way of life that is imbued with a deep religious sense ...[1]

Instead of religion being used to address these questions for the good of Nigerians in particular and the world at large, it has been used to achieve selfish purposes. Rioting, violent clashes or outright wars have been fought for religious conversion.This currently goes on unabated. Some go to the extent of supporting the unfortunate situation with the claim that there have always been wars in the name of religion. According to Mbon M.F,

> It is a well known fact that the tribal Roman and Greek religions have both chief gods of war and peace. In the ancient roman religion, Mars is depicted as the god of war while Ares is referred to as the Greek war god. Even in the religious systems of both Rome and Greece sacrifices, rituals,

[1] *Nostra Aetate*, (NA), no.1&2.

and omens were regular religious preludes to war. But at the same time Rome personified peace, Pax. The Greeks, on their part, had their Athene, Promachos, and Apollo as goddesses of peace, although even these goddesses of peace could also be invoked to give strength and victory to Greek soldiers at war. The notable Greek goddess of peace was Demeter, the goddess of harmony and peaceful co-existence, though she was also the goddess of agriculture – giver of grains and preventer of famine (although she was also believed to be able to bring about famine). The Greeks also had Eirene as another goddess of peace. Among European primal religions, too, there were gods and goddesses of war or even warring gods.[2]

Even if there is an element of truth in this claim, must we continue to live in the past? This madness does not stop with Nigeria. It is now a global problem as the religions in Nigeria belong to organizations or have connections with their likes outside the shores of Nigeria. One who listens to the world news on radios or televisions will surely be asking oneself many questions. Such world news call to mind the events like the Reformation, the Crusades, the expulsion of the Jews from Spain, the troubles in Northern Island, the April 1995 Oklahoma City bombing by followers of the Christian Identity Movement, the Holocaust, the assassination of Mohandas Ghandi, the attack on the Muslim holy sites by Hindu militants, the celebration by Jewish militants of the mass murder of Muslim Arabs in Hebron, genocide in Rwanda, Al Qaeda and September 2001 World Trade Centre bombing, the Madrid train bombing, ethnic cleansing in Bosnia-Herzegovina , the killing of Prime Minister Yitzhak Rabin in Israel, the London subway bombings and the various pogroms all around the world. When it comes to religion, the question should always be: Is religion a means of achieving peaceful coexistence, progress and harmony in the world or a means of spreading hatred, acrimony and wars?[3]

These well known incidents when compared with the Nigerian situation leave much to be desired from religions. This assertion is clear when one makes a short in-dive into the history of Nigeria and her religion-related disturbances which gained momentum since she gained Independence from Great Britain in 1960. Some of these religious disturbances are mentioned in

---

[2] Mbon, M. F., "Possibilities of Peace in a Multi-Faith World" in: *Dialogue and Alliance* Vol.7 No.1 Spring/Summer 1993, p. 6.

[3] Ebuziem, C. E., "Religious Tension in Nigeria Today: A Call for De-polarization" in: *Nigeria World,* January 2, 2008, p. 1

a nutshell for the purpose of this research work. But knowing fully well the fact that Religious Studies has to do with researches into all religions and religious phenomena through religious- history, -psychology, -sociology and other disciplines,[4] I wish to limit myself in this research to only the three major religions in Nigeria namely Christianity, Islam and African Traditional Religion (ATR). The question here is: could these three religions and their adherents peacefully co-exist in Nigeria?

II. Background of the work

Nigeria is a multi-cultural and pluralistic state. There is no type of human character that is wanting in her. Therefore, the citizens have to put up with diversified ideologies- both good and bad. These ideologies spread their tentacles everywhere looking for recognition and acceptance. They are bent on being heard as well as making every effort to gain influence. It is therefore a kind of a fight between the good, the bad and the ugly. For some, the trouble with Nigeria lies with her numerical strength. Accordingly, Gbogini Emmanuel as reported by Vellguth Klaus, remarked,

> We are not a nation. Nigeria is not a nation. It is a state which is made up of numerous nations fused together. Yoruba is a nation. Hausa is a nation. Fulani is a nation. Gwari is a nation. Edo is a nation. Igbo is a nation – there are many nations! But if all these nations are fused together, then we are a state, which is put together from different nations.[5]

Are these problems really based on the wrongful amalgamation of the different nations which produced the entity called Nigeria? Are they based on the improper method of evangelization on the part of our European Missionaries - Christian or Muslim as some people claim? These are plausible ideas that could be mastered if we decide to tackle them headlong. That is why Cardinal Arinze was more disposed to the possibility of finding the answer with the poor living condition of the people coupled with materialism, greed and seemingly spiritual bankruptcy. He emphasized,

---

[4] Schwachulla, W., (red.), *Der Brockhaus in einem Band*, Leipzig, F. A. Brockhaus, GmbH, 1998, p. 746.

[5] Vellguth, K., "Armut und Religionskonflikt in Nigeria“ quoting Gbonigi Emmanuel, in: *Stimmen der Zeit*, Heft 10, Oktober 2009, p. 698.

> We live in a world (country) threatened by materialism, selfishness and pursuit of pleasure and material progress at the risk of forgetting or undervaluing spiritual aspirations and respect for God and religion. There are also divisions among peoples, conflicts increasing polarisation and persistence of prejudices. There are social and economic concerns posed by hunger and malnutrition among millions of people, refuges, migrants, unemployment, poor living conditions and defective health care. And there are wars, actual and potential, with the hanging sword of a nuclear destruction threatening all mankind.[6]

This is exactly the problem with Nigeria. Reprieve could be sought in the suggestion proffered by Pope John Paul II. He urged that,

> Nations (Nigeria in particular) need to reform certain unjust structures, and in particular their political institutions, in order to replace corrupt, dictatorial, and authoritarian forms of government by democratic and participatory ones...For the 'health' of a political community – as expressed in the free and responsible participation of all citizens in public affairs, in the rule of law and in respect for the promotion of human rights.[7]

On the contrary, each group tries to develop its maxims to win attention. The groupings go along the line of ethnicity, sectionalism and religion. The most unfortunate side of this struggle is that religion which is meant to be a unifying force is most often compromised. It seems to have become a tool with which any dullard can easily fan the embers of violence. Some politicians are experts in this regard. So, in the face of this religious manipulation, what hope is left for the unity of Nigerians?

III. Statement of the Problem

According to Parrinder, E.G,

> Amid the more than 200,000,000 people of Africa...there must be great diversity of religion. Can one compare this with Hinduism or Islam? The desert nomad of Somaliland has little in common with the citizen of Dakar who knows no language but French, and the Cow Fulani of Nigeria

---

[6] Arinze, F., *Church in Dialogue, Walking with Others*, San Francisco, Ignatius Press, 1990. p. 206. (Bracket mine).

[7] John Paul II, *Sollicitudo rei socialis*, no. 44, 5, December 30, 1987, (Bracket mine).

must have a very different mentality from the miner of the Rand. Lacking a governing organization how can one speak at all usefully of African religion? ...the homogeneity of other religions is much less real than apparent. The central organizations of European Christianity are quite exceptional. Hinduism, of course, is a medly of ascetic philosophy and popular polytheism. But Islam also, for all its apparently uniform worship, has its "Two-and-seventy jarring sects"; and the mystical Persian Sufi is far removed from the stern Sunni of Arabia or Libya. Even in Christianity there is a vast difference in outlook and worship between the Maronite of Lebanon and the Quaker of England or the Adventist of America.[8]

This citation shows how diversified religion is. The African continent is worst hit by her religious plurality.This religious plurality also applies to other African countries.That is why Nigeria has been chronically infected by this infectious disease named religious pluralism. Nigerians, as unfortunate beneficiaries of this cankerworm are not helping matters. Each religious group claims to be the authentic one and must be exclusively accepted.

However, the Catholic Church has thought otherwise. In union of purpose and for the sake of peace, the Church declared:

The Church... acknowledges the good to be found in the social dynamism of today, particularly progress toward unity, healthy socialization...civil and economic cooperation. The encouragement of unity is in harmony with the deepest nature of the Church's mission, for it "is in the nature of a sacrament, a sign and instrument that is of communion with God and of unity among all men. It shows to the world that social and exterior union comes from a union of hearts and minds, from the faith and love by which its own indissoluble unity has been founded in the Holy Spirit. The impact which the Church can have on modern society amounts to an effective living of faith and love, not to any external power exercised by purely human means.[9]

With this, the Church urges the other religions to come together; at least, let the minds and hearts of all religious groups be united so as to co-operate in the ereas of spiritual, social and economic welfares of the populace with

[8] Parrinder, E. G., *African Traditional Religion*, 3rd Ed. London, Sheldon Press, 1976, p. 10.
[9] Gioia, F. (ed.), *Interreligious Dialogue, The Official Teaching of the Catholic Church from the Second Vatican Council to John Paul II (1963-2005)*, Pontifical Council for Interreligious Dialogue, Pauline Books & Media, Italy, 2006, p. 63.

the possible aid of the government. When these human necessities of life are provided, others will fall in line. Furthermore, "Since men are social by nature, they must live together and consult each other's interests. That men should recognise and perform their respective rights and duties is imperative to a well ordered society. But the result will be that each individual will make his whole-hearted contribution to the creation of civil order in which rights and duties are ever more diligently and more effectively observed."[10]

IV. Aim of the Work

To every Nigerian who closely monitors media reports of religious-oriented violence the following enumerations should neither be news nor a surprise. The most celebrated tensions in Nigeria include among others, the very well known post independence religious cum political crises which eventually led to series of coups d´etat and the subsequent Nigerian-Biafra civil war of 1967-1970, the Maitaitsine Religious riot in Kano between 1980-1984, the crises associated with the Archbishop Runcie´s visit in 1982, and the beheading of Gideon Akaluka in December of 1994. Not to be forgotten are, the Sharia crises of 1999-2001, the purported clandestine registration of Nigeria with the Organization of Islamic Conference (OIC) and subsequently as a member of the D8 countries which boiled in the nation between1975-1997, the issue of the Miss World Pageant in November of 2002, the incessant loggerheads between the Christian Farmers and Muslim Animal Herders in Central Plateau State that started since 1999 and reached to a feverish point in 2004, the February 2006 violent and occidental confrontations between Muslims and Christians triggered by the caricature of prophet Mohammed in far away Denmark, the recent crisis in Kagadama, an ancient Bauchi city[11] the Boko Haram of 2009, and of course the Jos riots of 2010 and 2011.

Despite these moments of conflicts, one cannot deny the fact that there have been moments of peace and tranquillity. But how long do these moments last? This question suggests that Nigerians live now on a keg powder or better still in perpetual fear of what may happen in the next hours. Uncertainty and constant fear have enveloped the nation. Today it is politically minded killing. Tomorrow it is religious minded killing, maiming and burning of shops of fellow Nigerians and their places of worship. This situation leads to another question that brings out clearly the aim of this work: Will

[10] John XXIII, *Pacem in Terris*, April 11, 1963, no. 31.
[11] Ebuziem, C. E., op.cit.

Nigerians ever live peacefully among themselves, taking into consideration its cultural and religious pluralism?

Simply put, this work sets out to look into the three major religions we have in Nigeria with the aim of finding out to what extent they have lived peacefully or have helped to inflame violence. The contributions of the political class and the religious leaders in curbing or encouraging riots and violence will also be examined. It will also proffer some steps that could be taken both by the government, the religious leaders and the citizenry themselves to maintain a relative peace (relative peace because no country in the world can boast of 100% peaceful co-existence, even where religious pluralism is not the case) where every citizen will be happy and live unmolested. To borrow an idea from Franz-Peter Tebartz-van Elst, 'The Beginning is the half of the totality.' Our steps towards this search for peace must be faster or fast-forwarded if we really want to bring order and peace in the world. There are so many steps on which every one of us is moving.[12] A stitch in time saves nigh.

V. Methodology

A research on a multi-cultural, religious country needs a multi-dimensional methodological approach in order to produce an acceptable and desired result. It is on the strength of this assertion that I, for the sake of effective and in-depth research on this topic, have chosen to adopt, the historical, comparative, analytical, instructive and descriptive approaches.

Historical: It is common knowledge that the three major religions in Nigeria did not begin all at once. It is for this that I tried to search for the situations that led to their successes or that militated against their establishment in Nigeria.

Comparative: Since this work deals with three major religions in Nigeria and how they could co-exist peacefully, it is understandable that comparative approach has been employed. At some stages, I have comparatively put the situations in Nigeria at par with the situations in other countries to drive home the fact that after all, Nigeria may not be alone in some issues. The disparity in method and system of each religion creates room for a comparative approach, particularly in the studies of African Traditional Religion. The differences in mentality and religious approach create a conducive atmos-

[12] Vellguth, K. (Hg.), *Missionarisch Kirchen sein, Erfahrungen und Visionen*, Freiburg, Herder, 2002, p. 155.

phere for turbulent moments and acrimony in Nigerian context for which comparison is essential.

Analytic-Expository: The visits made to different libraries helped me much to get information on different religions of the world. I tried to ex-ray the tenets of the three major religious groups in Nigeria. In doing so, efforts were made to expose the causes of conflicts and problems that from time to time shake Nigeria and Nigerians. The analysis of these exposed unfortunate situations exposes the causes and helped situate every event to its rightful place.

Instructive: The analysis of the different situations made it easier to suggest what could be done to avoid future conflicts and problems. It is a kind of instructive recommendation for the government and religious leaders as well as the citizenry.

Descriptive: Since some of the riots and violence that were discussed looked so similar to each other, care was taken to describe the actual event so as to remove ambiguities.

VI. Plan of Work

In order to give a detailed and lucid treatment of the topic of this work, it has been divided into seven chapters. Each of the chapters is made up of other sub-headings that helped embellish the content.

Chapter 1: This chapter names the three major religions in Nigeria: Christianity, Islam and ATR. It went on to briefly look at their historical emergence. While the three seem to be strange bed-fellows, I tried in this chapter to elaborate more on the tenets and notions of ATR so as to avoid unnecessary clash with the others in the main body of the work. As already said in the comparative methodological approach, ATR in Nigeria was often compared to its likes in other countries for authentic application in the Nigeria context. Two basic facts from this chapter are: (i) ATR is not a religion of the book while Christianity and Islam are. (ii) The three claim to teach and seek the same Creator of Mankind, though attributing different names to Him: God - for Christians; Allah - for Muslims; Supreme Being for all including ATR. However, the sharp and clear difference between them is that, Islam and Christianity claim to be monotheistic while ATR has been described as polytheistic.

Chapter 2 discusses to some detail the Islamic religion. Having seen the historical emergence of Islam in Nigeria in Chapter I, chapter 2 examines its means of expansion. It has been so much argued that Islam benefited much from the colonial masters who allowed them to maintain their Sharia laws. It was however countered by the Moslems who claim to have been deprived of their right to freedom of religion when their Sharia law was curtailed. On another note, the application of Jihad was said to be the most successful tool used in propagating Islam. Despite the claims and counter claims, the truth of the matter will speak for itself by the time this chapter is read. This chapter also considers some Islamic organisations and sects in Nigeria and the effect they have (politically, religiously and socially) in Nigeria and on her citizens. It carefully exposed the political game-plan of the far North even against the Middle Belts who are also Northerners. Despite the unfortunate Inter-religious battle witnessed between the Shiite and Sunni, the latest assault came from the Boko Haram group, a group that looked merciless in their approach, sparing not even their Moslem brothers whom they accuse of accepting the devilish western education.

Chapter 3 constitutes one of the most essential chapters of the whole work. Since the totality of the work is aimed at finding out the causes of the constant violence among the numerous religious groups in Nigeria, this chapter, together with chapter 6, unarguably has a central meaning for the whole work. The load of these conflicts was sometime laid on the population. Surely Nigeria is the most populous country in Africa, but not in the world. Some countries are more populous and yet they live harmoniously. This chapter therefore tells us to our face where our problems lie.

Chapter 4 looks the Catholic Bishops' Conference of Nigeria in the face asking the question: What are you doing about this situation? Surely their answer is not farfetched. They have been contributing their best quota through calls for prayers, through communiqués and also through constructive criticisms. But more is still to be done. The Church as a whole, the Bishops of Nigeria and of West Africa in particular have the duty of reminding the government of the implications of injustice and maladministration. They themselves have to live it out themselves as practical examples of what they teach. "Action speaks louder than word" is a popular maxim that we need to apply to ourselves as a Church and as a nation as Pope John Paul II applied to his Papacy.

Chapter 5 turns attention to the Moslems and adherents of ATR for answers to the question on what they have contributed to the peace and unity of the nation. The very first answer that one expects from the question is that Islam is a religion of peace. Surely there are so many peace-loving Moslems and adherents of ATR the world over. There are many of them also in Nigeria. The teaching on peace is also clearly written in the Qur'an. But the constant question that readily comes to mind is: why are all these riots and violence in Nigeria have their roots in the North known as Moslem area? This chapter x-rays what the Moslems have spoken or written about Islam. However, all that are written must be put into practice for Nigeria to continue to exist.

Chapter 6 after weighing the content of other chapters asks the question: With all these problems enumerated, what shall be done in order that Nigerians, with their numerous religions, will live in peace. In other words, 'to what extent have religion and the government contributed to the betterment of the life and well being of the Nigerian citizenry in the areas of enthronement of Justice and Peaceful co-existence? This chapter which is actually a solution-giving part of the work gives some useful suggestions on how to come together. It calls for dialogue among religions to work on the things that unite rather than dwelling always on that which divides us.

Chapter 7 evaluates the entire work. It is a kind of a follow up to chapter 6 but still possesses remarkable uniqueness. It gives a very important direction that the three major religions considered here should retain their key doctrines despite working together. It is however a thing of joy that the search for peace has been in motion as we read from chapter 6. Since some efforts are already on the way, it is hoped that this work if rightly applied will compliment the efforts so far made and fast forward them. It redirects all these divergent religious steps closer to one another, surely not under one universal religion but on the same express way with different diversions that eventually lead to the same common destination called PEACEFUL - COEXISTENCE.

For the sake of clarity and avoidance of obscurity, I want at this very beginning to make a very important observation that will help us through the whole work. There are some words in this research work which may have different spellings but still have the same meaning. They have to be used inter-changeably. Such words include: Sharia or Shari'a; Shiite, Shia or Shi'ite; Quran or Qur'an; Mohammed, Muhammad, or Muhammed; Muslim or Moslem; Spread or expansion.

CHAPTER ONE

MAJOR RELIGIOUS GROUPS IN NIGERIA

1. Introduction

The expression that Nigerians are religious people is no more news. This assertion becomes more glaring on any close observation of a typical Nigerian. He is in his whole being and activities encompassed in the search for the spiritual. Whether this assertion means that they are religiously pious is another question. However, this assertion is the reason for the numerous religions that we have in Nigeria. The basic ones which I intend to look into in this chapter are African Traditional Religion (ATR), Christianity and Islam. ATR will be given a more detailed treatment in chapter one. The other two would be given more detailed attention in other chapters of this work.

1.1. African Traditional Religion: Notions, Origin and Content

Writing in his contribution in the Journal of the American Academy of Religion, Awolalu explained that,

> When we speak of African Traditional Religion we mean the indigenous religion of the Africans. It is the religion that has been handed down from generation to generation. It is not a fossil religion (a thing of the past) but a religion that Africans today have made theirs by living it and practicing it. This is a religion that has no written literature, yet it is "written" everywhere for those who care to see and read. It is largely written in the peoples′ myths and folktales, in their songs and dances, in their liturgies and shrines and in their proverbs and pithy sayings. It is a religion whose historical founder is neither known nor worshipped; it is a religion that has no zeal for membership drive, yet it offers persistent fascination for Africans, young or old.[13]

For Bolaji Idowu, ATR is "(the body of) institutionalized patterns of beliefs and worship practiced by various African communities from time immemorial, in response to the ′supernatural′ as manifested in their different

[13] Awolalu, J. O., "Sin and its removal in African Traditional Religion" in: *Journal of the American Academy of Religion,* 44/2 (1976), p. 275

environments and experiences."[14]The attempt to solve the problem of the question relating to the origin of African Traditional Religion is not a simple one. Surely innumerable Authors have dealt with the questions relating to ATR. Most of them have dwelt only on its belief content. I wish however to rely heavily on J. Omosade Awolalu and P. Adelumo Dopamu borrowing from their deliberations on West African Religions which are invariably applicable to African Traditional Religion as a whole. They were of the view that ATR is a revealed Religion which has no founder. Its revelation claim stems from the fact of its being developed from the human experience of the mystery of the universe. It was conceived as they put it, in the timeless prehistory when the forebears of the African peoples observed the mystery of cosmos, gave it a thought, putting up questions and seeking answers as to who is the likely Progenitor of this physically inexplicable marvellous pieces of work. Unable to find a visible entity they landed to a conclusion of what constitute today a source of perplexity to millions of intellectuals.

For them, this mystery must have been from a Living Being with a supernatural power, who controls and maintains it in being. Because so many people reflected on their experiences coming up with their intuitive responses, we now have divergent religious approaches and views in ATR. But with educational, intellectual and spiritual growth many of the originally held views were discarded as ancient and archaic and therefore not ad rem to the spiritual needs of the human soul. Also unlike Christianity, Islam and other world religions which bear the names of their founder, ATR has no founder. It has no reformers, preachers or missionaries who change its contents or belief from time to time. Its changes take place simply as a result of the attempts to adapt to the living situations and spiritual awareness of the people. It is possible that powerful kings or influential priests may bring about some changes in religious beliefs of a people but not to the extent of changing the entire religious system. Even at that, they are not to be seen as Reformers as the latter come mainly with new ideas that could jeopardise and destroy the totality of the religious system.

As the name suggests, African religion is traditional. Although it is traditional, it is inappropriate to term it primitive. It rather points to it originating from African soil, evolving from the peoples' personal experiences, rather than being preached to the Africans, or being imported into Africa or Africans being converted to it. Each person is born into it, lives it, practices it and is proud to make its own. In this way African religion differentiates itself from any other religion which is brought through missionary zeal and by

[14] Idowu, E. B., *African Traditional Religion: A Definition*, London, SCM Press, 1973, p. 104.

propagation. African Religion is oral. The Forbears taught it orally to their descendants to pass them on to posterity. Their young ones learnt their beliefs and practices through participation in religious ceremonies. From the aforementioned attributes of ATR one can reasonably and conclusively say that it came into being with the oral traditions as its basic source.[15] Speaking on the viability and importance of these oral traditions Idowu unambiguously described them as the only sources or means of knowledge of anything about the peoples' interpretation of the cosmos and the super-sensible world, and what they think and believe about the relationship between the two.[16]

On the very first look at this sub-title, one would wonder why I am starting this work with a dive into the African Traditional Religion. It would be incomplete discussing the advent and expansion of Christianity and Islam in Nigeria without acknowledging the source that laid the foundation for their acceptance and adaptations. Before the emergence of these two great world religions, Nigerians in particular and Africans in general were already a religious people- thanks to their traditional beliefs and ways of living. Although the great world religions may have changed the notion and understanding of ATR and/or tried to wipe it off the earth, this aspect will enable us understand the background of faith which still influences most men today- Christians or Muslims.[17]

Basically because they were not lettered, nothing was documented and this constituted a big clog on the wheel of expansion. Writing on the topic, 'Ofo Na Ogu In Igbo Traditional Religion: The Meeting Point Of Christianity And Igbo Ancestral Religion' Cajethan Ajoku Duruji cited Professor Ikenga Metuh 'Religious Concepts in Igbo Proverbs' saying "The greatest handicap in the study of African Religion is that, unlike the major world religions like Christianity and Islam, African Religion is not a religion of the Book... Proverbs are one of the most reliable forms of oral tradition, and as such, are vehicles of authentic beliefs of peoples living in pre-literate societies."[18] This stand tallies unambiguously with Mbiti's opinion that African traditional religions "have no missionaries to propagate them...People sim-

---

[15] Awolalu, J. O. & Dopamu, P., *West African Traditional Religion*, Ibadan, Onibonoje Press & Books Industries, 1979, p. 27-29.

[16] Idowu, E. B., op. cit, p. 85.

[17] Arinze. F., "Pastoral Attention to African Traditional Religion" *Bulletin XXIII*/2:102-06, Rome, 1988, p. 102.

[18] Duruji. A. C., "Ofo Na Ogu In Igbo Traditional Religion: The Meeting Point Of Christianity and Igbo ancestral Religion" in: Okere, T. I. (ed.), *Religion in A World of Change: African Ancestral Religion, Islam and Christianity*, Owerri, International Symposium, October 8th-12th, 2002.

ply assimilate whatever religious ideas and practices that are held or observed by their families and communities."[19]

According to Oborji Francis, "Both magisterial teaching and theological investigations have shown that Africans knew of God ever before the coming of Christianity to the continent. It will therefore be incorrect to hold the view that the God which is known in ATR is totally unconnected with the God which African Christians worship today."[20] The situation would be better understood when one listens to the song in a German Hymn book "Gotteslob" where this period could be described as a time during which the people were still covered in 'darkness', and lack of understanding. It was until God extended his Spiritual hand, of course, through his light bearers (the Missionaries) that his message came to be clearer.[21] It is in line with this thought pattern that one may accept just the adjective ′benighted′ used and not the claim made by Prof. A.B. Fafunwa in his wrongful assertion that the British colonization of our dear country Nigeria was synonymous with Christian evangelism and so helped the benighted Africans to accept Christianity and Western civilization.[22]

The question of the colonial masters helping Christian evangelism in the North has been disproved by J.H. Boer. He said, "The government did not encourage mission work among the Muslims; in fact, it prohibited it. Judging from Fafunwa′s article, he knows this, for he refers to the protests against this government policy on the part of the Anglican Church. It was precisely at this point that the basic divergence in the respective impulses of missions and colonialism brought the two parties to continual loggerheads."[23] So the Christian and Muslim missionaries bore Jesus Christ and Prophet Mohammed respectively as the lights of God to enlighten the darkness. Citation of a text from a notable scholarly Icon of African Traditional Religion would help us understand the situation better. According to E.G. Parrinder, "...now come Christianity and Islam into tropical Africa, with their missionary fervour and clear theology, and the old God comes forth from his seclusion, with new attributes, but doubtless bringing some of his old features into the

---

[19] Mbiti, J. S., *African Religions and Philosophy*, 2nd ed., London, Heinemann, 1990, p. 3.

[20] Oborji, F. A., *Towards a Christian theology of African Religion, Issues of Interpretation and Mission,* Kenya, AMECEA Gaba Publications, 2005 p. 96.

[21] *Gotteslob, katholisches Gebet-und Gesangbuch*, Aufgabe für das Bistum Trier, 2001, Lied no.520, p. 502

[22] Fafunwa, A. B., "Educational Backwardness of the North: A colonial Phenomenon" in: *New Nigerian*, July 4, 1974.

[23] Boer, J. H., *Christianity and Islam under Colonialism in Northern Nigeria*, Abuja, Beacon Communications Ltd., 1988, p. 50.

new religions."[24] Unarguably for the Christians, the speech made by Paul before the Council of the Areopagus is an intrinsic missionary activity that could better explain what might have been before the emergence of Christianity and Islam. Paul said,

> Men of Athens, I have seen for myself how extremely scrupulous you are in all religious matters, because, as I strolled round looking at your sacred monuments, I noticed among other things an altar inscribed: To An Unknown God. In fact, the unknown God you revere is the one I proclaim to you...., he does not make his home in shrines made by human hands. Nor is he in need of anything, that he should be served by human hands; ... and indeed he is not far from any of us, since it is in him that we live, and move, and exist, as indeed some of your own writers have said: We are all his children.[25]

It was reported that after Paul had spoken, many who heard him got converted and became Christians.[26]This is a clear case of instant conversion after hearing the Word of God. Conversion in religion refers to "change in the religious life and behaviour of people. It generally involves a positive interior change in one's religious conviction, moral and spiritual fervour, from a state of unbelief, weak or lukewarm faith, to a holy and ardent religious life."[27] For Prof. Humphrey Fisher, there are three possible stages of conversion: adhesion, mixing and full conversion. Considering the conversions that occur from traditional religion to Islam or Christianity, he was of the view that people could go through the stage of "adhesion" during which they stood "with one foot on their side of the fence adopting their new worship as useful supplements" to the old. There could be a lapse from the orthodoxy and religious ardour of the first converts to a mixing stage, and people could later regain their fervency after a reform movement.[28]

As it is not our intention to dig into the conversion concept, it becomes pertinent here to consider some of the tenets of African Traditional Religion that helped its assimilation of, or conversion to either Christianity or Islam. Basically, Christianity and Islam are said to be Monotheistic religions whereas ATR is regarded as Polytheistic. In delving into this study we shall

---

[24] Parrinder, E. G., *African Traditional Religion*, 3rd ed. London, Sheldon Press, 1974, p. 43.
[25] Acts 17: 23-33.
[26] Acts17: 34.
[27] *Chambers Twenty Century Dictionary*, 1972 (ed.), p. 284.
[28] Ikenga-Metuh, E., *The Gods in Retreat, Continuity and Change in African Religions*, Enugu, F.D.P, 1986, p. Xiii.

try to make possible comparison of beliefs in different cultures of the African Continent with possible stress on the adherents of African Traditional Religion in Nigeria, West Africa.

1.2. Doctrines

In ATR, God is referred to as the Supreme Being with other small gods (divinities) with divine powers, who serve him by taking responsibility of aspects of human endeavour. In this regard, one hears of the gods of the land, sky, sun, water, life, moon etc. This Supreme Being is regarded as being too far removed from the living. As the living find it impossible to approach him directly, they go through the divinities, spirits and their dead relations through worship and sacrifice offered by their traditional priests. He is worshipped in Shrines and cults.

In ATR, those living have special connection with their dead whom they evoke for protection from the spirit world. These dead are called the "Ancestors". For this reason, some authors have miss-represented ATR as ancestor worship, thinking "that all that the people regarded as spiritual beings are no more than deified ancestors."[29] At this juncture we pose the question of the essential elements in ATR and their understanding: the place of God, the Ancestral cults and sacrifice, the spirits- good and evil, life after death and destination. All these are interconnected.

1.3. GOD: The Supreme Being in African Traditional Religion (ATR)

The place of God in ATR is not hidden either in the ancient times or in the modern era. It is to this effect that Obadiegwu thus argued: "In essence what the Christian missionaries taught the African (Aguleri man) was about Jesus (and the Holy Spirit) and Mary, how to worship the true God and not the concept of the Almighty God."[30] If one reads an article written by Msgr. T.I. Okere in the Leader News paper, as quoted by Dr. Cajetan Ajoku Duruji, in his presentation on the occasion of the International Symposium , Owerri, 8th-12th Oct. 2002, one is bound to pose questions like Okere did. He asked, "Chukwu a ndi Igbo naara efe oge ndi ozioma biara, obu ya bukwa God a ha ji ozi ya bia?"[31](This God (Chukwu) that the Igbo were worshiping prior to

[29]Awolalu. J. O & Dopamu. P., op. cit. p. 25.

[30] Obadiegwu, M., *The Catholic Church in Aguleri: A Centinary of Aguleri Parish* 1891-1991, Onitsha, Veritas Press, 1991.p. 43.

[31] Duruji, A. C., op. cit.

the advent of Christian missionaries, is it the same God whose message the Missionaries came with?). The difference lies in the notion and understanding of the nature of God and the true way of approaching Him. At times, the Supreme Being, God, has been misplaced with the gods or even with the dead warriors or dead societal leaders with acclaimed authority. There have been some authors on ATR who maintained that African belief in a Supreme God is dependent on a hierarchical structuring of society, and that God is nothing other than a glorified chief or ancestor.[32] This notion has since been discarded as more tenable positions and clarifications emerged. It is in line with this that Father Schmidt and certain missionaries maintained that Africans originally believed in one God, divinely inspired. Unfortunately they diverted from this belief into the polytheism of the present.[33] In affirmation to this stand, Farrow, a missionary in Nigeria, was of the view, "that the belief these people have in a Supreme God above many secondary gods "is plainly the remnant of an ancient monotheism."

Inasmuch as I don´t intend to undertake a detailed survey and understanding of the notion of ´God´ the Supreme Being in ATR and the belief in this Being, it is important to note some of the theories attributed to it that might assuage our quest, although they are not always totally accepted. In Sierra Leone, the people of Mende named God Ngewo. Simply put it means that "He existed from the beginning and is the author of all life, of the visible world and men and the invisible spirits....All power comes from God, who is omnipotent but not immanent...His name is frequently on men´s lips, in salutations, blessings and prayers: "God give you long life," "God take care of you." "God is judge," and similar words and proverbs indicate the finality and inevitability of God´s actions and judgements."[34] The notion of God by the Ashanti of central Ghana is acclaimed as the most explicit and simplest expose´ of the belief in God. For instance,

> They call God ´Nyame, and this name in one form or another (Nyam, Nyonmo, Nyama) is found widely distributed in West Africa....A few writers on the Ashanti have spoken off ´Nyame as female, the great Mother, who gives life to all and is symbolized by the moon. Under another aspect the sun appears as a personification of the supreme God. There is probably a duality of sex in this conception, the famous Dr. Aggrey spoke as a Christian of Father-Mother God....´Nyame rules over the

---

[32] Parrinder, E. G., op. cit. p. 31.
[33] Ibid, p. 32.
[34] Ibid, p. 33.

sky, a goddess of procreation over the earth, and old Mother Earth over the underworld, that is over the dead who "lie buried in her pocket.[35]

The Supreme God (Being) is surely viewed by the Africans as Omnipotent- possessing all powers, and described as the Creator of the Universe and the ultimate source of human life.[36] Not minding the part played by the divinities and the ancestors in the administration of the universe, the Supreme God is the Last Court of Appeal. He is beckoned not just in times of crises, but also in every life´s situation. Through ejaculation and silent prayers people seek favour from Him. The divinities and ancestors who receive worship are only approached as intermediaries; they have no absolute authority.[37]This stand is made more specific by Idowu who is of the view that the Supreme Being (God) not only maintains the universe, but also controls it pointing out that the sun, moon, stars, the created order in general as well as all the events in the universe are controlled by Him. Even the spirits, divinities and ancestors are always available for his use. He allows Himself to be seen through any of these. Without His permission other authorities remain non-functional.[38]

This concept of God as the Supreme Being is not hidden in the religious beliefs of the Yoruba people of southern Nigeria who call God Olorun, clearly pointing to him as "Owner of the sky". Under this name He stands out as the creator of all things, the almighty and all-knowing, who not only gives life and breath but also undertakes the last judgement of man.[39] This God-sky connection is a bit taken further by the Kikuyu of Kenya. They, according to Parrinder, " believe in a Supreme God called Murungu. He is believed to live on four sacred mountains, though he is also all-pervading and invisible. He is called "Possessor of Whiteness", perhaps because of his association with the sky. One finds in many parts of Africa this connection of the Supreme God and his priests with whiteness. God is the creator of all things. He shows his power in sun, moon and stars, in storm and rain, and in the rainbow."[40]

It is a common knowledge that the Igbo people of Eastern Nigeria refer to the Supreme Being with the name "CHUKWU, CHI-UKWU" (Great Chi) or

[35] Ibid, p. 33.
[36] Greene, S. E, "Religion, History and the Supreme Gods of Africa: A Contribution to the Debate" in: *Journal of Religion in Africa* XXVI/2: 1996, p. 122-138.
[37] Awolalu, J. O. & Dopamu, P. A., op. cit. p. 71.
[38] Idowu, E. B., *Oludumare: God in Yoruba Belief,* London, Longmans, 1962, p. 54ff.
[39] Parrinder, E. G., op. cit. p. 34.
[40] Ibid, p. 35.

Chineke (The Chi who creates). Implicit in this name Chi-ukwu, is their belief in other small gods -′chi-nta′ possibly referring to the subordinate spirits, divinities and ancestors in the spirit world who are under the beck and call of the Supreme Being- God. Following the prayer made by Queen Esther to God in her troubled moment one sees a biblical reference of Jewish/African tradition resemblance. This trend of thought, may rightly serve as a vindication of the Africans in their belief in the existence of minor gods. Esther prayed, "Remember, Lord; reveal yourself in the time of our distress. As for me, give me courage, King of gods and Master of all powers!"[41]She referred to him as the Lord, King of gods and Master of all powers. In summary, he is the God of gods. This is the God who, according to the Igbo name – Chima uchem or Chukwuma njo, has the knowledge of what is good and what is bad and judges the unspoken/hidden intentions of men.[42] It is his face that the adherents of traditional religion inadvertently seek in the spirit world through their so called gods (divinities) and ancestors as we shall now see.

1.4. Spirit- Mmuo

As the Western scholars were bruising themselves trying to unearth the life′s motivating force of the African life, thought and culture, asking whether Africans practice animism or animatism, materialism or spiritualism[43] a son of Africa went straight to demythologise the African thought pattern using the Igbo of Nigeria as a case study. Francis A. Oborji makes it clear that "The Igbo (of Nigeria) worldview explains the ultimate reality and life in terms of spirit rather than of the flesh. The Igbo is not materialistic. Indeed nothing was farther from his/her mind than a materialistic philosophy of existence. It makes no appeal to the Igbo."[44] This assertion is made stronger when we consider the meaning of the word "Mmuo" or "Muo" which "is a generic term signifying the beings inhabiting the spirit-world (ancestors, deities, etc.)."[45] If clearly understood, he does not argue that the Igbo do not need the basic necessities of life to survive.

Knowing that even amidst wealth and physical pleasure one can still not be fully happy, the Igbo repose their trust not wholly in the visible but also in

---

[41] Esther 4: 17r.

[42] Metuh, I. E., *African Religions in Western Conceptual Schemes*, Ibadan, 1985, p. 26.

[43] Parrinder, E. G., op. cit. p. 20-21.

[44] Oborji, F. A., op. cit. p. 50.

[45] Ibid, 54.

the spiritual. Employing his Yoruba terminology Ade Adegbola succinctly remarked that Modern materialism seduces man into thinking that his welfare is totally based on nutrition, health and hygiene. It is therefore not unknown for a healthy, well-to-do person to commit suicide. And it is noticeable how many insane persons seem to have no time to be otherwise ill- in spite of poor food and dirty living. For insanity is a matter of absence of áláfía [meaning ′well being′], not of ara líle [meaning ′bodily strength′].[46] So, Oborji argues from the point of view of religion, implying that the Igbo believe much in the spirit world, just like many other African countries but at the same time not denying the world of visible realities, the Earth (Uwa). This stand goes a long way to strengthen the belief that the Igbo are a deeply religious people as already mentioned.

A great missionary in southern Nigeria, Bishop Shanahan, must have been convinced of this claim and might have told his people so much about it. I assume this point considering what Joseph Jordon wrote in his book on this missionary. He writes: "It is an obvious fact of experience that the Igbo live a life of continual consciousness of their absolute dependence on the spiritual beings for a realization of life that is meaningful and rewarding."[47] This belief in the spirit world or according to Ezeanya, metaphysical reality, could be cited as one of the reasons why the Igbo, in line with their traditional belief make their sacrifices to Chukwu, (Supreme Being who is a Great Spirit) through the minor spirits in order to ward off possible calamities that may threaten their lives, its prolongation and preservation. This urge to protect life is summarised in the qualities they attribute to God evidenced in the names the answer or give to their children.[48]

A mention of some of these names can help broaden this claim: Muoka (spirit is greater), Muoma (spirit knows), Muozoba or Muonazo(may the spirit save or spirit saves), Muodum (spirit guides me), Muokwe (if the spirit permits), Muogboo (let the spirit intervene) Muoegbuna (may the spirit not kill), Muona-anu(the spirit hears), Muomuanya (spirit is awake), Muomailo (spirit knows where hatred exists), Muojekwu (spirit will [say] decide), Muojeke (spirit will judge), Eleodimuo (as the spirit pleases). These names explain the dignified position occupied by the spirits in the life of the Igbo for which they seek the face of the Supreme Being through their mediation be-

---

46 Adegbola, E. A. A., *Traditional Religion in West Africa*, Ibadan, Daystar Press, 1983, p. 281.
47 Jordon, J., *Bishop Shanahan of Southern Nigeria*, Dublin, Clonmore & Reynolds, 1948, p. 124.
48 Ezeanya, S. N., *The method of Adaptation in the Evangelisation of the Igbo-speaking People of Southern Nigeria,* Rome, Pontifical Urbaniana University Press, 1956, p. 24-25

lieving that the Supreme Being cannot be reached by the mortal man. They present their offertory to God through the spirits. Even as they make this offertory through the spirits, they invoke God´s name first.[49]

Their sacrifice is aimed at appeasing these spirits so as to obtain favours which in normal circumstance are above the reach of the human person. One sees their sacrifice as emanating from the fear of the unknown. In other words, "the philosophical principle that every effect must have a cause, finds an exaggerated application in the life of the Igbo: Prosperity and adversity, sickness and health, long-life and premature death, plenty and scarcity, fecundity and sterility, all these have a cause which is above human ability to explain. They are controlled by a multitude of spirits who supervise everything that a human being does. These spirits even the good ones are very sensitive to disrespect on the part of human beings and when offended, they swiftly strike the offender with untold calamities."[50] The mere mention in the given citation that ´these spirits even the good ones are very sensitive to disrespect on the part of human beings´ suggests the existence of different categories of spirits. So we acknowledge for instance the four categories of spiritual beings in Igbo worldview: The Supreme God (Chukwu or Great Spirit), leads the way, followed by a multitude of lesser divinities and spirits, then the ancestral spirits and finally the evil spirits.

The Supreme God otherwise called Chukwu is Creator God (Chineke), and is the maker of heaven and earth, sending the rain and making the crops grow. He is credited with the giving of life and honoured as the source from which human beings derive their Chi (personal god) which is conceptualized as a metaphysical personality, almost oriental in character.[51] This Chukwu because of his distant abode left the affairs of people´s daily life to the discretion of His subordinates. On this ground, He is looked upon as being so good and loving that He takes no pleasure in hurting anyone.

We must however observe that not all the Subordinates of God are good. Among them is the evil one. Ekwensu, who is also called Akalogeli, is at the helm of affairs among the evil spirits. This Akalogeli takes joy in working on earth, causing misfortunes, ill-health of differing grades, including handing out premature deaths to the people. At times it appears visible to a person or

---

49 Arinze, F. A., *Sacrifice in Ibo Religion*, Ibadan, University Press, 1970, p. 49.

50 Oborji, F. A., op. cit. p. 52-53.

51 Ezeanya, S. N., "God, Spirits and the Spirit world" in: K. A. Dickson and P. Ellingworth (eds.), *Biblical Revelation and African Beliefs*, Maryknoll, NY, Orbis Books, 1969, p. 35.

to a group of people and latter translates into a bad omen for his victims.[52] Among the good spirits we consider the ancestors and the Divinities.

1.5. Ancestors

In ATR the concept and influence of the ancestors vary. Whether the ancestors are worshipped or venerated, what we want to delve into presently is the existence of ancestors in ATR. We also intend to find out who they are and the qualities that qualify one as an ancestor. The ancestors are those important dead members of a family who being used by God, the Supreme Being, still remain connected to their families and influence the lives of the living. In some cultural settings, they are seemingly worshiped hence the coinage of the term "ancestor-worship"[53] while in some, they are venerated. For Awolalu and Dopamu,

> The Ancestors are also there for God′s use. They, acting as agents of God, also take part in the maintenance and control of the universe. They act as intermediaries between man and God, and between man and divinities. They still have interest in the day-to-day running of the affairs of the family to which they belonged while they were still alive. They are regarded as the guardians of morality. They can come down to help or hinder, to cause adversity or happiness...[54]

Chinua Achebe gives credence to this assertion in his book ′Things Fall Apart′. Although it is clear that Unoka was a failure, he still has to evoke the spirit of the dead, the ancestors, for protection. Achebe writes: "As he broke the kola, Unoka prayed to their ancestors for life and health, and for protection against the enemies."[55] This claim is in consonance with the stand taken by E.G. Parrinder in his attempt to solve the issue of the spiritual universe. He states: "The ancestors were human, but they have acquired additional powers and men seek to obtain their blessing or avert their anger by due offerings."[56] To be more specific we refer to Ulli Beier who asserts that, "The worship of the ancestor is based on a firm belief that the ′spirit′ of a human being never dies: it will continue to influence the life of the commu-

---

[52] Ezeanya, S. N., op. cit. p. 26.
[53] Parrinder, E. G., op. cit. p. 24.
[54] Awolalu, J. O. & Dopamu, P. A., op. cit. p. 71.
[55] Achebe, C., *Things Fall Apart*, London, Heinemann Educational Books, 1976, p. 5.
[56] Parrinder, E. G., op. cit. p. 24.

nity from another sphere after it has left the physical body, if at his death the necessary obsequial rites are undertaken..."[57] With this assertion, he underscores the fact that not every dead person belongs automatically to the circle of the ancestors.

A suitable burial ceremony must be accorded one before one qualifies to join in the circle of the Ancestors. In addition to this, one must have led a good life, being in good standing with his community members. For the Yoruba of Nigeria, the deceased "is thoroughly washed with warm and clean water, new sponge and soap. Great importance is attached to the washing of the corpse because it is believed that one has to be clean in order to be admitted into the abode of the ancestors...The grave is dug in either of the rooms or outside the house. This is with the belief that the deceased still forms part of the household, and should not be separated from his kith and kin."[58] For the Igbo of Nigeria, he must have been regarded as "Dike". This term is used to describe one who has proven himself a hero in his life time. In this sense, he must have been industrious, having many barns, and his children and must have managed them effectively.

His managerial ability and communitarian spirit play very important roles in the making of an ancestor as he will continue in the other world to influence the living. This is why a real Igbo traditional religionist prays to and placates the ancestors immediately he wakes up in the morning, at times using his symbol of office and authority, the ′ofo.′[59] He does this, first, by washing his face and breaking the kola nut[60] in his small hut. To break the kola, he first clears his throat and calls upon the Supreme Being, referring to him as Chukwu abiama, or Eke kere uwa depending on his dialect. He thanks him for life and for protection during sleep. He now breaks the kola which

[57] Beier, U., "The Egungun Cult" in: *Nigeria Magazine*, No.51, 1956, p. 380.

[58] Awolalu, J. O. & Dopamu, P. A., op. cit, p. 259.

[59] Ofo is the most important symbol of the ancestors. It is a portable stick made from the branch of a tree bearing the same name and which becomes effective after consecration. It is then regarded as the abode of a spirit, especially of ancestral spirits. It is used as a symbol of authority and as a symbol of all departed spirits, especially in the ranks of chiefs and priests. The ceremony for the consecration of an ofo stick is elaborate. Ofo sticks are handed down from generation to generation.Cf. Adegbola, E.A.A ed. Trad.Rel in West Africa, Daystar Press, Ibadan, 1983.p.204.cf also: Lucas, Religions in West Africa and Ancient Egypt, p.162).

[60] Kola-nut (Oji) is a symbolic seed for the Igbo. It is so symbolic that even when one gives a feast and kills thousands of cows without offering his guests a single kola, it would be taken that he has not given his guests anything. Usually a kola has four or more lobes. When a visitor comes and is offered a kola, it means that he is welcome. It is used in prayer to call down the blessings of the invisible spirits. Hence it is said that, the spirits listen when an elder clears his throat with kola in his hand.

has mostly four or five lobes. He throws a portion on the ground outside his hut calling on the ancestors (and as the case may be also on the divinities) to come and eat kola.[61] He does this believing that those ancestors are invisibly present, watching and listening. Convinced that he has given the ancestors their own share of the kola, he now asks them for guidance and assistance in the day′s activities.

It is after this brief prayer formula that he feels protected, ready for his day's work. In ceremonies involving these religious traditionalist, in which palm wine is used, they also pour out a little of the palm wine on the floor (libation) inviting their forefathers (ancestors) to come and drink. This practice is to some level also obtainable in Southern Ghana where the indigenes may never drink or eat without first throwing a small portion on the ground for their ancestors.[62] The Igbo do this because they see themselves as a deeply religious people.[63] "They believe that they live, move and have their being (see: Acts, 17:28) in an atmosphere in which they are constantly interacting with real, living but invisible and countless powers around them."[64]

For Idowu, "the practice of communion with the deceased or ancestor is a strong confirmation of the Yoruba belief in ′after-life′. There is a belief that the family life of this earth is extended to after-life′ in consequence of death. Dead ancestors are regarded as presiding spiritually over the welfare of the family or community"[65] In affirmation of this claim Parrinder writes "The ancestors are believed to have survived death and to be living in a spiritual world, but still taking a lively interest in the affairs of their families....they are believed to be watching over their families like a "cloud of witnesses". Everything that concerns the family, its health and fertility are of interest to the ancestors, since they are its elders and will also seek rebirth into the same family. The family land is their property, and they must be consulted when land is let out to other people."[66]

It must be emphasized that the requirements for admitting someone into the ancestral household are not always the same in all African countries. Every country in African has its own peculiarities in this regard. To clarify this, Bujo from Congo writes, "To be one of the ancestors, it is also necessary to have been married, been blessed with children, to have lived long,

---

[61] Awolalu, J. O & Dopamu, P. A., op. cit. p. 92-93.
[62] Parrinder, E. G., op. cit. p. 57.
[63] Mbiti, J., op. cit. p. 1
[64] Okolo, B. C., *To all Igbo Catholics- In their quest for understanding their Faith*, Obosi-Nigeria, Pacific College Press, 1985, p. 54.
[65] Idowu, B. E., op. cit p. 189-194.
[66] Parrinder, E. G., op. cit. p. 58-59.

and not to have died a violent death. These latter criteria were not generally valid among all ethnic communities and clans, since in some areas a virtuous life and heroic deeds are so stressed that some of the other preconditions could be left out."[67] Only women or men not younger than middle age who die of natural causes may pass on to become recognised ancestors within the patrilineage. Sometimes, however, one can pass on to become an ancestor even though one dies young, if while alive, one holds a responsible position such as being a "king" or ... "the overseer of the compound.[68] The ancestors are sources of encouragement to the living.

Every person wants to be accorded a befitting burial at death. At death, it is either you have lived a life worthy of emulation and have been admitted to the rank and file of the ancestors or be damned and banished to the abysmal, bottomless pit of forgetfulness. In this case, it is the belief that the person is chased away and he wanders about aimlessly in an unknown destination. To avoid this banishment and non-acceptance by the ancestors, the living tries to emulate the life models of the acclaimed ancestors with hope of joining them at death. Francis. A. Oborji captures and summarises the situation, thus, "At death, people hope to join the ranks of the ancestors in the spirit-world and to use their enhanced powers for the benefit of family and clan."[69] This is a welcome influence as it draws the living to an exemplary, noble life of good neighbourliness, dedication and duty consciousness.

If someone has a reputable father, living or dead, he tries to be like his father or to be better than him. At this point, one understands the brave Okonkwo´s outbursts, what was boiling in his mind as he yelled and almost cursed his son for not being agile and energetic. Fuming at his son's laziness he yelled, "I will not have a son who cannot hold up his head in the gathering of the clan. I would sooner strangle him with my own hands. And if you stand staring at me like that... Amadioha will break your head for you."[70] If he does not measure up to his father´s standard, he will surely be an object of unbearable caricature in the community or among his colleagues. It is in this sense that the ancestors could be seen as maintaining order and unity not only in their families but also in the community.

Anyone living according to the dictates of the custom feels protected and helped by the ancestors. In critical situations he tries to overcome hardships

---

[67] Bujo Be´ne´zet, *The Ethical Dimension of Community*, Nairobi, 1998, p. 16.

[68] Adegbola, E. A. A. (ed.), op. cit. p. 129.

[69] Oborji. F. A., *In Dialogue with African Traditional Religion, Studies in Interreligious Dialogue* 10/1: pp. 57-76, 2000, p. 66.

[70] Achebe, C., op. cit. p. 24.

with every trust in the helping power of the ancestors whom he believes have supernatural qualities linking him to God. Therefore, according to Nyamiti: "An ancestor is, according to African beliefs, one who enjoys supernatural status, which consists of sacrality, spiritual qualities, nearness to God and the consequent superhuman forces. As such the supernatural status is the basis of the ancestor´s mediation, exemplarity of conduct, and title to regular sacred communication with his earthly Kins."[71]

The veneration of the ancestors by the African Traditional Religionists as a fast means of reaching the Supreme Being, God, has continued to echo as one of the points of contacts between Christianity and African Traditional Religion. In his sermon in the mass marking the opening of the Synod for Africa held in Rome, Pope John Paul II said: "The Church of Rome salutes these peoples, especially their religious traditions, in which is expressed the ardent quest for the one God through veneration of their ancestors."[72] As a confirmation of this stand, Onwubiko quoted Pope Paul VI´s book, Africae Terrarum: "there is in all the traditions of Africa a sense of the spiritual realities...in reality, a living sense of God as the supreme, personal and mystical Being pervades the whole of African culture."[73] Pope John Paul II had expressed a similar view in his first encyclical Letter, Redemptor Hominis (RH 6) as quoted by Ownubiko "that non- Christian religious traditions were not lacking in the treasures of human spirituality."[74]

1.6. Divinities or Deities

As we saw earlier, the ancestors serve as intermediaries also between man and divinities. This is a pointer that the deities enjoy a more honorary position in the spirit world as the ancestors. For the African people, there is no question as to whether these divinities really exist. They really exist but incorporeally. Due to their elevated position in the spirit world, it becomes a problem categorising them among the created beings. They are in fact described as ´gods with small letter ´g´ who possess the attributes or qualities or characteristics of the Supreme Being, and consequently, offsprings of

[71] Ezekwonna, F. C., *African Communitarian Ethic: The basis for the Moral Conscience and Autonomy of the Individual,* Bern, Peter Lang AG, 2005, p. 188, quoting, Nyamiti, C., Christ as our Ancestor, Gweru, 1984, p. 107

[72] John Paul II, "Africa Exult in all your sons and daughters who have believed in Christ's resurrection" Nr. 3, in: *Observatore Romano*, weekly Ed. in English, 13 April, 1994.

[73] Onwubiko, A. O., *The Church in Mission in the Light of Ecclesia in Africa*, Kenya, Pauline Publications Africa, 2001, p. 14.

[74] Ibid.

God.[75] From the above clarification of the place of the ancestors and the deities, one observes that the divinities enjoy a higher cadre of reverence than the ancestors. But both the divinities and the ancestors are under the command of the Supreme Being who enjoys supreme worship from adherents of traditional religion.

When they call on the divinities or the ancestors in prayer, it is done with the belief that these are dependants of the Supreme Being who at the long run receives and addresses their supplication and sacrifices. Even when He is not directly worshiped, it is done so in the hope and belief that the worship to lesser gods is actually directed to Him and that it is not necessary to be disturbing Him as he has given the authority to the lesser divinities and spirits to administer to the daily affairs of the world.[76] Borrowing a leaf from the Roman Catholic Church as regards her categorisation of the worship to God (Latria) and the reverence to the Saints/Angels (Dulia) and to the Virgin Mary (Hyperdulia), Parrinder differentiates the categories of worship and honour accorded these Spiritual Beings. He says, "It might be helpful to speak of Latria for the Supreme Being alone in Africa, with Hyperdulia for the gods (divinities) and Dulia for the ancestors."[77] In the ATR, to displease or dishonour these spiritual beings is regarded as sin against both the deity and humanity. Sin is, therefore, going contrary to the will and dictates of the Deity and his functionaries which include among others: ritual mistakes, breach of covenant, any immoral behaviour, breaking of taboos and doing anything regarded as abominable and polluting.[78]

As already stated, divinities are among the good spirits in the ATR. In Africa, the divinities are so numerous that to name and talk of all of them will require writing volumes of books. Each tribe, town, village, family or kindred has its own divinities. For this reason, it is pertinent to select some of them from different clans or tribes and ex-ray. Naming the Igbo (Nigeria) tribal divinities in general for instance, we talk of Eke, Orie, Afor and Nkwo. These are the four market days for the Igbo. These four days are referred to as Igbo week (Izu). Every town has one/two market/s named after these divinities as protector. Also every baby born in Igbo land is automatically named after the market day on which he/she is born. For this reason we hear of Okeke or Nweke, Okoye or Nwoye, Okafor or Nwafor, Okonkwo or

---

[75] Awolalu, J. O. & Dopamu, P. A., op. cit. p. 72.
[76] Ibid, p. 122-124.
[77] Parrinder, E. G., op. cit. p. 66.
[78] Awolalu, J. O., op. cit. p. 279.

Nwankwo, for male issues; Mgbeke, Mgboye, Mgbafor, and Mgbankwo for female issues.

However, due to the influence of Christianity, many now take up different names so as not to be inadvertently dedicated to the gods to whom they owe no allegiance. Because the males are the heads of the families, the male names are therefore taken as the family name (Surname) while the female names are subdued. In the modern times it sounds both archaic and outmoded to give anyone such names except as a Surname to maintain the family root. We now consider some of the most known divinities in some areas. Among the Igbo of Nigeria, the divinities to be considered are Ala and Amadioha.

1.6.1. Ala, Ani or Ana (all meaning the same thing- the earth)

The concept of Ani readily comes to mind when one thinks of the divinities in Igbo land. This is the earth goddess, who is in-charge of fertility. She "is regarded as the queen of the earth and custodian of the human morality"[79] - a duty she carries out in union with the ancestors. The folk stories about this deity depict her as carrying a baby in her arms or dandling the child on her knees or laps. This is meant to show that she is the goddess who gives increase of life both of human beings as well as of crops in the farms.

It is for this very reason that farmers call on her for permission and protection before embarking on clearing of the land and the eventual planting of their seeds. "She is very close to man because it is on her that we move, walk, sit, sleep and plant our crops.... Crimes such as adultery (or Incest), stealing of yams, murder, poisoning, and abominations such as giving birth to twins and abnormal children, like the cripples, are regarded as offences against Ala (Imelu ala - desecration of the land), and they must be purged (Ikpu alu) by suitable sacrifices."[80] The Ala goddess enjoys an enviable veneration in Igbo society. Thus some people are of the opinion that life would be impossible for the Igbo without the Ala goddess because of the importance and sentiment they attach to the land.[81]

Just as sacrifices are made to her before the planting, she is also thanked at harvest times as the invisible queen of the underworld with some farm products as well as cocoyams, yams, wine, eggs et al. The powers attributed

---

[79] Oborji, F. A., op. cit. p. 51.

[80] Awolalu, J. O. & Dopamu, P. A., op. cit. p. 92.

[81] Uchendu, V. C., *The Igbo of South-East Nigeria*, Holt, NY, London, Rinehardt and Winston, 1965, p. 96.

to Ala goddess are so numerous that one cannot but hold her in high esteem. She is heralded by the Igbo as their mother and god on whose benevolence they live and without whose gifts they would be lost. A communal Ala shrine is erected in every village not only to serve as a medium of fostering their social unity but also as the invisible President of the community as no community is complete without it.[82]

Even in married life, the Ala plays significant roles. If a woman becomes pregnant, her husband has to offer a fowl at the shrine of Ala, who is the Earth goddess, asking for her protection over the woman. If she dabbles into extra-marital sex, she will have a difficult delivery for displeasing the ancestors which may even lead to death. To avoid this bad omen, she is often asked to confess any such sex before and during pregnancy. It was also recommended that the pregnant woman wears a cloth, most suitably white cloth as a sign of her union with the Mother Earth, Ala. It was believed that White clothes dispel the effects of the evil spirits. If a woman is having a difficult delivery, she is asked to confess her sins; Ala and Chukwu are beckoned in union with the ancestors to receive offerings to help achieve a successful labour.

In some areas among the Igbo, even after birth, the baby is washed with loose earth signifying its connection with Ala and serves as a means of informing the ancestors that the baby has safely arrived.[83] Any offence against Ala goddess has great consequences if she is not appeased and her ordinances followed. It does not matter who commits the offence or whether the offender did it inadvertently. A typical example of this is clear in Chinua Achebe´s Things fall Apart. It was during the funeral ceremony of Ezeudu. As the final rights of funeral were at its peak with gun shots renting the air, the unexpected happened. Okonkwo´s gun had accidentally discharged and exploded and a piece of iron had pierced the heart of the dead man´s sixteen year old son. He had committed an offence against Ala goddess by killing a clansman. Because it was a mistake, it was described as a female crime.

Notwithstanding, he had as the only alternative to flee the land and remain outside the town for seven years. Having fled, a group of men from Ezeudu´s quarter came in war cloths and set his house ablaze, and destroyed his belongings. His close friend Obierika was among them. He had no choice as that was their customary way of cleansing the land that Okonkwo polluted

[82] Ibid, p. 92.
[83] Awolalu, J. O. & Dopamu, P. A., op.cit. p. 183-184.

by spilling the blood of a clansman. If this cleansing was not done, the wrath of Ala would visit not only the offender but the whole land.[84]

1.6.2. Amadioha

The mere mention of the name Amadioha in the life of the Igbo strikes terror and fear in the ear of the hearer. This situation suits the name of this divinity. Amadioha is the God of the sky who is sometimes called the husband of Ana (earth) and he expresses his anger and authority by using lightening and thunderbolts.[85] Amadioha is feared by all, held as second in rank after the Ala and has the sun as his abode. One sees here the reason why the brave Okonkwo used Amadioha's name to remind his lazy son that he had to be agile and brave. He says: "And if you stand staring at me like that...Amadioha will break your head for you."[86] Okonkwo, boiling with anger and annoyance, expressed his disappointment at his son just like Amadioha uses thunder to manifest God´s wrath, even sending a desecrator of the traditions or moral offender to his/her early grave.

Just like one who commits suicide could not be mourned but only be buried by a particular medicine man, so also a person who is struck by thunder (Amadioha) is not mourned since his/her death is seen as suitable reward and punishment for the atrocities he/she has committed. Only the priest of Amadioha can bury such a person and sacrifice must be offered on the spot where the thunder struck. Being a victim of royal punishment, his wealth is forfeited to Amadioha and not usable by mere humans. So many highly placed Christians up till today indirectly revere Amadioha, attributing to him the power to fight for them even as they deny him the divine attributes. It is most often done in response to an annoyance, especially by exchange of bitter words where a case is being settled.

One expresses his annoyance by cursing and raining abuses on his opponent whom he accuses of not saying the truth. Pointing at the presumed defaulter one thunders, "May thunder break your head" (Just like Okonkwo as quoted before) or "if you do not say the truth now, thunder will cut you into pieces" Clearly, a divinity may have more than a task. It is based on this claim that one can say that Amadioha does not only punish immorality but also like the Ala - goddess, he sends rain and gives fertility. Sacrifices are

---

[84] Achebe. C., op. cit. p. 86-87.
[85] Ikenga Metu, E., *African Religions in Western Conceptual Schemes*, p. 41.
[86] Achebe, C., op. cit. p. 24.

made in his shrine where people go to ask him for their good and success in business.

This makes the Amadioha of Igbo similar to the Sango of Yoruba who is also the god of thunder and lightning. He however could kill by spurting fire from his mouth. His reign was tyrannical and cruel. Despite being the fourth King (Alafin) of Oyo, he was challenged by two of his ministers and was eventually deposed. Consequent upon this deposition, he committed suicide by hanging himself. He was however deified after his death taking the attributes of the original thunder divinity of Yorubaland called Jakuta- a name which signifies ′one who hurls or fights with stones. Due to his malevolence, he is more dreaded than any other divinity. He forbids and punishes lying, stealing and poisoning through lightning and thunder.

If one has committed any crime or one is not sure of one's moral stand, one becomes terrified at the sound of thunder or flashing of lightning. Just like the Amadioha of the Igbo, the victims of Sango can only be buried by a priest of Sango with suitable rituals performed on the spot of the incident since his death is regarded as a reward by Sango for the dead person's misconduct and wickedness. The worshippers of Sango wear necklaces of red and white beads. The priest of Sango by name Magba, hardly cuts his hear. Instead he plaits it like women. As legend has it, when he is possessed, he can carry fire on his head without getting hurt or burnt. He is prayed to for peace, long life, prosperity, material well-being and protection against danger and unseen calamities.

Songo had a wife Oya who is also worshipped as a deity. After Songo committed suicide, Oya wept bitterly. She uncontrollably shed tears for her dead husband that the tears from her eyes formed certain Rivers among which is the River Niger.[87] However, for Parrinder, these rivers are taken as the wives of Sango and are worshipped along with him with rainbow and thunderclap as his attendants. He opined that Sango committed suicide because the fire which he was usually able to call down from heaven with disastrous effects also disastrously destroyed his own house.[88] The god of thunder is in Nupeland called Sokogba. He has all the characteristics of the Yoruba Songo, representing the wrath of God. Sokogba actually means Soko Egba which literally means, "Soko′s axe" or "God′s axe". He does not only specialize in punishing offenders, he performs also the task of the Ala of the Igbo. He procures the fertility of childless women. Any child that was

---

[87] Awolalu & Dopamu, *West African Traditional Religion,* p. 83-94.
[88] Parrinder, E., *African Traditional Religion*, p. 7.

born came as a result of the intercession of Sokogba belongs to him for life. His children enjoy special protection from the god.[89]

1.7. Islam

To talk of Islam in Nigeria without having the Hausa/Fulani people in mind is to talk of Nigeria without mentioning Abuja (the capital) or to talk of Vatican without remembering the Pope. It simply points to the importance of Hausa/Fulani in the history of Islam in Nigeria. The Fulani are regarded as Immigrants or better put wanderers as their origin is not known. The Fulani is an English adaptation of the original name Fulbe. Just like one would talk of red or black India, one can as well talk of red or black Fulbe. The Fulbe could be easily identified anywhere following their physical appearances such as thin lips, straight hair, narrow noses. They appear taller and more slender than the people playing them host. Although without clear origin, their characteristic features according to M. Crowther and Fage led scholars to suggest of their possible emergence outside West Africa mentioning Semitic and Hamitic origins as most probable hypothesis.[90]

The possible movement of the Fulbe from West to East brought them to a place called Futa Toro, traceable between the rivers of Gambia and Senegal. Although they seemed insignificant, they now number over seven million with sizable representation in about fifteen countries with such names as Sidi and Seri from Fezan being associated with their founders.[91] The Fulbe could be classified under three groups:

I. Nomadic: they wander with their herds in search of greener pasture depending on the season of the year without fixed living location.

II. Semi-nomadic: this group are so named because of their double living standard- partly wandering and partly settled. It is possible to visualise them in Jos and Adamawa environs.

III. Settled: this group of Fulbe got mingled among the Hausa having become negroid, acquiring new social attitudes and economic values measuring in agriculture. With their mingling among the Hausa, they lost their freedom of movement, changing some of their customs even adapting a second language. The high point of the change in their life style is certainly traceable to their adoption of Islamic customs.

---

[89] Awolalu & co, op. cit. p. 84-85, 87&101.

[90] Crowther, M., *The story of Nigeria*, London, Faber and Faber, 1978, p. 11-36., cf. also Fage, J. D., A *history of West Africa*, London, Cambridge University, 1069, p. 6-10.

[91] Trimingham, J. S., Islam in West Africa Oxford, Clarendon Press, 1959, p. 11-20

This notwithstanding, they held tight to their strong feeling of racial pride and with Islam, they added religious superiority. With this tenacity came a day when a Negro Pulo cleric proclaimed a jihad as testified by Trimingham. With this jihad they rose, overwhelmed the pagans and found a state.[92] This conquest which took place in Futas, Toro, Bondu and Jalon, Masina, Hausaland and Adamawa made inroad into Northern Nigeria in 1802-1817 with the popular jihad of Usman dan Fodio and his successors. However, this should not be understood as marking the beginning of Islam in Nigeria. It serves only to show who the Fulbe/Fulani are and how they are connected in the spread of Islam not just in Nigeria but also in Africa. We shall discuss more about Islam in Nigeria and the contribution of Jihad led by a Fulani when we discuss the expansion of Islam in Nigeria.

Now still on the issue of the arrival of Islam in Nigeria, we look in the direction of the Hausas who occupy the extensive northern part of Nigeria for a comprehensive result. The denotation Hausa is maximally a terminology used to describe a language of a people rather than a people. It is the common language of the people living in Northern Nigeria spoken even by millions of people who have little or no Hausa blood. Till date, historians are not unanimous on the origin of the Hausaland. Though it is affirmed that they originated from a mingling of different tribes and races of Negro farmers and Nomadic Berbers from the desert, Onwubiko K.B.C maintained a strong stance that there is really no Hausa race or nation. They are simply a people moulded verisimilitude of a nation with possession of a common language and culture.[93]

This language is today used widely in Sudan stretching so into Timbuktu in the West and into Wadi in the East. In Nigeria, especially in the North it is spoken by over 20million people with or without Hausa blood. In the Nigerian case, legend has it that Abuyazidu or Bayajidda was named the found of Hausa land. His legendary marriage with Queen of Daura produced a son, Bawo, who gave birth to seven sons that later stood as the founders of seven Hausa states commonly referred to as "Hausa Bakwai" that encompassed Daura, Kano, Rano, Zaria, Katsina, Biram and Gobir. Through relationship with other women, Bawo bore seven more states with the names, Zamfara, Kebbi, Nupe, Gwari, Yauri, Kwararafa and Ilorin. Due to impropriety of their birth, they were commonly named "Hausa Banza" or "Bastards states.[94] Because of their common ancestral inheritance, it was easy for these states to

---

[92] Ibid.

[93] Onwubiko, K. B. C., History of West Africa, Bk.1, Nigeria, A. E. P, 1961, p. 40.

[94] Ibid, p. 41.

create functional city states. This functional city states which have governmental structures aided their speedy assimilation of Islam on its arrival.

1.7.1. Effects of the Hausa Traditional Religion in the Emergence of Islam in Hausaland of Nigeria

Before the arrival of Islam, the traditional Hausa were termed "Pagans or Idol worshippers". There is a strong indication that the belief in innumerable spirits popularly termed, iskoki, which were contacted through bori cult must have given rise to the idea of the Hausa being referred to as Pagans. In bori cult, the mediator, medium or celebrant was possessed by a particular iskoki. Despite the conversion of the Hausa the bori cult remains strong having resisted every attempt at wiping it out during islamization. As could be read in her autobiography, the Baba of Karo, an Hausa woman, echoed by Mary Smith unequivocally opined that the Hausa spirit cult has a parallel function to that of Islam.

However, in stressing the difference in the works of the mallams and that of the experts of bori cult, one needs to be cautious to avoid the mistake of mixing them up. Although these differences exist, they are commonly bound by the fact that at heart everyone loves the spirits.[95] A non-debatable effective machinery in the emergence of Islam among the Hausa is the belief in the notion that all living things have body, ray and *kurwa*. *Kurwa* is a vital force that animates the body and is acceptable in the moslem world as the personal spirit which goes to al-akhira.

The *Kurwa* is closely connected with the body during life and remains with it after death until disintegration. *Kurwa* must not be mistaken for *fatalwa*, which is designated as the ghost or apparition of a dead person or shadow *inuwa* or *boka* observable in magic This *Kurwa* is simply the 'double' (a copy) of a person which travels in dreams. It plays an essential role in possession when the spirit of an iska enters and dominates a human being but without displacing that of the possessed. It accounts for life in all living things, man, animals, insects and vegetation. From the above, it is clear that the Hausa are a people with already established religious background before Islam came to either reform or transform them. No wonder the early attempts made in Kano at destroying the religious belief of this community met a stiff-necked resistance and unyielding people.

---

[95] Smith, F. M., *The Baba of Karo*, quoted by J. S. Trimingham, in *Islam in West Africa*, op. cit. p. 44.

Despite the unyielding resistance of the traditional Hausa, the sacred place of Kano was eventually forcefully taken over during the reign of Sarki Tasamia between AD 1309 and 1343. Having been captured, the man in the sacred place fled for his dear life with the red snake and the wall and the sacred place was destroyed with whatever was associated with Tehibir by Sarki.[96] With this development, one observes that there has always been a religious struggle between traditional religion of the people and the Sarki especially in Northern Nigeria where the original Hausa traditional religion is still practiced despite the domineering influence of Islam.

1.7.2. Advent of Islam

Some unfortunate circumstances, especially religious and social disturbances in Nigeria between Moslems and non-Moslems, particularly with Christians in the North make the study of the advent of Islam a necessity. Indigenous religion formed however a real obstacle to Islam and vehemently resisted it at the very beginning.[97] Following this resistance, it took a long time for Islam to take root in northern Nigeria. To address this situation, the only option left for the spread of Islam was that of Jihad or Islamic war which was vigorously pursued.[98] The Jihad will be revisited in chapter 2 under the spread of Islam in Nigeria. Presently, we make do with how Islam came to Nigeria.

Attempts at the study of the advent of Islam in Nigeria in particular and Africa in general leave no one in doubt that the scholars of history are not unanimous in giving an acceptable date. Their suggestions point towards some historical events and centuries. It was a historical truth that Islam entered West Africa through Arab traders who plied their business along trans-Saharan routes acting at the same time as missionaries of their religion. By eighth century, the Arabs had conquered the whole of the coastal stripes of North Africa and installed new Arabic ruling families whose courts became strong abode for the spread of Islam.[99] C.F.M.A. al-Hajj holds a widely accepted belief among the Moslems that Islam found its way into Hausa land

---

[96] Ibid, p. 38-39

[97] Sundkler, B. & Steed, C. (eds.), *A History of the Church in Africa*, Cambridge, Cambridge University Press, 2000, p. 254

[98] Hirshfield, C., *The Diplomacy of Partition: Britain, France and the Creation of Nigeria*, 1890-1898 (Studies in Contemporary History, vol.2), cf. also Martinus Nijhoff, The Hague, 1979, p. 20.

[99] Stride, G. T. & Ifeka, C., *Peoples and Empires of West Africa 1000-1800*, Thomas Nelson Ltd., 1971, p. 133.

in the fourteenth century, maintaining that Sharia was not completely functional till late fifteenth century.[100]

In a historical marathon on African countries, A. Mazrui was of the opinion that the region between Lake Chad and the middle reaches of the Niger, until the eighth/fourteenth century, had formed a backbone in the spread of Islam. At the point in question, Hausa land had not been fully touched by missionary activities. It was on the strength of this argument that one believes that Islam first came to Nigeria by spreading to the North in the fourteenth century by entering the court of the Sultan in the region of Sarki Ali Yaji (Yagi), the prince of Kano (750/1349 to 787/1385), despite the fact that Sarki had resorted to the services of the Moslem 'Ulama' in his court for some time before his conversion. It was the Wangarawa from Melle (Mali) who were said to have brought the Moslem religion.[101]

This group of forty missionaries (Wangarawa) led by Abduraham compelled the Sarki to accept their religion and imposed Islamic prayer times on the people. In his unalloyed effort to make Islam stand, he appointed Moslem officials, built a mosque and encouraged the people to pray in accordance with Islamic prayer regulations. Unfortunately all his efforts did not implant a deep rooted Islam neither in his time in Kano nor during the time of his son Kanajeji. The traditional religion of the people (Barbushe) had taken hold of them and flourished despite strong attempts at suppressing it. This disappointment was not to last forever as the reign of Muhammad Rumfa (Rimfa) in the second half of the fifteenth century (1463-1499) became a blessing and a fortune changer for Islam. Under him, Moslem traders and scholars, including a well known writer in the person of Al-Maghili were allowed to settle in Kano. Al-Maghili´s writings and treatise, "The crown of Religion Concerning the Obligations of Princes" which deals with how a Moslem leader should govern, influenced not only Rumfa but also the entire West Africa. Rumfa was accredited with the elevation of Islam to a state religion in Kano for which his name rings bell among the who is who in the foundation of Islam in Hausa land.[102]

Before the arrival of Islam, the people of this area lived differently. But with Islam came also changes in history, economic, life, social, political and legal institutions of this people. This is as a result of their being under the

---

[100] Al-Hajj, C. F. M. A., "A Seventeenth Century Chronicle on the Origins and Missionary Activities of the Wangarawa" in: *Kano Chronicles*, 1:4 (1968), p. 11.

[101] Muzrui, A. A., *The Africans: A Triple heritage*, Toronto, Little, Brown & Company, 1986, p. 95.

[102] Hastings, A., *The Church in Africa 1450-1950*, Oxford, Clarendon Press, 1994, p. 60-61.

influence and dictates of their new Moslem Lords. More radical changes came with the expansion of Islam under the Jihad led by Usman dan Fodio (1804-1830) which we shall discuss later.

1.8. Christianity

Just like the discussion on Islam in Nigeria without the Hausa/Fulani is seen as a grave omission, it may be more so incomplete to discuss the history of Christianity in Nigeria without having the Igbo[103] in mind as they constitute the greatest percentage of the adherents of Christianity. In the internet Encyclopedia, Wikipedia one reads the following, "The Roman Catholic Church is the world's largest Christian Church, and its largest religious grouping. There are an estimated 17 million baptised Catholics in Nigeria, some 15% of the population....The boom in vocation to the priesthood in Nigeria is mainly in the eastern part (especially among the Igbo ethnic group) which accounts for over 70 percent of the country's Catholic population."[104] This does not mean that Christianity in Nigeria first arrived at the eastern Nigeria, especially among the Igbo. But if one is to talk of the eventual settlement of Christianity in Nigeria, one can authoritatively ascribe its success to this region.

The effect of Christianity on African Traditional Religion and Culture could be felt when one reads in-between the lines the inner sentiment with which Nwosu, V.A describes the conversion of a great adherent of Traditional Religion, Chief Samuel Idigo of Aguleri. It was considered an incomprehensible and regrettable omen that Chief Idigo abandoned his religious belief, his traditional religious symbols, rituals and staff of office to join Catholicism. So deep-rooted was the feeling especially that he left his highly revered position as the ruler of his people only to stay with numerous fellow converts in "Ukwu Ndi Uka" under the care of the missionaries in Aguleri.[105] It was as if the whole lot of the Igbo people have been converted to Christianity, at least 80% of them. The situation was comparable to the fall of the Jericho wall and this made Ayandele to title his reviewed article "The Collapse of 'Pagandom' in Igboland". His opinion was that the massive conver-

---

[103] The Igbo of Nigeria are the 3rd largest ethnic group in Nigeria who live in the eastern part of Nigeria. They led the popular Biafra war of 1966 under Chief Odumegwu Emeka Ojukwu due to alleged political and social marginalisation. Till today, they still agitate for the Sovereign State of Biafra as the marginalisation issue is not yet properly addressed.

[104] Cf. "Roman Catholicism in Nigeria"in: http://en.wikipedia.org

[105] Nwosu, V. A., *The Catholic Church in Onitsha, People, Places and Events*, Onitsha, EPL, 1985, p. 16-41.

sion to Christianity is "nothing short of an epic."[106] However, before we dwell on the issue of conversion to and spread of Christianity, let us find out how Christianity managed to creep into Nigeria.

What could be said of the arrival of Christianity would not be complete if one does not take cognisance of her effect on African continent as a whole. According to Mbiti, "Africa is caught up in a world revolution which is so dynamic that it has almost got out of human control... The man of Africa must get up and dance, for better or for worse, on the arena of world drama. His image of himself and of the universe is disrupted and must make room for the changing 'universal' and not simply 'tribal' man."[107] For the successful implantation of Christianity, it must be noted that the missionaries took advantage of the favourable climate already created by the effect of colonization by the Europeans in Africa. Contributing to this epoch success story were Urbanisation, Western culture civilisation, science and technology.

The viable evangelical method and mastery, strategies and expertise employed by the missionaries gave their hearers no room for questions and doubts. They did not stop at the open air-preaching but addressed the most pressing needs of the people, offering various humanitarian services including the rehabilitation of the slaves and socially disadvantaged people. Even Settlement abodes in the name of Christian villages were set up for the early converts.[108]Health-wise, medical care and attention were not lacking. This contributed much in disposing many adherents of traditional religion to accept the missionaries as well as their Christian message as a good substitute for their old belief. So many youths, male and female, were offered opportunities for vocational training. Their house-to-house missionary activity (visits) with its concomitant signs of friendliness with the people worked magic of its own.

Furthermore, the introduction and promotion of formal school education proved advantageous and was rated the most viable and effective instrument of conversion evolved by Christian missionaries among the many traditional African groups. In the schools, the people were drilled in the tenets of the new faith, and upon the acceptance of the new faith got baptised and eventually broke up with the old ancestral covenant. It was not long before these Christian religious denominations like the Roman Catholic Church, Anglicans, Methodists and Presbyterians began the fruitful harvest of their tireless,

---

[106] Ayandele, E. A., "The Collapse of 'Pagandom' in Igboland" in: *Journal of Historical Society of Nigeria*, (Vol. II, No. 1, Dec. 1973), p. 126-7

[107] Mbiti, J. S., op. cit. p. 216.

[108] Nwosu V. A., op. cit. p. 16-41.

vigorous evangelical effort.[109] The successful entrance story of Christianity in Nigeria, with its gradual, systematic and continuous forward-push could be dated from 1848 thanks to the Church Missionary Society (CMS) since all the past efforts by Nubians in the middle ages and that of Portuguese Missionaries hit the rocks.[110]

The attempts by these early missionaries from Portugal could be traced to the period stretching from 1472-1621. Their failure could be basically linked with the political intrigues between their home government and the government of their hostile neighbour – Spain. Following the Papal Bull of Demarcation of the Holy See that granted Portugal an uninterrupted-monopolistic control of commercial cum spiritual influence over the African Continent, Kings Alphonso, John II, Manuel, John III had launched a pioneering missionary enterprise in the kingdoms of Warri and Benin of Nigeria. Unfortunately they were more interested in the political and commercial areas rather than in the spiritual awakening of the people.

They made no efforts to understand the culture and mentality of the people they were to evangelise. B.C. Okolo regretted this attitude of the Missionaries pointing out that their non-adherence to the principles outlined in 1659 by the Sacred Congregation for the Evangelization of People contributed to their undoing. In line with these principles, missionaries upon entering a new land are expected to preach the Gospel, accept and purify whichever elements that might be found useful in the people´s culture without forcing the people to accept their own cultures. These early mistakes of the missionaries have continuously moved some Africans to advocate the revival of African cultures.

This new impetus at reviving the African cultures is seen as a way of decolonizing the Church in Africa, setting her free from those inherent cultural elements of Western and European nations. If you like, it could be interpreted as maintaining that the era of "missionary colonization" should be replaced with Africanization and adaptation of the Church.[111]Regrettably, instead of following these principles, the Portuguese sent priests who were not experienced in mission work together with merchants with the sole aim

---

[109] Tasie, G. O. M., "Christian Awakening in West Africa, 1914-18, A Study in the Significance of Native Agency" in: Kalu, O. U., *The History of Christianity in West Africa*, London, Longman, 19980. p. 293-306

[110] Makozi, A. O. & Ojo, G. J. A. (eds.), *The History of the Catholic Church in Nigeria*, Nigeria, Macmillan, 1982, p. 1-8. For further reading, see also "Christian-Muslim Relations in Nigeria" by Kenny, J., in: *Islamo-christiana*, Rome, 1986, p. 172.

[111] Okolo, B. C., *Towards Decolonizing the Church (An African Liberation Theology)*, Onitsha, Tabansi Press Ltd, 1975, p. 5.

of evangelizing and trading with Benin kingdom. As would be expected, they took no interest in the people and their culture. Instead they occupied themselves with political and economic merchandise that later degenerated into slave trade. Even the attempts made by the Spanish Capuchin priests who came with the right intention to save this ugly moment were mundanely blocked by these same Portuguese. They were not ready to share or cede part of their territory to Spain, reasoning that it would tantamount to political violation of their rights.[112] Even the efforts of the Italian Capuchin fathers met with failure due to uncompromising stance and self aggrandisement or selfish interest of the Portuguese. Suffice it to say that the ensuing rivalries and intrigues of the Portuguese in relation to other missionary groups sent the Catholic Church singing "requiem" to the idea of evangelizing Nigeria.

In 1856 efforts were made again. This time around, Rome encouraged the founder of the Society of African Mission (SMA) Bishop Melchoir de Marion Bresillae to take a second shot at evangelizing Nigeria. Any attempt at this stage to delve into the success or failure of the SMA in Nigeria would mean a research into the beginnings of Catholicism in Nigeria. That is not basically our concern here. Our concern is a general outlay of the entrance of Christianity in Nigeria, not even in Igbo land. So after the failed attempts of the Portuguese missionaries to bring Christianity into Nigeria, her beginnings had to wait till the mid nineteenth century thanks to the freed Slaves or 'better described as' the returnees from Sierra Leone, Latin American and Brazil that found themselves back to the coast of West Africa. Among these was Samuel Ajayi Crowther[113] who was seen as their leader.

With this group around, it was believed that the era of Christianity had eventually come. The Europeans saw them as reliable instruments for starting and spreading the Christian gospel not only in Nigeria but also in Africa as a whole. They would work towards making them self reliant and self-supporting, thereby using them as the source of civilization and through which the light would radiate to other neighbouring regions.[114] The reason for laying much emphasis on these returnees was basically sequel to a fatal blow and the disappointing total rejection they met in Northern Nigeria. With the supposition and high hopes that the uneducated Muslims in the North would easily embrace Christianity, they set out to propagate the faith. Unfor-

---

[112] Makozi, A. O. & Ojo, G. J. A., op. cit. p. 3.

[113] Samuel Ajayi Crowther was from Yoruba-land. He attended CMS colleges in Sierra Leone and in London. He became through active service and dedication to his missionary work the 1st African Anglican Bishop.

[114] Clarke, P. B., quoted Venn in: *West Africa and Christianity*, London, Edward Arnold, 1982, p. 62.

tunately, they met a stiff rejection and a clear cut embarrassment when they met the Emir of Kano (1890-1892). Having expressed their reason for the visit, the Emir told them to their faces that they were not welcomed. He said, "We do not want you. You can go, I give you three days to prepare: a hundred donkeys to carry your loads back to Zaria, and we never wish to see you here again."[115]

However, despite this disappointment, the Missionaries never learnt their lessons as they prized material gains and influence above the faith they intended to spread. Their fear was that building a self supporting Church through Crowther would rob them of their appointment and influence. So the wonderful idea of Venn was jettisoned overboard by his European colleague. But that never made Samuel Ajayi Crowther look back since his hand was already laid on the plough. In 1846 a C.M.S mission was brought into being in Abeokuta by Crowther and Townsend. This was seen as a great hope for C.M.S missionaries and actually the symbol of Christian missionary hope in Africa. It was even seen as 'the sunrise within the tropics'. Their great success was made simpler as they spoke not only English but the language of the people they evangelized. Crowther's effort earned him an unalloyed support of Venn. Consequently, Crowther was rewarded by being raised to a cradle of confidence (by being made a bishop) in his Church. Having considered the advent of these three major religions of Nigeria, I deem it necessary basing on the 2006 Census, to give a tabulated population of the followers of these religions as worked out by Dr. Christopher Nwankwo of Nnamdi Azike University and Catholic Institute for Development, Justice and Peace (CIDJAP), Enugu. Although this census is considered a hoax by many states, I use it since the government of the day, by publishing the census, recognised it. This state by state percentage is not officially published. It will however serve as a basis for further discussions and criticisms that will push the government to be alert to her responsibility.

[115] Kenny, J., "Christian-Muslim Relations in Nigeria" in: *Islamo Christiana*, Rome, 1986, p. 172.

NIGERIA POPULATION SKETCH INDICATING CHRISTIANS AND THE MUSLIM AND OTHERS[116]

Rank	States	Total Population	%	CHRISTIANS	MUSLIMS & OTHERS
1	Kano	9.383,682	6.702	2.210,000	7.173,682
2	Lagos	9.013,534	6.438	5.684,000	3.329,534
3	Kaduna	6.066,562	4.333	2.551,000	3.515,562
4	Katsina	5.792,578	4.137	26,001	5.532,568
5	Oyo	5.591,589	3.994	2.938,000	2.653,589
6	Rivers	5.185,400	3.704	4.574,000	6,114
7	Bauchi	4.676,465	3.340	31,240	4.364,065
8	Jigawa	4.348,649	3.106	89,246	3.456,189
9	Benue	4.219,244	3.014	3.562,000	657,244
10	Anambra	4.182,032	2.987	4.150,000	32,032
11	Borno	4.151,193	2.965	1.240,000	2.911,193
12	Delta	4.098,391	2.927	3.712,000	386,639
13	Imo	3.934,899	2.811	3.910,000	24,899
14	Niger	3.950,249	2.822	1.770,000	2.180,249
15	Akwa-Ibom	3.920,208	2.800	2.954,000	966,208
16	Ogun	3.728,098	2.663	2.138,000	1.590,098
17	Sokoto	3.696,999	2.641	91,251	2.784,489
18	Ondo	3.441,024	2.458	2.137,000	1.304,024
19	Osun	3.423,535	2.445	2.310,000	1.113,536
20	Kogi	3.278,487	2.342	2.520,000	758,487
21	Zamfara	3.259,846	2.328	23,984	3.020,006
22	Enugu	3.257,298	2.327	3.220,000	37,298
23	Kebbi	3.238,628	2.313	35,794	2.880,688
24	Edo	3.218,332	2.299	2.753,000	465,332
25	Plateau	3.178,712	2.270	67,784	2.110,928
26	Adamaw	3.168,101	2.263	34,967	2.418,431
27	Cross River	2.888,966	2.063	1.988,000	900,966
28	Abia	2.833,999	2.024	2.797,000	36,999

[116] Nwankwor, C. Unpublished tabulation of Nigeria Population by Dr. Nwankwor, C. of Nnamdi Azikiwe University and Catholic Institute for Development, Justice and Peace, Enugu based on 2006 Census, giving each state´s percentage of Christians, Muslims and others.

29	Ekiti	2.384,212	1.703	1.993,000	391,212
30	Kwara	2.371,089	1.694	1.340,000	1.031,085
31	Gombe	2.353,879	1.681	79,331	1.560,569
32	Yobe	2.321,591	1.658	1.066,000	1.255,591
33	Taraba	2.300,736	1.643	1.146,000	1.154,736
34	Ebonyi	2.173,501	1.552	1.970,000	203,501
35	Nasarawa	1.863,275	1.331	671,895	1.191,380
36	Bayelsa	1.703,358	1.217	997,321	706,037
----	Abuja F.C.Territory	1.405,201	1.003	907,137	298,064

Looking at this census result, any Nigerian will find it hard to accept that Kano state is bigger than Lagos state. On this issue, one can rightly understand the former governor of Lagos state, Bola Tinubu, who described the census as a hoax and therefore unacceptable.

1.9. Conclusion

This chapter which looked into the beginnings of the three major religions under consideration in this work is more historical. It however contained a detailed study of African Traditional Religion which claimed to have not documented its historical beginnings. That notwithstanding, it is clear that the three have common areas where they can co-operate. Some of these areas are: the belief in the Supreme Being/God/Allah to whom we all direct our supplications; the belief in the life after death and the sacredness of the human life. Be it as it may, it is clear that none of these major religions under consideration has had it easy. But one thing is clear, 'they have come to stay and must find ways of allowing one another be. With this in mind, we now turn our attention to Islamic religion.

CHAPTER TWO

ISLAM IN NIGERIA: SPREAD, ORGANISATIONS AND SECTS

2. Introduction

Every religion has its history. The history of Islam has been taken care of in the first chapter of this work. It is our intention in this chapter to consider how Islam, having come to Nigeria, spread its tentacles to catch followers. We shall also try to have a glance at her organizations and go ahead to face the contents of its numerous sects. This chapter will not end without us inquisitively peeping into the intra-religious conflicts in Islam.

2.1. Spread

The expansion of Islam in Nigeria has its high and low points. Many writers, both foreign and indigenous have given their best. According to Sundkler, "The spread and growth of Islam has been variously studied and classified"[117]. According to Enwerem, I.M,

> Islam's most rapid and extensive advance in Nigeria was from 1804 to 1810. This was the period of the Jihad (holy war) when Sheikh Uthman Dan Fodio and his followers unleashed a reform movement aimed at bringing the state and its populace to purity of Islamic religiosity in accordance with the Qadiriyya version of the Muslim faith... In a matter of six years, the movement was victorious over a very large territory constituting most of what is known as Northern Nigeria and parts of Niger Republic, the Cameron.[118]

In other words, talking about the spread of Islam in Nigeria would not be complete without mentioning Jihad, its coercive impacts, and the activities of the colonial masters in Northern Nigeria.

---

[117] Sundkler, B. & Steed, C., (ed.), *A History of the Church in Africa*, Cambridge, Cambridge University Press, 2000, pp. 646-648f

[118] Enwerem, M. I., *A Dangerous Awakening, The Politicization of Religion in Nigeria*. First published in IFRA/Institut Francais de Recherche en Afrique/French Institute for Research in Africa, Nigeria, University of Ibadan, 1995, p. 21-22.

2.2. Jihad: What is it?

Generally and fundamentally the term Jihad means 'effort'. But this has been interpreted both by Muslims and non-Muslims simply as referring to the stereotyped form of the jihad of the sword. This term was adopted by some groups of radical Muslims as a symbolization of their intent on changing the status quo, fight secularism and defend itself against Western domination.[119] Jihad, when led against the possessors of the revealed texts (ahl al-kitab, above all referring to Jews and Christians) do not aim at forceful conversion.[120] One thing is clear. In Qur'an the Moslems are emphatically called to Jihad, charged to Islamic duty, to strive with every effort towards the things of God (Surah 9, 41). This is clearer when one analytically follows the concept of Jihad and its dimensions.

It is necessary following the definition of Jihad according to the efforts of the heart or of the spirit (right intention or orientation), of the tongue (right speech, particularly bearing witness to the truth of Islam) and of the Hand (right behavior or attitude, that is behaviour that corresponds to God's will). The Jihad in the sense of fighting (the Jihad of sword) is a form of the Jihad of the hand. By this, one understands its direct connection in the beginning with the tradition of the Prophet of Islam, Mohammed. In the early Islamic legal teachings the idea of Jihad always experienced a new interpretation in which case under the great legal schools, consensus prevailed that the call to Jihad is first of all and primarily the duty to defend the Islamic faith and its region from the attack of the enemies, i.e. the unbelievers. Over and above that the Moslems have dutifully taken it as a duty upon themselves to make sure that God's law is instilled even among the non-Moslems making his rule to reign.

The call to Jihad is accordingly the duty of the Islamic community as such, a call which only achieves its aim when all men must have accepted Islamic faith. The duty of Jihad through military action or political means is now the changing of the house of war, that is, the non-Islamic world to the house of contracts or the house of peace, which then means the supreme leadership of Islam.[121]

---

[119] Robinson, D., *Muslim Societies in African History*, U.S.A, Cambridge University Press, 2004, p. 17

[120] Elger, R., „Islam" in: Eicher, P. (Hg), *Neues Handbuch Theologischer Grundbegriffe*„ Band 2, München, Kösel-Verlag, 2005, p. 223.

[121] Riße, G., „Der Islam, Religion der Gewalt oder des Friedens?" in: *Lebendiges Zeugnis*, 58. Jahrgang, Heft 1, Paderborn, Bonifatius GmbH, März 2003, p. 21-22.

2.3. Jihad in Nigeria

Clearly Jihad to every Tom, Dick and Harry in Nigeria means a holy war which the Moslems wage against the so called infidels – all those who do not profess Islam. But Jihad was not just an event that was thought out over night. It was embarked upon partly as a corrective measure (a reform) within the Islamic folk and as an instrument of conversion. This is evident when one considers that further development and expansion of Islam in Hausa land had waited till the jihad of Usman dan Fodio[122] in the nineteenth century. His aim according to his Manifesto was to teach, preach and propagate an uncorrupted Islam Musulinci Sahili and the establishment of a system of government based upon the Sharia.

To achieve this ideal, the non -Moslem or superficially islamized method in Hausa land must with its neighbouring territories be shown the way out.[123] It would therefore be pertinent to maintain that the zeal to promote the cause of Islam in Nigeria was, and still remains, connected to the numerous dreams, which started in 1789. It was the dream of the alleged divine mandate of Dan Fodio to unsheathe the 'Sword of Truth' against the enemies of God. He had no doubt as to the mission he received to reform Islam as the Mujaddid of his age.

In another term, he saw himself as the 'Renewer of Faith' who God is meant to send once in a century. For him the reinforcement of Sharia through Jihad is a way in the right direction of having this divine mission from Allah coming to fruition. For this reason and with the Hejira of 1804 when he was still 50 years of age, he withdrew from Gobir.[124] This withdrawal gave him ample opportunity to plan for his Jihad aimed primarily at corrupt Moslem emirs. Jomier writes, "The holy war of Uthman Dan Fodio was directed against the Hausa Muslim emirs, who were accused of practicing a perverted Islam and were attacked in the name of purity of the faith that the warriors of Sokoto came to be re-established."[125]

However, for a total islamization of Nigeria, Dan Fodio planned the implementation of the Dhimma. It is a covenant or legal agreement which was purported to have been drawn up during the reign of Caliph Umah Iben Ab-

---

[122] Dan Fodio was born of Hausa Kingdom in 1754 of a scholarly Fulani family, which lay more than a thousand miles east of Futa Jalon (north-east of Sierra Leone) and Futa Toro (north-east of Dakar).

[123] Rashid, M., "Political Dynamism of Islam in Nigeria" in: *Islamic Studies*, February 26, 1987, p. 181. cf. also, *West Africa and Islam, London,* Edward Arnold, 1982, p. 60.

[124] J. D., *A History of the West Africa,* London: Cambridge University Press, 1969, p. 147-151.

[125] Jomier, J., *How to Understand Islam*, London, Butler & Tanner Ltd., 1989, p. 32.

dal Azeez (717-720) and allegedly "agreed to" by the Christians of ria.[126]The sealing of this covenant meant a total subjection of the Christians or non-Moslems to the grade of mere on-lookers in the affairs of their country of origin. The spirit of this covenant, to some level is unfortunately still at work in Nigeria, at least indirectly. The Christians by appending their signatures to the covenant agreed to the following restrictions:

1. We will not build in the cities or in their neighbourhood any new monastery, church, monk's cell, or hermitage.
2. We will not restore any such buildings which fall into ruin, neither by night or (sic) by day, especially when the building is surrounded by Muslim compounds.
3. We will keep our doors open to people passing by and to travelers; moreover we will give food and lodging for three days to Muslims who stop at our places.
4. We will not harbor a spy in our Churches or houses.
5. We will not hide from the Muslims any plot to hurt them.
6. We will not teach our children the Qur'an.
7. We will not display our religion, or invite anyone to join it.
8. We will not prevent any of our relatives from joining Islam if he wishes.
9. We will respect Muslims, and give them seats if they wish to sit down.
10. We will not in any way imitate their way of dressing, such as wearing a cap, a turban, or sandals, or parting the hair.
11. We will not speak as they do, or use their surnames.
12. We will not use saddles in riding.
13. We will not wear swords or posses or carry any arms.
14. We will not use Arabic letters on our signet rings.
15. We will not sell alcoholic drinks.
16. We will clip our hair from covering our foreheads.
17. We will keep to same dress wherever we are, and will wear a belt.
18. We will not display our crosses or books in any way in the roadways or markets of the Muslims.
19. We will play the nagus only very lightly in our churches.

---

[126] Nwobi, S. O., *Sharia Law in Nigeria What A Christian Must Know*, Nigeria, Totan Publishers Ltd., 2000, p .5. cf. also Takaya, B. J., "The Kaduna Mafia and the Church in Nigeria" in: *Bulletin of Ecumenical Theology* 'The Power game: Kaduna Mafia and The Church in Nigeria' (Enugu: Ecumenical Association of Nigerian theologians, 1989), p. 13

20. We will in no way read the lessons loudly in our churches....
21. We will not have processions on the Palm Sunday and Easter.
22. We will not pray loudly while bringing our dead to the grave.
23. We will not at all display processional lights in the roadways or Markets of the Muslims.
24. We will not bury our dead near the Muslims.
25. We will take no possession of any slave who belongs to a Muslim through the division of war booty.
26. We will not have places where we can look down into Muslim houses.

Unfortunately for Dan Fodio, and very fortunately for the Nigerian Christians, before this devilish machination was to see the full light of the day of its planned implementation, the British overpowered him. But before they overpowered him, he had achieved some measure of success. His religious revivalism was supported by the king of Gobir. Majority of Hausa leaders assisted in the expansion of the Muslim religion and a unified system of government as witnessed in the emirates of Sokoto and Gwandu in 1808s, four years after launching the jihad of the sword[127].

Despite the alleged Fodio's noble intention of embarking on Jihad, some Moslems did not support the timing of his so called noble duty. They had divergent opinions as to when to engage in this sword warfare. The strictest view had it that Jihad is an unavoidable duty or obligation of continuous process of warfare which a believer has to carry out until dar al-harb is turned into dar al-Islam. Majid Khaduri, a strong scholarly member of this group holds the view that God mandated believers to kill the non-believers wherever they may be found until they believe.[128] Jihad is a strategy that leads to violence. It is a poor way of spreading a religion. A great Sheikh, Mohammed Said, of the popular University Al-Azhar in Kairo once granted interview in 'Süddeutsch' newspaper. In this interview, he was asked about the wars that the Prophet Mohammed and his successors led which made Islam spread up to Southern Spain. The interviewer asked if violence is not inherent in Islam. The Sheikh was quick to give the expected answer:

---

[127] Eneh, J. O., *The Sharia and Islamic Philosophy: The Nigerian Experience*, Nigeria, Snaap Press, 2001, p. 44.

[128] Khadduri, M., *War And Peace in the Law of Islam*, London, John Hopkins Press, 1952, p. 16-17.

Impossible and impossible and impossible. A religion cannot be spread through force. All the wars which were undertaken during the time of the Prophet – God bless him and grant him salvation- and the wars in the epoch of his successors were only aimed at protecting the land, the world, the honour, the human dignity and the punishment of the attacker. Wars which will be undertaken for the spread of religion or to deny other people their rights are banned.[129]

His view not minding, the position of Mohammed as regards violence is a dark capital in the biography of the religious founder which till today is a big problem for Muslims.[130] It would also not be surprising that the great Sheikh gave the defensive answer that is expected of him. After all, the issue of the spread of Islam is a delicate issue that should not be discussed in Islamic context not to talk of criticizing it. The fact remains, however that civil wars within and attacks without helped the coming into existence and spread of Islam in its early beginnings. Even in the power struggle over the caliphate, as well as the successor of Mohammed the religious and political aims were hardly differentiated from one another. Islam was not only a religion but also a worldly and war leading Kingdom. The bitter struggle over the successor of Mohammed basically led to fragmentation of Islam as it is still today seen among the Islamic Shiite and Sunnis.[131] When mouth watering promises are made, believe it or not, sky will be the limit of those who lack self control. That is why the promise made in Qur'an is surely a fertile land for violence. The Qur'an stipulates that those who engage in Jihad will be richly rewarded: "And who fights on the way of God and is killed there or defeated, we will give him a wonderful price."[132]

2.4. Conversion and Coercion

In religion, conversion refers to a "change in the religious life and behaviour of people. It generally involves a positive interior change in one's religious conviction, moral and spiritual fervour, from a state of unbelief, weak or lukewarm faith, to a holy and ardent religious life"[133]. If one takes this definition as authentic, a question would arise as to whether the system of the

---

[129] Riße, G., op.cit. p. 18.
[130] Ibid.
[131] Ibid, p. 18-19.
[132] Ibid. cf. also Surah 4, 74.
[133] *Chambers Twenty Century Dictionary*, 1972 (ed.), p. 284

spread of Islam in Northern Nigeria qualifies as conversion. Considering the speculated percentage of Muslims in 1978 and its present percentage, one can easily see a huge numerical leap. The question is how believable is this speedy growth?

Following the study by Alford T. Welch in 1978, the Muslim population in Nigeria was put at 13,000,000 estimated at 47.0% of the total population. This figure is seen as a hoax and criticised as unacceptable inflation which gives advantage to Islam against other religions, particularly the Christian folk.[134] As the dust raised by this claim seemed to be settling down, a different figure was put up in August, 1998 by Nance Profiles web site giving Muslims 39%, Christians had 49% while maintaining that one –fifth of the population are adherents of the traditional tribal religions. Evangelicals among the Christians claim a whopping 14%.[135] Still in the same year, 1998, John Owhonda believed that Islam has more followership amounting to 48% of the population, apportioning 34% to Christianity leaving the remaining percentage to the followers of other ethnic traditional religions.[136] It was even canvassed openly in 2000 that the population of the Muslims stood at 61,195, 200 being a 45.40% of the population. All these uncertainties were as a result of the unfortunate, pitiable or laughable argument of the federal government that including religious denomination in the census formula would cause disunity. This stand is suspicious.

It is however the opinion of many that Islam did not spread through conversion. Contrary to some claims that Islam in Nigeria spread through conversion, Mbukamma referred to a statement attributed to Chris Enyinnaya in The Punch, "Islam spreads by coercion or violence, even though it is said to be a religion of peace. The instrument of coercion is the Sharia Law. It will first and foremost seek and than (sic) capture political power. Then they foist the Islamic law which determines people's way of living and conducting business on Moslem (sic) and non-Moslems alike."[137] It is a common knowledge that Muslims pray fervently for that day when Islam will be the world religion. It will be a day of triumph for the religion of the presumed last prophet of Allah – Mohammed. It is not clear how and when this day will occur. But for them it will surely come - the enthronement of God's govern-

---

[134] Welch, A. T., "Islam", in: Hinnels, J. R., (ed.), *A Handbook of living Religions*, New York, Penguin Books, 1991, Ist published in 1984), pp. 164-165; cf. also http://www.adherents.com: Religions by location.

[135] http://www.adherents.com

[136] Owhonda, J., *Nigeria: A Nation of Many Peoples*, New Jersey, Dillon Press, 1998, p. 6-7.

[137] Mbukanma, J. O., *Preaching & Crisis of Faith*, Ibadan, Newborne Enterprises, December 2001, p. 115.

ment. It is therefore to this effect that the world experiences religious intolerance perpetrated by some uninformed Muslims aimed at the infidels – both Christians and even Muslims who are seen not to be living according to the principles of Islam. Writing on this, Ndiokwere said,

> As far as Moslems are concerned, the enthronement of God's government must be achieved, damn the consequences. Islamic proselytism is really pursued by force rather than persuasion. Often violence and intimidation are the only option to dialogue and negotiations; and this is inherent in the islamic holy war ideology. The Islamic fundamentalists are ever ready to perpetrate atrocities against those they refer to as infidels and these atrocities range from wanton destruction of property, including Churches and residential buildings to massacre of innocent people[138]

Nigeria as a nation has gotten more than enough of this religious massacre and wanton destruction of lives and property in the bid to spread the Islamic religion. As an impetus to the reason why Islam must be spread by all means, it was adduced that the revealed truths which Islam teaches and expounds is universal but also appeals and applies to all and sundry, meaning to all mankind, colour, place and race notwithstanding.[139]In his attempt to clear some probable doubting Thomases on why he held this opinion about Islam, Abdul-Rauf said, "Muhammad's message is therefore eternal. It has replaced all past religions; and Muhammad is the last and the seal of the noble series of the prophets. Moslems are urged to invite others to consider and to accept – if they are persuaded – the faith of Islam. The desire to spread our faith is because it is the surest measure towards peace, progress and happiness to all mankind."[140]

Another possible reason for which the Muslims seem determined to implant Islam by all means is due to their understanding of other religions as being intended for limited human communities. Some find it even bamboozling to hear that Jewish religion and Christianity still exist. According to Troll, "Islam is the one true, perfect and enduring religion. It has absorbed into itself everything of any worth in the other religions. The Muslim who thinks in traditional terms is therefore astonished that there are still Jews and

---

[138] Ndiokwere, N. I., *The African Church Today and Tomorrow, Prospects and Challenges*, Vol.1, Onitsha, Nigeria, Effective Key Publishers Limited, 1994, p. 78.
[139] Abdul-Rauf, M., *Islam: Faith and Devotio*n, Lagos (Nigeria), Islamic Publications Bureau, 1982, p. 7.
[140] Ibid, p. 9

Christians today, for with the advent of Islam these religions essentially became irrelevant. Judaism and Christianity are of a provisional nature and at best only partially true. They were intended for limited human communities. Outside Islam religion is of no genuine value because Islam is the only religion that is truly universal."[141] For the Moslems, it is this belief that makes it sensible when members of other religions convert to Islam but a taboo for a Moslem to convert to other religions.

Troll further wrote, "There cannot be a right to change religion. A person is born as a member of a given religion and must stay within it as it constitutes an essential element of personal, collective and national identity. Conversion to Islam is of course an exception, because here it is a case of entering a society and a structure which replaces all other identities and make (sic) them unnecessary."[142] Conversion from Islam to another religion on the other hand is in most cases punishable by death. The Qur'an clearly orders that the,

> polytheists must believe or be put to death (9:5; 48:16). On the other hand, the 'People of the Book' (Jews and Christians) are offered the status of protected people (dhimma): they may maintain their religion – even though it is faulty and has been superseded by Islam – along with its hierarchy and its rituals, but they must pay a special tax (jizya) and remain 'small' (i.e. inconspicuous and subordinate) (9:29). The Muslim who abandons his religion, either through conversion to another religion or by deeds or words clearly directed against Islam, will be condemned by God(3:85-90; 4:137; 16:108) and must be punished with death (2:217 has consistently been interpreted thus by legal scholars, and this interpretation has been reinforced by numerous hadith).[143]

To avoid this death, the only option is a participation in the spread of the religion of Islam till the whole world believes and becomes an Islamic community called Umma. In the case of political-religious wellbeing of the people, the Umma seeks the exclusion of the regions of those who do not belong to Islamic religion. This region of the non-Muslim, 'dar al-harb' will be regarded as the house of war.[144] The aforementioned reasons really helped Islamic religion in her spread in Nigeria as her members due to fear of being attacked or being put to death found it hard to convert to other religions.

[141] Troll, C. W., *Muslims Ask, Christians Answer*, India, Anand Press, 2005. p. 106.
[142] Ibid.
[143] Ibid, p. 108.
[144] Riße, G., op. cit. p. 21.

There were however other factors that influenced and encouraged the tenacity with which the Muslims were glued onto their religion. A typical example is Colonialism.

2.5. Colonial Masters

Viewed with an eagle eye, one cannot but admit that Islam gained much from colonial administration in Nigeria. Its spread got heightened in Northern Nigerian emirate under the colonial masters who allowed the use of Sharia. Lugard introduced for political and economic reasons the system of an indirect rule by which the Islamic leaders were not hindered from continued ruling of the Muslim communities. In this case, the emirs were authorized to apply the Sharia law both to Muslims and non-Muslims.[145] With this 19th century system it means that they were still part of the government of the time but with regional autonomy. So instead of the domineering power of ruling the whole land, they were to rule only in their region.[146] Eneh stated that,

> what Lugard did in 1902-1903 was to restrict and prohibit the Sharia sanctions for theft, fornication and adultery with the creation of customary courts that dished out punishment and imprisonment in order to protect the British acquisitions and loots and to allow prostitutes free movement to pay attention to and distract the pro-British African workers and labourers. The production of bastard, immorality and infidelity in marriage increased with the non-sanction of adultery....The Lugard's prohibition remained in force in Nigeria even after the Nigerian independence in 1960 until 2000 when the Muslim states in the North adopted the total application of the Sharia code.[147]

Because of the peculiar and precarious nature of Nigerian situation, Lugard did not apply the same system adopted in Egypt in the time of the French and British colonial rules. In the case of Egypt, the Sharia courts were replaced with civil law. In other words, as Egypt was invaded in 1798, Napoleon and his allies brought with them social and political changes. Taking a stand from the Lugardian system, his successors totally prevented missions among the Muslims. According to Jan H. Boer, "Lugard´s successors tended

---

[145] Eneh, J. O., op. cit. p. 50.
[146] Elger, R. (Hg.), *Kleines Islam-Lexikon, Geschichte. Alltag . Kultur* Band 383, BPB, p. 237.
[147] Eneh, J.O., op. cit. p. 51.

to oppose missions in general, but especially missions amongst Muslims. Girourd, his immediate successor, a Canadian Catholic, is said to have had bitter hatred for missions and considered them a "menace to the peace and good government"[148] This Nigerian experience could be affirmed taking a narrative from Bongo tribe. Here Kumm narrated a vivid example of this opposition to Missions by Colonial government related to him by their young Chief.

According to Boer, "He was told of this people´s hatred for the Muslims because Arabs had for years waged war against them until they were reduced to an insignificant few, though they never succeeded to enslave the Bongo. After the arrival of the European and the resulting peace, Muslims were sent to the area in various colonial capacities and clothed in considerable prestige. What the Muslims had been unable to achieve through violence, the British achieved through peace. Aided by government appointment, Islam infiltrated the tribe. Bongo warriors had begun to wear Muslim robes –"fetters".... The young were beginning to follow the Muslims to their mosque."[149]This is a case of conversion by means of political maneuver perpetrated by the colonial masters. Talking of a case of a Chief in Bauchi province, Kumm was informed that when he (the Chief) applied to have Christian teachers sent to him, a Muslim secretary was sent to him by the government to facilitate his correspondence with the British Resident.[150]

This was more or less a continental problem than a Nigerian problem since many people from different countries reported such government preferential treatment in favour of the Muslims. This is clear from the analysis given by Kumm. Writing on the influence of the government Kumm elucidated "how the Traditional tribes in the Eastern Sudan who had formerly successfully kept Islam at bay were now subjected to it through the direct policy of the government which had introduced Muslim teaching, appointed Friday as the day of rest for the soldiers instead of Sunday, saw to the teaching of Islam to the children of these soldiers in regular classes under government supervision. These soldiers were predominantly of Traditional origin, but immediately upon their enlistment they would be circumcised and turned into Muslims."[151]

---

[148] Boer, J. H., *Christianity And Islam Under Colonialism In Northern Nigeria*, Jos, Nigeria, Institute of Church and Society, 1988, p. 8.
[149] Ibid, p. 9.
[150] Ibid.
[151] Ibid, p. 9-10.

The colonial Master even went to the extent of seeing in this unfortunate situation reasons for boasting. As an affirmation to this claim, an American Missionary startled many during the 1910 Edinburg Conference, an international ecumenical missionary conference, where he quoted a British colonial official saying that missions may as well pack, for "we make ten Muslims to your one Christian"[152]. Cases abound where Traditional boys were enrolled in a government schools where Moslems are employed as their teachers. Even Christian boys in industrial schools were normally required to work on Sundays. Textbooks which were as good as Moslem handbooks were prescribed by government for the use of the students.

As these impositions became unbearable, a student vowed to resist this unfavourable tyrannical approach. However, a visiting white government official warned him insisting that he should subject himself to the Moslem way. There was also the common British practice of extending the rule of Moslem emirs over traditional tribes that formerly were never under Moslem governorship. A small mining town called Bukuru near Jos in Nigeria is a reference point in this regard. As soon as the tin mines were beginning to be developed, Hausa market sprung up to be followed soon by Moslem teachers. By the end of 1912, their call to prayer was heard where only a little while ago there was nothing but wilderness. The entire Bukuru area was politically placed under the Moslem Emir of Bauchi, while judicially Muslim influence was extended to the appointment of a Moslem judge. The missions suffered under such regime. An unfortunate case was reported of the ill treatment meted to Mumuye people in Gongola state. The mission had approval for opening a station at Kona, on the border of Mumuye territory. A month later the approval was withdrawn by the government because of objections submitted by government-appointed Moslem Chiefs.[153]

2.6. Organisations

The Islamic organisations in Nigeria are many. Among them are: the Council of Mallams, the Jamaata Nasril Islam and a host of others. For the purpose of this work, I tend to dwell on the Jamaata Nasril Islam and give a detailed account of it. This is because of the important roles it played in Islamic matters in Nigeria when it really mattered.

---

[152] Ibid.

[153] Ibid, p. 10-11.

2.6.1. Jamaata Nasril Islam (JNI): Formation

The period of formation of this Organisation was said to be in 1961 by the Sarduana.[154] At this period the spiritual authority over the Dan Fodio Kingdom was in the hands of the Sultan. So having dawned on him that he has no strong grip again on the spiritual authority, Sarduana looked for a way of winning back what he has lost with what was readily available - the political power of the Dan Fodio Kingdom. It was within this context that the conversion campaigns were hatched.[155] In this case, he used his political power to look outside the shores of Nigeria. He turned his gaze towards the Islamic world in search of importance and recognition as a leader of Islam in Nigeria.

No matter how one looks at it, he seemed to have made a great success by achieving what he aimed at. He made no mistake of giving the least opposition to the theological stance of the Arab and Islamic world. For this single stance he was globally acclaimed and honoured. Citing Paden's book, "Ahmadu Bello" Kukah said, "Muslim leaders like those of Libya, Pakistan, Tunisia, Morocco, Senegal, United Arab Emirates, Saudi Arabia, Jordan, Iran, Sudan, Lebanon conferred the Sarduana with all sorts of *honours* and sang his praises as a champion of Islam. There were millions of dollars pouring in for the promotion of Islam in Nigeria."[156] Apart from these fleets of honours and monetary gains, his international acclaim heightened. We read for instance that, "The crowning glory was his elevation as the Vice President of the World Islamic Council, and in his address, the Sarduana announced dubious numbers of conversions and the existence of a million Koranic schools in northern Nigeria."[157]

Feeling fulfilled with the attainment of this prestigious international recognition as a World Leader of Islam, especially the encouragement from the Arab countries, the sky was to be his limit. So, "with the flow of Arab money, the Sarduana had set up the Jamaatu Nasril Islam as an all-purpose umbrella for the channelling of finances for the propagation of Islam in Northern Nigeria in all its forms, including the building of Koranic schools and overseeing the propagation and practice of Islam."[158]

---

[154] Kukah, H. M., *Religion Politics and Power in Northern Nigeria*, Ibadan, Spectrum Books Ltd., 2003, p. 43.
[155] Ibid, p. 20.
[156] Ibid, p. 21. cf. also Paden, *Ahmadu Bello*, p. 533.
[157] Ibid.
[158] Ibid, p. 42.

2.6.2. Effects of Jamaata Nasril Islam (JNI)

Before this Organisation was put in place, the political manoeuvre in the country was at its peak. Ironsi was accused of "Ibonisation of Nigeria" with his fellow Igbo after the coup of 1966. This was sequel to his insistence on maintaining the oneness of Nigeria through his Decree 34- Unification agenda. In order to convince their people, the traditional Northern ruling class filled the whole north with the theory that, if this decree is allowed to see the light of the day, the obi of Onitsha could become the Sultan of Sokoto or the Emir of Kano and vice versa. Even the northern soldiers came under verbal attack by their northern ruling class who seemed to see power of ruling Nigeria slipping off their stronghold. These soldiers were criticised as being weaker than women.

To oppose this negative image given them, the soldiers staged a successful coup which Billy Dudley termed the "Return Match of 29July, 1966."[159]The danger and political game machination was far from being yet over. Instead of power moving to the North per se, it remained in Middle Belt under Gowon. Here, the adage becomes very *ad rem* that, 'one who is on journey must continue until he reaches his destination' or 'the tongue cannot rest until what is in the mouth finishes'. Not satisfied that the power to rule rests now in the hand of their ever subordinate Middle Belt, the North continued their quest to regain the ruling might.

In the spirit of Machiavelli, they proposed what they called the political interests of the North through which they brought together three erstwhile political enemies meant to represent the three northern political blocs. Under the codename "Leaders of Thought" the group made up of Alhaji Aliyu Makaman Bida (leader of the defunct NPC), Alhaji Aminu Kanu (NEPU) and Mr. Joseph Tarka (UMBC) toured the whole nook and corner of North as an evident manifestation of the Northern Unity or Oneness.[160] Even as this artificial unity lasted, the core Northerners continued in search of their greener pasture- the total re-capturing of political power.

This opportunity seemed to present itself when Gowon in September 1966 convened an Ad Hoc Constitutional Conference to enable the Nation articulate and map a new road to national political future. The North ceased this opportunity and asked their soldiers to drop their old secession bid as a green light to their plans seemed to be materialising. This advice was planned and executed by Alhaji M. D. Yusuf and Justice Mohammed Bello.

---

[159] Dudley, B., *Instability and Political Order*, Ibadan, University Press, 1973, p. 134-143.

[160] Kukah, H. M., op.cit. pp. 38-40.

They made the soldiers see the inherent dangers in their insistence on declaring their will to secede. The conference eventually began with Gowon calling on all present to try to find a common formula for the continued existence of the nation. The East and West were for one Nigeria as a Federating unit[161]. After some argumentation and arm-twisting, the North came up with an unbelievable turn-around mea culpa or declaration. With Sir Kashim Ibrahim as their spokesman they said,

> Nigeria should not be allowed to disintegrate. No Nigerian has anything to gain in the long run if this nation disintegrates. We shall all be losers. My delegation therefore believes there must be a strong effective central government. The conference may wish to note that this represents a modification in our stand as indicated in our original memo. To embody the right of secession of any part of this country from the rest is to invite a breakup of the country...Accordingly, the relevant section in our memo is hereby withdrawn...the principle of state creation must be agreed.[162]

To clarify this stand, one of the northern delegates further elucidated their position, "What we have always objected to, is the attempt by people from outside the North to draw up imaginary lines creating new states in the North in order to satisfy political ambitions. If people in the North want more states, let them say so."[163] With this common acceptance of Federalism, some states were created from the old North which the new states saw as ushering in independence from the Hausa-Fulani domination. It may however not be the case. As such, an avenue termed Interim Common Service Agency (ICSA) was created to see to the clearing of assets that the new states as a whole inherited from the former northern government. But for the ruling class, ICSA was hijacked and translated into a means of blackmailing the new states of old North who thought that they had achieved sovereignty from the old North that used to humiliate and degrade them.[164] The speed with which the new states embarked on self development speaks volumes. But the unfriendly disposition of the old North to help the new North made it clear to the new North that all that the old North said was simply a Greek gift. Hence, Gomwalk, one of the governors of the new northern states turned and sought helping hands from the South-West. By the time Gowon was

---

[161] Ibid, p. 40.
[162] Dudley, B., op.cit. p. 159, cf. also Kukah, H. M., p. 41.
[163] Kukah, H. M., op.cit. p. 41.
[164] Ibid.

overthrown in 1975 and Gomwalk killed in 1976, the Benue-Plateau state was already waxing strong and had translated to a strong symbol of what the non-Muslim members of the Middle Belt had always aspired and strived to achieve.[165] It was this turn of events that made S.K. Panter Brick and P.F. Dawson as quoted by Kukah to declare that,

> The idea of one North is dead. Its ghost lingers on, but it is no longer practical politics...there was something bizarre about the way in which the former region set the pace along a road which hitherto, it has always refused to travel, or had said it would only travel in the company of others. The dominant view had always been that the region must be maintained intact, any contrary point of view as expressed by the people of the Middle Belt, was firmly overruled.[166]

The formation of this organisation has a very big connection to Sarduana's conversion intent. Having dawned on the northern ruling class that their political calculations had misfired, they then decided to seek the way forward by negotiation. This time around, they moved towards using religious institution founded by Sarduana. By this they intended to parade themselves as the legatees of Sarduana so as to reclaim their legitimacy as the defenders of Islamic faith.[167] They achieved this by falling back on the organisation formed by Sarduana called Jamaatu Nasril Islam. With this claim, the Middle Belt indigenes who were Muslims remained connected and loyal to them, at least in matters concerning Religion.

The claim was that, "Every muslim in Northern Nigeria, male or female, young or old is deemed a member of the Jama'a. It only remains for him or her to choose whether to be an active or sleeping member."[168]But the formation of JNI was not without its side effects.

After the formation, even his fellow Muslims viewed the reason behind its formation with a pinch of salt. They wondered why the North has the Council of Mallams as well as the JNI? The explanation for that was immediately given to avoid further deterioration of the already heated situation. For the northern government, while the Council of Mallams dealt with the matters of the implication of the government's pilgrimage policies on Mus-

---

[165] Ibid, p. 42.

[166] Kukah, M., Ibid, p. 42, cf. S. K. Panter Brick & P.F. Dawson: "The Creation of New States in the North" in: Panter Brick (ed.), *Nigerian Politics*, p. 128-131.

[167] Ibid.

[168] Ibid, p. 43 cf. Paden, J, "Religion and Political Culture"

lims,[169] the JNI sought to encourage Islamic literature in Nigerian vernacular languages, build mosques and encourage Islamic centres of learning.[170] Furthermore, to avoid suspicions that may still be subsisting, the Sarduana himself was quick in pronouncing that the organisation in its conversion campaign will not be financed with the state money. The more he tried to let them find reasons to believe him, the more he was faced with stiff opposition with concomitant questions. This is clear from the stand taken by some inner caucus who ironically questioned the veracity of his statement. They argued, "what type of state funds did the JNI need when all its staff were on the payroll of the government as civil servants? What funds did they need when the JNI was like Religious Affairs Department in the Ministry of Education in the regional civil service? What else did they need when one of its members was the chairman of the regional civil service Commission?[171]" Giving credence to this assertion he explained that, "Alhaji Abubakar Imam, Chairman of the Public Service Commission, was a member of the Committee, obviously co-opted to see to the systematic deployment of manpower to areas of Islamic needs."[172]

It will not be out of place if one says that the formation of JNI created disfavour and disunity among the Islamic folk. This led to his forming one movement after another none of which is worth our mentioning here. Even after Sardauna's death, JNI faced yet another acute test of authenticity as it could not hold her members together. Infighting and jostling for enviable positions was for them the order of the day as they sought to use her as a means to advance personal and group interests. One of the reasons why it could not unite the Muslims was that even the South viewed it as a means established by the North to extend their Hausa-Fulani hegemony as it succeeded in bringing together only the Emirs and traditional Mallams.[173]Her critics also picked holes with the administrative system that was employed. For Dr. Junaidu Mohammed, "Alhaji Dasuki is running the JNI like a personal venture, rendering no accounts to anyone, and claiming that he is the sole financier of the JNI."[174]

---

[169]Ibid, no. 62. p. 61, There had been embarrassing stories of the problems of pilgrims in Mecca and the government sought to deal with this matter. Alhaji Isa Kaita told him (Kukah, H. M) that he had travelled to Mecca and had prepared a report for alleviating these problems, part of which lay in control of numbers.

[170] Ibid. cf. Paden, J, *Ahmadu Bello*.

[171] Ibid, p. 44

[172] Ibid, no. 69, p. 62.

[173] Ibid, p. 48.

[174] Ibid, p. 43.

2.7. Sects

Discussions on the Islamic sects in Nigeria will always suffer elaborate studies due to the dearth of study materials. An attempt to get help from the Muslims themselves is itself a herculean task that ends mostly bearing no fruit. This is sequel to their non-preparedness to provide you with valuable link to the resource materials. That is my personal experience. As evidence to this assertion, one reads from Kukah´s own experience as he intended getting information about the Jamaata Nasril Islam. He wrote,

> When I asked Alhaji Ibrahim Dasuki (who had been Secretary General of JNI since the death of the Sarduana) for information about the organisation, he told me that not much information was available and a revised Constitution was only being drawn up, based on an earlier document which was mainly a statement of objectives.[175]

The disappointment with which Kukah narrated this shocking answer could be easily felt especially considering the fact that even the secretary of the organisation could not readily provide the requested material to him. With this in mind, we shall try our best to look at some of the Islamic sects existent in Nigeria. There are so many sects among the Muslims in Nigeria that sprang up to spread their presumed authentic Islamic faith. Out of these sects, two are very prominent as obtained in all other Islamic world. These two are the Sunni and the Shiite Muslims. Outside these two, I must not fail to talk of the most recent sect that cropped up to rain havoc on the people - the Boko Haram.

It is important to note right away that these two mostly known and acclaimed sects in Nigeria and of course in the Islamic world –Sunni and Shiite - differ on matters concerning the theological interpretation of their articles of faith while they hold the same basic religious tenets. We ask ourselves now what these differences are. Before going to specifics, one reads from the Book, "Im Namen Allahs, des Allbarmherzigen" that, the background history as it concerns the misunderstandings between the Sunni and Shia Muslims lies in the schism that occurred when the Islamic prophet Muhammed died in the year 632 (CE). His death blew open a dispute over who is to succeed him.This dispute over the caliph of the Islamic community spread across

---

[175] Ibid.

various parts of the world.[176] Ever since this dispute reared its ugly head, Islamic religion has known no peace since these two groups have always been tangled in fearful war of who rules Islamic world. The constant collision in Iraq should be a good example of this war for control. Nigeria is not spared of these clashes between the Sunnis and Shiites.

2.7.1. The Sunni

The word Sunni refers to the majority.For this sect therefore the legitimate religious leaders are those appointed by consensus, by the majority. They believe that the heirs of those leaders are connected to Muhammad's first four successors, his Caliphs.[177] It is on this note that we believe the following statement as seen in ′wikipedia.org, where it is maintained that, "Sunnis hold that Abu Bakr was Muhammad's rightful successor and that the method of choosing or electing leaders (Shura) endorsed by the Qur'an is the consensus of the Ummah, the Muslim community.... Sunnis follow the Rashidun "rightly-guided Caliphs", who were the first four caliphs who ruled after the death of Mohammad: Abu Bakr, Umar, Uthman Ibn Affan, and Ali."[178] It is therefore not out of place to say that the Sunnis are more democratic than the Shiites.

2.7.2. The Shiite

As the Sunnis talk of electing their religious leaders by consensus, the Shiites believe that religious leaders must descend directly from Muhammad's bloodline. His Fourth Caliph was Ali, the husband of Muhammad's daughter- Fatima. For this the Shiite Muslims believe that Ali is the true source of Islam and all religious leaders should descend from him. The other three, who held sway as caliphs before Ali are seen as power ussurpers since they have no direct blood relationship with the Prophet [179]Hasan ibn Ali and Husayn ibn Ali were the sons of Ali, the husband of Fatima who was to the most beloved daughter of the Prophet. On this account, it was a common belief among the Shiite Muslims that Mohammad divinely ordained this his cousin and son-in-law Ali (the father of his grandsons Hasan ibn Ali and

---

[176] Butzkamm, A., "Im Namen Alllahs, des Allbarmherzigen" Eine kleine Einführung in den Islam, Paderborn, Bonifatius GmbH Druck, 2002, p.114.
[177] Ibid, p. 114-115.
[178] htpp://en.wikipedia.org/wiki
[179] Butzkamm, A., op. cit. p.115.

Husayn ibn Ali) in accordance with the command of God to be the next Caliph, making 'Ali and his direct descendants Muhammad's successors.[180] Consequently, the Shiites discount the legitimacy of the first three caliphs of the Sunnis (Abu-Bakr, Omar and Uthman) and believing that Ali, after Mohammad, is the second-most divinely inspired man and that he and his descendants by Muhammad's daughter Fatima, the Imams are the sole legitimate Islamic leaders. Ali is for the Shiite therefor the first Caliph. Following him was his son Hasan who being poisoned, died after only six months as a caliph. His brother Husayn was considered as the third caliph by the Shiite although he was through a gruesome murder debarred from ever ascending to the caliphate. His martyrdom is celebrated every year by the Shiites. [181]

Critically considered, one can see that the clear summary of the difference in the two sects is depicted in their etymology. The term Sunni Islam is a shortened form of ahl al-sunnah wa.l jamaah (the people of the custom and Community). The Sunnis emphasise the traditions (Sunna) of Prophet Muhammad as authoritative and approve the historic order of Mohammad's first four successors. On the other hand, "Shiite takes its name from the Arabic word Shi'ah meaning "party of" or "Supporter of" and refers specifically to the supporters of Imam Ali, the cousin and Son-in law of the Prophet."[182] It is however important to note this clear difference between the two sects. The Imamate of the Shi'ah encompasses far more of a prophetic function than the Caliphate of the Sunnis. Unlike the Sunnis, the Shiites believe that special spiritual qualities have been granted not only to the Prophet Muhammad but also to 'Ali and the other Imams.[183]

2.7.3. Intra Sectarian Conflicts in Islam

Most often in Nigeria, stories are heard of the inter-religious conflicts. A statement attributed to one Shiite Muslim leader, Shiekh Ibrahim Zakzaky and his likes is what normally fans the embers of religious tensions in Nigeria as a whole and in North in particular. The statement reads, "Nigeria must become "wholly Islamic" and "Allah pronounced Lord of the entire nation."[184] Such statements as this do not extinguish the intra-religious conflicts

---

[180] Ibid.

[181] Ibid. p. 114-115

[182] Jones, G. W, Karin, S. M., "Islam, the State and Population" p. 14-15, cf http://book.google.de). Cf. also Butzkamm, A, op. cit. p. 114

[183] Cf. htpp://en.wikipedia.org/wiki

[184] Aymer, E., "Nigeria: Clash of Religions" 1996, cf. hppt://www.yale.ed/inforum/nigeriaWin96.htm

that are found within a given religion- Christianity or Islam. Our intention here is to x-ray some bones of contention among the Islamic sects- Shiite and Sunni- in Nigeria which have experienced more conflicts than cooperation among themselves.

There is constant in-fighting as one group tries to impose its theological tenets on the other. This in-fighting can be best described as a tussle "where the two main sects of the Religion of Peace are battling for dominion."[185] The Shiite Muslim sect has fewer followers than the Sunni in Nigeria. But the Shiite sect is more militant in nature. It gained importance in Nigeria during the 1970s as a consequence of the Iranian Revolution. On the other hand, the establishment of the Sunni dates back to 19th century when Usman Dan Fodio with his Jihad terrorised the entire northern and central Nigeria. It is therefore no surprise that the Dan Fodio's legacy held sway in Northern Nigeria both politically and religiously under the leadership of Sultan of Sokoto until it fell to the more powerful European authority in 1903.Till today, the spiritual leadership authority of the Sultan of Sokoto among the Sunnis is still intact.[186] Fodio, with his charismatic power of the sword and word – he was both a warrior and a scholar- united the North under the banner of Islam. Unfortunately the Shiite Muslims lost trust in the capability of the modern Sultanate accusing it of collusion with the Nigerian corrupt government thereby deviating from the very principles that Usman Dan Fodio outlined. Because of this lack of trust on the Sultanate, many northern youths saw the only way out by joining Zakzaky's movement as an act of opposition to the disappointing and corrupt political and religious establishments. In this way, the Shiite group was growing.

The Sunnis however saw this episode as an affront and a threat to their own religious hierarchy and were ever ready to defend their heritage no matter what it takes. The Shiites were angry because their place of worship in the heart of Sokoto was razed down by the Government. The Shiites held that the government felt threatened by their non-acceptance of any authority other than Allah. For them, that was the reason for the government's support for the Sunni.[187]But the Sunnis were in full support of Government's action. They accused the Shiites of being blasphemous in their preaching. The stand of the Sunnis could be seen in the statement attributed to one of the members, Hussein Abdullahi, "If people want Sokoto to be like Iraq, with people killing each other every day, then let the Shi'ites stay. If they want Sokoto to

---

[185] "RoP Burns Govt't Building in Nigeria" June 6, 2005 cf. http://rcm-images.amazon.com.

[186] Aymer, E., op. cit.

[187] Frank Umar et. al., "Challenging Authority" cf. http://www.reuters.com/article/africaCrisis.

be its old peaceful self, then let the Shi'ites go."[188] This unsavoury relationship between the two sects led to recent conflicts within Islam in Nigeria.

The 2005 clash was memorable as it eventually led to the destruction of innumerable human lives and government property. The unfortunate incident was said to have begun when the Sunnis refused to allow the Shiites the use of the central Mosque in front of Sultan's palace. This situation was not unexpected since Sokoto is the home and seat of the Sultan, the spiritual leader of the Sunni Muslim sect. Details of how the situation, prior to the clash, looked like are readily available. One of the witnesses recounts that, "In the past three weeks there has been fighting every Friday, the Islamic days of prayers, between the two groups at the city's main mosque as Shi'ites tried to gain access and Sunnis tried to keep them out. Two weeks ago a Sunni mob attacked the Shi'ite seminary in the city and burnt it down, and last Thursday a prominent Shi'ite leader was attacked and killed in his house."[189]

Judging from the charged situation, the Sunnis might not be wrong entertaining the fear of the Shiites staging a counter attack. That could be the unpronounced reason for not allowing them the use of the Mosque. But the Sokoto State Governor (a Muslim) pleaded with the Sunnis to allow the Shiites the use of the Mosque. Angered by this request, Dan-Maishiyya, a Sunni preacher, was alleged to have preached against this action. He was consequently arrested for provocative preaching. His arrest provoked a violent reaction. According to the Sokoto State government spokesman, Mustapha Shehu, "Hundreds of protesters who besieged the Sokoto North local government secretariat and set it alight (ablaze) on Friday were angered by the police arrest of a Sunni cleric, Umar Dan-Maishiyya, accused by the authorities of inciting violent attacks against the Shiite minority...In their anger they completely burned down the secretariat building."[190]

As usual, the deployment of hundreds of armed riot police men saved the situation that could have continued unabated. After a year in detention, precisely in 2006, Umar Dan-Maishiyya was released and he became again a free man. The consequence of his release was another experience of accusation and counter accusation of each other by the Sunnis and the Shi'ites. Despite the attempt of the government spokesman to do his job of playing down the extent of damage, the witnesses were clear that many people were injured and as many as about five houses destroyed. The Shiites accused the

[188]Ibid.
[189] Ibid.
[190] RoP Ibid.

Sunnis of molesting a Shiite woman. Sa'adu Labbo said, "A group of radical Shia followers launched an attack on Thursday against a Sunni mob in the Marmaron-Garo area of the city for molesting a Shia woman, saying they would no longer condone assaults on their members."[191]

According to the spokesman of the Sokoto Shiite community, Ibrahim Atiku in reference to their Shiite members, "This group... has vowed to retaliate against any attack on any Shia follower from now on because they can't fold their hands while they are being attacked, maimed and killed...We believe the renewed attacks on our members were caused by the release of Dan-Maishiyya which emboldened the Sunni mod."[192] Even as these glaring conflicts that led to the destruction of lives and properties were raging, a group believed to be of Shiite sect under the umbrella of Islamic Movement denied the existence of any rift between the two sects. According to the group, "We the members of the Islamic Movement in Nigeria religiously believe in and advocate for Muslim unity as a matter of policy and do not in any way believe in any Shiites-Sunnis conflict. In this regard we declare that there was not any Shiites-Sunnis crisis in Sokoto before or even now."[193] This article was a response to the purported incisive article written by Aminu Muhammed and published in Daily Trust on 22 October 2007. The Daily Trust newspaper was accused of allowing biased journalists the use of its newspaper to defend a murdered political thug against the Movement. The newspaper was also accused of fronting for the incapable State Governor. A member of the Islamic movement remarked,

> We have noticed the efforts of the Trust newspaper in two of its past editions of trying to link the Islamic Movement in Nigeria with the murder of political thug in Sokoto, Umaru Dan Mai Shiyya. Uninvestigated reports that are detrimental to the reputation of the Islamic Movement which is of international calibre were made in a biased tone by the same Daily Trust, Sokoto correspondent. We are truly disappointed with the newspaper for preferring to be on the side of the irresponsible, morally degenerate Sokoto Governor, Alu Magatakardan Wammako, who could not defend himself before the Political Petitions Tribunal on charges of gross miss-conduct, in his battle against the Islamic Movement.[194]

---

[191] AFP, "Nigeria: Scores injured in Sunni-Shia violence" cf. http://www.joomla.org.
[192] Ibid.
[193] Abdul, M. G., "Re-Shiites Sunnis Clash Again in Sokoto...3killed" cf. www.islamicmovement.org. (Abdul, M. G is the secretary, Media Forum of the Islamic Movement in Nig.).
[194] Ibid.

Inasmuch as I am not writing as a judge to confirm the killing of Umaru Dan Maishiyya, I deem it necessary to disagree with the group on the issue of conflicts between the Shiites and Sunnis. In trying to deny that there was a rift between them, the group ended up unfortunately confirming it. Painting their own picture of the real and undeniable situation the group said,

> What actually happened was a clampdown on the innocent members of the Islamic Movement in Nigeria in Sokoto who are also under the revered leadership of Sheikh Ibraheem Zakzaky (H) by the state government, her security wings and paid hoodlums. This is in fulfilment of Wammako's promise of wiping out the Shiites sect which has no political inclination in the State in order to please their rival Sunni brothers who actively participated in voting him into office. Henceforth, even those who rivalled Wammako's political ambitions, most especially the rival DPP members who are also supporters of Bafarawa were declared Shiites by him and his supporters. This act of terrorism reached its peak when a political thug in the person of Umaru Dan MaiShiyya was shot by gunmen near the Shehu Mosque at Kan Wuri in Sokoto and died some hours later in the hospital. The members of the Islamic Movement otherwise referred to as Shiites were hypocritically accused of killing 'A SUNNI CLERIC' immediately after the death of the political thug Ummaru Dan MaiShiyya.[195]

The very fact that the 'innocent members' of the Islamic Movement are loyal to Sheikh Zakzaky, who himself is opposed to the 'inordinate political and religious leadership inclination of the Sultan of Sokoto' coupled with the claim that Wammako is simply trying to wipe the Shiites out to please their rival Sunni brothers leaves no one in doubt that there is a conflict between the two rivals- Sunnis and Shiites.

2.8. Boko Haram

Apart from the two principal sects mentioned above, there are many others that have emerged but seemed to have no strong hold even among Muslims themselves. Not having foothold even among Muslims, they either evaporated into thin air and died off or regrouped and came out in another disguise and name. Since most of them are militant by nature, they bring

[195] Ibid.

with them untold havocs which they often wreck in the name of Allah on innocent citizens. Thanks to some peace-loving Muslims who spoke out in condemnation against them. We cannot name or dwell on all of them. One of such sects that emerged recently is the Boko Haram led by Mohammed Yusuf. Born on 29 January 1970, Yusuf hailed from Girgir Jakuso in Yobe State of Nigeria. He had four wives and twelve children.[196]

2.8.1. Meaning and Doctrine of Boko Haram

Boko Haram in Hausa language means, "Western education is evil." So this group opposes all forms of western education and civilisation. Mathew Kukah was more critical in his approach as he tried to unravel the conceptual confusion of the term by first seeking to dismantle its etymological import. He wrote, "Although the group has come to be popularly known as Boko Haram, it is not clear whether the group actually called itself by this name. This is because the words, Boko and Haram are two different nouns which merely describe rather than define what you might call a system of beliefs...the words have no theological meaning and could not in themselves become a set of beliefs as such."[197] Dwelling on the etymology of the term, he reasoned,

> In the mind of the Muslim every act is either **Halal**, *permissible* or **Haram**, *impermissible*. So, from within this context, while *Ilimin Islamiyya* was considered **Halal**, *permissible*, *Ilimin* Boko was **Haram**, *impermissible*. Against this backdrop, anyone getting Western education was therefore a sinner, carrying out an impermissible act....It is interesting that even within the Muslim community there are conflicting notions to what the word Boko itself really means. It crept into the vocabulary right from the beginning of the incursions of the colonial state and its Western educational system. Boko was often used in relation to a second noun, *Ilimi*, meaning education. Thus, the full expression, *Ilimin* Boko, was used to derogatorily refer to Western education as distinct from what the Muslim community understood as the only form of education, namely, *Ilimin Islamiyya*, that is *Islamic education*.[198]

---

[196] Kilete, M., "Military in Control – DHQ" in: *Daily Sun*, July 31, 2009, p. 7.
[197] Kukah, M. H., Boko Haram: "Some reflections on causes and effects" in: Dr. Otmar Oehring (ed.), *Human Rights,* Aachen, Pontifical Mission Society, Human rights office, 2009, p. 22.
[198] Ibid.

Having gone far in trying to unmask the meaning of this term, one does not do justice to it without mentioning some schools of thought that view the word 'Boko' from a different angle. For one of such groups, Boko is a corruption of the word *Boka*, meaning sorcery or witchcraft. This claim therefore highlights the idea that Western education was as debased as sorcery or witchcraft and should by all means be avoided since it is viewed as a tool the enemy intends to use in destroying Islam just as the colonial master destroyed Islamic polity. The second group sees Boko as referring to a *counterfeit* or *fake* thing. This concept is evident in the Islamic marriage rite. *Amaryan* is a term used for a new bride. *Amaryan Boko* refers therefore to a fake bride. In marriage procession, the Amaryan Boko leads a procession dressed as the future real bride. As the invitees rise to follow the Amaryan Boko, the fake bride, the Amaryan, the real bride appears to the jubilation of the crowd. This period is regarded as the high point of the ceremony. The argument for all this is meant to convey the view that as the white Christian missionaries used the words pagan and witchcraft interchangeably to connote the African beliefs and culture, the coinage of the word Boko was meant to situate the new but strange and suspicious education of the white man within the Muslim community in a negative stand.[199]

The question which constantly comes to mind is: Why do these militant sects crop up and mostly in northern part of the country? One of the reasons is lack of education. The traditional religious education of the Muslims has failed to prepare them for the sought-after technical and commercial jobs.[200] Kukah vividly wrote,

> Hordes of Muslim children who today roam the streets are graduates of the Islamiyya schools who often graduate after four or five years under the tutelage of an itinerant teacher, Mallam. The Mallam instructs them, earns no salary and has to rely solely on the proceeds of his students' daily rounds of begging on the streets or in private homes. In the course of their training both they and their teacher have no other forms of support except the proceeds of their begging. These hordes of young children are unleashed on the streets of almost all the Northern cities and towns with no means of self-support. Their population runs into millions across all the major cities and towns in the Northern states. They are the cannon

---

[199] Ibid, p. 23.

[200] Aymer, E., op. cit.

fodder that feed sects like Boko Haram and other similar millenarian movements that sprout occasionally in the North.[201]

After the Kano riot in 1983, Paul Lubeck, a professor of Sociology from the University College of Los Angeles, after studying the situation published a resume of his finding which he entitled 'Islamic Protest Under Semi-Industrial Capitalism'. According to Kukah, Professor Lubeck made a touchy revelation as to the problems of these rioting youths who were referred to as Gardawa. His write-up which focused on Kano incident could easily pass for the situation in all of the Northern States. His findings "reveal that these Gardawa are the victims and products of the contradictions of a semi-industrial economy which had not fully developed or expand to absorb these youths. The training they were receiving in their Koranic education was for a world that was fast vanishing, while the new one could not accommodate them."[202] However, considering the fact that their leader was very articulate, Kukah had some reservations in believing that the Boko Haram group was totally against the Western education as such. He tried to find another cause of the unfortunate attitude of these youths by looking more critically into the Nigerian hopeless situation. He emphasised that the evil effects of bad governance, corruption, total lack of security and welfare have all become part of our daily lives. Clearly, in the eyes of the sect members the persistence of corruption, collapse of public morality, injustice and so on could be attributed to those who govern. In their reasoning, those who govern, do so because they have acquired their tools by gaining Western education. These same people call themselves Moslems, but they persist in things that are Haram, impermissible in Islam. It is their acquisition of Western education that has polluted public morality. This line of thinking had resonance among the poor and the victims of society.[203]

Another possible explanation for their violence could be their charged and changing environment with themselves now feeling uneasy in their own locality. Kukah reasoned that following the tornado of changes around them, the ordinary Moslems feel overwhelmed. This feeling could be due to their inability to access the tools of modernization for which they have to a visible extent remained outside the loop of power. To worsen this feeling, the very people they had always regarded as foreigners, mainly Southern Christian traders, were seen in the very inner recesses of their major cities in Northern

---

[201] Kukah, H. M., op. cit. p. 24.
[202] Ibid.
[203] Ibid, p. 25.

region engaging in almost all kinds of businesses. Their habits of taking alcoholic drinks, partying and generally indulging in lifestyles which the Moslems consider dysfunctional made ordinary Moslems nervous and they became afraid of the future of their families and faith. Sensing that they had become too weak to fight, people like Mallam Mohammed Yusuf, the leader of Boko Haram, took an advange of this situation by arguing that turning inwards, away from contamination, was a greater source of strength than looking outwards by means of acquiring Western education and other tools of modernization.With ninety percent of his followers not having Western education and being surely graduates of the Islamic education system, this approach naturally would have made a big sense. The situation was made more fertile for any form of rioting since the environment harboured some educated Moslems who were not gainfully employed. They found a new community in Boko Haram with the claim that it had offered them security and cathered for their welfare. This new found community translated for them into an alternative state and their leader an alternative to their so-called political class that have undoubtedly failed them.[204]

Despite the backwardness of the Northerners in education, this group came up in this modern era to denounce Western education and culture insisting that only the enthronement of Islamic ideals in Nigeria will guarantee peace and morality. Just like the Shiites, the Boko Haram simply have their minds set on the eradication of un-Islamic values in Nigeria. These un-Islamic values include also the attitude of some Muslims who are adjudged corrupt, probably because they are not against the Western culture. But to the utmost surprise of some of these youths who made themselves easy prey to some insincere politicians in the North, they found out that even those who seemed to be fronting for Islam were simply working for their personal gains and glory. Their tenures as governors were a total failure marred with corruption and self-enrichment. For instance,

> In 2000, many ordinary Muslims were excited by the announcement first from the then Governor of Zamfara that the state would adopt Sharia law. The euphoria that followed this announcement spread as other states similarly made the same promises....Sadly, ordinary Muslims have come to realize that their own governors and public officers, the so called holy men of yesterday and apostles of Sharia have been caught in the same web of corruption like all their contemporaries. They realized that these

[204] Ibid, p. 26.

apostles of Sharia shared in the same looting of their state treasury and were hypocritical in their claims. Thus, abandoning Sharia, as the elites are now being accused by ordinary Muslims, has added to the feeling of shame, embarrassment and powerlessness among Muslims. Sharia, as it has turned out in the hands of these elites, has not proved to be the solution to national and community problems, contrary to their hopes.[205]

This new awareness on the part of the ordinary suffering Muslims did not make things easier in the North. Since justice is said to be highly priced in Islam, the poor Muslims in such situations have no alternative than to revert to misplaced wanton destruction of property in line with the caliphate war mentality. In trying to see that justice is done, they end up inflicting untold hardship on the innocent citizens going about their genuine businesses which in itself, is an unjust act of the first order. This stand makes it easier to note that Islam has remained prone to violence in the Northern states. In the North, they still think in terms of wars of the caliphate and other wars of resistance in the last one hundred years. This is due to the experience they had where the state in collaboration with the colonial state used its monopoly and control of violence to destroy the entire communities. Mahdism went beyond the borders of the colonial states in Nigeria. In the face of injustice and the perception that the state has abandoned them, some of these Muslims have often decided to take laws into their hands. In Islam, Justice is highly priced so that the words of the founder of the Caliphate and the first Sultan, Othman dan Fodio, are often recalled: A nation can live with unbelief, but cannot live with injustice. With a justice that commands very little respect and is suspected to be subject to manipulation by the powers that be, ordinary Moslems find no other outlets than the secondary targets, such as innocent civilians, their properties, churches or police stations, onto which they release their frustration.[206]

The level of injustice being perpetrated by the wealthy in Northern Nigeria was a source of great concern for many Muslims. Their attitude towards the poor among them is nothing to write home about. While the rich swim in abundance of wealth, looting the state treasury, the ordinary Muslim wallows not only in ignorance but more so in abject poverty. These poor ones are usually gullible and can do anything possible or join any type of group that can guarantee their daily bread. It is therefore not surprising that so many of

---

[205] Ibid, p. 30.
[206] Ibid, p. 31

the visible members of Boko Haram are poor. According to Kabiru Lawanti, Northerner,

> We have in the North today an elite that takes pride in seeing fellow citizens live in abject poverty and squalor, an elite that is happy to be the only educated and enlightened ones in their villages and neighbourhoods, elites that pride itself with being the richest in their communities while the majority cannot afford to feed their families... Our governors have turned their States into fiefdoms. They steal with impunity. They arrogantly convert State resources to their own. They have deliberately destroyed the public school system which most of those who have found themselves in the Boko Haram sect are supposed to attend. They denied them access to education. They deprive them from living a decent life.[207]

2.8.2. Beginning

The notorious sect that inflicted mayhem on innocent citizens is not relatively new in Nigeria. They have been in operation for some time even with the knowledge of the government. It is unfortunate to note here, according to the Director, Defence Information (DDI) Colonel Mohammed Yerima, that this group started its operation as far back as 1995. He explained that,

> A certain group of Islamic fundamentalists, led by one Mohammed Yusuf had in the recent past been engaging in some suspicious activities with security implications. The group named Boko-Haram...did not emerge just of recent. They have been in existence as far back as 1995 under different names such as Ahlulsunna wal'jama'ah hijra. Securty agencies have over this period been monitoring and containing their activities even when they transmuted to other names but with the same doctrine of intolerance. For instance, on November 13, 2008, the group's leader, Mohammed Yusuf and quite a number of his followers were arrested by the security operatives and handed over to the Inspector General of Police for prosecution. However, they were subsequently granted bail by an Abuja High Court on January 20, 2009. Before then, in 2007, one of his ardent disciples, Al-amin who was also the Kano State leader of the group was arrested along with some of their members after an attack on a police station in Kano, he was also handed over to the police for prosecution. Similarly, between February and April 2009, Yusuf's second in

[207] Lawanti, K., "Boko Haram and the Culpability of the Northern Elite" in: *Daily Trust*, August 3, p. 12.

command named Kilakam, a Nigerien, was on two occasions arrested and repatriated to his country.[208]

The above quotation actually shows that even the Security outfits did not know when exactly when this group started. However, it is clear from above that the sect did not just start in 2009 when the great havoc that brought them into limelight was caused. This uncertainty contributed to the criticism in which Kukah sees the Security agents as part of the problem. According to him, "Most of these rantings of Boko Haram discontentment sounded every (sic) familiar. The government and the security agencies knew what was happening. But like all previous crises no preemptive measures were taken."[209]Regretting and reporting the extent of havoc that this sect caused the nation, Timothy Olanrewaju, as given by a source in Maiduguri hospital writes, "the corpses are countless...Some of them are still lying in the streets and around the police headquarters...Our hospital is full to capacity...Some of the patients who are injured from the fighting are lying on the floor of the hospital for lack of space."[210]

Both defenceless citizens and the sect members numbered among the casualties. Reporting further he said, "Troops raided the Islamists headquarters in Maiduguri, killing no fewer than 200 followers of the self-styled Taliban sect along with its deputy leader."[211]A much later account put the casualty figure at 650 including of course the sect members and all those shot by the police under the suspicion that they belonged to the sect. Some Christians totalling about 300 were said to have been forced to convert to Boko Haram firebrand of Islam after their capture. Those who swore never to deny their Christian faith were summarily martyred. Among them were three clergy men who were purported to have been gruesomely beheaded.[212]

2.8.3. Sponsorship

It is obvious that this violent sect in Nigeria has some sponsors. State government officials and the security agents seem to be implicated in this activity. The extrajudicial killings of some of the members of the sect by the

---

208 Kilete, M., op. cit. p. 7.

209 Kukah, H. M., op. cit. p. 27.

210 Olanrewaju, T., "Islamist militant leader, Mohammed Yusuf, flees" in: *Daily Sun newspaper*, Friday, July 31, 2009, p. 6.

211 Ibid.

212 Ola, T., "Revealed! How they killed our Father – Mohammed Yusuf's family" in: *Saturday Sun*, August 8, 2009, p. 13.

State security agents seem to be a distraction and a cover-up. Reacting to the killing of some of the members of the Boko Haram, The Nigerian Bar Association through their President remarked, "We note the effort of the security operatives for rising to the occasion and nipping the horrific incident in the bud. We must also strive to unmask the real sponsors of these deviants and punish them appropriately"[213] Further the President of the Nigeria Bar Association (NBA) said, "We must however...hasten to equally condemn the reported extra judicial killing of some of those captured by the security operatives. It was widely reported that the leader of the Islamic extremist group, one Yusuf, was captured alive. The killing of this man in the police custody, however reprehensible his deeds must have been, must not be encouraged in a civilized society"[214]

The Afenifere Renewal Group through their spokeman, Yinka Odumakin said that their group, "...unequivocally condemns the extra-judicial murder of the leader of Boko Haram, Mohammed Yusuf... We fear that his murder could have been a cover-up to shield his backers from justice. This has again exposed Nigeria to the sane world as a country founded on deceit and being sustained by siege."[215] Without slightest ambiguity, the Nigeria Labour Congress, (NLC) stated that "Most of the blames should go to the government. There were reports that the group had been existing for a long time. What we know about security operatives is that because of preventive measures, these security operatives are made to infiltrate into suspicious groups to find out whether they are dangerous groups or not and then make appropriate reports. If this was done and government followed it and did the right thing, those innocent citizens would not have been wasted. There is no doubt that innocent people were killed and valuable properties destroyed during the violence. But today in Nigeria, all the security agencies in the country are concentrated around politics and politicians while other segments of the society are left unattended to."[216]

One is more likely to suspect a cover if it is provable that the security operatives and the State government were informed of the impending anarchy before it happened. The brother-in-law of the deceased leader of Boko Haram, Baba Kura Fugu, regretting that the security operatives killed his father decided to let the cat out of the sack. He narrated how he wrote a letter

[213] Anaba, I, Akoni, O. et.al, "Police uncover Boko Haram arms depot in Bauchi" in: *Vangurd newspaper*, August, 3, 2009, p. 5.
[214] Ibid.
[215] Ibid.
[216] Ibid.

on behalf of his father, Alhaji Baba Fugu Mohammed, to the state government two weeks to the crisis. His father was later assassinated by the police. Realising that Mohammed Yusuf, their son-in-law and his group were threatening the peace and security of the state, he went to the office of the Secretary to Borno State Government five times but did not meet him. On another occasion he was told that he was having a meeting. He then submitted the letter to his PA for onward transmission to his oga. He gave him the original copy and he endorsed the duplicate with his signature and date, as an acknowledgement of receipt of the letter. But through negligence of government or security agencies all his recommendations were not followed and what he predicted in the letter came to pass because they noticed the level of their preparedness, the unusual in-flow of Mohammed Yusuf's supporters from neighbouring states.[217]

As evidence that the above claim was authentic, the content of the purported written letter was made known with a reference no 26/PERS/13/2009 and the title, 'Threatening Situation to Peace and Security of the State Posed by Mallam Mohammed Yusuf and his Disciples'. The content indicates, "The spate at which disciples of the Boko Haram flung Maiduguri and paying solidarity to their leader shows they were busy preparing to launch an offensive attack. In addition to that, they are targeting many government agencies and departments such as courts, the state House of Assembly, police stations and formations across the state, the university and other tertiary institutions. They are also targeting all democratic institutions and structures and political office holders"[218] As part of his contribution to help avert this calamity, he proffered some solutions. Convinced of the ignorance of the landlord as to the activities of this group, he suggested that he should be called and rightly schooled on the danger of harbouring such a group. As a follow up, all the law enforcement agencies and security formations in the north eastern sub-region should be made to know of this danger and then get ready to contain any possible spread of this group in their areas of jurisdiction.[219]

This laisser-faire attitude on the part of the government provides a strong ground for suspicion. It is a nonchalant behaviour that could lead any right thinking person to suspect an attempt to cover up. It is one of the banes of Nigerian democracy bedevilled by endemic corruption. In a democratically developed country, such a gross mark of irresponsibility is enough for the

[217] Ola, T., op. cit. p. 13.
[218] Ibid.
[219] Ibid.

concerned government official to wilfully resign from office. It is consequent upon this that the chairman of the Civil Liberty Organisation (CLO), Sadiq Makaramba described this government attitude towards this purported pre-information as irresponsible. He regretted that the president did not help matters when he failed to call for proactive action, having confirmed that the government truly received security alert. This awful irresponsibility has led not only to the killing and maiming of innocent citizens but sent huge resources to the world of no return including riot policemen and soldiers[220]

This stand by Sadiq is a clear pointer to doubts in the claim of the police that Yusuf, the leader of the Boko Haram sect was killed when he attempted to escape from their custody. Ikenna Emewu writing under the caption, 'Let's clap for northern governors' was more direct and had neither the time to rigmarole nor the room for economy of words. As he boldly put it, "Nobody would be convinced that the summary killing of the financier of Boko Haram fanatics, Buji Fai, and their leader, Mohammed Yusuf by the police after they were handed over to them alive was a coincidence. Yusuf, from what BBC displayed even had a bandaged arm from an injury he sustained in the hands of the soldiers who captured him. They treated the injury to make sure he lives and speaks, but in the hands of the police, 'he tried to escape', and the solution to stopping the escape of an unarmed detainee was to snuff life out of him to be very sure he does not live to tell the world who he works for."[221]

He unambiguously directed his searchlight in the direction of the northern governors describing their coming together to make laws that would deter further offenders, as a jamboree. Speaking as if he has first hand information on who sponsored the sect, Emewu said, "Of course the originators of the problems won't be far from the northern governors and other politicians. Watch out for these planned new laws and see if they will ever come...It is all deceit. It is a grand design to escape from tackling the problem. It is just another baseless jamboree to deceive themselves. Nobody needs any new laws. But what all of us need is that you implement the laws you already have which contain enough provisions to punish the offenders adequately. Stop playing games and just admit you have failed by sponsoring these riots and killings and turning around to look for scapegoats and escapes from the reality."[222]

---

[220] Ibid.
[221] Ibid, p. 41.
[222] Ibid.

The alleged action of the government in killing the leaders of Boko Haram and destroying any possible incriminating evidence resemble the case of Maitatsine whose corpse was completely burnt after he had been killed.[223] With this assertion, Kukah unambiguously pointed accusing finger to the government and politicians as sponsors of this group. Courageously he mentioned names and the possible reasons for their identifying with the leaders of such sects, damning the consequences. He explained that,

> The deputy leader of the Boko Haram, Alhaji Mamman Foi, was an influential man who had served as a commissioner in the present government of Adamawa State. He was said to have had direct access to the State House and Governor. He obviously had access to resources because he was said to be the financier of the movement. He and the Governor are said to have originally hailed from neighbouring Niger. All these point to one thing: the occasional complicity of politicians who, in search of spiritual legitimacy, often befriend men such as the leaders of the sect in question. In exchange for the patronage a politician or a follower of these *holy men* secure what is called in Islam Al Barka, that is blessing. In the popular mind of the politicians this Al Barka can be a source of protection in many forms. It can ward off political enemies, ensure success, ensure physical or political longevity, ward off demons...[224]

2.9. Conclusion

Considering the immediate quotation above, it is clear that many religious problems in Nigeria are not caused by the common man out there in the street. These riots or violence are mostly planned by men and women who are well place and even respected in the society. It is either that they plan them and employ the unemployed poor ones roaming the streets of Nigeria to execute them for a fee or they indirectly lead the violence themselves. It is in this case that we can see that the plan for the spread of Islam in Nigeria which is partly peaceful and partly coercively made was planned by well placed men. Unfortunately, the Jihad that was used in the attempt to expand Islam in Nigeria turned out to be a problem even for those who employed it. It is for this reason that the Moslems now carry the Jihad against themselves. Typical examples are the Maitatsine and Boko Haram episodes. These groups did not spare their fellow Moslems accusing them of renega-

---

[223] Kukah, H. M., op. cit. p. 28.
[224] Ibid, p. 27.

tion. Unfortunately, members of these groups are themselves Renegades having separated themselves either from Sunni or Shiite Moslem groups. It will surely not be an over statement to hold tight onto the view that these problems within these sectarian Islamic groups have refused to remain only within the Islamic fold. They have spilled over to the religious and political life of Nigeria on the whole. It is therefore on the strength of this assertion that we shall now consider the conflicts and problems that militate against peaceful co-existence in Nigeria.

CHAPTER THREE

PROBLEMS AND CONFLICTS

3. Introduction

This chapter could be seen as one of the basic chapters of the whole of this work. It addresses the question of whether there are really conflicts and problems in Nigeria. It goes on to consider differing opinions adduced as the root causes of the problems and conflicts that disunite a nation. It is even suggested that the root of these problems could be found outside the shores of Nigeria. We intend first of all to consider some divergent opinions or statements on the conflicts before we take on some of the basic conflicts on their merits.

3.1. Divergent Opinions on the causes of the Conflicts

In discussing the problems and conflicts militating against the peaceful co-existence of Nigerians, one has to pay attention to the two powerful elements adduced by Bloomfield and Reilly which H.B Yusuf quoted as being the tap roots of many problems. Referring to these powerful elements Yusuf said, "The first is identity, which is defined as 'the mobilitation (sic) of people in communal identity groups based on races, religion, culture, language'. The second is distribution: 'the means of sharing the economic, social and political resources within a society."[225] He went further to explain that,

> Where perceived imbalance in distribution coincides with identity differences, where, for example, one religious group is deprived of certain resources available to others, we have the potential for conflict. It is this combination of potent identity with wider perceptions of economic and social injustice that often fuels deep-rooted conflicts....These conflicts have a tendency to recur because identity issues cover a wide range of elements that are at the core of a people's sense of being, such as race, religion, culture, heritage, history, language, etc. They are therefore more complex, persistent and prolonged. They are also much more difficult to

---

[225] Yusuf, H. B., "Managing Muslim–Christian Conflicts in Northern Nigeria: A Case Study of Kaduna State" in: *Islam and Christian – Muslim Relations*, Vol. 18. No.2, 237-256, April 2007, USA, Taylor & Francis Group, p. 241.

resolve since the core issues are difficult to negotiate and not amenable to compromise.[226]

It is in concordance with the above citation that Vellguth Klaus made reference to the conflicts in the African soil as a whole accusing his fellow whites of being insensitive to the African situation as they demarcated the Africa nations. For him, the foundations for conflicts in African land were laid at least in 19th Century when the European powers marked out the boundaries of Africa with lines. In making this demarcation they failed to consider ethnic connectivity but were particularly oriented towards the European power hegemony.[227]The above quotation though referring to Africa as a whole, could be applied to Nigeria. This application is possible following some opinions that the improper amalgamation of Nigeria in 1914 is one of the root causes of Nigerian conflicts. It could therefore be said that the same inconsiderate system used in the whole of Africa was extended to individual countries without considering their identity or amenability in mind. It could be said in general that economic selfishness and power hegemony on the part of the whites have helped leave the African continent in general and Nigeria in particular vulnerable to conflicts. The above assertions give at a glance the general causes of conflicts.

Since it is our concern here to discuss the conflicts in Nigeria, it sounds more reasonable that we refer to the result of an investigation carried out in Kaduna in 1992 to indicate possible causes of conflicts in Nigeria. It is carried out in form of an interview and the results stated in percentage. Regarding the question on the causes of conflicts between Muslims and Christians in Kaduna State, respondents attributed it to the following:

(a) competition over scarce resources: 22%
(b) clash over values: 32%
(c) elite manipulation: 68%
(d) hoodlums who cash in on peaceful demonstrations: 40%
(e) poor, unemployed and frustrated people: 58%

When asked whether the conflicts were religious, ethnic or economic, respondents stated as follows:
(a) religious: 50%

---

226 Ibid.

227 Vellguth, K., ,Wenn Religion als Vorwand dient, Unruhen in Nigeria haben vielfältige Ursachen' in: *Heilung und Heil*, Heft 3/2009, p. 12.

(b) ethnic: 46%
(c) economic: 62%.

Politics, envy and frustration have also been identified as possible causes.[228] From the above data it becomes easier to observe that the high scores on economic, religions, poverty/unemployed/frustrated people and elite manipulation really speak volumes about the conflicts in Nigeria. Christianity and Islam remain to date the two largest religious groups in the globe and neither of them is showing any sign of giving up the exclusive claim to uniqueness and authenticity. Nigeria is also touched by this assertion. It needs to be clearly noted that religions do not bring about conflicts. It is their misuse that does. Thus according to Isizoh, it has to be said without fear of contradiction that:

> It is not the issue of religion that provokes violence. Religion, when truly practiced, brings peace and harmony in the society. Our love of God is manifested concretely in our love of our neighbours. It is indeed the abuse of religion that creates tension, brings division and hatred, and leads to violence in the society. Sometimes some individuals exploit and manipulate the religious sentiments and the religiosity of others to their selfish ends. This is to be condemned.[229]

It is this exploitation and manipulation of religious sentiments and religiosity for selfish ends that can be characterized in the words of John Paul II as "shadows"[230] or as George Carey puts it "Darker side"[231] of religion. Bemoaning this darker side, it can be observed that,

> The same religions which have such potential for creating community have, sadly, all too often divided and alienated people from one another...I am also very much aware that the medieval conflicts between Islam and Christianity cast a long shadow. No modern Christian is happy with the way our forebears sought to settle the divisions of the past. The Crusades severely damaged relationships both between Christians and be-

---

[228] Yusuf, H. B., op. cit. p. 244-245.
[229] Isizoh, C. D., 'Exhortation: On IRDC-AECAWA during their 2002 Study Session in Accra-Ghana' published in *Missio Korrespondenz MISSIO/MWI* 6.März 2008, Bibliothek/Doku, p. 49.
[230] John Paul II, Homilies and Addresses in Nigeria: Address to Christian families, no.1
[231] Carey, G., 'Documentation: The Challenges Facing Christian-Muslim Dialogue' being a lecture given on October 4, at Al-Azhar University Egypt in: *Islam and Christian-Muslim Relations,* Vol.7, No. 1, 1996, p. 95.

tween Christians and Muslims....But religious disputes continue today and, sadly, violence is often linked to passions which become associated with different faith communities.[232]

These Shadows are unarguably the multitude of dark angles that look hidden. These shadows notwithstanding, only some people who are totally biased would not want to see and acclaim some positive aspects that will be discussed later in another part of this work. Unfortunately, the problems are becoming daily more pronounced among the two great world religions, even with ATR, each laying claim to the possession of absolute truth and peace. A typical example is a speech by an adherent of ATR at a wake service for their deceased member. It shows the bias people can have about religions such as Islam and Christianity in Nigerian context. It was a total and deliberate manipulation of a quotation from Christian Holy Bible. It was a critique of both Islam and Christianity. But it contains some important lessons. He started by telling his fellow adherents to rejoice for they were blessed to be on the right holy and divine train/track. He accused the Christians of ignorance and blindly reading the Scriptures without wisdom and out of context in which case they misled the people by misinterpreting the content to fit them and their devilish masters.

The text he was quoting was a popular verse "many are called but few are chosen". Interpreting this verse, he quoted another biblical text. The road is wide which leads to doom and many people follow it, while the road is shallow and hard which leads to Heaven and only a few follow it.[233] He was of the view that Christianity is a simple and easy straight road that leads to doom and that is why so many follow it. He sees ATR as that very difficult, rigorous shallow road that leads to Heaven and that is why a few follow it. For him therefore, ATR is the religion of the wise and informed people of the African continent. They may be listened to when one considers the degree of destruction and acrimony going on between Christianity and Islam as each tries to stamp her authority as the authentic, revealed religion.

Despite their laying claim to being religions of peace, evidences abound of their rivalry presumably rooted in some texts of their holy books. Thus according to Thomas, D,

232 Ibid, p. 96.

233 Mt. 7:13-14.Here, we read the authentic text that was quoted out of context to fit his confusion.

> It cannot be denied that acts of violence have been committed in the name of religion with depressing regularity. Nor can it be denied that, although religion may have been manipulated by cynical rulers and governments to support acts of cruelty and warfare, both Christianity and Islam have within their arrays of scripture and belief sufficient to provide contexts in which acts of violence and barbarity can be legitimized. The sacred texts themselves provide undeniable evidence for this, and the histories of both religions speak eloquently of it...The problem that stands before Christians and Muslims has its roots in the very principles that each proclaim. These appear in many aspects to be strikingly similar, but they actually cut across each other in ways that have driven followers of both faiths to mutual condemnation and complaint. When they are set out schematically, their similarities and differences become dangerously apparent.[234]

In buttressing their similarities, one notes that Christianity and Islam believe in and teach about the existence of God, the creator from whom all things come into being and to whom they owe their sustenance, depending of course on act of the creative grace. With these assertions one sees clearly the many factors that contribute to the innumerable conflicts jeopardizing the much desired peaceful co-existence, and enveloping the most populous African nation and religious- pluralistic Nigeria. Some of these problem-laden areas have been unambiguously enumerated by M. Kukah. He remarked that, "Since the country attained independence, regional, ethnic and religious tensions have marred its progress."[235] In another instance he mentioned, suspicion, accusation and counteraccusation as part of the problems. We must however not deny the impact of history and economy. Having seen the divergent opinions on the root causes of conflicts and problems in Nigeria, let us now look at the basic and generally accepted root causes on their merits.

3.2. Historical Problem

God created the world where man can find meaning and as a context in which his moral intention could be discerned and understood. Because he so

---

[234] Thomas, D., "The Past and the Future in Christian-Muslim Relations" in: *Islam and Christian-Muslim Relations,* David Thomas, ed. et al. p. 33-34, U.K, CSIC, Birmingham, Vol.18, No.1, 33-42, January 2007.

[235] Kukah, M. H., "Christian-Muslim Relations in Sub-Saharan Africa: Problems and Prospects" in: *Islam and Christian-Muslim Relations.* Vol.18, No. 2, 155-164, April 2007, p. 156.

much loved the world and his creatures, he fortified them with the level of intelligence to seek his face and communicate with him. In order to communicate with him, he allowed some signs of his care to be evident. Man should appreciate these deeds of love from God by following his loving examples since he has been endowed with the grace to differentiate between right and wrong. Failure to act rightly merits one condemnation on the day of judgment- a clear pointer to the events to mark the end of the world when the good will be separated from the bad.

Christianity and Islam are in accord on this point of moral imperatives of the last days. This does not remove the very existence of historically substantial disagreement. For Mathew H. Kukah, "Christian-Muslim relations, even at the best of times, have always been disturbingly marred by suspicion, accusations and counteraccusations over interpretations of history and experiences"[236] Commenting on this issue Thomas, D opined that in Christianity,

> History is seen as a process of loss and regain, with humanity losing its first innocence through disobedience to God, and thereafter being barred from full relationship with him. But humankind lives with the promise of a decisive act by God to heal the rift and restore the lost relationship. Prophets come to make God's promise known, and finally God himself, in the form of his Son, comes to take the weight of sin and to save humankind. In the climatic event of Christ's appearance on earth, his life and death are seen as God's supreme act of love in which humankind is restored and the relationship between God and his creatures can be resumed in its fullness. What this story means is that, in traditional teaching, Jesus Christ is seen as the climax of history, to whom the prophets whose sayings are recorded in the Jewish scriptures pointed, and after whose coming the whole of history is one of hope and expectation. After his dramatic appearance on earth and his atoning death, there is no further need for God to act in a new way, because the ongoing path of history is that of the Church whose function is to proclaim the life and death of Christ and to bring all people to believe in them.[237]

Having dwelt summarily on the Christian doctrinal stand (taking the line of history) that puts her at loggerhead with Islam, Thomas, D went on to survey the Islamic stand. He maintained that,

---

[236] Ibid, p. 155.
[237] Thomas, D., op. cit. p. 34-35.

> History is a process of instruction, with God sending teachings to the communities of believers in order to help them in their effort to live lives in obedience to and love for him. For Muslims, humankind are (sic) placed as representatives of God on earth, with a stature that fits this role. Human's reason enables them to perceive the existence of God behind creation and to understand their relationship with him. But to help them and to clarify his intention for them, God has sent through history a succession of instructions by which they can fulfill their relationship of servant with him as master. These revealed messages, which contain teachings identical in substance, all look forward to the last message and messenger who will bring it. This is the Prophet Muhammad, who is the seal of the Prophets and sent to all humanity rather than to single community as earlier messengers were, and the message is the Qur'an, the revelation that comes to confirm and guarantee the contents of all the earlier messages and to correct them where they have been allowed to admit errors.[238]

The observable negative effects of the positions taken by these two religions are the continuous squabbles that emerge between them. Basically, Christian teachings maintained that the climax of God's love for the world he created is evident in his sending his only begotten son to die for the salvation of his creatures. Since his plans and creative will are perfectly fulfilled in Jesus Christ, it becomes senseless for anyone to come after Jesus with the claim of superiority. It is therefore unacceptable to suggest that Mohammed who came 600 years after Jesus has any connection with God's will for the world. Against this claim was the counterclaim by the belief in Islam that the events in history point to the coming of Mohammed with intermittent appearances of some messengers, including Jesus the Messiah. They claim that Jesus was an infallible, created human prophet to whom the message referring to the coming of Mohammed was revealed. This Jesus just like other Prophets before and after him taught that there is only one God and that this God alone is divine. On this hinges their criticism of the Christians doctrine that Jesus is more than a human and maintained that the idea of Jesus being God on earth violates the unanimous belief and revealed teachings of all the prophets, as well as Reason itself[239].

These historical-doctrinal conflicts that raged between Christians and Muslims since the emergence of Islam has dealt a deadly blow to prospects

[238] Ibid.
[239] Ibid, p. 35.

of peaceful co-existence as each religion tried to deny authenticity to the other. It has made it extremely difficult for the two religions to trustfully create a common ground where dialogue could meaningfully offer solutions to subsequent conflicts. Instead, mockery and disdain towards one another have been the resultant effect, creating a seemingly insurmountable barrier. It is on this foundational problem that basically other problems rest, as is evident in the Nigerian situation.

The religious conflict in Nigeria obliterates its kind anywhere in African continent. Kukah has no doubt in stating this obvious Nigerian situation. According to him, "It has to be stated though, there must be something peculiar about the Nigerian situation because nowhere else in Africa has violence by adherents of both religions manifested itself the way it has done in Nigeria."[240] Giving this assertion, despite the general historical background of religious conflicts in Africa as given above, he traced that of Nigeria to the attitude of the British colonial masters as it regards their indirect rule.[241] He remarked that the British sought with their indirect rule to ward off all the laws that they felt were repugnant to natural justice found in Sharia and customary laws. It is however important to remember that at the back of their minds, the British took Africa as a black, dark continent to which they intended bringing the rays of light. In as much as they welcomed some aspects of Sharia and customary laws, these laws are not deemed worthy of being incorporated into the modern Nigeria. It resulted in the simple removal of these repugnant laws.

Among others, the following were considered repugnant: execution by the sword, cutting off of hands and banishment. In their places, hanging and imprisonment were to be introduced. The question of repugnancy was for the Moslems another ploy by the British to perpetuate and further their colonial domination. It is for this reason that they were not ready to accept it especially when they reasoned that Sharia, which was the sacred Laws of God is immutable. Surely this instance sowed the seed of enmity between Muslims and the British with their system. This confused situation remained unresolved and continued to trot on.

A typical good example was in 1957 where a case in Gwandu, the second most powerful Emirate after Sokoto in the Caliphate was upturned by the

---

240 Kukah, M. H., "Religious Liberty in a plural society: The Nigerian Experience" in: *Religious Liberty: A theme for Christian-Muslim Dialogue*, Vatican City, PCID, 2006, p. 105.

241 Indirect Rule was the platform under which the British administered Nigeria. Through this system, the British sought to extend their authority and the rule of law to the various communities using British colonial administrative offices and traditional rulers to enforce law and order. Cf. Kuka, M. H., op. cit. p. 107.

British against the Sharia. It was a popular case where Mallam Gubba was tried and found guilty by Gwandu Sharia court having been accused by Gwwnda Native Authority of murder. Mallam Gubba took advantage of the court of appeal instituted by the colonial masters and appealed against his condemnation. Fortunately for him, the appellate court set aside the judgment of the Sharia court. Instead of the murder he was accused of, he was sentenced for manslaughter and was sent to jail contrary to the death sentence ordered by the Sharia. This however scored a high class mark for some Muslims and non-Muslims alike. It curtailed the excesses of the Sharia Judges who had entertained some cases of non-Muslims who were dragged to them thereby dispensing 'unjust justice' over who they have no jurisdiction.

On the part of Muslims themselves, it was clear that their Sharia was not completely to the advantage of their common good. It became unfortunately clear to them that Sharia courts because of its corrupt justice systems, had become a tool in the hands of the wealthy against the poor, and the political big weights against the common politicians. The Emirs and their political fronts had siezed the Sharia court to fight their political enemies. Unfortunately as it became evident that the British must go, it was clear to them that they had not solved the problem they created with this indirect rule. The resultant effect is that they were leaving behind disjointed pieces of legal system that seemed irreconcilable; a Nigeria ladled with religious, economic and social conflicts which evidently has continued unabated.[242] Since the scope of this work is not to apportion blames, I deem it sufficient in this chapter just to mention and discuss some of the areas of conflicts in Nigeria.

3.3. Religious Problem

There is no denying that religious politicking is an entrenched phenomenon which may be difficult to expunge from Nigerian politics. [243] For Carey, "In much of the world we have underestimated for too long the ability of cultures and religions to create divisions. We have failed to grasp what they can mean, particularly for the young. As has been observed: 'Even more than ethnicity, religion discriminates sharply and exclusively among people. A person can be half-French and half-Arab and simultaneously even a citizen of two countries. It is more difficult to be half-Catholic and half-Muslim.'

---

[242] Ibid, p. 106-108.

[243] Miles, W., "Muslim Ethno-politics and Presidential Elections in Nigeria" in: *Journal of Muslim Minority Affairs,* Vol. 20, No. 2, 2000, p. 237.

"[244] In order to emphasize the effects of religion he cited Hans Kung saying, "Without peace between the religions, war between the civilizations. No peace among the religions without dialogue between the religions. No dialogue between the religions without investigation of the foundations of the religions."[245] In this text, Kung emphasized the role of dialogue among religions as a strong source of peaceful co-existence. This issue of dialogue is discussed in chapter 6 of this work. It is pertinent here to look at some unfortunate instances where religion has been used to impact negatively on the psyche of Nigerians as a whole or on some of them.

Historically, one can trace the religious conflicts and problems to pre-independent days when some Christian missionaries made concerted efforts to reach the Northern emirates but were rebuffed by the Emirs of Kano as I already mentioned in chapter one of this work. After the colonial era, the post-independence period as it is called, Nigeria witnessed some devastating periods of religious unrest. The first of this looked like a 'peaceful unrest' that was well executed. According to J.J. Onotu in his description of the period between 1960 and 1965 as regards the Christian-Muslim relationship, this period can be called Sir Ahmadu Bello of Sokoto jihad revival time; it was carried out on a non-violent, low-keyed and classical strategy. It needed just a little more time to escalate into real religious civil war on account of the systematic and the down grading way Christianity and adherents to Christianity were persecuted, victimized and ruthlessly put in the then Northern Region under Sir Ahmadu Bello, the Sarduana of Sokoto.[246]

This situation was seemingly only an iceberg in the line-up of the worse days ahead. Because Sarduana saw himself as a man entrusted with a mission, he had to work tirelessly towards achieving this goal. As a means to this direction, he instituted some organic entities among which was the Jama'atu Nasril Islam – being a group mandated to ensure victory for Islam-whose membership consists mainly of Mallams working as advisory body on Islamic affairs. This associations empowered by their founder turned in the direction of the non- Muslims to unleash untold hardship with the sole intent of getting them converted. Particularly the Jama'atu Nasril Islam metamorphosed into the well known and of course feared "Kaduna Mafia" whose escapades would still be touched. Onotu describing this situation opined:

---

[244] Carey, G., op. cit. p. 96.
[245] Ibid.
[246] Onotu, J. J., "Muslim Master Plan and Method" (Anim. Seminar Paper, published by Anim Diocesan Priests Asso., 1988, p. 17

Throughout this time and when the various machineries for conversion spree had been set up, Sarduana coded the "Operation Jihad", a metaphor which referred to a variety of organs, strategies, modes to enlighten educated Muslims and non-Muslims alike on Islam; to victimize, persecute, harass, degrade and down-grade both Muslims and non-Muslims who were opposed to his views; it was indeed a crude and unorthodox method of conversion which he used effectively for his religious zeal and growing fanaticism.[247]

But he employed all known tricks to let his voice vibrate to the ends of the world. He was actually heard but with little attention to his bickering. If other religions had reacted so negatively in retaliation to this provocation, it would have been a different story. It would have been for him a great opportunity to declare his planned 'Jihad'. Some of our Newspapers carried the news making his name at least popular, a situation which he of course cherished. According to the news, "Every day, as the conversion campaign heated up, the Nigerian Newspapers came out with the following headlines, much to the chagrin and most understandable shocks to Middle Belt and Southern Nigerian Christians. Such headlines as these were noteworthy: "ISLAMIC CAMPAIGN BREAKS CHRISTIAN FORTRESS...9000 BECOME MUSLIMS IN JOS". SARDUANA DECLARES HOLY WAR"[248]. This attitude of Sarduana could not have come as a surprise to many who knew of the escapades of his great grand Father, Uthman Dan Fodio.

At least, this period of Sarduana, though unfortunate, woke some lukewarm members of other religions, including also some Muslims, to consciousness. It is on this ground that one would not be totally wrong if one calls this time a 'period of Sarduana's enlightenment'. People were moved to defend their faith with the intention of doing God a holy service. People observed but refused to succumb to the idea that they could lose their work positions because of their religious affiliation or even be promoted or demoted. This event was basically happening in the North. But due to human insatiability, he set off his fleet of fighters to the Southern and Eastern region where Christianity has no parallel. Unfortunately, before he could step further, he met his waterloo, kicking the bucket in 1966 following the military coup that jolted the nation. But his boldness had emboldened the Christians

---

[247] Ibid, p. 21-22.
[248] Ibid, p. 23.

especially the missionaries who became aware of the dangers lying ahead. According to Onotu,

> Naturally, the Christian missionaries saw the Sarduana as a threat to the work and the evangelical success they had achieved earlier on especially among the non Muslim and Middle Belt areas. They had to device a means of making the Middle Belt Christians rise up against a second attempt by Hausa/Fulanis to dominate and enslave non-Muslim minorities, this time, through religion. The people were vividly reminded by the missionaries of the atrocities of Sokoto Jihad perpetrated against them by Sarduana's great grand Father Uthman Dan Fodio in the 19th century[249].

With the death of Sarduana and the coup issue, it was thought that all was over. That was not to be. Before his sudden death, he had already galvanized and cornered many followers who took up his struggle, holding steadfast on his religious notions and convictions that run counter to the wellbeing of the adherents of other faiths. As these ideologies of Sarduana were becoming unbearable, especially for the Northern Christians, they had to form their Christian group known as 'Northern Christian Association, (NCA)'[250]. The worst problem in Nigeria is that some of the conflicts that are mainly political often wear the religious label. The Nigeria civil war is such a case study. For many Christians, it was another camouflaged Jihad meant to eliminate the Christians living in the North. As a result of this riot that led to the 1967 civil war, many Christian Churches were destroyed or burnt and no one was brought to book. For many decades now, religious conflicts seem to have become a way of life for Nigerians. In an Interview he granted the Guardian Newspaper to the question concerning fruits of the Religious dialogue as it affects the inter-religious conflicts in Nigeria, Archbishop Val. Okeke remarked,

> One can say that inter-religious conflicts in Nigeria are recurrent decimals. In the last one year, for instance, Nigeria has experienced at least three serious religious crises, namely, Jos, Bauchi and Niger State, which claimed many lives with property worth billions of Naira destroyed: It is very unfortunate that Religion is employed to bring unrest in our society... I can say without fear of contradiction that all genuinely religious

---

249 Ibid, p. 24.

250 Duniya, F., "The Challenges of Religious Intolerance in the Third Republic" in: *The Nigerian Journal of Theology*, no.1. June 1993, p. 42.

people do not resort to violence to settle issues be they Christians or Muslims.[251]

Since Nigeria in her present composition needs peace to survive, it must here be made clear that this search for peace when combined with violence cannot be promoted just as violence will not be used to dethrone violence. When love becomes the dominant virtue, hatred will surely take to its heels under a one-way journey ticket as a return ticket will not be issued. Expressing the same recurrent decimal in Nigeria, Nwobi, S.O pointed out that, "There has been at least one religious riot every year especially since 1980s with the uprising of Maitatsine riots in Kano – a town in the Northern part of Nigeria during which lots of lives and millions of naira worth of goods were destroyed. This very riot is seen even till today as the bloodiest riot in the history of religious riots in Nigeria."[252] This riot remains really evergreen in the memory lane of many Nigerians. It could be seen as a result of long accumulated retaliatory plan.

Alhaji Muhammad Marwa was the brain behind this genocidal riot that took place in Kano. Later called Maitatsine, Marwa was notorious for his undiluted doctrines. Following his religious fanaticism, he fell out of favour with the Kano authorities including the emir of the city. As the emir could no longer bear his overbearing intrusion, he ordered that he should be put in chains. Not satisfied with the jail order, he commanded that he be repatriated to his country, Cameroun. Still breathing furry for what he considered unjust deportation, Muhammad Marwa came back later to Kano with his group. This time, nobody was spared- both Christians and Muslims were brutalized and many paid great price with their lives especially those considered to be unfit to live, the infidels. The aftermath of this gruesome human slaughter that took place in North between 1980 and 1984 still hold many spellbound today as this Maitatsine group took swipe even among their Muslim brethren. Thanks to the concerted efforts of the Nigerian Police and the army who matched force with force and subdued them. This notwithstanding, the devastating effects of this unexpected attack has since been a clog in the wheel of the socio-political and economic emancipation of many.[253]

---

[251] Okeke, V., "In what areas has the dialogue across religions been successful in that it has not engendered the kind of tolerance that would douse inter-religious conflicts?" being Interview granted in *The Guardian Newspaper*, June 21, 2009.

[252] Nwobi, S. O., *Sharia Law in Nigeria: What Christian must know*, Ibadan, et. al., Totan Publishers, 2000, p. 31.

[253] Ekwunife, A. N. O., *Politics and Religious Intolerance, the Nigerian Experience*, Nigeria-Enugu, Spiritan Publications, 1992, p. 28.

The pogrom committed by Marwa was so ruinous that both the peace-loving Christians and Muslims joyously heaved sighs of relief when the news of his death in 1980 Kano riot broke out. But the relief was only temporal. For those who had heaved sighs of relief believing that all was then well, with Marwa out of the road to peace, were dumbfounded and shocked when his footsoldiers struck the city of Kano again. It was not Uhuru for Nigeria. Just like their leader re-appeared after he was sent parking back to Cameroun, so also, his followers went into hiding only to regroup, re-strategize for yet another Kano onslaught. As Metu captured it,

> Although the leader of the Maitatsine sect, Muhammad Marwa, was killed during the 1980 uprising, his lieutenants went underground, regrouped and struck again repeatedly. The first, in October 1982, took place simultaneously at Bulunkutu near Maiduguri, Rigasa in Kaduna and parts of Kano States resulting in over 175 deaths including some members of the police force. They struck again in February 1984 in Jimeta, in Gongola State where about 763 casualties were recorded. Yet again in April 1985, in Gombe in Bauch State, at which many people, Muslims and non-Muslims alike were ritually killed and Mosques and Churches were destroyed. The Maitatsine uprisings, though an intra-Muslim conflict (the Maitatsine group claimed to be a revivalist though syncretist Islamic movement challenging certain Muslim teachings and practices...) appear to have created a precedent. They not only inspired a string of religious riots in the country within a decade, but spilled over and resulted also in inter-religious conflicts.[254]

If we take our minds back to 1982, we remember two great religious events that took place- the first ever Papal visit to Nigeria followed by the visit of the Anglican Archbishop Runcie after two months of the papal visit. The visit of the Pope excited no commotion. The head of the world wide Anglican communion had also come and gone when it all started again. Some Muslims were irked by the fact that Runcie had laid a foundation stone of an Anglican church in a place that was dominated by Muslims in Kano. For them it was a slight on their face and they vowed that such a building should not be allowed to stand. For this reason, they were determined to destroy the church. If not because of the timely intervention of the security

[254] Ikenga-Metu, E., 'Two Decades of Religious Conflicts in Nigeria: A recipe for Peace' in: *Bulletin of Ecumenical Theology, on Power, Authority, and Leadership: Africa and Christian*, 6/1: 1994, p. 69.

agents, they would have had their way. As they failed in their plan option A, they followed an alternative option B, and vented their anger on other churches. Kukah described the situation vividly:

> The Muslim rioters came to destroy the church because they claimed that it was close to their mosque. Sensing the doom, the church members alerted the police whose immediate arrival averted a serious clash. But, in frustration, the rioters made for other churches, set some on fire, burnt and severely damaged others. By the time the rioters were brought under control, eight churches had been variously desecrated.[255]

After this riot, a panel in which Muslims were majority was set up. The result of such a panel is every one's guess. Part of the recommendations of the panel was that the church should be removed from the site where it was built and a compensation be paid to the Anglican Church which owned it. This recommendation was a clear injustice by a panel that never wanted to work for peace since they were judges in their own case. This report was upheld by government without taking cognizance of the fact that the two Christians out of the seven members of the panel protested against the report.[256] In his normal erudite way Kukah quoted by Nwobi never saw it as a surprise that the recommendation was indirectly aimed at frustrating the spread of Christianity. He commented that, "It is not surprising therefore that the committee finally recommended that, whenever a new church or mosque is going to be built in areas already settled, the opinion or the consent of the community in the vicinity of the proposed site must be sought. This should be done by public announcement of the proposed building through advertisement in the newspapers and other means. The people are free to indicate their response either for or against."[257]

The claim that the unfortunate report of the panel was consciously conscripted against Christianity became clearer as it has become an Achilles' hill securing an approval of a plot to build a Christian Church. Taking bearing from this fact that the heavy presence of Christianity and its seemingly spread in Northern Nigeria was a headache to the Muslims, it is unquestionably a presumable intentional provocation for Christians, no matter how religious, pious or even peaceful it may appear, to march through the streets of Ilorin the capital city of Kwara State. This looked impermissible with or

---

[255] Kukah, M. H., *Religion, Politics and Power in Northern Nigeria*, p. 158.
[256] Nwobi, S. O., op.cit. p. 34.
[257] Ibid.

without the acclaimed constitutional religious freedom in Nigeria. The fateful day in question was on a Palm Sunday of 1986 when some Christians were on procession. The offence was that this procession passed through a Muslim dominated area. So the Muslim youths had no option than to descend on this 'purported lawless offenders', many of who were wounded.[258]

Despite all we have said so far, Muhib Opeloye traced the beginnings of the Christian-Muslim conflicts back to 1979 Sharia controversy which spilt over to the OIC issue of 1986. For him, "The genesis of the Christian-Muslim conflicts in this country is traceable to the 1979 controversy over the introduction of the Sharia in the Appeal Court. Since then the relationship between the two groups has been characterized by mutual suspicion, rivalry, acrimony, rancor, discord and hostility. This was the mood that ushered in the 1986 debate over the desirability of Nigerian participation in the Organization of the Islamic Conference (OIC) which further aggravated the strained Christian-Muslim relations."[259]He was however of the view that very few of the conflicts were as a result of religious intolerance and inconsistent religious policy of the government.[260]Most of the conflicts were ethno-politically motivated. Even the very few he selected and dimmed religious, he saw the Muslims as sacrosanct and as only peacefully protesting against a seemingly injustice meted on them, having been provoked. According to Opeloye,

> The Kafanchan riot in Kaduna State, described as one of the most destructive, started on the campus of the college of Education, Kafanchan on 6 March 1987. According to the Denli Commission of Inquiry, the crises erupted as a result of the Reverend Abubakar Bako's provocation of the Muslim students by his offensive interpretation of the Qur'an and the misrepresentation of the prophethood of Muhammad in the course of his preaching. When the Muslim students protested, they were overrun by the Christian assembly and their mosque was immediately burnt. Twelve Muslims named in the Denli Commission report were murdered in Kafanchan. The news of the massacre resulted in public disorder throughout the state and the situation was so chaotic that it took combined teams of soldiers and anti-riot police several days to bring it under control.[261]

---

[258] Ibid, p. 35.
[259] Opeloye, M. O., "The Socio-political Factor in the Christian-Muslim Conflict in Nigeria" in: *Islam and Christian-Muslim Relations,* Vol. 9, No. 2, 1998, p. 231-232.
[260] Ibid, p. 234.
[261] Ibid.

Another riot which begs for attention was that of 1991 that took place in Kano. Opeloye reported that the riot,

> Was sparked off as a consequence of the permission granted by the Federal Government to the famous German Christian revivalist Reihnard Bonnke to evangelize in the country. Bonnke, well known for his fiery preaching, came to the country at the invitation of the Kano State branch of the Christian Association of Nigeria (CAN). The arrival of the world proselytizer in Kano would naturally be a surprise to the people of the city, who are homogeneously Muslims, because early in the year the government had refused permission for the veteran Islamic preacher Ahmad Deedat from South Africa to preach in Kano. The aggrieved Muslims of the city naturally wondered why the same treatment had not been applied to both preachers. This singular action of the government was enough to confirm suspicions that the Ibrahim Babangida regime was hostile to Muslim interests in the country. The protesters, numbering about 8,000 Muslim youths, were unresponsive to the passionate appeals of the Emir of Kano and members of his Emirate Council to shun violence. The promise of the council to intervene in the crisis came too late. The protesters withdrew from the Emir's palace to the Central Mosque. Before long, what started as a peaceful demonstration became a mob action descending on the city suddenly like a violent thunderstorm.[262]

This religious violence is not restricted to cases between Muslims and Christians. The adherents of traditional religion at times are also involved. From the office of the U. S Missions in Nigeria one hears that there were instances in which individuals or groups were targeted primarily based on religious issues/or because of their religious affiliations. An incidence in July was mentioned in which animists destroyed Christian homes and businesses in Nkalaha, Ebonyi State in retaliation for the nonparticipation of Christians in animist rites and traditions. Animists in Ebonyi State insisted that all individuals pay cultural respect to the traditional ruler. Many Christians refused, and in retaliation the animists flogged the Christians. The Christians later complained to the police, who then beat the animists involved in the flog-

[262] Ibid, p. 235.

ging.[263] Cases also abound where the Christians and the Muslims burnt down the Pagan shrines.

3.3.1. Sharia as a Source of religious conflict

In order to delve into the implications of the introduction of Islamic legal system, Sharia, in some Northern States of the Federal Republic of Nigeria, one needs to be aware of the basic stipulations of the Nigerian constitution on freedom of religion. Surely, the constitution guarantees every one the freedom to belong to and practice any religion. The constitution states:

> Every person shall be entitled to freedom of thought, conscience and religion, including freedom to change his religion or belief, and freedom (either alone or in community with others, and in public or in private) to manifest and propagate his religion or belief in worship, teaching, practice and observance.[264]

It further stipulated, "No person attending any place of education shall be required to receive religious instruction or to take part in or attend any religious ceremony of observance if such instruction, ceremony or observance relates to a religion other than his own, or a religion not approved by his parent or guardian."[265] Furthermore, it stated that "No religious community or denomination shall be prevented from providing religious instruction for pupils of that community nor denomination in any place of education maintained wholly by that community or denomination."[266] All the above citations though important to address the issue at stake, have not answered the question of the introduction of Sharia. A look into chapter One part One section 10 of the constitution gives us the necessary answer as a working tool. It reads, "The Government of the Federal or of a State shall not adopt any religion as State Religion."[267] This helps us to appraise the clear stand of the Catholic Church on the issue of freedom of religion and worship. In its document, 'Declaration on Religious Liberty',

---

[263] U.S Missions in Nigeria, "Religious Violence in Nigeria" cf. International Religious Freedom Report 2004.

[264] *1999 Constitution of the Federal Republic of Nigeria with Fundamental Rights* (Enforcement Procedure) Rules 2009, Chapter IV, Fundamental Rights, Art.38, no.1, p. 47.

[265] Ibid, p. 47-48..

[266] Ibid, p. 48.

[267] Ibid, p. 29.

> The Vatican Council declares that the human person has a right to religious freedom. Freedom of this kind means that all men should be immune from coercion on the part of individuals, social groups and every human power so that, within due limits, nobody is forced to act against his convictions nor is anyone to be restrained from acting in accordance with his convictions in religious matters in private or in public, alone or in associations with others. The Council further declares that the right to religious freedom is based on the very dignity of the human person as known through the revealed word of God and by reason itself. This right of the human person to religious freedom must be given such recognition in the constitutional order of society as will make it a civil right.[268]

This is exactly what the Nigerian constitution has done. To clarify the basis of their declaration, the Council Fathers further stated,

> The reason is because the practice of religion of its very nature consists primarily of those voluntary and free internal acts by which a man directs himself to God. Acts of this kind cannot be commanded or forbidden by any merely human authority. But his own social nature requires that man give external expression to these internal acts of religion, that he communicate with others on religious matters, and profess his religion in community. Consequently to deny man the free exercise of religion in society, when the just requirements of public order are observed, is to do an injustice to the human person and to the very order established by God for men. Furthermore, the private and public acts of religion by which men direct themselves to God according to their convictions transcend of their very nature the earthly and temporal order of things. Therefore the civil authority, the purpose of which is the care of the common good in the temporal order, must recognize and look with favor on the religious life of the citizens. But if it presumes to control or restrict religious activity it must be said to have exceeded the limits of its power.[269]

With this information one can affirm with certainty that the issue of Sharia in Nigeria is a wind that blows no one good, neither the non-Muslims nor the Muslims themselves. It has brought much grief to so many families, including the Muslim families.

---

[268] Dignitatis Humanae (DH), no. 2.
[269] Ibid, no. 3.

3.3.1.1. Sharia: Meaning and Sources

The root of the Muslim legal code 'Sharia' cannot be seen as coming undiluted from God (Allah). It is rather a fusion work carried out on the hadith and the Qur'an that gave rise to it. The hadith, described as the traditions about the Prophet's life, and collected over a longer period of time was a source used by early Muslims to shape Islamic culture and obligation.[270] According to Robinson, "For many Muslims the hadith provided crucial guidance to the moral life, because they dealt with the human instrument who founded the faith. Some of them have elevated Muhammad to a very important status, as someone who ascends to heaven..., appears in dreams bearing the messages of God..., or inspires reformers to take courageous action....The hadith that tell the Story of the Prophet are often called Sira."[271]

In trying to put up a standard legal code, the Sharia, some well known Islamic legal scholars employed two principles namely, 'consensus' and 'analogy'. The term consensus was used to refer to the views of the main doctors of law. It simply means the prevailing learned opinion. Analogy was very instrumental in the making of the Sharia as it aided the scholars in bringing in precedents from other practices not excluding Jewish, Christian, Zoroastrian, Roman and Sasanian links. It is on this ground that it could be taken as contacts made to other traditions when the Arab Muslims confronted new realities or conditions in their bid to expand.[272] Robinson further explained, "Using the two sources (Quran and hadith) and the two principles (consensus and analogy) scholars gradually built up a body of doctrine to guide individual and collective behaviour. This code was called the Shari'a, divinely ordained law..."[273] But as Yusuf Hajiya Bilkisu put it, "Shari'a is defined as the divine and complete code of conduct. It entails the whole system of Islam, covering worship, personal attitudes and conduct, social norms, laws, roles and responsibilities of citizens, and the political, social, intellectual and legal systems. It is therefore broader than the narrow scope of a definition that limits Shari'a to a legal code that, in the Western legal tradition, is enforceable by the state."[274] Therefore for the Moslems, Sharia is

---

[270] Robinson, D., *Muslim Societies in African History*, UK, Cambridge University Press, 2004, p. 12.

[271] Ibid, p. 14.

[272] Ibid.

[273] Ibid.

[274] Yusuf, B. H., "Managing Muslim-Christian Conflicts in Northern Nigeria: A Case Study of Kaduna State" in: *Islam and Christian-Muslim Relations*, Vol.18, No.2, 237-256, April 2007, p. 237.

seen as "The Way or Road in the religion of Muhammad, which God has established for the guidance of his people both for the worship of God and for the duties of life"[275] But for Kate Zebiri quoting Nasr 1994, 96-98, it is,

> The blue print of the ideal human life...a transcendent law which is at the same time applied in human society, but never fully realized because of the imperfections of all that is human. The Shar'iah corresponds to a reality that transcends time and history.... The Shar'iah is for Islam the means of integrating human society. It is the way by which man is able to give religious significance to his daily life and ... to integrate this life into a spiritual centre... In this way the whole of man's life and activities become religiously meaningful. Were it to be otherwise man would be a house divided unto itself in a condition of inner division and separation which Islam tries to avoid.[276]

Qur'an therefore expects the Muslims to live their lives completely in obedience to the dictates of Sharia, without leaving any aspect unobserved and to the letters. Any diversion from the path of Sharia is unambiguously interpreted as following the way of the uninformed and is condemned in the strongest word possible- apostasy. Qur'an stiüulates, "Then we have granted you a clear path (Shari'a) regarding the religious affairs, so follow it and follow not the whims of those who have no knowledge."[277] Qur'an however did not condemn the divine scriptures before it. It rather claims to be the fullness of the revealed truth, superior to those others before it and enjoins the Muslims to disregard any teaching contrary to the content of Qur'an, since they are misleading. It rather stipulated,

> And unto thee have we revealed the scripture with truth, confirming whatever scripture was before it, and a watcher over it. So judge between them by that which Allah hat revealed, and follow not their desires away from the truth which hath come unto thee for each we have appointed a divine law (Sharia) and a traced-out way. Had Allah willed, He could have made you one community. But that he may try you by that which he

---

[275] Ndiokwere, N. I., *The African Church Today and Tomorrow, Prospects and Challenges*, Vol.1, Onitsha, Nigeria, Effective Key Publishers Limited, 1994, p. 83 qouting Paden, J. N., *Values and Leadership in Nigeria,* Zaria, Nigeria, Hudahuda Publishing House, p. 54.

[276] Zebiri, K., "Muslim Anti-Secularist Discourse in the Context of Muslim-Christian Relations" in: Esposito, J. L., et al. (eds.), *Islam and Christian-Muslim Relations*, Vol.9, USA, Taylor & Francis Ltd, No. 1, 1998, p. 53.

[277] Ibid, p. 238, cf. Surah 45, 18.

hath given you. So vie one with another in good works. Unto Allah ye will all return and he will then inform you of that wherein ye differ.[278]

It is obviously in the spirit of implementing the Sharia law that the Kano State government in 2007, lacking proper knowledge of Qur'an, introduced the Islamic dress code for all the students in the State without adequate consideration of its possible implications. As a reaction to that, the government was criticized by the Northern States Christian Elders Forum (NOSCEF) labelling such unfortunate move unconstitutional. For them, "the right of a large segment of the population of the state is being infringed by those that have sworn to protect and defend those rights as enshrined in the Nigerian Constitution."[279] They therefore called on the government to desist from such unhealthy introductions that is detrimental to the constitution of the Federal Republic of Nigeria which recognises and protects harmony in diversity. It is however clear that many Muslims claim that Sharia is simply for the Muslims and should be incorporated into the Nigerian constitution since it will surely not affect other non-Muslims. For many, this stand is clearly a political statement.

3.3.1.2. Political Sharia and Sharia Protagonists

If one is well versed in the Islamic political theory of Sharia, one cannot but be afraid. The theory holds Sharia law in higher esteem than the constitution of Nigeria. Accordingly, Suleiman emphasized that, "...the state is subordinate to Sharia and it is Sharia which lays down the general norms and functions of the state and all the public institutions of the state."[280] It becomes clear with this assertion that the introduction of Sharia is the enthronement of Islam as the State religion which the law of the land forbids in strong terms. The hidden agenda in the Sharia introduction would be clear if one takes note of the statement accredited to Suleiman Kumo in one of the seminars held in Zaria pre-emptive of the final unslaught on the debate on the floor of National assembly. In his anger, he thundered, "Why should the transplanted English law which, let it be recalled, was imposed on the coun-

---

[278] Ibid, cf. Surah 5. 48.

[279] Shiklam, J., "Sharia: Northern Christian slam Kano Government" in: *Daily Champions Newspaper*, August 7, 2007.

[280] Suleiman, K., The Organization and Procedure of Sharia Courts in Northern Nigeria, London, SOAS, 1972, p. 41.

try by the colonial regime, be allowed to remain the common law of Nigeria? ...from its very existence, it has been an architectural eyesore."[281]

It is unfortunate for Suleiman Kumo who is a member of the Constitution Drafting Committee (CDC) to have taken this stand. One wonders what type of constitution he might have helped to draw up. An English adage holds that birds of the same feather flock together. It is not surprising that Suleiman's position was echoed by his colleague Shani. For him,

> The law of the land is the law which commands the approval of the majority alone. Minorities have a right to demand safeguards for their legitimate rights and interests and we are bound to concede this demand as Islam enjoins us to do so. But it is not fair for minorities to ask us to throw our ideology overboard and introduce laws which are against our convictions merely for the sake of appeasing them. When we were helpless because of foreign domination, we tolerated the supremacy of un-Islamic laws. But we are now the masters of our destiny.[282]

Under the Islamic spell, they even turned deaf ear to a voice of reason and wisdom. This voice, showing itself true to its statute put forward some mind boggling questions that could have made every peace loving mind to be hammered into the right track. The questions which the then Rector of College of Advance Business Studies (CABS), Dr. C. Abashiya, wanted everyone to ask himself are as follows,

> Can we have Sharia up to the Federal level without running two legal systems in the country? If the Muslims have the Sharia, how do we deal with the possibility of the proliferation of demands by all other religious groups across the country? If we are all in one country, should we not seek to have one law for all? Should the Sharia cover only personal matters or criminal matters also? Is it possible for us to have one legal system with sub-divisions?[283]

Although some of them hold that the solution would be to make Sharia supreme or at least favourable to Muslims, these questions marshalled by

---

[281] Suleiman, K., "Judiciary Under the Draft Constitution" in: Suleiman Kumo & Abubakar Aliyu (eds.), *Issues in the Nigerian Draft Constitution: Report of the Conference on Issues in the Draft Constitution* , A.B.U. Zaria, 21-24 March, 1977, p. 209-212.
[282] Shani, M. B., "Sharia Debate" in: *New Nigerian*, September 15, 1977.
[283] Abashiya, C., "Sharia Debate" in: *New Nigerian*, March 27, 1977.

Abashiya in their debate in Minna remain yet unanswered. It is clear that any sincere answer to this question would work against any demand for Sharia law. Due to the dangerous nature of the Sharia problem, Kukah invested so much time trying to lay bare the hidden intentions behind its protagonists. He made researches and interviewed some important personnel. Eventually he had the opportunity of meeting Alhaji Balarabe Musa (former governor of Kaduna State) who with his group made it clear that the high-wired intrigues coupled with the Ostrich-like type of hide and seek attitude of the Northern politicians leave no one in doubt that the intent was condemnable. They are trying to use Sharia for political gain. According to Balarabe,

> In the face of the new political programme, the ruling class in Northern Nigeria knew that they were threatened by the new democracy. They had no foothold or any solid base for political competition as a block with the rest of the country. In view of this political bankruptcy, it became clear that Islam would offer the only alternative for the protection of their class interest. But even this was not an easy card to play. The so-called muslim North no longer existed, but all the same, it was that to seek to defend it would enhance their position. So, they held on to the issue of the Sharia in the Assembly as their only weapon for mobilisation in the North.[284]

In his own opinion, another educational heavy weight, Mahmud Tukur, the late Head of Department of History in Ahmadu Bello University, Zaria, went beyond pinning the debate on the political intention of the Northern elite blocks. It was for him an unfortunate chance for both southern and northern politicians to play their political cards well. To be seen not just as political champions in their region but also as religious faithful of their different religions would give them political advantage. He argued that certain groups from the North and the South with political aim decided to use the Sharia debate as a means of mobilising support, the advantage being that either way, these individuals would still use the support they had earned in presenting themselves as defenders of Sharia or defenders of their people from the cloak of Islamic domination. The idea then was for either side to build up a pool of supporters that should be relied on for electoral advantage in the second republic for the advancement of their collective class interests.[285] With the aforementioned utterances one cannot but see the reasons

---

[284] Balarabe, M., Interview granted to Mathew Kukah in: Kukah, M. H., *Religion Politics and Power in Northern Nigeria*, Ibadan, Spectrum Books Ltd. 1993, p. 121.
[285] Ibid.

for this new attempt to reintroduce the Sharia. The Sharia that was claimed to have been thrown overboard would soon be 'regurgitated' or resurrected. So with this in mind, it becomes hard to accept that the Sharia when introduced, will affect only the Muslims. Let it be clear to us that the above arguments for and against Sharia is a debate before debate. It is only the tip of the iceberg in the expected debate that is yet to engulf the Constituent Assembly (CA). What happened in the Constituent Assembly seemed to follow the trend that went before it. The core north was bent on the enthronement of Sharia while the Middle Belt seemed to be moderate as the South was clearly against the move. To set the ball rolling, the chairman of the CDC, Rotimi Williams, tried to clarify the place of the Sharia as is already drafted in the constitution. He explained,

> It is obviously desirable that our constitution should ensure that there are no embarrassing conflicts of judicial decisions as to what Islamic law is on any particular point as interpreted by the Sharia court of appeal from state to state...Everyone, however biased he may be on this issue, must accept that there is need for a court which will exercise appellate jurisdiction from the various Sharia courts of appeal. The only question that the honourable members have to consider is whether there is a better substitute for the solution proposed in the CDC, namely that there should be a Federal Sharia Court of Appeal.[286]

The fact that the Chairman of the CDC made this observation at the very beginning of the debate seemed to have put a blockade on the road to successful consideration. He seemed to have taken sides at the very beginning. This was suspicious. But the Moslems added salt to an already very painful injury. Exuding with smiles and appreciation for what Rotimi said was a very big eye opener for the opposition camp. They suspected that some handful of water has passed under the bridge. Let me here give a detailed opinion of some Muslim members of the Assembly in support of what Rotimi said. Alhaji Abdu Mashi from Kaduna argued, "To deny Sharia which governs the life of millions of its adherents is like passing a bill in particular or enacting a law in the constitution suspending all Christians in the country from attending Sunday worship."[287]As if in alliance with him Adamu Ciroma from Fika/Fune took his argument beyond the Sunday worship. He appealed to his

[286] Kukah, M. H., op.cit. p. 122. cf. also Proceedings of the Constituent Assembly, Official Report. Vol. 1, Federal Ministry of Information, Lagos, 1978.
[287] Ibid.

religious freedom stressing that, "if we agree to freedom of religion, there is no need truncating my freedom. I must be given the chance to do it fully. If I am not subject to Sharia, I will regard myself as not having freedom of religion."[288] In a seemingly comparative tone, Alhaji Ibrahim Dasuki of Sokoto toed more the path of the value of Sharia. For him, "Without religion, people become materialistic....Sharia to me is everything. Sharia tells me that when you frown at me as the leader, I should sit down. Sharia tells me that when a Rev. Father is speaking, I should listen."[289]

In his own input, Yahaya Gusau, from Gusau was more apologetic maintaining that, "if we really believe in unity and diversity, if we believe in live and live, if we really believe in mutual co-existence, if we really believe in respect and accommodating lawful and legitimate peculiarities of each other, there is no reason why Sharia Court of Appeal should not be established throughout this country."[290]As these arguments in favour of Sharia were being voiced by the 'Moslem North', there were contrary opinions from the same North, emanating both from Moslems and non-Moslems. Most of these took their stand cueing from a pre-colonial and post-colonial Sharia experiences. Most of such voices were of the Middle Belt origin that saw the insistent on the Sharia as coming from the Hausa-Fulani hidden plan to recapture their seemingly lost political importance since after the independence. Speaking without equivocation against Sharia, Paul Unongo who himself is a former member of CDC, left no one gazing where he has pitched his tent. He remarked,

> I would like to assure my friends that I came here to perform a political function. When I went to the CDC, I performed a technical function...There is no basis at all to even discuss the possibility of providing a court structure or system which by definition is a religious court and use federal funds to maintain such a religious court in a basically secular state...Sharia system runs counter to the political objectives and the social on which we seek to build our nation.[291]

Borrowing a leaf from Unongo's input but going a bit beyond it, Udoji Jerome, a Christian from South representing Ihiala/Nnewi/Idemili argued that "those who oppose the courts on religious grounds argue that to establish

[288] Ibid.
[289] Ibid.
[290] Ibid.
[291] Ibid, p. 123.

on a national level and with national funds, a court which will only deal with the laws of a particular religion, is not only giving that religion a preferential treatment, but is tantamount to making that religion a state religion."[292] Dr. A.U. Jalingo from Jalingo, a Moslem, made it clear that he was there to represent his constituent. He was therefore sent to say the opinion of his constituent taking into account what they have experienced or are still experiencing as Moslems under Sharia. In a pool of regrets he pointed out that, "slavery is still being practiced in this country... Sharia condones the practice of concubinism. The area I come from is one in which a lot of people are still being regarded as slaves. I have a mandate from this area to come and appeal to the conscience of man who has respect for the essence of human beings and human rights to do something."[293]

What one could see as a consolation price came the way of Moslems when Akinjide, Richard, a Christian, evoked no Christian sentiments in his speech. His opinion was that, "those who do not want Islamic law system will not have it. It will not be forced upon them...As a matter of fact, even those areas of the North who do not want the Islamic law system could abolish it through their legislature...anybody who feels that this country is being turned into a Muslim state is simply being mischievous."[294] Arguments and counter arguments raged on to the point that the members started seeing no green light. It became also so boring to many that they had to ask some questions as to what direction the debate was heading.

Although the ATR members were not officially invited, an indirect reference was made to them when C. C. Onoh from Enugu passionately called his fellow assembly members to emulate the example of their forefathers in settling disputes. He urged the members, "...all I am trying to beg this house for is that we should learn from our forefathers...they resolved many things without the acrimony we have in this house... I ask in all honesty, is there no Sadat? No Begin? Is there no leader that can resolve this conflict so that we can move ahead?"[295] Although all these could not drive deep into their psyche, one thing was clear. The fear of the army take-over did not spare them. It became clear that to avoid the ugly situation that may befall the nation if the army should take over, some of them, who sang uncompromising hard-tuned songs, changed the tone and started singing songs that seemed better in accord.

---

[292] Ibid.
[293] Ibid.
[294] Ibid
[295] Ibid, p. 124.

At the end of it all, it was agreed that a sub-committee made up of few members should be formed to fashion out what could be generally acceptable. In forming this sub-committee, the chairman said, "I have, with the authority which you have vested in me, appointed members of this and their assignment is to devise a way whereby anybody aggrieved by the judgement of an appeal court in the state dealing with Islamic law will be able to appeal to the Federal Court of Appeal."[296]Despite some initial difficulties arising from the so called Moslem hardliners among the committee that was almost forced into submission, the report was eventually submitted. The submitted report stated, "whenever there was a Sharia case on appeal, the Federal Court of Appeal would be constituted by three judges learned in Islamic law. They are not called Panel. They are not called a division. They are called a Federal Court of Appeal and for that purpose, they are the Federal Court of Appeal."[297]

This report enraged another round of three days of argument. The bone of contention this time was what name to be given to the recommended court- a Panel or a division. This recommendation alone was a kind of visible and clear red card being given to the Sharia issue. This gave rise to some of the Moslems staging a walkout after submitting officially their letter of withdrawal from the debate. This walkout was however termed to be a political calculation to stop any possible passage of the committee's report. Unfortunately the report was adopted despite their walkout thereby deleting the controversial provisions of section 180(1) (c) as it appeared in the CDC's Draft. A clear sign of disappointment on the Moslem circles was clearly written in their faces and undertakings. It was so devastating that protesters took to the streets in Zaria with inscriptions that read, "No Sharia, No Peace, No Sharia, No Constitution, No Sharia, No Muslims, No Nigeria etc."[298]

The chairman of the CDC sub-committee explained that the Moslems by staging a walkout hypocritically shot themselves on the leg since that became a boomerang. Reacting to an interview on the implication of the walkout, he said, "the walkout was hypocritical, it was not done in favour or against Sharia, it was for people to enhance their political future."[299] Unongo maintained that it was, "a political weapon and part of the arm twisting meant to effect a constitutional crisis which would make the prospect of a military intervention a very good means of frightening the Southern delegates into

[296] Ibid, p. 125.
[297] Ibid.
[298] Ibid. p. 127.
[299] Ibid.

submission. But it was an act of political miscalculation on the part of its architects for it woefully failed."[300]

To the Moslems it was a big loss. As some of them were pointing accusing fingers at the Christians for their failure Balarabe Musa took a swamp on the Moslems for the failed project since they, as a block were in disarray. In his view, "it was when the Christians saw that there was some confusion among the Muslims, listened to their contradictory positions and utterances, that they became worried and frightened. The Christians concluded that if the Muslims do not trust one another, how can we trust anyone of them on what they are saying about Sharia? It was the Muslims who gave their game away."[301] Really it was a very bitter pill for the Moslems. Assessing their representatives at the concluded CA, the traditional ruling class felt disappointed with their inputs and failure. They believed therefore that the loss of the Sharia was clearly an indictment on the political immaturity of the northern intellectuals who made a mess of a project entrusted to them."[302] The seemingly defeat of the Sharia inclusion in the constitution was actually not the last to be heard about it in Nigeria since it has now and then reared its ugly head.

3.3.1.3. Sharia: To whose benefit?

Having seen that Sharia was a product of an inseparable marriage between the contents of the Qur'an and the Speeches of Mohammed, the hadith, it becomes clear that this laid foundation for the life styles that Moslems should lead. However, in the course of formulating the Sharia between 7th and 13th century, a detailed presentation of the use of violence against the non-Moslems and of limited possibility for peace with them was developed.[303]The concept of Umma will play a considerable important role in clarifying this issue. Taking our bearing from Qur'an, the term Umma is clearly explained. However in later usage of the word, Umma referred to the community of believers as well as to a nation in modern usage. For the classic Islamic legal system, the concept, Umma, describes specifically the Islamic faith community, not minding the colour, ethnicity or nation as differentiated from other religious groupings.

---

[300] Ibid.
[301] Ibid, p. 128.
[302] Ibid.
[303] Riße, G., *Der Islam – Religion der Gewalt oder Religion des Friedens?* p. 20.

Following this, members of Umma could therefore be only Moslems since if there is only one God and one true faith in him, then accordingly there could also be only one community of believers. The adherents of other religions do not belong to the family of Umma. According to the Prophet Mohammed and the classic Islamic law, the polytheistic religions have only the option of accepting Islam if they live in Islamic community. The people of the book, 'ahl al-Kitab', Jews and Christians would only be tolerated. Through a contract of protection, 'dimma', would the 'ahl al-Kitab' be permitted to some extent to practice his religion though with some discriminating restrictions. The Sharia which is really meant for the Moslems in the Umma, applies indirectly to the Jews and Christians through the protection contract.[304]

With this analysis of Sharia application and who it affects, one understands clearly the reason for fears of non-Moslems. Addressing the issue of the claims being always forwarded by Moslems that Sharia will not affect the non-Moslems, J.O. Mbukanma under the sub- topic, 'Islamic Militancy' echoed the view expressed by Chris Enyinnaya in his contribution on the Sharia controversy as reported in The Punch Newspaper. He wrote, "Forget about their claim that Sharia will not affect non-Moslems. It will. How? "Under the Sharia environment, if you are a Moslem, you get juicy jobs, promotions, contracts, positions etc. If you are a non-Moslem, you get peanuts or nothing."[305] It implies that non-Muslims are not entitled to complete rights of a citizen in the States where Sharia is in vogue. A typical example could help us understand what the situation could look like if Sharia is allowed. Bemoaning what has already started to happen in education sector, Ndiokwere said,

> There is discrimination against Christians and non-indigenes of Northern states at all levels, both in admissions and services. The troubles in schools in Kaduna state in 1989 were sparked off by the discriminatory attitude of the government of the state while reviewing school fees in Kaduna state. According to government directive, non-indigenes, comprising mostly Christians were to pay higher amount than their moslem counterparts. Elsewhere in the North, where education is free, non-indigenes, once again Christians are made to pay heavily or their children would not

[304] Ibid.

[305] Mbukanma, J. O., *Preaching & Crises of Faith*, Ibadan, Newborne Enterprises, December 2001, p. 115.

be admitted in school. Medical treatment and the enjoyment of other social amenities follow the same discriminatory trend.[306]

Such a situation breeds much injustice and acrimony since the non-Moslems are deprived of the opportunities of getting lucrative Jobs. Clearly the aim for which the Sharia law was introduced was simply to Islamize the country. To give credence to this claim, we refer to the comments of one of its major proponents, the former Zamfara State governor, Alhaji Ahmed Sani, which he made in Gusau during the official unveiling of his Sharia project. In the statements attributed to him in the Tell magazine of October 27, 1999 which were widely published, he said that the,

> launching will be marked in the annals of not only Zamfara State but throughout our beloved country, Nigeria, as the culminating point in the actualisation of the hopes, ideals and aspirations of majority of our citizens, the Muslims...The Muslim Ummah in this nation had for too long been dormant, inactive and indeed, in a state of slumber which had given the impression that we are a silent majority. The Muslims have for long yearned for the freedom to exercise their full rights since the period they were invaded and colonized by the British. We only partially achieved victory with independence but our neglect of planning robbed us the fruits of our struggles...the struggle had not gone in vain for the Islamic order we envisaged has now emerged...what we have embarked upon now is the continuation of the struggle started by our foresighted leader, the late Sarduana of Sokoto, Sir Ahmadu Bello of blessed memory[307]

To make sure that he convinced his people to accept and support his selfish political interest in advocating the introduction or adoption of Sharia, he stopped at nothing. This is evident in the report as given by the Civil Liberties Organisation in their report after their trip to Zamfara lasting from 11-13 Feb, 2000. It was clear from the report that Governor Sani as part of his preparation to proclaim Sharia as the supreme law of the land, saw to it that the people were mobilized "95 percent" to support his programmes. First of all, he released N240 million (apparently from the state's internally-generated revenue estimate of N400 million) to his Ministry of Religious Affairs to buy grains to feed the masses during the month of Ramadan. He gave the Islamic preachers N3 million as their expenses for the month. He

---

[306] Ndiokwere, N. I., op. cit. p. 81.
[307] Cf. "Sharia Time Bomb" in: *Tell Magazine*, November 15, 1999, p. 12-13.

bought "tokunbo" buses and taxis which were reserved exclusively for the use of women and distributed 100 motorcycles to unemployed youths and hundreds of bicycles to messengers to the state civil service. He also introduced N5, 000 as the minimum wage in the state. Besides these welfare programmes, he created a preachers council, a Zakkat collection and distribution board and the Zamfara Youth Council (a vigilante group).[308]

It was a consideration of this attitude that led Danjuma Byand to articulate the following, "The real issue here is not whether or not moslems should have shari'a courts to determine their personal matters, but whether such courts should be established and run with public funds. One thing we have to understand is that shari'a courts are religious courts that apply purely religious laws to try personal matters. No non-moslem has any objection to the moslems expressing their faith by means of shari'a. But the demand based on the existing situation in which our scarce resources are channelled to help propagate the practice on only one religious faith, is both unconstitutional and unjust"[309] Toeing the same pathway, Chukwulozie, an acclaimed expert in Islamic studies and affairs, opined that "the establishment of the shari'a court by the government with state powers and funded by the state means that islam is indirectly accepted as the 'right religion' of the state of the federation. The Constitutional provisions for the shari'a court go against the secular nature of the state and the principles of democracy in a pluralistic society"[310]

A critical look at this philanthropic gesture of the governor as aforementioned reveals that he was doing it just to score a political mark rather than as an evidence of his deep religious convinction. To the delight of the Zamfara Governor, the other Northern State governors, seeing the mouth-watering political implications that this insistence on the introduction could bring them, joined the crusade, claiming that Sharia will not be used against non-Moslems. One interesting thing is that even among the Moslems, there was no agreement on the sharia issue. To clarify this, I deem it very necessary here to refer to the personal experience or a firsthand information given by Mathew Kukah having been invited by the President of the Supreme Council for Islamic Affairs, SCIA, (Sultan of Sokoto) to Chair a section of the national seminar of Sharia put together by Jama'atu Nasril Islam. He wrote,

---

[308] Report of the Civil Liberties Organisation, in: *Guardian Newspaper*, March 2, 2000.
[309] Ndiokwere, N. I., op. cit. p. 85.
[310] Ibid, p. 87.

First of all, the political class had a different view of the Shari'a. Many of the Governors of the 11 Northern states who had adopted the Shari'a had been literally stampeded into doing so to avert political disaster and chaos. They had also seen political capital to be made as a result of the excitement of ordinary Muslims. But there was a world of difference between what these ordinary Muslims wanted and what the politicians themselves wanted. For the ordinary Muslims, the Shari'a was the shortest cut to addressing the problems of corruption, injustice and social degeneration that had taken hold of society. In second place, there were the traditional ruling classes. These, being on the payroll of the Federal and State Government, were living in two worlds and had an ambiguous response. On the one hand, they had to show their followers and adherents that they were truly the custodians of religion whilst, at the same time, they tried to calm frayed nerves on behalf of the Federal Government. Finally, at the intellectual level, there was a small group which openly argued that the adoption of the Shari'a was an exercise in futility because it was not possible to superimpose a Shari'a state on a post-colonial modern state fashioned on western democratic models. This group believed, therefore, that if Muslims wanted to live in a Shari'a state, they would have to conquer the present state before they should transform it.[311]

Even if it will not be applied against non-Moslems, these Sharia protagonists would have asked themselves a critical, people-oriented question. As they failed to do so, Martin Nwanne quoted by Nwobi in National Post called their attention to a thought provoking-situation in the North. He indicated that many parts of the Northern Nigeria were arid, sandy, crusty, dry, forlon, unhabitable and forsaken. In the rural areas of the same North, most people live in abject poverty, in huts and shanties, the kind that hardly exist anywhere else in the world. Even the framed Sabon Gari in Kano is still a ghetto and an anachronism in the 21st century. It is a wonder that these Northern governors have never given any thought about how to address the desert encroachment, they had claimed at revenue allocation moments that ravage

[311] Kukah, M. H., "Religious Liberty in a plural Society: The Nigerian Experience" in: *Religious Liberty: A Theme for Christian-Muslim Dialogue*, by The PCID, The Commission For Religious Relations with Muslims,Vatican City, Tipografia Vaticana, 2006, p. 119-120. The last stand was according to Kukah, the position canvassed by El Haj Zack-Zacky, the Iranian trained cleric who had had many brushes with the Nigerian state while he himself claimed he wanted a Shari'a State for Nigeria.

the North.[312] Taking the claim that the adoption of Sharia will not affect non-Muslims with a pinch of salt Nyiam Tony argued,

> We saw the whole issue of using Islam as a cover to create a situation where they have a monopoly of power. For example, if the Sharia they want to adopt is allowed to stay, it means that in all those states you have a Muslim-guided polity which means any non-Muslim will have no political right in those states. And if you now add up it means that for a number of states in Nigeria there will be no-go areas for non-Muslims. So it's all another ploy to regain what power they think they've lost[313]

Giving his view that is totally in line with the immediate past argument Kukah went beyond his already stated view on the Sharia issue to assert with vivid reference to why they may have opted for Shria adoption. It is very clear that the Moslem North have been in the corridors of power since after independence. Unfortunately after the Presidential election of 1999, a Southerner was announced the winner. This new president was not only a Southerner but a Christian who claimed to have been 'born again' after his rule as a soldier many years ago. Christian. The Christians, especially the Penticostal wing, celebrated this success with in a unique style. As if salt was added into an injury, the new President on taking office built a Presidential chapel in the Presidential Villa. Occasionally, prayers and services are transmitted on the Federal Television. There is no gain saying that such situations must have created anxiety among the Moslems that they saw the imposition of Sharia as the only consoling option to assert that they are still in reckoning.[314]It was therefore a shocking dismay as the Human Right group, after their fact-finding mission in Zamfara State, narrated in a state of unbelief and regret their experiences thereby confirming the fears expressed by many. The Human Rights Group reported,

> Now, there is an absolute violation of all these provisions of the constitution by the Zamfara state government. The establishment of a ministry of Religious Affairs and a preachers Council as well as the constitution of a council of Ulamas who are the custodian of Sharia are pointers to this. There also exists a mosque at the government house with a Chief Imam. Right to freedom of expression and the press is also being violated. This

[312] Nwobi, S. O., op.cit, p. 44.
[313] Nyiam, T., "Sharia Debate" in: *Sunday Punch*, March1, 2000.
[314] Kukah, M. H., op. cit. p. 118-119.

is in respect of the fact that Islamic religious instructions are being aired on state radio while debarring Christian religion from enjoying the same. An indication of this was given by Venerable Danbo of the Christian Association of Nigeria who told us that the state radio no longer takes advertisements or tapes from Christians in the state[315]

Worried by the attitudes of these governors, John Onaiyekan could not hide his stand against the use of religious sentiments to score a cheap political gain. For him, "Sharia is not about religion. It has to do with who does what and who has which right in this country. It is eminently political and those who are quietly pushing it are doing so for the political reasons not because they love Allah. If it has to do with religion, there is enough freedom in this country for any Christian and Muslim to practice his religion to the fullest."[316] And if it is political, it is then to be seen in the same self-service oriented Nigerian politics in which the poor Moslem masses will be at the unfortunate receiving end of these Sharia laws. As the helpless poor Moslems will be suffering to live in accordance with the Sharia law, the so called Sharia 'adoptionist governors' will be smiling to the banks with what they steal from their state purse without facing the wrath of the Sharia law.

Some of these Sharia 'adoptionist-governors' if critically scrutinized must have at one time or the other helped themselves from the public fund. Embezzlement of the public funds has been the unfortunate hallmark of the political class in Nigeria. It would have been wonderful if these governors are spared of this political cankerworm. Some of them were unfortunately accused of stealing public property and abusing of the office entrusted unto them. Even some were accused of securing their political posts through the back door. How could such a person or persons champion the cause of Allah through Sharia, yet they escape being amputated. If the truth be told, we have to question them, borrowing a leaf from Don Adinuba who argued,

> How many of the Sharia advocates can swear they never fornicated, let alone engaged in extra-marital relationships, including the commercial sex workers? How many do not drink alcohol habitually, though often in secret? Which governor or legislator or commissioner or any public officer can agree to be tried before a religious court rather than a civil court?

---

[315] Cf. "The Report of the Findings of the Human Rights Group on the implication of Sharia law for non-Muslims in Zamfara State" in *Guardian Newspaper*, March 27, 2000.

[316] Onaiyekan, J., "Expressing his opinion concerning the Sharia Problem" in: *The Punch*, March 8, 2000.

Which security agent can have the audacity to stop a 'big man' in a big car to find out if this female companion is actually his wife or mistress or commercial sex worker?[317]

Unfortunately, it is the poor masses out there that suffer the whole lot of the Sharia legal code, while those who are clamouring for its adoption and the haves in the North go about as sacred cows living like Kings and Emperors even amidst their corruption. Clearly, Sharia infringes on the rights of the totality of the citizens since Nigeria is a multi-religious nation. The report by Dipo Laleye in Minna, on the banning of hugging in an institution of higher learning is a case in point. He wrote, "In line with the provision of the Islamic legal code, the Vice Chancellor of the Niger State government-owned Ibrahim Badamasi Babangida University Lapai, Professor Ibrahim Adamu Kolo, has outlawed hugging of female students in the university... anyone caught "embracing or hugging" any female students would be severely dealt with...Describing hugging and embracing of female students as immoral, the vice chancellor said the management had decided to "forgive" those caught in the act but said those affected had been noted and would be closely watched by authorities."[318] Some of these 'Sharia-adoptionists' see Sharia as a way of converting others to Islam. In this way, they even wash their dirty linens in the public by manifesting their ignorance of the Nigerian constitution which they swear to protect and even of Qur'an. The Nigerian Constitution and the Qur'an (cf. Qur'an 2:256) are unanimous in support of religious freedom. In explaining the content of this Qur'an 2.256 Ibrahim M. Zikirullhi emphasized, "This injunction of the Quran removes the misunderstanding that Allah desires Moslems to use force for propagating their religion. It does not only forbid Moslems, in most emphatic words, to use force for converting non-Moslems, but also gives reasons why force should not be used for this purpose. It is because truth stands out distinct for using force"[319]

Despite this clarification, it was clear that these 'Sharia adoptionist governors,' had the Islamisation of Nigeria in mind coupled with their political future. This is evidently and unarguably contained in the statement attributed to former Zamfara state governor, Ahmed Sani, where he made it clear that he was out to finish the work started by Ahmadu Bello. Throwing more light

---

[317] Adinuba, D., "Reaction to Sharia Case" in: *Guardian Newspaper*, March 27, 2000, p. 61.

[318] Laleye, D., "Sharia: VC bans hugging of female students" in: *Tribune Newspaper* October 27, 2010 cf, also http:/www.tribune.com.ng

[319] Zikirullhi, M., "Reaction against Sharia Imposition" in: *Guardian Newspaper*, September 12, 2000.

on the gravity of this claim, Ubaka, C.O gives us a gentleman's knowledge of the work of Ahmadu Bello born to a Sokoto royal family. He wrote,

> He was the Sarduana of Sokoto, the president general of Northern region. He therefore used his position to campaign for the total Islamisation of the North. His northernisation policy was actually an Islamisation policy. Government resources and machinery was employed in his religio-political strategies to win the whole North, nay, the country to Islam. He went on pilgrimage to Mecca and while there he held talks with Muslim leaders at the international level. He was elected the vice president of the Muslim World League and thus attracted foreign personnel to support Islam in Nigeria....When he returned from the pilgrimage in 1962...he co-opted the emirs and local traditional leaders in his expansionist programme. Some of the non-Muslim traditional rulers were forced to convert or be dethroned. With regard to Sharia, Ahmadu Baello advocated the implementation of the whole sharia...[320]

Although he did not live to execute his ideas, it has continued to plague the country till date. What happened in 1978 was common knowledge to all. It was a situation where some Islamic protagonists fought tooth and nail to get Sharia approved and included in the Nigerian constitution. The drama played out in the assembly was everywhere in the air. With the likes of Shehu Shagari, who refused to be so fanatical about it, it was defeated. Many more attempts have been made by these protagonists before the Zamfara State governor eventually politically set in. It is to be taken from the action of the likes of Shehu Shagari that not all the Muslims are in favour of the plan to adopt Sharia. Even some Moslem sects like the Shiites and the Izala, are against the adoption of Sharia, at least for now. For them, the application of Sharia law should wait till such a time when religious leaders have taken over political leadership of the country. It is in lieu of this that both Zakzaky and another Shiite leader, Abubakar Mujahid, promote a thorough Islamic revolution to reclaim society for the Moslem faithful.[321] As a resume on these riot-oriented governors, Ubaka said,

---

[320] Ubaka, C. O., "Sharia in Nigeria: Its Implications for Non-Muslims" (being a paper presented at the 29th Convocation Ceremony of Bigard Memorial Seminary Enugu on the 10th of March 2000).

[321] Pike, J., "Nigeria Christian / Muslim Conflict" cf. http://www.göobalsecurity.org

> If they succeed in achieving their set target which is the total Islamisation of the country, with the sharia as the constitution, the non-Muslims will either be killed or they will be subjected to series of suppression, subjugation, oppression and discrimination until they submit to the religion of the state (din al daula)....The influence of foreign Muslim countries in the sharia issue in Nigeria cannot be over emphasised....Its strategic position, its economic riches and human potential makes it the country of their dream. If they win Nigeria over to Islam, other smaller countries will easily be conquered for Islam. No wonder the struggle for sharia in Nigeria.[322]

However,the implementation of this plan is becoming impossible on daily basis as other non-Moslem religions are now aware of all these plans and are ready to face any uprising headlong. In a four paged strong petition written on June 18, 2009, to the late President of Nigeria, Umaru Yaradua and the Senate President, David Mark, the non-Moslems condemned the actions of the Hisbah as they tried to implement the Sharia law, accusing the State Governor, Ibrahim Sherakau and the police of silent conspiracy. It is therefore unfortunate that the Hisbah has taken over the duties of the NDLEA in the State, mounting road blocks in their search for alcoholic drinks and directing these attacks mainly at the non-Moslem residents in Sabon Gari. Giving an account as to what exactly was the problem, Cosmas Ekpunobi wrote in daily Champion Newspaper,

> Very fresh in memory is the incident of March 30 when Hisbah (an agent set up by the state government to implement Sharia legal system in the state) intercepted a truck conveying drinks to Maiduguri, after a thorough investigation by the Nigerian police, they charged the truck to a magistrate court which later released the truck upon finding that it was on transit plying a federal high way, but to the consternation of law abiding citizens, Hisbah after the court verdict, re arrested the truck at court premises, confiscated and destroyed the drinks...a number of bus drivers and owners of drinks have been arrested and detained by the police and taken to court of their choice.[323]

---

[322] Ubaka, C. O., op. cit. p. 47.
[323] Ekpunobi, C., "Religious Violence looms in Kano" in: *Daily Champion*, June 29, 2009.

3.3.2. OIC as a Source of religious conflict

Another hydra-headed monster that could have eclipsed the unity of Nigeria is the secret registration of Nigeria as a member of the Islamic Union. It is for me an explosive, poisonous gift of the 'Maradonic' and Machiavellian administration of the Ibrahim Badamosi Babangida regime. Critically observed, one sees it as the continued attempt to implement the religious agenda of the late Ahmadu Bello – the Islamisation agenda. The aim of the secret deal is not far-fetched. For him or them, Nigeria has or must become an Islamic country. This single act nearly set Nigeria again on a religious war part. He maintained that this Organization which has its aims and objectives will benefit Nigeria. But the charter of the organization was unambiguous in stating the reason for its existence. It works according to articles 2 - 6 of this charter "to promote Islamic solidarity among member states...to co-ordinate efforts for the safeguard of the Holy Places, and support of the struggle of the people of Palestine, and help them to regain their rights and liberate their land...to strengthen the struggle of all Muslim peoples with a view to safeguarding their dignity, independence and national rights."[324]

This organization was formed in Jedda in 1971. Nwobi reported that, "At the founding of the organization in 1971 Nigeria, under General Yakubu Gowon (Retired), was given observer status. In January 1986, under General Ibrahim Babangida (Retired), the federal government decided to regularizes its membership during the organization's conference held in Morocco"[325] This secret regularization process was what helped to heighten the tension and suspicion. Nwobi further remarked, "This suspicion became justifiable when Christian members of the ruling military junta claimed that they were not aware that the Nigerian government had regularized its membership in the OIC."[326] But in defense of Islam, Z. T. Ayyuba, maintained that,

> No one knows Nigeria to be an Islamic State as many of the members of the OIC are well known to be...we are well aware of the fact that our Constitution has not been replaced with the Sharia law. Until Sharia law is attempted to be introduced we cannot conclude that Nigeria is on the path of Islamisation... Not only Islamic states are members; those secular states like Sierra Leone and Senegal are members. Only God knows how

[324] Nwobi, S. O., op. cit. p. 42.
[325] Yusuf, S., "Nigerian's Membership in the OIC: Implications of Print Media Coverage for Peace and National Unity" in: *Journal of Muslim Minority Affairs*, Vol. 19, No. 2, 1999, p. 237.
[326] Ibid.

long they have been members of the organization but that did not make them Islamic states...Let me say categorically here that I am not advocating that Nigeria should be declared an Islamic State now, as I know that the time is yet to come. That might be when we are physically, mentally and spiritually ready to accommodate the idea and it shall be acceptable to even Christians and other non-Muslims willingly and without any hue and cry.[327]

Even the defense given by Ayyuba is itself pregnant since Ayyuba had the hope that Nigeria will one day come to be an Islamic state. It boils down to the fear that OIC, through the 1972 charter is primarily and purely for the propagation of Islam in its entire ramification. Professor Aluko considered it 'nonsensical' for anyone to assert that the OIC's membership does not make Nigeria an Islamic State, maintaining that it is "a threat to our survival... the greatest single threat to the survival of this country as an entity since the civil war...with only two aims: to secure support against the Israelis and to expand Arabic cultural imperialism. He thereby declared that we must be left alone to chart our course."[328] Chief H. D. Davis, advising that the sleeping Dog should be allowed to lie blasted and dismissed the argument of those fronting for OIC as foliage of tendentious and fallacious irrelevancies, describing the real issue of the matter as an imposition of Islamic faith on the nation.[329] So whatever may be the reasons, the Christians saw it as a snail speed Islamisation of Nigeria. By implication, every State which belongs to this group would be governed by Islamic law. As Obemeata argued,

One of the implications of Nigeria's membership in the OIC is that Nigeria has become a recognized Muslim country. Another leader may emerge in the near future who will declare Nigeria an Islamic republic and in justification of his action may, like President Babangida, claim that he merely upgraded the status of Nigeria because Nigeria has been a Muslim country for many years by being a member of OIC.[330]

Still in an attempt to justify the claim that Nigeria has been secretly dragged into OIC, Sunday Tribune, as regrettably quoted by Yusuf Salahu-

[327]Ayyuba, Z. T., "OIC Debate" in: *Sunday Sketch,* Feb, 1986.
[328] Aluko, Prof., in: *Sunday Sketch*, Feb 9, 1986 also cf. *Guardian News paper*, February10, 1986.
[329] Davis, H. D., "OIC Problem" in: *Guardian,* February 12, 1986, p. 9.
[330] Obemeata, J., "OIC debate" in: *Independence Newspaper,* February 23, 1986.

deen, carried this information, "... talks in the past about attempts to turn Nigeria into an Islamic state has (sic) been dismissed as a wolf cry. No greater credence could be lent to that allegation than Nigeria's so-called membership of OIC which may be a ploy to test public reaction before further steps are taken to consolidate the Islamization process."[331] In the course of these debates, some newspapers were vehemently pro-OIC. Among them was the New Nigerian. Yusuf, S., quoted it as saying, "... the wide-spread interpretation of this is that the state should not be seen to touch anything remotely religious, and obviously the OIC has its roots in a particular religion...."[332] The paper then went on to admit that the Christians were justified in their hostility towards Nigerian membership of the OIC. But then it added: "...still the hostility is mistaken. The OIC is not purely a religious organization, otherwise countries like Benin, Cameroun, Uganda, Burkina Faso, Lebanon, Senegal, Chad which are either predominantly Christian or secular, would not be members... At any rate, Nigeria and the Vatican have diplomatic ties at ambassadorial levels and the Vatican is a Christian theocratic state whose relationship with us unlike with say Saudi Arabia, a Muslim theocratic state, is purely spiritual."[333]The Triumph was another newspaper which was supportive of the OIC membership. It wrote an editorial on 25 January 1986 entitled 'IOC (sic): Needless Controversy'. In this editorial the paper argued that it was wrong to give the secular nature of Nigeria a negative interpretation which would mean an outright neglect of religious factors in our national life, since religion occupies a central point in our daily affairs.

The paper further argued, "... that Nigeria is a secular state is no excuse for us not to join the international body. We should exploit the happy coexistence of Islam and Christianity to reap benefits the two religions offer."[334]Then it went on to enumerate the benefits that could accrue to Nigeria, particularly from the OIC's soft loan and solidarity fund, which had been so maligned by the anti-OIC newspapers. In addition, the paper stated that membership of the organization would provide another front for Nigeria to fight racism and imperialism, as highlights of the OIC's charter include elimination of all forms of colonialism and racial discrimination.[335]In line with Ndiokwere[336], the summary of the Moslem/government stand on the OIC issue could be given as follows:

---

[331] Yusuf, S., op. cit. p. 240.
[332] Ibid.
[333] Ibid.
[334] Ibid.
[335]Ibid, p. 241.
[336] Ndiokwere, N. I., op. cit. p. 92-94.

I. The Topmost agenda in the OIC objectives is how to ensure cooperation and friendship among countries with Moslem inhabitants, not minding how small they are in number;
II. They strive to achieve enviable economic, technical, cultural and diplomatic matters as well as support moves for the promotion of international peace, eradication of racism, colonialism and standardizing of unity among member nations;
III. It directs its business efforts strictly towards international cooperation with the hope of developing economically that will eventually open the avenues for self-dependence as is the case with United Nations and other agencies like FAO, UNESCO, and WHO. Apart from the above stand, the Nigerian president gave his personal argument for the Nigeria's membership of OIC thus:

I. Because of its advantages, many of Nigeria's neighbouring States are members despite their being secular States with relatively non-Moslem population. In some cases, even the delegations from these States were led to the organization's conferences by Christian ministers.
II. Member nations are characterized more by the common denominator name, 'Third World' than by religious affinities.
III. It is not possible for a religiously pluralistic country like Nigeria to be dragged into OIC with the hope of making Islam a State religion. Therefore, the decision to regularize its membership cannot be out of pressure from Moslem leaders and fundamentalists. But on the part of the opponents of OIC, the secrecy involved in the inclusion of Nigeria in the league of OIC member states, only to be revealed by a foreign press was the big clear reason for suspicion. Their stand could be thus summarized:

I. The OIC affair is seen as part of the Moslem grand plan to Islamize Nigeria. It is equally a world – wide design rooted in Islamic culture to propagate Islamic faith and interest.
II. As far as the horrified Christian leaders were concerned, the way in which Nigeria was secretly and hurriedly smuggled into the OIC on January 9, 1986 showed in clear terms that government, already accused of showing open and committed interest in moslem religion was solidly behind moslem campaign to islmize Nigeria.
III. To Islamize Nigeria, moslems have demanded that the shari'a laws should be incorporated in the constitution of the country. The membership of the OIC is a full – drawn plan to declare Nigeria and (sic) Islamic republic;

IV. There had been consistent attempts to accomplish this long-standing Islamic objective – dating back to the Sokoto jihad, led by Islamic reformer and crusader, Shehu Othman Dan Fodio – cutting through the period of Sarduana of Sokoto – down to Shehu Shagari – down to Idiagbon/Buhari regime and lastly, the Babangida administration. No matter how hard the OIC protagonists tried to clear the cloud of mistrust and suspicion that enveloped the OIC issue, as it regards the above cited clarifications, Christians, emboldened by historical facts insisted that the introduction of Nigeria into OIC has purely and unambiguously religious background and motives. They therefore maintained that:

I. Right from its foundation in 1965 and its first conference, the organization had had the primary motive of uniting the Islamic and Arab theocracies for the purpose of propagating the Islamic faith.
II. Very other objective of the organization should be seen as 'an appendage', fruit of a later reflection, meant to attract and sustain the interest of member nations, while pursuing the Islamic religious interests.
III. Islamic solidarity among member states is the soul of its charter meant to preserve Islamic spiritual, ethical, social and economic values.
IV. The extension of membership status to nations with small moslem population is a type of bait meant to convert their leaders to Islam and thus hasten the islamization programme of the countries concerned. This is particularly true of the poor African countries who must have been attracted to the organization primarily on account of economic reasons. As all these arguments (in favour of and against Nigerian membership in OIC raged, an observation was made that the members of ATR were not included in the panel set up by the government. Surely their stand would have been more devastating if we consider their usual and normal claim to authenticity. Writing on their behalf, Sola Oke simply reminded both Christians and Moslems that they (Christianity and Islam) were both, adherents of "foreign religion" who engaged in an open denigration of traditional values.[337] In the wake of this accusations and denials or counter-accusations, the Catholic Bishops did not hide their stand on the issue after their mature deliberations. Part of their press Release on February 22, 1986 in Lagos reads:

We feel distressed that this issue has tended to sour the cordial relations that should exist between us and our Moslem compatriots who share with us the hope of building a united, virile country based on equity and social justice,

[337] Oke, S., "In Defence of Secularism" in: *Guardian Newspaper*, April 4, 1986, p. 9.

and on respect for fundamental rights of all, irrespective of creed. While holding to these ideals, we are compelled in the interest of truth to declare our stand on the burning OIC issue. The fact that secrecy and rumour eventually gave way to belated admission that Nigeria has joined the OIC cannot but disappoint us. With the majority of Nigerians, we have come to expect openness and free debate from this Government. The lack of previous debate on such a sensitive matter, either in public or in government is a blow to the trust and the hope that freedom loving Nigerians have been led to repose in the present administration. Yet we believe that all is not lost if the authorities take immediate and necessary action to repair the damage. Now that the fact is clear, after mature deliberation and having listened to the pleas of numerous representations from Christians, non- Christians and some Moslems, we have come to this inevitable conclusion: we do not and shall not agree to Nigeria's membership of the OIC. In the overall national interest of unity, peace, equity and progress, we strongly advise the Government to withdraw the country from the Organization of Islamic Conference. Our continued membership is perceived by many as indirectly but effectively making Nigeria an Islamic State despite all assurances to the contrary. To elevate one religion to the status of a state religion is clearly against our Constitution (section 10).[338]

The above Press Release by the Catholic Bishops' Conference really touched every aspect of what could be said about the OIC issue. Despite the denials that Nigeria's membership of OIC has nothing to do with islamization of Nigeria, evidences abound to the contrary. The very fact that even some Moslems were against this move was a big plus to those who oppose the regularization attempt. The secrecy with which it was done after several months and years of denials made the whole issue suspicious. As the Bishops demanded, only the withdrawal of Nigeria could guarantee freedom of worship and peaceful co-existence.

3.4. Ethno-Political Problem

Acknowledging the contributive effect of instability of a particular region in fomenting trouble, the Sultan of Sokoto called on the Northern traditional rulers to avoid anything that could trigger the coming back of the bloody sectarian clashes which rocked the region in the past decade.[339] This secta-

---

[338] CBCN, Press Release in Lagos, February 22, 1986.
[339] Shiklam, J., op.cit.

rian problem is not applicable only to the North but also to the South. Since Nigeria is a pluralistic nation, the slightest problem in a section of the land, spreads to the whole land, as those in the troubled section have their relatives residing in other parts of the land. The government, which has the wherewithal to help the traditional rulers enhance security monitoring in their respective areas of jurisdiction thereby laying a strong foundation for peace, most often seems to look the other way while the riots rage on. These sectarian squabbles have been often hijacked by politicians to whip up religious sentiments. Surely the conflicts in Nigeria today come wearing religious outlook/garment but they have really other remote causes.[340] Kukah, M. regreted that such a situation was allowed to stay. And neither the Christians nor the Muslims were spared of this political good fashioned trap. He emphasized,

> Although the adherents of Islam and Christianity form the dominant majority in Nigerian society, neither religion has been able to overcome the obstacles laid by the political class, which continues to manipulate religious sentiments to set one group against the other. Tensions have continued to mount over the status of Islamic Law, the Sharia. The nation has been unable to benefit from the return of civil rule since 1999 due to the decision of the Muslim elite in Northern Nigeria to turn to religion as a means of compensating for their seeming loss of political control and power. The adoption and application of Sharia Law by some of the states in the region led to violence in many parts of the country.[341]

With this assertion, one can rightly hold the view that despite the fact that most of the riots in Nigeria are presumed to be religiously motivated, there is no denial of elements of ethnic and political interests as Opeloye asserted. A typical example of this assertion could be the Kaduna riot - specifically in Zangon Kataf 1992 as well as the Tafawa Balewa in 1991 and 1995 in Bauchi. In the case of Tafawa Balewa of April 20th, 1991 the sale of suya sparked of the riot. As the story had it, a Christian (Sayawa) sold suya alleged to be from pork meat to a Moslem Fulani. Fundamentally, the Muslims don´t eat pork meat which for them is defiled. As a result of this allegation, quarrel ensued between them. Their voices of accusations, denials and counter-accusations rented the calm atmosphere thereby creating a scenario. The

---

[340] Vellguth, K., „Wenn Religion als Vorwand dient, Unruhen in Nigeria haben vielfältige Ursachen“ in: *Heilung und Heil*, Heft 3/2009, p. 12.

[341] Kukah, M., op. cit. p. 156.

attracted passers-by took sides and the next action is a free-for-all Mike-Tyson-like punches.

Many lost their lives in this pandemonium while some sustained injuries. The seemingly uncontrollable commotion spread fast to other parts of the State including Bauchi, the capital city. Prior to this stage, it wore the look of a religious riot being ignited by doctrinal fanaticism. However, the timing of this unfortunate incident was unfavorable for any fast hope of peaceful settlement. The problem that rocked the Tafawa Balewa Local Government had not been solved. The Muslim (Hausa/Fulani) butchers and their Christian (Sayawa) counterparts were still at logger-heads over the use of the joint abattoir facilities. A panel of enquiry was set by the Federal government to unravel and clarify the misunderstanding as well as proffering solutions. The commissioner of inquiry under the chairmanship of Justice Bala Babalakin pinned the problem on a rock side where the Hausa/Fulani had been slaughtering their animals for public consumption for more than a century. The Christian Butchers following their increasing animosity towards the Muslims started slaughtering their own animals in the church premises. After the local government constructed a new abattoir, unlicensed Christians demanded an equitable allocation of space within the abattoir to both themselves and the licensed Muslim butchers.

The suya episode only compounded a problem that was already clamouring for a solution. Solutions for lasting peace in the area were worked out and recommended by the panel among which is a suggestion for a creation of chiefdom for the Sayawa. This was not to play out as planned. In July 1995 a cabinet reshuffle sparked off another unrest. The Bauchi State government dropped a Christian replacing him with a Muslim (Hausa/Fulani). It was for the Sayawa a clear confirmation of the all time claim of marginalization and discrimination policy of the Bauchi State government against their tribe. The resultant effect was no less catastrophic than that of 1991.[342] The year 1992 was not spared of such confrontations. This time around it took place in Zangon Kataf. Duniya Francis describing what happened said,

> On Thursday 6th February, 1992, there was a massive destruction of lives and property in Zangon Kataf. This was the day set aside for the Zango Kataf market to be moved across the road leading to Saminaka and Samaru-Kataf in order to locate it at a better site prepared by the Zango-Kataf local government council. On getting to the new site on the fateful day, unsuspecting early market goers, largely Christian Kataf natives, were at-

[342] Opeloye, M. O., op. cit. p. 232-233.

tacked by the largely Muslim Hausa Fulani settlers. It is the premeditated action of the Muslims using dangerous weapons such as machine guns and daggers, which caused the riot leading to loss of lives and massive destruction of property.[343]

Just as the above account seems to put the blame on the Muslims, Opeloye's account following the findings of the panel of inquiries put it on the Christians. Opeloye reported that what is known as immediate cause of the February 1992 Zangon Kataf[344] riot was the decision of the Zangen Kataf local government chairman, who is a Kataf Christian, to move the Zango weekly market from its old site in the heart of Zango town to a new site without complying with the necessary constitutional requirements. The discontent of the Katafs with the old market was due to the fact that most of the stalls there were owned by Hausa/Fulani with no room for expansion. The Zango people, who were predominantly Hausa settlers, were strongly opposed to the relocation because the new site was unfavourable to them. The ensuing disturbance rocked the whole Kaduna State.[345]

Whether the Muslims or the Christians are to blame, what is to be taken from these accounts was the fact that they pin point ethnic upheavals as the root cause. The riots cropped up as would a sleeping Lion whose tail was touched. It was like an already over pumped balloon into which more air is added. The resultant effect is not to be doubted. It was an explosion of a long accumulated ethno-political rivalry which had been gathering in Tafawa Balewa town since 1945. With this, we can see that tribalism or ethnicity and injustice are part of the root causes of Nigerian problems. Even the riots of 1991 and 1995 were seen as an outward bursting of a long overdue incubated anger of the Sayana against the hemogenic tenacity which the Bauchi Emirate Council had on administrative power in Tafawa Belawa, especially political appointments of District Heads. Their anger found an outlet in the uprisings of 1945 and 1959, even leading to the murder of the district Head in

---

[343] Duniya, F., "The Zango Kataf Crisis In Retrospect of Minority Culture in Northern Nigeria" in: *Bulletin of Ecumenical Theology, Violence and State Security*, 7: 1-2, 1995.

[344] Zangon Kataf is situated in the South Eastern part of Kaduna State and it is a Hausa settlement in Kataf land. The Hausa arrived there in the fifteenth century as traders under the leadership of one Malam Mele. The Kataf allowed the Hausa to settle there and the Hausa then named the settlement Zango Kataf, meaning a station for the Hausa in Kataf. The Town is 99% Muslim, but it is surrounded by Kataf villages inhabited by non-Muslim and non-Hausa people - cf. Yusuf, H. B., p. 242.

[345] Opeloye, M. O., op. cit. p. 233.

1977.[346] It was due to the clear application of political maneuvers of some acclaimed religious disturbances that Pastor Ayo Oritsejafor did not hide his bitterness in pointing accusing fingers on and condemning the former Zamfara State governor, Alhaji Ahmed Sani Yerima, referring to him as a religious fundamentalists and directing his appeal to the President of the Federal Republic of Nigeria for necessary action as reported in Sun News on-line of March 2, 2009. He wondered why wanton destruction of the houses of Worship should be carried out in the name of religion. He appealed to the President Yar' Adua administration to do something before the angry youths take laws into their hands. He emphasized,

> It is preposterous for a human being created by God to burn places built for the worship of the same God. Not even in the Middle East...After consultation with Christians leaders, especially the youths who rolled out frightful statistics to show how many persons that have been killed in different parts of the North since 1999, I am left with no other option than to make this passionate appeal to the Yar'Adua Administration....They told me in tears that after losing their commercial ventures to some mindless religious bigots, they can no longer continue on this path of turning the other check because they had been beaten on both checks...They youth leaders vowed to employ any means available to defend themselves, their places of worship and their businesses in any part of the country.[347]

As one of the solutions to this unrest, as well as acting as a deterrent to the future occurrence he suggested punishing the past sponsors and offenders. He wrote, "We, therefore, strongly appeal to the Federal Government to, as a first step to the resolution of the protracted crisis, all identified sponsors and perpetrators of past crisis in different parts of the country must now be brought to just justice in the interest of peaceful co-existence."[348] Apart from this, one calls to mind the unfortunate riot of Jos in 2008, in which so many lives were lost. Reacting to the riot, the then State's chairman of CAN, Most Rev. Ignatius Kaigama wrote, "We were taken aback by the turn of events in Jos. We thought it was political, but from all indications it is not so. We were surprised at the way some of our churches and properties were attacked and some of our faithful and Clergy killed. The attacks were carefully planned

[346] Ibid.

[347] Oritsejafor, A., "Bauchi crises: Stem religious violence or....Oritsejafor warns FG, Slams Senator Yerima" reported by Osewele, B., in: *Daily Sun Newspaper,* March 2, 2009.

[348] Ibid.

and executed. The questions that bog our minds are why were churches and Clergy attacked and killed? Why were politicians and political party offices not attacked if it were a political conflict? Why were the business premises and property of innocent civilians destroyed? We strongly feel that it was not political, but pre-meditated act under the guise of elections."[349] On the same note, the CAN's National Secretary, Engr. Samuel Salifu pointed out that, "CAN is sick and tired of these type of repetitive crises that keep happening in Jos, Bauch, Kano, Maiduguri, Zangon Kataf, Kaduna and host of other places in Nigeria with attendant loss of lives and properties. We are calling on all the people of the state to be calm and also calling on the state government to promptly put a stop to the killings and burning and find a way of addressing future issues before they degenerate into killings."[350]

But as a way of drumming it deep into the ears of those that may care to hear, who said that it was not political, the National Secretary of Action Congress, Alhaji Lai Mohammed on behalf of their party condemned what they referred to as, "the government's gross insensitivity in going ahead to release the results of the elections, especially that of the Jos North that precipitated the crises, even as the smoke was yet to clear from the ruins of the violence."[351] The Jos crises seem to have defiled all solutions. It has continued to re-occur up till January 2011. It has led to an unfortunate 'Shoot-to-kill Order' given to security operatives. This Shoot –to-kill order as reported by Jon Gambrell of the Associated Press allowed the soldiers to quicken the death of anyone found trying to hurt another person or destroy a home, church or or mosque. They are expected to try to stop the person or group of rioters even if it involves taking the person's life. This order was as a result of the killing of a Moslem election worker by a Christian mob who went ahead to set his body on fire.[352] Even before this incident, an earlier report had it that following the political congress of the Congress for Progressive Change (CPC), Angwa Doki area of Bukuru in Jos South local government area witnessed some unfortunate and regrettable scenery that involved borning of houses. The state Commissioner of Police, Mr. Abdulrahaman Akano testified that some irate youths set houses of people ablaze at random when

---

[349]Kaigama, I., "Death Toll in Jos Rises to 350" as reported by Okocha, C. et. al., in: *Thisday Newspaper*, November 30, 2008.

[350] Ibid.

[351] Ibid.

[352] Gambrell, J., "Shoot-to-kill orders issued in Nigeria after riot" January 18, 2011 cf. http/www.wtop.com

they had left for Sunday church service.[353] For this reason, an Igbo group called, 'Izu Umunna Cultural Association Nigeria' warned of that enogh is enough with the killing of their innocent brothers. Connecting the unfortunate event of 2010 Christmas eve bombing and the recent episode of 2011burning of houses, they made their stand known through their president Prof. Zebelum Okoye who said, "It is with utmost sense of sadness that we lament the chronic and cruel killing of Igbos in Jos which reared its ugly head again on the eve of Christmas and as recent as last Saturday with the bombing of innocent souls in some parts of Jos...For whatever the intentions or reasons of this terrorism may be, we want to strongly warn that political, religious and ethnic disagreement should not be settled with the blood of a single Igbo man or his property and indeed any other Nigerian for that matter."[354] It is not to be doubted that politics in Nigeria is a strong contributive element in the riots and bloodshed in the Nigerian Nation. As a summary to highlight the influence of religious politics in Nigeria, a differentiation between religion and politics of religion is necessary. On this note Ehusani argued,

> To appreciate the infinite potential for good in the collaboration or cooperation of Christians and Muslims in modern pluralistic societies we must first make the distinction between the practice of religion and the politics of religion. Living in a country where Christians and Muslims each claim fifty percent of the population, I am able to say without fear of contradiction that the genuine practice of Islam and Christianity will hurt no one in our land or in any land whatsoever. Instead, the faithful practice of these religions, which include private and public prayer, fasting, and acts of charity, and the dissemination of the fundamental teachings of the religions, should normally ensure a just, peaceful and united polity. Because of the transcendental values they share in common and the elementary moral principles by which good is sought and evil is avoided, the faithful practice of Islam and Christianity can only lead to a better human society, one that thrives on justice and peace. On the other hand, it is often the politics of these religions and the manipulation of religious sentiments for selfish individual interests that fuel the intolerance, discrimination, perse-

[353] Adinoyi, S., "Nigeria: Jos- House Burnings Escalate" January 10, 2011 cf. http/www.thisdaylive.com
[354] Ibid.

cution, hatred, vengeance and violence that we have witnessed in the recent past in our country and in other countries.[355]

From the above quotation, it becomes no exaggeration to maintain that the Nigerian problem is a man-made problem. Every religion in Nigeria has in her elements that will ensure peaceful co-existence. It is however regrettable that some of those who should lead others to genuine practice of their religion have diverted all their efforts towards appealing to religious sentiments to gain political importance or influence. Until this politicization of religion in Nigeria is done away with, the hope of peaceful co-existence will remain forever a mirage. If peaceful co-existence remains a mirage, economic wellbeing of the citizenry will continue to retrogress.

3.5. Economic Problem

It is a regrettable tale of shame that a country like Nigeria which, because of her divine economic natural endowments should be one of the richest country in the world is today referred to as one of the poorest in the world. It is referred to as a poor country because it cannot boast of helping her numerous children maintain a standard living style. As a testimony to this, the President of Missio in Germany, Msgr. Klaus Krämer after his travel to Nigeria with the President of the German Bishops' Conference, Archbishop R. Zöllitsch did not hide his feelings about the situation in Nigeria. He summarized his experience thus: "Nigeria, a country with the support of oil is a wealthy country, in which very many people live on abject poverty."[356] Kößmeier Norbert captured this situation with a descriptive accuracy. For him, "Despite the fact that Nigeria makes much income from her oil-production- about 80 percent of the total income of the country-, it is eventually the ruling Elites who benefit from it. A betterment of the situation of the population, especially in the North but also in the Niger Delta is not guaranteed. It is the opposite. Poverty level has increased."[357] It is therefore no surprise that her inhabitants, especially the youths engage in atrocities of divergent magnitude- religious, economic, social and cultural. Following the aforementioned observations, one sees their necessary link to the general

---

[355] Ehusani, G., "Case Study of Nigeria" in: *Human Rights, Opportunities for Christian-Islamic Co- operation in upholding human rights and establishing civil societies'* Conference in closed session 11/3/2002 – 14/3/2002, Berlin, Vol. 2, PMS, Aachen, p. 90-91.

[356] Krämer, K., „Der Emir und der Erzbischof" in: *Kirche+Leben*, Oktober 18, 2009, p. 8.

[357] Kößmeier, N., „Leben auf dem Pulverfass" Quelle: *Herder Korrespondenz* 63, 11/2009, p. 583ff.

message sent by Pontifical Council For Interreligious Dialogue to Moslems as they marked the end of Ramadan in 2009. The message read,

> The attention, the compassion and the help that we, brothers and sisters in humanity, can offer to those who are poor, helping them to establish their place in the fabric of society, is a living proof of the Love of the Almighty, because it is man as such whom He calls to love and help, without distinction of affiliation. We all know that poverty has the power to humiliate and to engender intolerable sufferings; it is often a source of isolation, anger, even hatred and the desire for revenge. It can provoke hostile actions using any available means, even seeking to justify them on religious grounds, or seizing another man's wealth, together with his peace and security, in the name of an alleged "divine justice". This is why confronting the phenomena of extremism and violence necessarily implies tackling poverty through the promotion of integral human development that Pope Paul VI defined as the "new name for peace.[358]

As if talking directly to the Nigerian citizens, the council was re-echoed in the words of Pope Benedict XVI where he, on the occasion of the World Day for Peace on 1ST January 2009, distinguished between two types of poverty: poverty to be combated and poverty to be embraced. These two types of poverty are just what Nigeria is suffering from. Under the poverty to be combated we have some normal daily life's problems that make life bitter if they are lacking. They include: hunger, lack of clean water, limited medical care and inadequate shelter, insufficient educational and cultural systems, illiteracy. Added to these are those problems visible in the so called advanced wealthy nations which include among others: evident marginalization, as well as affective, moral and spiritual poverty. Talking about the poverty to be embraced, one thinks of a style of life which is simple and essential, avoiding waste and respecting the environment and the goodness of creation. Poverty to be embraced is helpful since it calls us to fasting and frugality. It also predisposes us to go beyond ourselves, expanding the heart.[359]

To lend its weight to the truth that poverty is one of the strongest causes of upheavals in Nigeria, a German newspaper, '*Die Tagespost*' gave a sum-

---

[358] Pontifical Council for Interreligious Dialogue, 'Christians and Muslims: Together in overcoming poverty' being the Message for the end of Ramadan 2009 cf. www.vatican.va, cf. also Encyclical Letter, *Populorum Progressio*, 1975, no. 76.

[359] Ibid. cf. also Message for the World Day of Peace, 2009, n. 2.

marized detail of the happenings in Niger Delta - a State in Southern part of Nigeria where the most talked about oil well is located. According to the Newspaper, "Twenty million people live in abject poverty in Niger Delta, surrounded by oil industries which are dominated by foreign companies. These companies pay millions of dollar as tax but the locale inhabitants hardly benefit from it. On this account, the Movement for the Emancipation of Niger Delta (MEND) legitimizes her act of kidnapping the employed foreigners of the oil companies and the destruction of their oil rigs and pipelines, although the real target of their struggle is the government. It is therefore not surprising that USA, an old ally of Nigeria, always warns of the breakdown of law and order in a Nigeria."[360] The above citations allude to the unfortunate results that Nigerians harvest after hard-fought elections and point out clearly why so many have taken politics as their only business. These business politicians could be classified in Nigeria as enjoying a first class life style. They take the first class seats whenever they want to fly by air. What is more worrisome is that even what they promised the people during the electioneering campaigns are never met. Instead, they use the monthly allocations from the federal government meant for the people to enrich themselves. Their accounts and shares overseas are bottomless. The best word for this situation is 'corruption' which begins with selfishness and gluttony. The poor masses who are aware of their corrupt nature often remain unrestrained and take laws into their hands. The effect of this is not hidden especially when one considers that the youths who have not been gainfully employed despite being qualified are involved. The level of poverty cries to the high heavens. Decrying this unfortunate situation and the wide divide between the rich and the poor that more often than not breeds violence, Vellguth Klaus in line with the Daily Sun Newspaper report, wrote,

> At the same time there is a little group of people who are boundlessly rich – mainly because of the income from the state oil business ... Approximately 60 percent of the youths are unemployed. A great number of people because of their precarious living situation exhibit a great measure of readiness towards violence; many eventually fall back to criminality. Above that, the peaceful co-existence of the different ethnicity in Nigeria has been poisoned through bribery and corruption.[361]

---

[360] Gregory, M., „Nigeria braucht die Zusammenarbeit seiner Religionen und Völker" in: *Die Tagespost*, Januar 9, 2010.

[361] Vellguth, K., „Armut und Religionskonflikt in Nigeria" in: *Stimmen der Zeit*, Heft 10, Oktober 2009, p. 702.

A driving force in Nigerian politics which is very clear to everyone who cares to know is selfishness and the greed for wealth rather than the intention to serve. It is the urge to partake in the 'national cake'. It is no wonder then that a whole President of a nation would declare an election "a do or die" affair thereby pointing out glaringly why people can maim and murder their opponents or make charms in order to win elections. Many voters who are ready to kill in the name of religion or ethnicity to make sure that a politician of their faith or town emerges are most often ignorant of their being exploited. Having found the strong influence that religion plays in Nigerian politics, many politicians these days appeal to religious sentiments of some less informed to achieve their economic and materialistic political aim. Appealing to the political class, especially from the North whom he accused of religio-politico cum economic manipulation of the poor, illiterate and unemployed youths, Oritsejafor Ayo said, "Please save this country from imminent danger of a major religious war, which if begins might be too catastrophic for the nation as a whole...If you love this country so much and you must fight to defend it through religious wars, then bring your children from oversees (sic) to carry cudgels, arms and petrol."[362]

Just as we have seen before, these politicians are actually not driven by their strong religious convinction. Their political adventures are rather economically motivated, for the moment they emerge as winners, they plan how to accumulate and enrich themselves, siphoning what in reality should belong to the electorate. Often the voters who voted them into power are booted and foot-marched. There is no gainsaying that even some of the electorate themselves vote, not because the politician will work for the general good but, because of the inordinate gains they hope to get from the politician they voted for. I mean their selfish gains. Many are ready to change their religion, at times temporarily, for political-economic gains. The report of Justice Aniogolu's commission of inquiry into the 1980 Maitatsine showed no pretension in condemning economic and social factor as part of the root causes of the riots in Nigeria. The commission was of the opinion that the,

> lack of employment opportunities for young men in rural areas encourages a drift to the cities, especially after the harvest. On getting to the cities, they invariably remain unemployed. They eventually constitute a reservoir of human potential to be exploited and used by anybody for any pur-

[362] Oritsejafor, A., cf. Osewele, B., "Bauchi crisis: Stem religious violence.." in: *Daily Sun Newspaper*, March 2, 2009.

> pose. Members of the society, whether as individuals or groups, who have an axe to grind use this reservoir to settle old scores. These people, mostly vagabonds, juveniles and touts having been brought up in extreme poverty, generally nurse a grudge against the privileged, whose luxurious and ostentatious way of life they detest. Because of the wide gap between the rich and the poor, they are ever prepared to rise against society and perpetrate insurrection at the slightest opportunity.[363]

A particular reference could be found in Northern Nigeria where some children are not being well cared for. At this, they do not have the opportunity to go to school except the school of Qur'an. They are brainwashed that the only language they hear is the language of violence. The activities of this almajiri, cannot be freely excused if they are critically looked into. The almajiri is described as a corruption of the Arabic al-muhajir, which is actually used to refer to immigrants. They are a less privileged group of poor children who can neither go to school nor cloth themselves neatly due to poverty. However, they still make effort to find a way of making both ends meet, being sent out in the mornings after their morning session in the qur'anic school. In this line, they now take to begging on the streets. Whatever they get from the benevolence of the people, they use for their qur'anic learning. Unfortunately, they remain on the streets more than they remain in their places of learning. They gather whatever remnants (either money or food) from what they got and send them to their masters (mallams) who use them to take care of them. The operational routes of the almajiri include among others the motor parks, markets and railways. With this dangerous and unfortunate exposure, they are liable to catch in on any slightest commotion to explode like tightly closed bottle that fell into a furnace. In such situations, they ransack, loot, vandalize as well as cause arson.[364]

Even in the period when the expatriate held sway in Nigeria, Christians did not find it easy. Lugard, a well known colonialist, for political and economic reasons, and not wanting direct confrontation with Islam, introduced an indirect rule system allowing the continued leadership of the Muslim community by their fellow Muslims but on behalf of the British. This situation was therefore not favorable to Christians who saw themselves as shortchanged. Although they would naturally have wanted to protest, they could not due to numerical incapacitation. The only way out was the maxim: if you

---

[363] Opeloye, M. O., op. cit. p. 235.
[364] Ibid.

cannot beat them you join them. So, many of the Christians simply for economic survival converted to Islam.[365]

3.6. Conclusion

In this chapter, we have been able to search out the causes of disunity and violence in Nigeria, placing some of the riots in their rightful contexts. But one thing is clear: The country Nigeria is very sick, overburdened by seemingly foreign and locally induced sicknesses that seem to have defeated all medications. It is a general consensus that all is not well with Nigeria and Nigerians. Poverty, endemic corruption, lack of know-how could be the class name for the sickness. After surviving the first shock of colonialism, it has continued to push herself to the wall of mistrust, mutual suspicion, politics of rancor and antagonism, insincerity, corruption and above all, religious fanaticism. The visible effect of this madness is that the country has shamefully and regrettably nose-dived to the notorious state of 'one week (month), one trouble' resulting from abject poverty and hunger. If this situation is not fast attended to, the fear of possible suicide bombing in Nigeria may not be far fetched since people no longer find much meaning in life.

On this note, the speaker of the house of Assembly, Dimeji Bankole in November 2010 used the occasion of the Moslem Eid-El-Kabir to call on all Nigerians to faithfully pray for peace in the country, noting that the fervent prayers by various religious bodies and individuals have accounted for the peace that we enjoyed as a nation in recent times. He asked Nigerians to be steadfast in love of one another, adding that it is in doing so that we can be committed to what is just and right for our nation.[366] The Christian Association of Nigeria, CAN, also called on the Moslems to maximize the season of their feast to pray for peaceful co-existence among different ethno-religious groups in the country.[367]Surely Nigerians use every slightest opportunity to bombard the heavens. But 'God cannot work for us but with us'. So the solution still lies with us – I mean the cooperation between the government, the governed and religious groups. Without living out the principle of 'Igwe bu ike' (togetherness is strength) our country will be re-baptized with the name, 'doomed to fail' instead of Nigeria. If this mistakenly ever happens, we all,

---

[365] Eneh, J. O., *The Sharia and Islamic Philosophy: The Nigerian Experience*, Enugu, Snaap Press Ltd, 2001, p. 50-52.
[366] Eyoboka, S. et. al., "Sallah: Jonathan, Mark, others tasks Muslims on peace" in: *Vanguard News paper*, November 16, 2010.
[367] Ibid.

according to the members of Congress for Progressive Change (CPC), shall be accountable to God for the failure no matter what religion one professes. "As a Muslim, Christian, (ATR) or what have you, we shall be all accountable to our creator for negligence of our responsibilities in any form at the appropriate time...we all have the duty to ensure that our society is ideal for all."[368] The 'we' here refers both to the government and the governed. But the president, Goodluck Jonathan summarized a possible solution in his Sallah good will message thus, "Nigeria will make quicker progress towards the fulfillment of its great potentials as a nation if its citizens foster peace, security and stability which are essential for development by showing greater respect for national safety and public order laws."[369]This is a good sermon. But it is directed to the wrong people who have nothing to eat.

The question remains, 'why can't the government provide for the teaming poor, unemployed people of Nigeria the dividends of democracy so that they can peacefully co-exist despite their differences? Who will bail the cat? The government is calling on the citizenry and the citizenry are beckoning on the government for action. Who has the required solutions? It is like Nigeria needs divine intervention to recuperate. The citizenry seem to know it and the government seems to know it too. That is why both the government and religious leaders are all calling for prayers because Nigerians, as religious people believe so much in signs and wonders. But must we only pray and wait for wonders? The sure answer is a capital NO. We must use the abundant human and natural resources, with which our dear country is blessed, to solve our nagging problems instead of wallowing in laziness and corruption, waiting for divine intervention. It is on this note that we turn our attention, in the next chapter, in the direction of the Catholic Church hierarchies to see what solution they have for peaceful co-existence in Nigeria.

[368] Ibid.
[369] Ibid.

CHAPTER FOUR

CATHOLIC CHURCH DOCUMENTATIONS ON CALLS FOR PEACE IN NIGERIA

4. Introduction

In chapter three of this work, we have been able to establish that Nigeria is swimming in the wave of conflicts and problems. This situation seems to offer no hope of any fast solution in the near future. That is why many have called for prayers as we saw in chapter three. But there are many peace loving Nigerians who wish to see Nigerians live in peace. Among them are some Moslems, Christians and adherents of Traditional religion. There are also many who are not Nigerians who wish Nigeria well and work for peace in the world level which if applied to Nigeria will put us on the right track to peace. It is on this instance that I wish to consider in this chapter the general attitude or contributions of the Catholic Church towards peace in Nigeria. This chapter will take three groups into consideration - the Magisterium of the Catholic Church, Nigerian Catholic Bishops' Conference (CBCN) and the Association of Episcopal Conferences of Anglophone West Africa, (AECAWA).

4. 1. Contributions from the Magisterium / Holy See

Inasmuch as we are dealing with Nigerian situation as the topic suggests, it is not out of place to bring in the stand of the Magisterium of the Catholic Church which if applied in our search for peaceful co-existence in Nigeria would yield good results. To do this, we shall not restrict ourselves to statements accredited only to the Magisterium. We go further taking some contributions of various offices within the Holy See. In a message calling both Christians and Muslims to promote a culture of peace, the Vatican Information Services (VIS) emphatically pointed out that religious freedom is not limited to freedom of worship and also condemned all violence in the name of religion. It read, "In the troubled times we are passing through, religious believers have, as servants of the Almighty, a duty above all to work in favour of peace, by showing respect for the convictions of individuals and communities everywhere through freedom of religious practice. Religious freedom, which must not be reduced to mere freedom of worship, is one of the essential aspects of freedom of conscience, which is the right of every individual and a cornerstone of human rights...."[370] It further stated,

> We know that violence, especially terrorism which strikes blindly and claims countless innocent victims, is incapable of resolving conflicts and leads only to a deadly chain of destructive hatred, to the detriment of mankind and of societies...As religious believers, it is up to us all to be educators of peace, of human rights, of a freedom which respects each person...No individual in the national community should be excluded on the grounds of his or her race, religion, or any other personal characteristic...We are particularly responsible for ensuring that our young people, who will be in charge of tomorrow's world, are formed in this spirit, providing everyone an education appropriate to his or her particular circumstances, especially a civic education which invites each young person to respect those around him or her, and to consider them as brothers and sisters with whom he is daily called to live, not in indifference, but in fraternal care.[371]

It is however regrettable that all these are said but are not hearkened to and are not put into practice by those who should know better. Pope John Paul II on his part praised the norms and conventions being put together by international community. But he emphasized that much still need to be implemented. He was very direct in mentioning human rights that are violated without proper attention or reaction being given them. He remarked,

> When the violation of any fundamental human right is accepted without reaction, all other rights are placed at risk (n.12). It seems to me that this truth needs to be seen in relation to all juridic norms. International law cannot be the law of the stronger, nor that of a simple majority of States, nor even that of an international organization. It must be the law which is in conformity with the principles of the natural law and of the moral law, which are always binding upon parties in conflict and in the various questions in dispute.[372]

---

370 Tauran, J. L., "Christians and Muslims called to promote a culture of peace" in: VIS (*Vatican Information Service)*, September 28, 2007.
371 Ibid.
372 John Paul II, speaking on the "Right Conditions for effective Freedom of Religion" in: Gioia, F.,(ed.) *Interreligious Dialogue, The Official Teaching of the Catholic Church from the Second Vatican Council to John Paul II* (1963-2005), Boston, Pauline Books & Media, 2006, p. 699.

The above quotations are ad rem when one considers the Nigerian situation where laws are seemingly made for the poor while the rich are mostly set free when the corrupt Judge has been bribed. The unfortunate thing about this situation is that those in authority look the other way while these atrocities are being perpetrated in their very presence. As it is obvious that a leader should be successful if he leads by example, Pope John Paul II showed himself true to his teachings. He had met world religious leaders in Rome and during his apostolic journeys. His visit to the Supreme Buddhist Patriarch of Thailand on 10 May, 1084 (cf. La Civilta′ Cattolica 3216 (16 June 1984) 583f) was a high point in his endeavour for peace. On 19 August 1985 he visited Casablanca in Morocco, a State that is officially Islamic and addressed about 80,000 Muslim youths; a visit which till today rings bell worldwide. Again on 13 April, 1986, he paid a visit to the Jewish Synagogue in Rome. This visit from the angle of history is said to have spanned almost two millennia. This Synagogue is however, only two kilometres away from Vatican. It was symbolic as it marked a millennium hand of friendship extended by the Catholic Church to the people of the Hebrew faith for dialogue and collaboration.[373]

In articulating a possible means of achieving this desired goal, dialogue has been suggested as a viable option. According to Cardinal Arinze,

> In this spirit, the pursuit and intensification of dialogue between Christians and Muslims must be considered important, in both educational and cultural dimensions. Thus all forces can be mobilized in the service of mankind and humanity so that the younger generations do not become cultural or religious blocs opposed to one another, but genuine brothers and sisters in humanity. Dialogue is the tool which can help us to escape from the endless spiral of conflict and multiple tensions which mark our societies, so that all peoples can live in serenity and peace and with mutual respect and harmony among their component groups...This is the ardent hope I share with you: that Christians and Muslims continue to develop increasingly friendly and constructive relationships in order to share their specific riches, and that they will pay particular attention to the quality of the witness of their believers.[374]

---

[373] Arinze, F., "Interreligious dialogue: Problems, prospects and possibilities" being a Paper presented at the Celebration of 150th Anniversary of Nashville Diocese, at Nashville, USA, March 19, 1987.

[374] Ibid.

The Catholic Church has done much to encourage inter-religious dialogu. Seminars have been organized. Notably, the first Seminar organized by the Catholic – Moslem Forum was held in the Vatican City. The Forum was established by Pontifical Council for Inter-religious Dialogue and Muslim representatives in the wake of the Open Letter sent on 13 October 2007 to His Holiness Benedict XVI and to other heads of Churches and ecclesial Communities by 138 Muslim leaders, and of the reply, sent by the Cardinal Secretary of State in the Holy Father´s name on 19 November 2007.[375] Critically speaking, I describe this Seminar as a move in the right direction as no meaningful peaceful-coexistence will be achieved under violence. With this Seminar put in motion, I have the strong belief that some other heads of Churches and ecclesial Communities will still join the chorus when they have seen the fruits of such Seminars. Nigeria surely will be one of those to join. In this Seminar, the interesting theme, -"Love of God, Love of Neighbour" was expected to be treated from the standpoints of theological and spiritual fundamentals as well as the dignity of the human person and mutual respect. Each side was expected to present 29 people, including experts, religious authorities and advisers for this exercise at the end of which there was to be a presentation of the Joint Declaration approved during the course of meeting.[376] Participating in the 63rd session of the United Nations General Assembly in New York with the theme "Culture of Peace" Cardinal Jean-Louis told the Assembly on behalf of the Holy See that,

> Believers in contributing to public debate and participating in the societies to which they belong, feel themselves called to co-operate in promoting the common good, which rests on a platform of values shared by everyone, believers and non-believers alike: the sacredness of life and the dignity of human beings, respect for liberty of conscience and of religion, practice of responsible freedom, acceptance of different opinions, correct use of reason, appreciation for democratic life and care for natural resources, to mention but a few.[377]

He urged that believers cannot use religion to attack freedom of conscience, justify violence, spread hatred and fanaticism or undermine political and religious authority. He remarked that individual believers and communi-

---

[375] VIS 081104 "First Seminar of the Catholic-Muslim Forum" Vatican City, 4 November 2008.
[376] Ibid
[377] Tauran, J. L., "Religion Carry a Message of Peace and Reconciliation" in: *VIS* 081113, November 13, 2008.

ties of believers have their role to play and that Religions, despite the weaknesses and contradictions of their members, carry a message of reconciliation and peace.[378] All the above assertions are in tandem with all the messages of His Holiness in 1982 and 1998 during his visits to Nigeria. Speaking to Islamic religious leaders in Kaduna on February 14, 1982, the Pope gave reasons why peace must be given a chance. According to him,

> All of us, Christians and Muslims, live under the sun of the one merciful God. We both believe in one God who is the Creator of man. We acclaim God's sovereignty and we defend man's dignity as God's servant. We adore God and profess total submission to him. Thus, in a true sense, we can call one another brothers and sisters in faith in the one God....Because of this faith that we have in God, Christianity and Islam have many things in common: the privilege of prayer, the duty of justice accompanied by compassion and almsgiving, and above all a sacred respect for the dignity of man, which is at the foundation of the unborn child. We Christians have received from Jesus, our Lord and Master, the fundamental law of love of God and love of neighbour (cf. Mt 22:37-39). I know that this law of love has a profound echo in your hearts, too, for in your sacred book, together with the invitation to faith, you are exhorted to excel in good works (cf, Sura 5, 21).[379]

He went on still to mention additional areas where cooperation is possible for peace to reign. He suggested engaging in dialogue both at the level of the scholars, of person to person relationships as well as in the family and places of work so as to understand one another better. When this is achieved, there would be a proper promotion of honesty and discipline in private and public life, greater courage and wisdom in politics which can lead to the elimination of political antagonisms and discrimination due to person's colour, race, ethnic origin or sex. Christians and Moslems can unite to usher in religious freedom in which case they try to give their children proper religious education. If the right of each child to worship God is genuinely complemented by his or her right to proper religious education, our future society is enriched and ensured. Religious education is today of utmost importance since so many unscrupulous elements are bent on forgetting or destroying the spiritual

---

[378] Ibid.

[379] Gioia, F., (ed.), *Interreligious Dialogue, The Official Teaching of the Catholic Church from the Second Vatican Council to John Paul II* (1963-2005), Boston, Pauline Books and Media, 2006, p. 289.

aspect of man.[380] With these points he addressed the very core problems that militate against peaceful coexistence in Nigeria. After addressing the Moslem leaders, he admonished the Catholic Bishops on the following day on the importance of living out what they teach and preach so as to give people reasons to hope for peace. He urged them to avoid antagonism and to respect other peoples' cultures. He declared,

> In practice, the Church's vocation to evangelize means above all living the Gospel ever more deeply....An important aspect of your own evangelizing role is the whole dimension of the inculturation of the Gospel into the lives of your people....The Church truly respects the culture of each people. In offering the Gospel message, the Church does not intend to destroy or to abolish what is good and beautiful. She recognizes many cultural values and through the power of the Gospel purifies and takes into Christian worship certain elements of a people's customs. The Church comes to bring Christ; she does not come to bring the culture of another race. Evangelization aims at penetrating and elevating culture by the power of the Gospel.[381]

As the youths are more vulnerable to the temptation of indulging in religious riots, induced by poverty and inordinate desires, the Pope made it clear that these youths should be brought up in such a way that they be able to avoid being used by some unscrupulous, 'do no goods' - call them sects members or the 'ungodly'. Addressing the Nigerian Bishops in Rome on December 18, 1993, the Pope said, "Catechesis is especially important for young people, for whom an enlightened faith is a lamp to guide their path into the future. It will be their source of strength as they face the uncertainties of the political and economic situation now evolving in Africa. Firm and humble submission to the word of Christ, as authentically proclaimed in the Church, also forms the basis for your relationship with other Churches and ecclesial communities, and for the dialogue which you seek with the followers of Islam and African traditional religion."[382] Speaking to the religious leaders on the need for peace in Nigeria would not be sufficient to address the issue without the co-operation of the Nigerian government since the government should be seen as a co-traveller or partner in the ordinance of peace.

---

[380] Ibid, p. 289-290.
[381] Ibid, p. 291-292.
[382] Ibid, p. 557-558.

It is consequent on that that the Pope seizes every opportunity to express his desire for peace in the world as a whole and in Nigeria in particular. Such an opportunity presented itself on May 24, 2004 as the New Nigerian Ambassador to the Vatican, H.E. Kingsley Sunny Ebenyi presented his letter of Credence to the Holy Father. In accepting the letter, the Pope made it clear to the newAmbassador that in any dealing requiring peaceful co-existence, peace and truth must be seen as indissolubly united. He said, "Indeed, there exists an indissoluble bond between peace and truth that must be recognised if men and women are to live in freedom, justice and security ...Honesty in the supply of information, equity in legal systems, openness in democratic procedures give citizens a sense of security, a readiness to settle controversies by peaceful means, and a desire for genuine and constructive dialogue, all of which constitute the true premise of a lasting peace."[383] Explaining further with indirect reference to the importance of education in the search for peace, the Pope said, "When people more fully grasp the meaning and consequences of events in their own lives and in the world, they are better equipped to make effective contributions to peace, especially through the proper use of societal structures and mechanisms – juridical, political, economic – to serve the common good."[384] Presenting his letter of credence, the new Ambassador made mention of the fact that the Nigerian government is working towards stabilising and uniting the country. It was welcome news to hear of such a development. But the Pontiff did not just accept that message as raw as it was given without some observation. He was quick to point out the implication of such a claim. He remarked,

> Of course, as the Federal Republic seeks ever greater national stability and unity along the path of increased democratization of society and institutions, challenges are not lacking. Moral courage and political wisdom are necessary....Through a resolute commitment to work tirelessly and steadfastly for the cause of peace, for the defence of human dignity and human rights, for the integral development of every individual, these challenges can be met and the way will be prepared for heightening awareness of the common destiny and interdependence that links all Nigerians, and indeed all peoples, as members of the one great family of mankind.[385]

---

[383] Ibid, p. 1082, cf. also, *L'Osservatore Romano*, weekly Edition in English, no. 8.
[384] Ibid.
[385] Ibid, p. 1082-1083.

His remark could be described second to none since the past Nigerian governments lacked the sincerity required for the integral development of every Nigerian. However, he commended the Nigerian government for peace initiative in Africa led by Nigeria. He pointed out, "Increasingly, Nigeria has emerged as a country predisposed to serve the cause of peace and development through international institutions such as the African Union and the United Nations. I encourage Nigerian leaders to be steadfast in their solidarity with other nations in order that a free and just world may become a reality."[386] It was clear from his writings that the Pope praised the importance of religion in nation building. He called on the government to involve the religious groups in this search for peace if it must succeed. With this call he emphasized on the vital role of religion in the service of peace and so remarked that violence could never claim religious justification. According to him,

> In the service of peace, which is also the service of truth, religion has a vital role to play. It makes its most effective contribution in this area by concentrating on those things that are proper to it: "attention to God, the fostering of universal brotherhood and the spreading of a culture of human solidarity" (cf. OR.N.9). Now, when communities or peoples of different religious convictions or cultures live in the same area it can sometimes happen that tensions will develop or increase, which, because of the strong passions involved, can turn into violent conflict. For this reason, it is of paramount importance to recall that recourse to violence in the name of religious belief is a perversion of the very teachings of the major religions. I reaffirm here what many religious figures have repeated so often: the use of violence can never claim a religious justification, nor can it foster the growth of true religious feelings.[387]

He concluded this with an assurance that the Catholic Church is ever disposed to peaceful co-existence and to promote the course of peace. He left no ambiguity on his stand when he declared that the Catholic Church in Nigeria is committed to the peaceful advancement of the nation, especially through her presence in the fields of education, health care and social services. The effective guarantee of the right of religious freedom will enable Catholics to continue to work for the spiritual and material progress of society. He expressed his fervent hope that tensions between diverse ethnic and

---

[386] Ibid.

[387] Ibid, cf. also Message for the 1999 World Day of Peace, no. 5.

religious communities, escalating to the point of violence and even murder in some parts of the country, will be defused by sincere dialogue and efforts aimed at reconciliation and mutual understanding and cooperation.[388]Without doubts, a sincere adherence to these suggestions or admonitions from the Magisterium will put Nigeria on the world record as a pluralistic, peaceful nation. The value of peace is immeasurable. Peaceful co-existence cannot be achieved in Nigeria without open, sincere cooperation between government and the religious groups in general and among the religious groups themselves. This is what the Magisterium has tried to call our attention to.

4.2. Contributions of Association of Episcopal Conferences of Anglophone West Africa (AECAWA)

If I should traverse the whole of African countries in order to seek out solutions to the multi problems that face the religious Africans, it would amount to going too far in search of what is readily available. It is readily available because the opinions of the Anglophone Bishops' Conference would present us with enough materials that cover the opinions of the entire African Bishops. This notwithstanding, the opinions of the Nigerian Bishops will still enjoy a separate treatment. It is based on this fact that I want only to take into consideration, pronouncements of Anglophone West African Bishops' Conference known as 'Association of the Episcopal Conferences of Anglophone West Africa' (AECAWA). This group of Bishops dedicate themselves to a common goal- 'building a common front for the spread of the Gospel of Jesus Christ without undermining the worth and dignity of adherents of other religions.' In this way they try to create conducive atmosphere for peaceful co-existence among all the creatures of One Almighty God through dialogue and proper catechesis. This Conference at times invites also the laity to dialogue with them on the best way forward. In one of such gatherings and consequent deliberations, they made clear their intention in the statement:

> Our search for dialogue with Islam is motivated by several factors. Our Church finds itself in a multi-religious society. In their daily life, our faithful have to relate on all levels to Muslims and adherents of the Traditional African Religions. It is therefore necessary that we find or devise ways and means of living in peaceful coexistence with our brothers and

[388] Ibid.

> sisters who do not follow our religion. It is our view that Christians and Muslims must be free to practise their religion without hindrance.[389]

In pursuing this goal, one should not pretend that it would be an easy task taking into consideration the differences that exist. It is in the knowledge of this fact that the Conference made it clear that some areas will be a hard nut to crack in order to achieve their aim. This notwithstanding, the Conference refuses to shy away from the effort and determination to lawfully succeed. Declaring their readiness for such an odious task, the Bishops stated,

> We are, therefore, determined to explore all lawful avenues for fostering and maintaining good relationships with our brothers and sisters of the Islamic faith in our sub-region. We think of meetings, exchange of ideas at the intellectual level, but also daily practical dialogue at the grassroots level in the homes, workplaces, schools, playgrounds and so forth...In this resolve we take into account the fact that there are areas of convergence in theological thinking between Christianity and Islam. Both Christians and Muslims believe in the one Unique Creator God. But we are also not oblivious to the vast differences that exist between us, such as those with regard to the Person and role of Christ in salvation. We note, as well, that terms such as salvation, democracy and politics often have a connotation for Muslims which is different from the meaning that Christians attach to them. For example, for Muslims religion and culture are the same. It is also observed that within Islam itself there are serious divergences in theological thought and religious practices.[390]

The Conference commended some aspects of Islamic practices which if translated into reality will surely enhance peace. Sequel to this, the Conference expressed deep desire friendly relationship with Muslims. The Conference did not hide its respect for Moslems and their religion. It also appreciated the good aspects found in Islam mentioning in particular their prayerfulness, their edifying ascetic fasting as well as their inspiring almsgiving and pilgrimages to Mecca. For all these the Conference declared itself ready to make friends with Islam. This friendship is hinged on the command of Our Lord Jesus Himself calling us to universal love and to prayer even for our

[389] AECAWA, "Christianity and Islam in dialogue" being Communiqué, Resolutions and Recommendations after its Fourth plenary assembly, Lagos, October, 20-27, 1986, p. 237.
[390] Ibid, p. 238-239.

enemies (Matt. 5:43).[391] We Christians should have no enemies. This mandate of the Lord to pray for our enemies is a strong support and call to peaceful dwelling with one another irrespective of one's race, colour or religion. Despite this call to identify with all, efforts must be made to see to it that one does not compromise his faith so much that one loses the bearing. Christians are therefore advised to try to avoid complacency. In this case we have to reject all that is anti-communal living found in Islam. The Conference declared,

> However, in faithfulness to our traditions, we must reject many tendencies in Islam: the treatment of non-Muslims as second rate citizens; the identification of religion with culture and politics; the classification of non-Muslims as infidels; the discriminatory nature of Islamic laws; the heavy penalties meted out to Christian converts from Islam or Muslim women who marry Christians. We cannot accept any situation where our rights as citizens of our nations are denied us because we are not Muslims. We believe in the unity and solidarity of mankind but this does not make us forget our duty to preach the gospel, the good news, welcome or unwelcome, in obedience to the Lord's own injunction.[392]

In calling all Christians to be steadfast in living out their faith, the Conference made it clear that only prayer and exemplary Christian living can achieve peace and conversion. For the Conference therefore prayer is the best means to improve our relation with Moslems. The faithful were called upon to pray without ceasing to the Father of us all since he is the only one that can propel the unification of mankind. The Christians were reminded that they can bear witness to Christ by the way they comport themselves in their daily life. Listed among the things that could draw Moslems and Christians together were: life of love, mercy, compassion, justice and peace were mentioned.[393] The Bishops called upon the different government in the sub-region to be impartial in their dealings with different religions. For them, secularity as opposed to secularism is the only viable form of democracy which could be applied in the sub-region that is clearly religiously pluralistic. The Bishops emphasized, "Secularity in the state implies that the state does not favour any one religion to the detriment of others. Such a secular state assures the common good and obviates common harm. It respects the con-

---

[391] Ibid, p. 239.
[392] Ibid.
[393] Ibid, p. 239-240.

science of all citizens and allows the full range of religious practice. Secularism, on the other hand, is the systematic muzzling of religion and the exclusion from society of religious influence on public opinion and life."[394]

One interesting thing about the gathering of the Anglophone Bishops is the commendation they accorded African Traditional Religion (ATR). It was a big departure from what used to be where ATR is regarded as profane. The conference acted as Plädoyer for ATR. They remarked,

> We realize that if the Church's presence is to be felt in our sub-region, then inculturation should be expanded to embrace theological thinking and moral behaviour. We observe that our traditional religion is tolerant and friendly to Christianity. Many of the elements, such as the concept of wholeness of life, the use of symbols, the respect for the sacredness of human life, communal existence and friendship, and the close contact between the living and the dead, could enrich the Christian experience to an enormous degree.[395]

In order to lead by example, the Conference called on the administrators of the various learning institutions under their control to include the study of Islam and ATR in their school curriculum. It is necessary because these will enable the- would be formators of tomorrow to be knowledgeable about the teachings of the other religions in order to appreciate them more. They wrote, "We recommend that the phenomena of Islam and of our Traditional Religion be studied systematically in our centres of formation. We particularly call upon CIWA to establish contact with the universities in the sub-region with a view to creating a centre of research on Islam and Traditional Religion. We are anxious that our major Seminaries should be an on-going concern for priests, religious and other pastoral workers after their formal training."[396] The Conference called on their Moslem brothers to join hands in this unalloyed desire for the institution of peace everywhere it is lacking. In this appeal the Bishops said,

> We extend the hand of friendship and fraternity to Muslims in our sub-region to join us in promoting human values such as the dignity of life, freedom of conscience, liberty of the human person and the importance of morality. We open doors to dialogue of experience. We wish to share our

[394] Ibid, p. 240
[395] Ibid.
[396] Ibid, p. 241.

mutual experience of the mystery of God, of love, of revelation and of mercy. This ardent desire of ours is not motivated by a spirit of proselytism. Our aim is the mutual promotion of the Kingdom of God, which is the Kingdom of truth, holiness, unity, peace and love. We pray that our good and well-meaning intentions will be met by a correspondingly sincere response from our Muslim brothers and sisters.[397]

In the year 2000, this Conference expressed happiness over the past efforts of the government and religious organizations that tried to fashion out ways that could lead to peace. In their own case this Conference of Anglophone Bishops made far reaching decisions and suggestions. As enumerated in their communiqué:

"1. There is need for cooperation and participation between Religious Leaders and Governments to create a vibrant civil society based on education and economic empowerment of the masses in order to prevent the poor people from being used for political and economic gains under the cover of religion.
2. The leaders of Christianity, Islam and African Traditional Religion should come together to fashion out a comprehensive standard of values for nation-building in the West African sub-region.
3. Religious leaders should continue to identify and promote ways of combating moral decadence and corruption in the sub-region.
4. Leaders of the major religions of the sub-region should form a joint Commission that will, from time to time, identify the problems of the sub-region and advise the respective governments on how to solve them.
5. Adherents of Christianity, Islam and African Traditional Religion should allow their religious ideals to guide them in their day-to-day living.
6. Religious leaders should be in the forefront for women empowerment through education, economic and political opportunities.
7. Through their teaching and preaching, Religious leaders should conscientize their followers against the evils of child abuse, prostitution and drug abuse which are rampant in the sub-region.
8. The Governments should create an enabling environment to allow our citizens overseas to contribute meaningfully towards the development of the sub-region.

---

[397]Ibid.

9. Finally, we sincerely recommend that religious studies be taught as a core course at all levels of our educational system."[398]

In 2003 Nigeria witnessed yet another round of wanton destruction of lives and property blamed on religious intolerance. This conflict was so remarkably touching and devastating that it moved everyone who witnessed or read of it to pity. It was in line with this and in their effort to bring peace to where it was lacking and consolation to those who seriously need it that Aecawa to hold its study/workshop in Kaduna- Nigeria with the theme, 'Offer Forgiveness and Receive Peace: A Challenge to Multi-religious Society.' Even this theme suits our Nigerian situation. According to the commission their aim of coming to Kaduna was to pray and be united in prayer with the unfortunate people of the State who suffered the ravage of religious intolerance. They wanted to use the opportunity to express their solidarity with the many commendable efforts towards reconciliation and recognize the efforts of all who have contributed and may still be contributing to peace building.[399] Regretting the situations and events associated with religion in African continent, especially in sub-region of Aecawa, the commission said,

> We recognize the fact that religion must not be the reason for hatred, violence and conflict in our sub-region. Rather, the three major religions, as reemphasized by their representatives at this seminar/workshop, encourage forgiveness as against revenge and hatred. At the same time, the representatives recognize the duty of the government to curb violence and injustice to take steps to prevent violence and lawlessness when there are warning signs. They are also bound to demand accountability from public officials.[400]

The involvement of the government in peace making in any nation is not to be neglected. It is understandable that government should be in the front in the match towards building a peaceful atmosphere. It is regrettable to say that the reverse is the case in Nigeria where political opponents help to instil disunity for their political gains. They often forget that peace implies pro-

---

[398] AECAWA, Communique by Aecawa Inter-religious Dialogue Commission at the end of the 2000 Annual Study Session/Workshop held at the Pastoral Institute, Ibadan, 3rd – 6th October 2000.

[399] AECAWA, A Communiqué on 14th November 2003 published in: Borrmans, M., (ed.), *Islamochristiana, PONTIFICIO INSTITUTION DI STUDI ARABI E D'ISLMISTICA*, Rome, p. 210.

[400] Ibid.

gress and peace is a must for any country that aspires to authentic nationhood. Deliberating on the need for peace and its implications, Aecawa maintained that, "...peace is a gift and not a wish. Peace is a plenitude of fulfilment, well-being and wholeness. It comprises security, tranquillity and harmony. It embraces justice and forgiveness. It is everybody's responsibility therefore to contribute towards the realization of that peace which is the universal hope of human family and a religious value for all."[401] Despite the clear fact that peace is not negotiable, it is unfortunate that peace continues to elude us in the African continent in general and Nigeria in particular. At its worst, religion which should be in the forefront of peace-making efforts falls constantly short of its mission. Aware of the unfortunate negative influences of religion and its polarization of its followers, the Conference offered the following as possible solution: "Principles of inter-religious co-existence and dialogue should be taught at the grass-root level: homes, schools, communities, churches and mosques.

Information concerning other religions should be sought from the competent and legitimate custodians and authentic sources of these religions. On their part, these custodians should be eager and ready to ensure that correct information about their religion is readily available.

We appeal to the governments in our sub-region to continue to create an enabling environment for peace, reconciliation, justice and inter-religious activities.

While we recommend the efforts of the Christian and Muslim youth towards inter-faith activities, we appeal to them not to allow themselves to be manipulated under the guise of religion by whomsoever. Rather, through seminars, workshops and conferences, they should be empowered to play a more positive role in the pursuit of justice and peace.

We strongly recommend the interchange of dialogue at all levels, namely, national, provincial, diocesan and parish levels.

We appeal to the local and foreign media to positively report inter-religious dialogue initiatives, since negative reporting do not help to create peace, forgiveness and harmony.

We recognize that in almost all instances, inter-religious conflicts are preceded by clear warning signs. We therefore call on governments and communities to set up safeguards to address issues before they escalate.

We encourage collaboration with all agencies committed to the promotion of peace, justice and development.

---

[401] Ibid.

Recognizing that peace is a gift from God, we call on all people of goodwill to pray to God to give us this gift and make us instruments of peace..."[402]

It is my conviction that these recommendations of the AECAWA have given in block what Nigeria needs to do for the interest of peace. From there stipulations for Africa, ones sees the unfortunate picture of Nigeria painted in black and white. It is therefore hoped that the voices of the Bishops of AECAWA will reach the ears that can implement it for the sake of peaceful co-existence in the world and Nigeria. This message from AECAWA will surely be made present in Nigeria with the help of the Nigerian Bishops' Conference whose contributions we now intend to consider.

4.3. Contributions of the Catholic Bishops' Conference of Nigeria (CBCN)

In an attempt to sincerely contribute their quota to finding a lasting solution to the unfortunate disturbances, wanton destruction of life and property and establish a permanent conducive atmosphere of peaceful co-existence in Nigeria, the Nigerian Catholic Bishops under the umbrella 'Catholic Bishops' Conference of Nigeria' assumed the honourable but hard task of speaking for the poor in Nigeria. As directors of moral they saw in it their role to proclaim the truth not minding the consequences knowing that the masses look unto them as their mouthpiece. The Bishops declared,

> As shepherds of God's people in our land, we are called to bear witness to Christian hope...the church has the mission to proclaim the truth which guarantees the dignity and right of the human person. If hope is not illusory and deceitful, it has to be based on truth...we cannot stand aside when the dignity of God's children is being trampled upon. That is why we insist that ethics and morality must never be divorced from politics. We would be failing in our mission if we do not speak and teach to direct the hearts and minds of the citizens to shun evil and do good in order to usher in true development and lasting prosperity...[403]

---

[402] Ibid, p. 210-211.

[403] CBCN, "The Church in Nigeria: Keeping Hope alive" Communiqué after its 1st Plenary Meeting for the year held at Divine Love Retreat and Conference Centre, Abuja, March 6-11, 2006.

Just as the bishops would not want to fail in their duties of giving ethical and moral directions, it would be a failure on the part of the government if it fails to carter for her subjects, providing for them a conducive atmosphere to live anywhere in Nigeria, and in peace. In the book titled 'The Voice of the Voiceless', being a compilation of their past Pastoral letters and Communiqués the Bishops made known their stand in difficult times between the years 1960 and 2002. One finds their contributions not only in religious matters but also in matters concerning the general wellbeing of the citizenry that impede progress or may lead to it if not well addressed. Speaking about the responsibilities of the government and the Catholic Church in Nigeria, the Conference stated,

> The Catholic Church in Nigeria and worldwide has, by the grace of God, a good record of massive and effective involvement in works of charity and human development. In those projects, whether they are schools or hospitals, orphanages or rehabilitation centres, the poor and needy are assisted irrespective of their creed. We look around us and see the growing misery in our land. As a Church, we are committed to giving solace and comfort to all whose cries of anguish rise daily to the ears of heavenly Father. This is an essential part of our mission. In the name of God and of the voiceless poor, let no one put any unnecessary obstacles in the way of our accomplishing this mission. Government has the duty to God and to the people to promote and facilitate the social and charitable services of genuine religious bodies, and other truly charitable organisations.[404]

This citation has brought to fruition my expressed hope that the recommendations of the AECAWA would be made known in Nigeria by the Nigerian Bishops Conference. Their warning that nobody should put unnecessary obstacles in their way towards accomplishing the mission of instilling peace is a positive sign. It is a practical sign of their burning desire to see peaceful co-existence in Nigeria come true. The Catholic Bishops have continued till date and of course unambiguously to take stand whenever the need presents itself. They give praise to whoever deserves it and blame or advice where it is necessary. We shall now see some of their statements in the past years.

---

[404] Schineller, P. (ed.), "*Voice of the Voiceless*" being a compilation of the Pastoral letters and Communiqués of the Catholic Bishops' Conference of Nigeria 1960 – 2002, Ibadan, Daily Graphics Nigeria Ltd., 2002, p. 226.

Already in the year 1987 as was published in the Easter edition of the Magazine 'Catholic Life', they prophetically cried out stating without equivocation that the Nation is in jeopardy. Considering the extent of tragic and heart-breaking damage inflicted on the innocent and helpless people of Nigeria by fellow Nigerians, they refused to be silenced. Being very much concerned, they went searching for a way out, in which they asked the question, "What must we do to save the nation?"[405] Even as they waited and searched for an answer to their question they took a stand and declared,

> 1. We condemn outright recourse to violence in the name of religion. 2. Crime has been committed: there has been wanton destruction of life and property. Of particular concern is the fact that the property destroyed is Churches and places of worship. In order that justice may be done now, and to prevent a re-occurrence, a thorough, honest and speedy investigation should be conducted to identify the culprits and bring them to book. It is absolutely essential that this investigation covers also the remote causes and sanctions should extend to those who support, abet, encourage and defend the criminals...3.We call on all in position of authority, trust and influence, especially religious leaders, to join hands by using words that build up to avoid anything that would worsen the situation.[406]

Continuing they left no one in doubt about their readiness to commend, support and encourage what is good and to condemn and help remedy what is evil. They maintained

that action rather than words, giving more than promising, sincerity more than show are what we urgently need. The well known problem is how to turn words into deeds, thoughts into purpose and plans into realization. Referring to the spirit of Assisi, they beckoned on other religious leaders, no matter their creed, to join hands with them in the name of God our common Father, to rid the nation of fanatics and misguided elements who are misusing religion for their selfish motives. In this way, they give religion a bad name. To give religion a bad name is to give truth a bad name. At the root of our present conflicts lies not truth. With the misapplication of religion, the truth of religion is falsified and negated which eventually gives way to crimes committed in the name of misapplied truths. This explains the spirit

[405] CBCN, "The Nation is in Jeopardy" in: *Catholic Life*, Easter Edition, Lagos, Toklast Enterprises, 1987, p. 17.
[406] Ibid.

that refuses to live and let live.[407] Aware of the close connection between hunger and violence the Bishops bemoaned the evident yawning gap between the rich and the poor in the country stating clearly that they could not keep silence in the face of situations they deemed unjust, inhuman and therefore unacceptable. They warned of the possible, though momentarily seemingly unforeseeable, catastrophic consequences. They remarked,

> There are yawning gaps within our nation that give rise to conflict. There is an enduring gap between the rich and the poor. There is a developing gulf between the elected officials and the people. What of the gap between the energy an average worker expends and the wages he or she receives? It would seem that in Nigeria, it is not so much what you know or how hard you work that counts, but rather whom you know, and with whom you are connected. There are still instances of widespread child abuse and discrimination against women. We should also mention the gap between ethnic groups that engender suspicions and fears. There are also serious cases of conflict among various religious groups, arising not from religion itself, but abuse of religion for their selfish agenda. We urge Nigerians, as individuals and groups, to address these issues urgently for an enduring peace to reign in our land.[408]

Considering that Nigeria is a multi-religious nation, they commended the freedom of religion as inscribed in the Nigerian constitution as that would guarantee the safety of all Nigerians to worship God unmolested as and when due. They stated, "We welcome the religious freedom that is written into the Constitution. Through this guarantee the human right and duty that every man has to worship God as well as he can is respected. In this connection too we note that no state religion exists in Nigeria and that there is no state church. It follows that no religious group may claim an exclusive right to mark state occasions by its own particular form of religious worship."[409] Furthermore, expressing their readiness for peaceful co-existence as evident in their respect and acceptance of other religious bodies in the country, the Bishops emphasize,

---

[407] Ibid, p. 17-18.

[408] CBCN, Communiqué issued at the End of their First Plenary Meeting held at St. Leo's Catholic Church, Ikeja, March 13th – 18th 2000, cf. also *Leader Newspaper*, Vol. XL II No. 6, April 2, 2002, p. 3.

[409] Schineller, P., op. cit. p. 43.

> We, Catholics, have never made any secret of our conviction that Christian truth is to be found in its complete form within our communion alone. But that conviction does not hide from us the way that many other Christians know and love Christ....We express sentiments of fraternal love towards our Muslim fellow-citizens. We share with them a sense of reverence for the One God. We appreciate their deep spirit of prayer and their striking fidelity to penitential fasting. Christians and Muslims can work together for the good of the country. We are united against tendencies towards materialism and secularism. It is a comforting sign of hope for Nigeria that the vast majority of people in our country are convinced that man's first duty is to God and that life has no meaning without religion.[410]

The constant mention of Islam as dialogue partner should not give the impression that ATR is not seen as a possible dialogue partner. The Nigerian bishops' Conference in particular and the Catholic Church in general have always committed itself to authentic dialogue with ATR for the enthronement of peace especially in areas of belief and interest common to both religions. In this regard, the Bishops enumerated the following: "(a) Belief in the moral principle that 'good must be done and evil avoided'; (b) Belief that humans are a composite of soul and body, beings who live in webs of relationship; (c) Belief in the metaphysical communion that exists between the living and the dead; (d) Belief in the imperative of justice as a cardinal virtue of social co-existence; (e) Belief in the existence of the Supreme Being."[411] As an attestation to that, we refer to the list of areas of dialogue as proposed by the Bishops' Conference. But as this call for peace seemed threatened by the secret elopement of Nigeria into OIC, they spoke up in condemnation of the initiative. Requesting that Nigerian membership in the OIC be immediately withdrawn, the Bishops emphasized,

> Withdrawal in no way infringes on the fundamental religious rights of our Moslem compatriots. OIC membership is not one of the pillars of Islam. The Charter of the Organisation has easy provisions for such a withdrawal (cf. Article X)...We urge withdrawal because we have carefully

[410] Ibid, p. 44.

[411] "The Church in Nigeria, Family of God on Mission" (A Pastoral Exhortation of the Catholic Bishops' Conference of Nigeria (CBCN) to the Clergy, Religious and Lay Faithful on the First National Congress), Enugu: CIDJAP, 2004. cf. also Ani, I., in: *Forum Mission*, Jahrbuch Band 1/2005, p. 147.

> examined the arguments put forward in favour of continued membership- religious, economic, political, diplomatic etc., and we find them all unconvincing...With its religious pluralism, Nigeria cannot as a State become a member of an international body whose objectives are essentially the promoting of one particular religion (cf. Articles II and IV). To do that would mean injustice to other religions and to their adherents. This basic injustice in an area so all embracing and sensitive as religion, is bound to manifest itself also in other areas of national life- political, economic, social, cultural, legal, etc. ...the Charter of the Organisation of Islamic Conference clearly implies that the Head of State and Foreign Minister of a member nation shall be Moslems (cf. Articles IV and V). How can Nigeria guarantee this, unless it entrenches the absurdity of making political leadership the exclusive preserve of a particular religious group.[412]

They accepted the glaring truth that our country is economically moribund. However, they did not see Nigerian membership in the OIC as a way out of this poverty. But just as Nigeria rejected the IMF loan and decided to look inward for economic salvation, OIC should be rejected since our economic advancement does not lie in it. The OIC adventure is a distraction that needed urgent termination. This will help the nation battle with undivided attention for the restoration of our bastardized economy. The Bishops' great concern for unity, peace, justice and mutual harmony of all Nigerians, irrespective of religious affiliation is the reason for making this appeal. As a demonstration of their genuine concern for the peaceful resolution of the impasse, they took part in the presidential panel on the OIC problem. They were convinced that their worries were the same with that of the vast generality of Nigerians who wish and deserve to live not only in peace, enjoy religious freedom but also pursue individual and national development in an atmosphere devoid of sectional rancour and social exploitation.[413] Deliberating on the real way out, while warning the Nigerian leaders of the sycophants who may be out to mislead them, though wearing the garment of a 'non-blemish lamb' the Bishops wrote,

> Those who lead the nation must be doubly vigilant: not to allow themselves to be misled, and not to mislead the nation. Government must strive to eschew what looks like lopsided involvement in religious mat-

[412] Schineller, P., op. cit. p. 180.
[413] Ibid, p. 180 – 181.

ters which leads to political crises in the land. The OIC and Sharia, for example, are cases in point. Our government must strive to see that in these issues it complies with its declared intention "neither to adopt any religion as a state religion nor show favouritism towards any religion or religious organisation" in the nation. In that way, peace and mutual trust will be restored. Only then will the atmosphere be created for religion to perform the wonders of national salvation which God alone can bring about.[414]

The atmosphere for wonders of national salvation will never be possible if the religious leaders are at war with one another. It is for this that the Bishops expressed their desire for all Religious leaders in Nigeria to foster mutual understanding and collaboration. The Bishops maintained that the time had surely come to take more seriously the need for leaders of major religious groups in the country to seek ways to forge forums for mutual understanding and collaboration, free of government interference and political manipulation. They expressed their intent to make every effort to promote such dialogue and collaboration in the spirit of truth and mutual respect, freedom, and according to the wise directives, rich traditions and fruitful traditions of the church in this matter. They made this resolution in line with the injunctions of the Apostle Paul to the Christians of ancient Rome: 'Do all you can to be at peace with everyone' (Rom.12:18).[415]

This statement is a clear and direct call for dialogue between the major religious groups in Nigeria. In order not to be misunderstood or to be seen as not being direct in their appeal, they left no one in doubt that their appeal was directed mainly to the recognised Moslem religious leaders in the country. They emphasized, "We address ourselves especially to the authentic spiritual leaders of the Islamic faith in our land. We hope that our open heart and sincere invitation will meet a positive response, for the overall good of our nation. May the almighty and merciful God "guide our feet into the way of peace."[416] At this far, they felt that they have said enough for even a deaf ear to hear it and bear witness to them. Hence they warned that, they would not be silent and passive as their flock is being molested and misled. They expressed their determination to form a common force with other Christian denominations for the defence of the rights of Nigerian citizenry. The option is surely there. Accordingly they remarked that their commitment to Chris-

---

[414] Ibid, p. 225.
[415]Ibid.
[416]Ibid, p. 226.

tian solidarity in Nigeria remains firm and irrevocable. They hoped to continue to join forces with their brethren in the Christian faith, especially through CAN, to resist any attempt from whatever source and by whatever means to impede the fundamental rights of Nigerians to freely choose, proclaim, practice and propagate the Christian faith which according to them is not only their God-given right but also a duty.[417]

As evidence of their desire for peace in the land, they outlined some unfortunate problems that stare the land in the face which are capable of instigating people to take laws into their hands. They mentioned among others: "serious unemployment, breakdown of social services, hospitals being still often no more than consultation clinics, hunger and malnutrition, despair and moral disorientation of the youth, misery and neglect of the aged, social and political insecurity, corruption and incompetence among the leadership..."[418] They went on to particularly mention in the context of justice some of the implications of neglect and inaction. Where the government is inactive or does not fulfil its obligations to the citizenry, social disorder becomes the order of the day. Even amidst this social disorder which is caused by the government's neglect of its duty, some citizens embark on protests to show their displeasure with the situation. At times, the protests become very fatal with wanton destruction of properties arising from the menace of hunger and lack of education. Some wanton arrests are made and people put in prisons that are very unfit for human beings. Some of the arrested ones are released fast because they are highly connected while the unfortunate, poor ones languish in prisons for years without trial. Even amidst this situation, the government goes on to service foreign debts that have never impacted on the lives of the people. This is insensitivity on the highest level and man's inhumanity to man. These are typical cases of corruption and injustice. Injustice is of course the grandmother of disorder while disorder is the mother to peacelessness. Corruption and bribery are the senior brother and sister of peacelessness respectively. These maladies are unfortunately, the major problems with Nigeria. On the long run, it is the country and the populace that suffer since a nation's economy does not grow in the midst of social disorder. The Bishops gave a more vivid and detailed account of the situation especially on the issue of prisons and economy. According to them,

> Prisons have become overcrowded with inmates detained in deplorable conditions. Suspects have often been detained for years without trial. We

---

[417]Ibid.

[418]Ibid, p. 227.

appeal to those responsible to organise a systematic visitation of prisons, release those unjustly held without trial, and devise a prompt and equitable dispensation of justice....Using a good percentage of our national income to service doubtful foreign debts has not helped the plight of our people. Political freedom and independence are important, but unless they are accompanied by economic and social justice, they are meaningless. All the slogans for economic revival will do the country little good unless there is an all out war on economic exploitation, bribery and corruption in all facets of society. We believe that present revenues if effectively collected and judiciously managed will to a large extent raise the falling standard of living of the average Nigerian. The problem is not merely one of scarcity; it is largely one of inequitable distribution of the available resources. Economic decisions are at the service of man. Whenever they negate man, especially the poor, they should be denounced as deprivations.[419]

Clearly part of the root causes of all these abnormalities is lack of proper education and poverty. They therefore called for the upgrading of our educational system to a standard that will guarantee gainfully employment after school days. The Bishops offered the government hands of fellowship by declaring their readiness to join hands with the government to standardize our educational system. They bemoaned the poverty level that makes it impossible for some to have basic education. According to them,

> We have for long seriously called to question the value of our present educational system no longer leads to that happy productive and successful life that once characterized it. Because of the present loss of confidence on the benefits of education, many bright boys find more meaning in going for business without basic education...What are the moral consequences for these youths?....As religious leaders, we take the social and temporal order seriously as part and parcel of our prophetic presence. We call for an integral education of our children, an education that embraces the moral, intellectual and the practical....We demand once again the right to participate fully in the running of public schools....Perhaps unknown to the government, the ordinary Nigerian citizen has never had it so bad within memory....Widespread malnutrition in children of tender age is particularly devastating, since this leads to stunted physical and

[419] Ibid, p. 227 – 228.

mental growth....A more comprehensive solution to the food crises has to be found before it is too late.[420]

The above statements of the Bishops show the chain reactions that could arise from lack of education. It is a chain reaction which like a network is interconnecting. Until this chain reaction is punctured and each part treated on its merit, peace will remain on the platonic level in Nigeria. In their untiring spirit, the CBCN in the year 2000, specifically on 28th February, made a statement concerning the disturbances in the North emanating from the Sharia question. Parts of their statement with the title, 'Let there be Peace', read,

> We call on Government at all levels – to ensure the prompt restoration and secure maintenance of law and order in all the troubled part of the country –to make immediate emergency relief available with utmost urgency to the wounded and to those rendered homeless and destitute: many are in dire need of food, clothing, medical attention and shelter; we condemn violence on whatever excuse, and from whatever direction. We condemn it, above all, when its perpetrators blasphemously and fraudulently claim religious justifications. Those who say they love God while hating their fellow human beings, even to the extent of killing them, are liars. It is the duty of government to ensure law and order, not only by arresting disorder, but above all by taking steps in time to prevent it breaking out. It is our strong conviction that the present tragedy could have been avoided if Government had heeded our warning as contained in our Memo to government as early as October 1999. Even now, it is not yet too late for government to take vigorous action to halt this mad rush to national suicide.[421]

It is indeed a national suicide, for a nation that knows the cause of the death of its citizens and seems to look the other way, instead of attacking and up-rooting the cause is leading her populace to national suicide. For those who know but are pretending not to know, the CBCN went on without any fear or favour and elucidated unambiguously that Nigeria as we know it cannot sustain a Sharia legal system parallel to the law of the land in any part of the nation. The Nigerian Constitution has already carefully circumscribed the limits and scope of the Sharia, after long and bitter debate, especially in

---

[420] Ibid, p. 228.
[421] Ibid. p. 407 – 408.

the 1978 Constituent Assembly. It was for the sake of peace that Christians tolerated a compromise at that time. It must however be made clear to all concerned that it is not possible to bring in through the back door of state legislation what has already been clearly rejected in the Constitution. Those who are insisting on this, by declaring a wider scope for the Sharia in their states, must bear the full responsibility for the conflict situation we now find ourselves in, as well as for any further degeneration of the situation. No one should therefore underestimate the firm resolve of all Nigerian Christians in this matter.[422] Also in the same year after their Second Plenary meeting which took place at the Catholic Social Centre, Kaduna from 11th -15th September they issued a Communiqué entitled, 'Let us Live and work together in Peace and Harmony'. The topic of this Communiqué speaks volumes. It shows their burning desire for peaceful co-existence of all adherents of different religions, stressing their belief in one undivided Nigeria whose Constitution if democratically strengthened and corruption doggedly fought, will surely produce a new Nigeria where love of neighbour and peaceful co-existence will reign. They pointed out, "We wish to affirm our belief in and commitment to Nigeria as one nation under one God who cares for every Nigeria, irrespective of religion, ethnic origin or language. By the same token, we reaffirm our commitment to one national Constitution to safeguard our human and social rights and to one judiciary to defend every Nigerian against any assault on his or her person and rights."[423] In their burning desire for peace in the land they pointed out some grey areas that needed urgent attention which they sincerely believed will strengthen our hard fought democracy. They condemned the regrettable attitude of some States which were adamant in pursuing their Islamization agenda through the adoption of Sharia. They remarked,

> Notwithstanding the unfortunate bloody crisis in Kaduna early this year, that claimed many innocent lives of Christians and Muslims alike, some states in the North have adopted, while others are still bent on adopting the Sharia legal system as state criminal law...We were told that there was nothing to worry about; that the Sharia would not affect non-Muslims, and that their rights under the Constitution would be fully guaranteed. Now, from reports reaching us and from what we have observed, it is sad to have to say that our original fears were well founded. The reality on ground in the states that have adopted the Sharia shows clearly that non-

[422] Ibid, p. 408.
[423] Ibid, p. 415.

Muslims are being negatively and unjustly affected. They are being deprived of their legitimate means of livelihood. Fanatics are being encouraged to molest law-abiding citizens without cause. Under the prevailing circumstances, freedom to practice and propagate one's faith, guaranteed in our Constitution, is being progressively eroded....The civil authorities of the states involved cannot claim ignorance of what is going on. No one is deceived by utterly empty statements of useless assurances....We cannot continue along these lines and still pretend that we want a united, peaceful and prosperous nation.[424]

To the claim by the proponents of Sharia that people should live according to God's will in their private lives and that this should be reflected in the public laws as far as possible, the CBCN made no denial of the correctness of the assertion but went further in making the claim more intelligible. According to them, "We Christians subscribe to the same premises. They are not the exclusive preserve of Muslims. At the same time, we believe that all that is required is that our laws should give room enough for everyone, Christians, Muslims and others to follow their consciences in searching for and carrying out God's will in their lives. To ensure a permanent solution to all these problems, we are convinced that Nigeria will now have to review our Constitution along these lines. There should no longer be room for special provisions for any religion within our Constitution."[425] As a solution to these problems they handed a sound fraternal advice to both the government and the politicians. They cautioned, "Government should desist from favouring one religion over others. Politicians too should refrain from using religion to further their political ambitions and sectional interests, knowing how this can easily divide the people and erupt into violence. The people, on their part, should be vigilant and refuse to be used as tools for the prosecution of the selfish agenda of unscrupulous politicians and other agents of destabilization."[426]

As it is their style to blame and praise where it is necessary, the CBCN commended the initiative of the Ulamas who sent delegates to their meeting in the following words, "...we are happy to have received a courtesy visit during our meeting, a delegation of the Committee of Ulamas of Kaduna State under the leadership of Alhaji Muhammad Baba Yan Gusau. We com-

---

[424] Ibid, p. 416.
[425] Ibid, p. 417.
[426] Ibid.

mend this friendly and cordial gesture."[427] They however regretted the seemingly failure of the government to handle the Sharia issue to a reasonable halt thereby weakening the nascent democracy. This critic notwithstanding, they praised her on the new laws against corruption. They remarked,

> The fact that government and the political class have so far failed to deal decisively with the Sharia issue is one indication, among many, that our new found democracy needs very much to be strengthened. To begin with, the ongoing review of the Constitution of the Federal Republic of Nigeria should aim at removing the many inconsistencies and ambiguities that give room for conflicting interpretations of its provisions. There is need to return the nation to the practice of true federalism, as against the unitary and arbitrary form of government that was foisted on us by the military....The civil service should be returned to its pristine status of independence from the political establishment so as to ensure continuity in the conduct of government business, irrespective of what political party is in power at any given time.[428]

A critical re-examination of past decrees from the government will reveal that Nigeria has had good laws and decrees that if well applied would maintain relative peace. However the problem of applying the laws only to those who have no high connection or to perceived political enemies, real or imagined has always held Nigeria on the wrong side of progress. This is why the Bishops after praising the government for the enactment of the corruption law did not fail to chip-in that it should not be business as usual. They took the president on his words in declaring that there should be no sacred cows. On the corruption law they said, "The enactment of an anti-corruption law by the Federal Government is in line with our "Prayer Against Bribery and Corruption in Nigeria... We urge that the law be applied without fear or favour. In the words of President Olusegun Obaasanjo there should be no sacred cows. Anyone found guilty of infringing the law should be brought to book, no matter how highly placed he or she may be in the society. In the same vein, we commend the efforts of the government at tracking down the staggering sums of money that were stolen from our national treasury and stashed away in banks at home and abroad...we call on Western financial institutions to stop the corrupt practice of co-operating with fraudulent public servants who loot public coffers by accepting stolen money for safe keeping

---

[427]Ibid.

[428] Ibid, p. 418.

in their banks."[429] It is a warning to the government not to evoke religious sentiments in handling any matter. As a Christian president, he has to treat any Christian defaulter as he would a Moslem defaulter. Contrary to this, the other group will give a wrong interpretation. As all efforts made to fight Sharia seemed not be supported by the government, the CBCN continued to speak against it as an ill wind that will blow no one good. In their Meeting in 2001 they called attention to their rejection of any State religion no matter how it is figured. They stated,

> In the past, we have stressed the secular nature of the state, understood as the non-adoption of any religion as a state religion or giving preferential treatment of one religion, promote the principle of equality before the law. Given the existence of multi-religious groups with divergent interest in the country, the violation of the secular nature of our nation cannot occur without grave threats to peace and stability. We wish to state anew that the adoption and the full implementation of shari'a law by some states in the Northern parts of Nigeria is a flagrant violation of the secular nature of the Nigerian nation. Its introduction and extension into the domain of criminal law have given rise to the trampling of the rights of innocent law-abiding citizens who cannot seek redress in law courts on account of the well-grounded fear of threats to their lives and property and those of their families.[430]

Inasmuch as the Catholic Bishops are spiritual leaders, they have also their civil rights as every other Nigerian citizen to speak out on matters needing attention- social or political. It was to exercise this civic right that they made their voices heard in 2003 after the general election. They wrote, "We note with relief that Nigerians are now in a position to stand for their rights in the face of arbitrary and unjust impositions by the Government, as exemplified by the mass protests during the recent increase in fuel prices."[431] Surely, every uncoordinated critical mind will not be blamed if he criticises the CBCN for seemingly supporting violence and civil disobedience. But a careful and well tailored, positively critical mind will see beyond their statement, an unalloyed appreciation to God for signs of democratic maturity in

---

[429] Ibid.

[430] Catholic Secretariat, Statement by the Catholic Bishops' Conference of Nigeria, September 10, 2001.

[431] CBCN, "Hope for a Better Nigeria" A Communiqué Issued at the End of the Second Plenary Meeting at the Assumpta Pastoral Centre, Owerri, September 1 – 6, 2003.

our beloved country Nigeria. Democratic process goes with the right to make one's voice heard in a manner devoid of violence, peaceful protestation inclusive. Continuing however, they raised eyebrow against attitudes they described as unwholesome for peace and democracy and firmly condemned all fraudulent behaviour, violence and rigging, which took place during the elections. They called on all who engaged in irregularities to examine their consciences taking in into consideration what scandal and damage they have caused. They therefore called on men and women with proven integrity to join politics for the good of Nigeria instead of living politics in the hand of the do no goods who constantly use politics to inflict pains on their fellow citizens. The involvement of people of good will help reduced corruption and deceit to the barest minimum.[432]

The well known adage that when one part of the body is sick, the whole parts are affected is a truism. In the same vein, when any part of the land knows no peace, the whole land is invariably bleeds also. The incessant unrest in Niger Delta is a big minus for the land being the major source of the nation's economy. It is worse because it is well known to every Nigerian who wants to stand on the side of truth that the central government has not done enough for that area. Standing up for the truth, the Bishops condemned the incessant destruction of lives and property in Niger Delta area. Although they sympathised with the people of the area for the obvious neglect from the government, they condemned the way they were going about their claim which has dented the image of our country. They concluded by calling on the government to do something urgently to benefit the people of the area as well as compensate and make life again meaningful for those who have lost hope and courage to live due to the physical and mental torture l they experienced through the loss of their property.

> The wanton destruction of lives and property in the Niger Delta has continued to dent the image of our nation and to retard progress. We condemn the use of violence as a means to achieve any end, no matter how legitimate or noble. We pray for victims who died in the feuds and condole with those who suffered losses. While appreciating the efforts made by the Government to maintain peace in the areas, we call on the government to set up a commission to identify the causes of the perennial violence, as well as those responsible and proffer an enduring solution to

---

[432] Ibid.

the crisis. Meanwhile, we appeal to the government to compensate and rehabilitate those who have suffered losses.[433]

Apart from calling on the government to protect the property and lives of her citizens, the bishops called on the citizens to live a life worthy of good ambassadors of their peace. Calling on all to a sober lifestyle, they maintained that that alone can guarantee peace and survival of our nation and anything against it will be seen as handing our dear nation to the hands of the wicked enemies, "So, be very careful about the sort of lives you lead, like intelligent and not like senseless people. This may be a wicked age, but your lives should redeem it. And do not be thoughtless but recognize what is the will of the Lord."[434] One may contribute to the wicked taking over this age if one feels unconcerned in times of election. If an eligible citizen refuses to exercise his or her franchise by joining hands with the rest of the citizenry in electing credible people to lead his country, state or local government, he or she is making it faster and easier to for the wicked to take over. Once they take over, the one who, without cogent reasons fails to exercise his franchise is culpable of a grievous offence of hatred and negligence against his fatherland. Therefore, participating in elections is a first step towards helping to install peace. In recognition of this fact, the CBCN rejoiced at seeing their beloved flocks doing the right thing and did not waste time in praising and encouraging them. "Indeed, politics offers our lay Christians a great opportunity to contribute to the development of our country, following the light of the Gospel. Being a Christian includes the civic responsibility to contribute to good governance and the transformation of the society. The Church renews and will sustain her action for the promotion of a healthy democratic process in our land. We call on Nigerian Christians to study and practice the Church's Social Teaching in order to sanitize our society and be truly leaven in our nation."[435] Because of this task of sincere involvement in the deciding the future wellbeing of all through the exercise of one's franchise, they (CBCN) called on all as responsible citizens to start early to prepare for the next elections in 2007 to assure a smooth, successful and effective election even as they left no one in doubt that the past election was not 100 percent perfect as some of the results are being contested in the court of law.

---

[433] Ibid.
[434] Ibid. cf. also Eph.5:15-17.
[435] 2nd Plenary Meeting of CBCN at Pope John Paul II Pastoral Centre, Markurdi, September 13-17, 2004.

As responsible citizens, we should begin early to prepare for the 2007 elections. We lament that justice is being purposely delayed over the affairs of the past elections even as we prepare for the next elections. We should learn from our past mistakes to lay a good foundation this time around for free and fair elections. Plurality of parties is essential for the healthy sustenance of democracy. We regret a situation in which opposition is subverted and sabotaged, or opposition easily succumbing to such pressures. We should reject the temptation to one party state and work towards the promotion of a multi-party state which encourages debates and freedom of choice at all levels.[436]

What beats ones imagination is the extent some people can go so as to win the election. It is against such greed for power or quest for wealth and misguided source of security that the Bishops warned when they called on all citizens not to vote unfit politicians into power. Such people when they ascend the throne will surely work with ruthless conscience. Their target will never be to serve the people who voted them into power but to amass wealth. It is a bitter truth that such people mostly bribe the INEC workers and are rigged into power instead of being voted in. There is no extent such people would not go as long as they are assured that such sojourn would help them win elections. They can get involved in political killings (even of one's child or parents, wife, husband or neighbours), maiming, name-calling, charms and joining of secret cults. The CBCN spoke bitterly against such attitudes. "We condemn all fetish practices and regret the involvement of some Christians in perpetrating evil practices. We are appalled and vehemently condemn the activities associated with the Ogwugwu shrines in Okija and similar shrines in other parts of the country. We condemn nefarious practices like ritual killings, cultism and other diabolic activities as means to wealth, security and power. We warn against such recourse to the power of darkness."[437]There is no doubt that whoever gets elected through abnormal means will run an abnormal government. In such a case, the abnormal government hides under the umbrella of political immunity to enjoy police protection. Consequent upon the poor salary the police receive, they are ready to do any bidding of the abnormal government who promises to make life meaningful for them. For this reason, the police who are meant to keep order unfortunately join to put disorder and brutalise the people they are supposed to protect. That is

---

[436] Ibid.
[437] Ibid.

why there have been reported cases of police joining the protesting, riotous group to cause mayhem.

At times, the action of the police is tied to religious sentiments. In such a case, a policeman who is a Moslem joins his rioting Moslem brothers to cause havoc against Christians by providing them with security. The same could also be said of Christian policeman. Disorder surely means absence of peace. At times the police are themselves extortionists, even killing a citizen who refuses to offer them 20 or 30 Naira bribe at numerous checkpoints. When such is the case, accidental discharge will be blamed for the incident. Agreed that they are not well paid and maintained, the poor, penniless and defenceless citizens should on no account be the scapegoats on whom they now dump their bitter complaints. Knowing that a hungry man is an angry man, government should take serious the welfare of the security men and women. That to some extent will assuage the unfortunate accidental discharge claims and make them carry out their duties with joy and contentment. To this effect, the Bishops' conference said,

> We observe that the security on our roads has generally improved...It is due to the presence of more police on our roads...we note that there are now too many checkpoints. They seem to have become new 'de facto' tollgates where citizens experience harassment, extortion and intimidation with seeming impunity at the hands of some policemen...We acknowledge the poor condition under which the police have to live and work. We call on the government to pay the just salaries of the police men and women as and when due, and improve their conditions of service. We equally call on all members of the police force to shun corrupt practices. They are to uphold the law, protect the rights of the citizens and promote a positive image of a civic democratic society.[438]

It may not be out of place to say that the name police should have been made synonymous with the word 'Peace'. But when they turn to become confusionists, in conjuction with their pay masters in power, then the country is in jeopardy. As a remedy to that the Bishops anchored the root of this disorder on lack of well-directed training. The government take-over of former mission schools strongly contributes to all these destructive and deep eating cankerworm that continually hold this nation to ransom. While not denying the visible efforts of the government to rid the nation of some unscrupulous elements or political cabal, the CBCN maintains that until the

[438] Ibid.

government accepts this naked truth and hands the mission schools over to its real owners for proper and efficient management, Nigeria may still for a longer time to come witness this unnecessary, man-made logjam – both political and religious. The Bishops' conference therefore called the government to make them partners in the educational system of the country as some state governments thankfully have done. This will surely help to some extent to reduce the irresponsive and cabalistic tendencies of our youths.

> We will continue to offer our services in partnership with government towards the provision of quality and functional education for our people. We thank the state governments which have handed some schools back to the Church. Some of these governments have begun to assist in renovating the infrastructures, as well as provide grants-in-aid to the mission schools. We urge other state governments to follow these examples which further help in the moral education of our youth and raise the ethical standards of our people.[439]

The conference of Nigerian bishops being a gathering of great minds and moral, has never failed to be positive where necessary. It is in that regard, as earlier stated, that they praised the remarkable progressive strides of the government in matters of provision of some basic communication gadgets that provided employment opportunities for our youths. Closing their first plenary meeting for the year 2006, held at Divine Love Retreat and Conference Centre, Abuja from 6th to 11th March, the Bishops conference issued a communiqué with the caption, "The Church in Nigeria: Keeping hope alive". As part of the fruits of the communiqué one reads that the achievements of the current political dispensation offer us hope. Nigeria plays commendable peace-keeping roles in war-affected areas of the continent of Africa. The telecommunications industry has made it possible for Nigerians to stay in touch with one another and with citizens of other nations, and has provided employment for many of our youths. The national census about to begin is a step in the right direction. As stakeholders in the progress of Nigeria they did not hide their desire and opinion as a conference that religious affiliation and ethnic origin are vital statistical data of individuals in any nation. They called on all Nigerians to take part in the head count.[440]

---

[439] Ibid.

[440] CBCN, "The Church in Nigeria: Keeping Hope alive" being its 1st Plenary Meeting held at Divine Love Retreat and Conference Centre, Abuja, March 6-11, 2006.

Since an idle mind is the devil's workshop, the above quotation basically praised the impact of provision of employment opportunities in peace maintenance in any nation. These communication gadgets will help the citizens alert the security men and women of any suspected danger before it goes of hand. However, I want to warn and clearly state that the offering of hope by the government does not mean that all is now Uhuru for the suffering masses. It is a Nigerian system to offer hope to the people only to end up on a very disappointing tone. It is therefore pretence on the part of government to give fake and unrealistic hope to millions of the poor masses without commitment. Hope should be translated into reality. Even the conference was of the same opinion when they said, "Despite these rays of hope, the experiences of Nigerians have not matched their expectation. Nigerians are still in dire need of stable electricity supply, clean drinking water and more good roads. Insecurity of life and property makes citizens live in fear and scars visitors, investors, and tourists away from our land. The scourge of poverty is still with us despite the indices of economic growth with which we are presented."[441] The presentation of the nation as being on the right track while the opposite is the case is what the Bishops' Conference saw as a deceit.

A nation that cannot properly address its many problems cannot be said to be on the right track. With the level of riots and violence erupting here and there without the government finding its sponsors and punishing them accordingly, there is little to hope for. But the Bishops' conference has vowed never to allow itself to be silenced. Commenting therefore on the most recent riots, they said, "Examined more deeply, it would appear that these riots have been orchestrated by people with dubious intents. There is therefore an urgent need for government to live up to its responsibility by identifying, isolating, disarming and prosecuting murderers and arsonists. Government should also ensure that those who are behind this latest round of riots are brought to justice, and that its promises of compensation are kept."[442] This demand of the Bishops' Conference would have been taken seriously if the government is not totally aware of the perpetrators of the unfortunate incidents. The promises of the government over the years to deal with the masterminds of riots in Nigeria have never been matched with action. Clear to Nigerians, it was to be another bundle of empty promises.

Nigerians have learnt to live with the lies told by government. The knowledge of this fact is no doubt clear to the Bishops. No wonder they directed their thanks to God's grace and mercy instead of unfoundedly con-

[441] Ibid.
[442] Ibid.

gratulating the untrustworthy government for the relative peace in the country in 2008. The Bishops thanked the good Lord, especially for the relative harmony and peace that Nigerians had enjoyed in the land. This is not because the April 2007 elections and subsequent local government elections went well. It is rather because God's grace and mercy have sustained the patience of Nigerians in the face of blatant and crude provocation. This does not, by any means, justify complacency on the part of those responsible for the public affairs. The way to show gratitude for God's mercy is the way of doing things right.[443]This indirect critique on the government is consequent upon the day light robbery on the part of the government and her co-travellers on the route of corruption where people were denied their hard fought and won elections thereby denying many good and eligible people of Nigeria their franchise. The Bishops were vexed with the way the federal government could just wake up and simply call for amendment of the constitution just to benefit his selfish policies without recourse to the electorate. The people have democratic right to contribute their quota through public debate of issues affecting the general wellbeing. Mostly, the government comes up with inhuman and unintelligent policies that will make it and its cronies win elections. The Bishops' Conference captured and described the situation as nothing other than pure violation of human dignity. According to the Bishops,

> The flawed federal and state elections of 2007, and the subsequent local government elections, represent a brutal reminder that there is a culture of violation of human dignity in our country. The rights of every Nigerian as human beings are violated by some policies which are ill-conceived with little or no input from the people. Even some good policies are poorly implemented. Nigerians observe that many of our leaders, at all levels of government, assume that they are omniscient and omnipotent by the mere fact that they head an office or government parastatal. Our people witness many manifestations of the erroneous presumption that power is knowledge (in direct opposition to the truth that Knowledge is power) and that to be in office is to monopolise wisdom. This kind of thinking encourages arbitrariness in policy making and execution. It violates human dignity because it excludes the people from the process of governance. The human dignity of the Nigerian is also violated when his or her rights as a citizen of Nigeria are not recognized beyond the boundaries of his ances-

[443] CBCN, Communique at the end of the First Plenary Meeting held at Divine Love Retreat and Conference Centre, Abuja, February 11-16, 2008.

tral home. This is the "indigene-settler" dichotomy that shows itself in ethnocentricism.[444]

When such happens, the only option left for the people is mostly rioting and destruction of property. At times, such situations present good opportunities for the bandits to loot and maim. It must be said loud and clear that the best knowledgeable government is the one that carries the electorate along. It is a government of the people for the people. This is exactly what democracy is all about. Unfortunately for Nigeria, democracy is the government of the cabal for the cabal. On the other hand, in allusion to such policies that may be considered good but lacking proper application, the Conference declared, "We appreciate the wisdom of the principle behind the 'quota system' and 'federal character policy'. But the operation of this policy sometimes amounts to making some Nigerians second class citizens or even outright aliens in their own county and deprive Nigeria of her most competent sons and daughters."[445] No true Nigerian that worth the name can claim ignorance of what the Conference is referring to. One such clear unfortunate and obnoxious policy is the quota system applied by the ruling party, the PDP. Their rotation of the presidency between the North and the South has continued to make Nigeria a lame duck progressing with a snail speed. As the Bishops were calling for service with dedication, the new product of the condemned policy, Umar Yar'Adua (s)elected[446] as the new President, seemed to have known their mind-set and without wasting time, hammered on what seemed to have given the political direction a new lease of life. He made the statement that his election should be seen as an act of God and his leadership style as that of a servant-leader. He made this statement during his inaugural speed. Such a declaration can uplift the spirit and inspire hope for peace. The Bishops welcomed this stand with joy and admiration. However, as people who are not new in the Nigerian political terrain, their praise of the speech of Yar'Adua was not to end without a caveat knowing full well that some before him had made similar promises but later reneged . The danger was that even if the president may have sincerely had the good intention to serve his people, he may be led astray by those he might appoint as ministers and commissioners. The Bishops pointed out,

---

[444] Ibid, (bracket mine).
[445] Ibid.
[446] The use of the term '(s)elected' is in line with the claim of many Nigerians that, the then new President, late Umar Yar'Adua was not elected by the electorate but was single handedly selected by his predecessor, President Olusegun Obasanjo and hoisted on Nigerians against their political will.

> We note with satisfaction the pledge of President Umar Yar'Adua in his inaugural address to be a servant-leader. The fact that this notion has strong biblical roots enables us to identify ourselves with it. Christ Jesus himself has taught us: "Whoever wants to be first must place himself last of all and be the servant of all" (Mk 9:35)...While we commend the President for this pledge, we appeal to him to ensure that only those who share this notion of leadership are appointed to be in his government. For it is not enough to hear this from the President, it is also necessary that this be manifest in the utterances and conduct of his ministers and heads of parastatals. We urge public office holders to respect every Nigerian citizen in the discharge of their duties. Then they will be veritable civil servants and not lords and masters of the citizen.[447]

The warning of the Bishops was later proved to be well founded and timely. It is a common knowledge that the president had good will but most of his governors, associates and ministers were greedy, corrupt politicians who never allowed the president carry out his promises. The situation was made clearly with what played out as the hand of death hovered around the president. It was clear that the people around the president had never had the good of the country and its citizenry in mind. They showed themselves to be morally corrupt, feeding the country with false information just to hang on to power. This situation is only a drop of water in the ocean. The disregard for human dignity could be linked to the adoption of Sharia which we have discussed before. It has been happening with the past administrations that had always taken the dignity of the citizenry for granted. The dignity of the citizenry was for them a no issue. They were ready to continue to squander the wealth of the nation. They jettisoned the idea of development of the entire person into the ocean of selfishness.

We must take note of the fact the notion of human dignity is all inclusive. It is the building of the totality of the human person which does not only mean economic advancement nor its exclusion. It embraces also the moral aspect of human life since man is made up of body and soul. "Authentic development is centred on the human person and orientates the human person to his supernatural destiny in God. It is the attainment of self-fulfilment within our collective fulfilment. It is not just the availability of infrastructure, neither is it just a matter of enviable economic indices. While all these are necessary, they do not suffice where respect for human dignity is lacking.

---

[447] CBCN, op.cit. 2008.

Our country experiences the absence of authentic development because of our abysmally low record of respect for human dignity. It is because our humanity is impoverished that we experience economic poverty. The economic poverty itself leads to insecurity of life and property in a land where corruption and incompetence have crippled our police, and many other institutions and sectors of our national life..."[448] Being fully aware of the importance of moral principles in political ethics, the Conference called on the Christian politicians to lead the way so that others will follow, making clear their readiness to help fight the menace. It is not a call to religious dichotomy but a call to show the way.

The Bishops, having made it clear time without number that they acknowledge the moral values that exist in Islam, made this call on the Christian politicians so that their Moslem counterparts would follow suit. They declared, "On our part, we as a Church recommit ourselves to stand up against injustice, abuse of human rights, corruption and discrimination both in the Church and in the society. We challenge our Christian politicians to stand up for Christian values and work vigorously for a better society...."[449] It was a call to be "the salt of the earth and light of the world." It was a wake-up call on all Christian politicians to chart a new course and put an end to all violence and conflict and to construct a society built on traditional African values of love, solidarity, justice and peace.[450] Despite all the efforts of the Bishops and their pleas, it looks like the addressees are deaf and dumb. Instead of peace and tranquillity emerging, fear, rioting, maiming and killing of innocent citizens are becoming normal part of existence in Nigeria. But the Bishops refused to be down-spirited by this situation hoping that one day, the effect of their constant plea for peace will penetrate the hearts of the wicked and thieving politicians. The unfortunate, hopeless and disappointing state of the nation was thus captured by the CBCN, Ibadan Province. They remarked that another year has again begun in which many Nigerians feel betrayed and see their hopes and aspirations dashed. Our leaders continue to feed Nigerians with half-truths and downright falsehood in things that deeply affect their lives and nation. They regretted that in addition to serious disillusionment in the provision of regular power supply, security of life and property, provision of essential petroleum products and other infrastructure, Nigerians, after two months of the absence of the President, Alhaji Umaru Musa Yar'Adua, can-

---

[448] Ibid.

[449] Ibid.

[450] CBCN, Ibadan Ecclesiastical Province, A Communiqué issued at the end of their two days Meeting at Pastoral Institute, Ibadan, January 18-19, 2010.

not confidently state where and in what condition their President is. Yet, the leaders continued to pretend that all is well. This irresponsible state of uncertainty was regrettable and can have dangerous consequences for the nation.[451]

This incident can really be dangerous for the nation as political jobbers could use it to inflame the polity. The citizens have right to know about the state of their sick president but were denied. Such a situation was enough to cause civil unrest thereby disturbing the peace of the nation. Apart from that, the most recent mayhem in Jos, Plateau State that took place in January 2010 exposed the hypocrisy and ineptitude of our beloved but amalgamated land Nigeria to the world scorn and ridicule. It is regrettably on record that such happenings in the near past have never been thoroughly investigated and addressed. Such situations do not show Nigeria as a nation which is really serious with the rebranding crusade that will make her again be seen to be on the path of development and national integration.[452] Taking a stand, the Bishops declared their condemnation over the barbaric action: "We denounce all perpetrators of this shameful conspiracy against a particular segment of our nation and we call on the competent authorities to act decisively before things get out of hand."[453] As the dust of the January violence that claimed about 200 lives and multi-million Naira worth of property lost, the country witnessed another epic massacre in the wee hours of the same month, Sunday 7th 2010.

I deem it however unnecessary dwelling on this latest massacre episode. Suffice it to say, that the much given cases of rioting, rooting and maiming of innocent citizens are enough proof that all is not well in Nigerian state. However, the contributions curled out from the different submissions of the Catholic Church hierarchy if adhered to will surely be good recipes for peace in Nigeria. It would however be more fruitful if the contributors be in the forefront in living out what they have suggested. Accordingly, Archbishop of Kaduna, Mathew Manoso Ndagoso during the African Synod challenged his fellow prelates to this life of witness as reported by Vellguth, Klaus:

> The topic of the African Synod (...) reminds us that God has raised us as a Church that we may be for all that visible Sacrament of unity that brings healing. Furthermore the topic challenges us, as Sacrament of unity to bear witness to the Gospel with our lives in which case we reveal to the world the power of God in Christ, uprooting all barriers, be it of ethnic,

[451] Ibid.
[452] Ibid.
[453] Ibid.

religious or political nature....And that we are urged and challenged, in a land...that is visited by conflicts and divisions, together to bear witness to reconciliation, justice and peace.[454]

I now state in brief the core messages of the Catholic Bishops' Conference of Nigeria to the issue of peaceful co-existence of the three major religions in Nigeria.

1. Lagos, March, 1987: 'The Nation is in Jeopardy'; We have been overtaken by the tragic and heart-breaking events that have struck and left the nation stricken. It is a Statement made after their plenary meeting under the theme: 'The Bible: the Word of God for our Times'.
2. Lagos, 1989: They took time to discuss with the utmost sense of responsibility before God and the nation, the raging issue over 'Nigeria's membership in the Organisation of Islamic Conference' (OIC).
3. 28. Feb, 2000: 'Let there be Peace'. In their statement during the 'Sharia controversy', they condemned violence on whatever excuse and from whatever direction. They condemned violence above all when its perpetrators blasphemously and fraudulently claim religious justification.
4. Lagos, March, 2000: 'The Jubilee and National Reconciliation'. They declared that most of the problems causing conflicts in the nation can be prevented, and what has gone wrong put right, if there is a commitment to dialogue.
5. Kaduna, Sept. 2000: 'Let us live and work together in Peace and Harmony'. The Bishops affirmed their belief in and commitment to Nigeria as one nation under one God who cares for every Nigerian, irrespective of religion, ethnic origin or language.
6. Owerri, Sept, 2003: 'Hope for a better Nigeria'. In this meeting, they deliberated on several issues concerning the state of the Church and the nation.
7. Makurdi, Sept. 2004: 'Mission to serve'. They called on Nigerians at all levels to examine their life styles and the consequences of their actions on the people they should serve.
8. Abuja, March 2006: 'The Church in Nigeria: Keeping hope alive'. They maintained that they will not allow themselves to be silenced. Even as the maintained that the experiences of Nigerians have not matched their ex-

---

454 Vellguth, K., „Wenn Religion als Vorwand dient, Unruhen in Nigeria haben vielfältige Ursachen" in: *Heilung und Heil* 3/ 2009, p. 12.

pectation. Nigerians are still in dire need of stable electricity supply, clean drinking water and more good roads.

9. Abuja, Feb. 2008: 'Restoring our Nation'. Here they called on government to make policies that will benefit every Nigerian. This policy will make it possible for every citizen to live and work in any part of Nigeria without molestation.
10. Abuja, March 2009: 'Reinstate spiritual values'. They stated that corruption and theft of public funds, which have largely remained unabated despite their call for prayers, have brought our country to its knees.

4.4. Conclusion

Reading through the above selected statements and themes of different Communiqués made by the Magisterium, the Nigerian Bishops' Conference, and Aecawa, it is easy to decipher what is uppermost in their minds. It is their basic intention as Good Shepherds to actually speak for the good of the citizenry; to strive to sue for peace; to call for the enthronement of people oriented policies; to see that all these are achieved trusting on the Word of God who created us to live in His peace which if well interpreted would translate to living in harmony. Their statements and Communiqués answer the question posed in the concluding part of chapter 3 of this work: 'Must we only pray and wait for wonders?' In addition to the answer already given before, the Bishops maintained that God has given us all we need to survive. We must therefore co-operate with God by sincerely making good use of all he has blessed us with. They are at the long run to be seen as that what they claim to be, 'THE VOICE OF THE VOICELESS'.

CHAPTER FIVE

THE EFFORTS OF THE MOSLEMS AND THE ADHERENTS OF AFRICAN TRADITIONAL RELIGION FOR PEACE IN NIGERIA

5. Introduction

He is a dullard to its highest level who pretends not to see or not to know the great danger facing Nigeria at the present time. It is the danger of religious intolerance and bigotry. Most often, the Moslems are blamed for the religious riots and violence in Nigeria especially considering the fact that all disturbances usually begin in the Moslem populated area - the Northern Nigeria. Some Moslems and also members of other religious groups in Nigeria and the world over, claim that Islamic teachings are simply the root cause of the Moslems' attitudes. One then wonders if Islam really teaches violence and hatred. It is for this reason that I intend to consider the opinions of Moslems towards these accusations which I believe will inform us of the efforts the make towards peace in Nigeria. The adherents of African Traditional Religion are not many in Nigeria. They are hardly connected with any violence. This notwithstanding, I deem it necessary to look into their contributions towards peace in Nigeria.

5.1. Islam and Peace

Nigerians in Northern Nigeria live in perpetual fear of the unknown. It has been a common occurrence in the North for some families to go to sleep only to be woken in the morning by sounds of guns with consequent indescribable sights of violent destruction of lives and properties. The unfortunate connection of this barbaric action to religion and politics is shameful. This situation worries peace loving Nigerians and calls for a proper examination of consciences. The situation was thus described,

> The occurrence of some intra- and inter-religious crises in recent times in Nigeria has been giving lovers of peace some concern. This is in view of the wanton destruction of life and property which such crises usually occasion. The situation is so bad that many people wonder whether religion, at least in this society, has shirked its primary role of sustaining peace between man and God, and between man and man. It is unfortunate that this

laudable purpose of religion has been defeated and anarchy and chaos have been given free rein.[455]

Following this situation we x-rayed in the last chapter the stand and contributions of different categories of Catholic religious leaders on matters concerning Peace and Justice in Nigeria. It is worth it if we also examine some Islamic tenets that can sue for peace especially in the Nigerian context. It is very important here to note that peace in this realm does not mean a situation whereby the entire Nigerian populace will completely become Moslems, Christians or Traditional religionists. It is rather a situation where the adherents of these religions will always feel free to worship in a manner that does not constitute problem to others. It is a situation where every Nigerian will feel free to carry his business and go about his daily activities without fear of molestation. It is a situation where a Nigerian will be happy to be identified as a Nigerian and is at peace whether he is in the Northern or in the Southern part of Nigeria. It therefore calls for tolerance and appreciation of one another as a people of the same nationality.

The Moslems as detailed in the Qur'an see themselves as champions of peace. This is consequent upon the belief that Islam is made up of two parts which are complementary and inseparable from each other. Qur'an is clear on this, as given by Abdul. He wrote, "Good deeds cannot come without faith, because faith is a way of thinking, and doing depends on thinking. If you think in the wrong way, you will also act in the wrong way."[456] It is in the light of this that Muslims are always described in the Qur'an as "those who have faith and do good deeds."[457] The implication of this assertion is that anyone who does not promote peace and good neighbourliness with both Moslem and non-Moslem neighbours is not worthy of being a Moslem. A Moslem is therefore called upon to perfect what have been handed over by Prophet Mohammed. This is sequel to the fact that "Islam does not see itself to have started and ended with Prophet Mohammed...Rather, his role is just to complete and perfect the way of life and code of conduct recommended by Allah for humanity right from the time of Adam...our progenitor. Although differences between the levels of understanding, coupled with exigencies of

---

[455] Abdu-Raheem, M. A., "Islamic Concept of Tolerance and the Task before the Nigerian Muslim" in Olupona, J. K. (ed.), *Religion and Peace in Multi-Faith Nigeria*, Nigeria, Obafemi Awolowo University, 1992, p. 70.
[456] Abdul, M. O., *Islam as a Religion*, Lagos, Islamic Publications Bureau, 1982, p. 18.
[457] Abdu-Raheem, M. A., op. cit. p. 71.

time have affected the outlook of the divine revelation at various stages, its essence is largely the same."[458]

It is the talk of the day that Moslems want to Islamise Nigeria. Part of the reasons for this misrepresentation of Islam is due to the attitude of some disgruntled elements who do not know exactly what Islam teaches but go about carrying out their unholy duty in the name of Islam. According to Abdu-Raheem, "Islam teaches freedom of religion in such a way that it does not sanction forcing people to convert to it. According to Shari'ah, he who forces or intimidates anybody to become a Muslim is guilty of a great sin because his action is against the express teaching of the Qur'an which says, "There should be no compulsion in religion.''[459] To clarify this claim he further pointed out, "One of the distinctive features of Islam is its recognition of the fact that there is bound to be differences between human beings in the various aspects of life including the spiritual. This is largely due to the privilege of free-will bestowed on us to choose what to do and how to do it."[460] Consequent upon this free-will, everyone should live without fear. This should particularly be applied in Nigeria where we experience constant rioting, killing and maiming of innocent citizens in the name of religion. This situation is completely against the official teaching of Islam as given in Qur'an:

> Under no circumstance should they begin hostilities against them (non Muslims who call on the name of Allah) either for spiritual or mundane motives. It is only when they rise against Muslims that the latter are allowed to protect and defend themselves. Even in such a situation, it should be upper-most in the Muslims' minds to find ways and means of bringing about peace as soon as possible. Those who do not practically take part in the hostility should not be made to suffer at all.[461]

5.2. Nigerian Experience

In his attempt to convince the world that Islam in Nigeria had been a religion that encourages and supports peaceful co-existence, Abdu-Raheem appealed to history to make himself clearer. According to him,

---

[458] Ibid.
[459] Ibid, p. 72, cf. also, The Holy Qur'an, 2, 256.
[460] Ibid.
[461] Ibid. cf. also Qur'an 60, 9-10.

> The Sokoto Jihad of the 19th century established Islam as the state religion in most parts of Northern Nigeria extending as far South as Ilorin. Adhering strictly to the teaching of Islam that prohibits forcing people to become converts, the Jihadists allowed those who preferred their traditional religion to Islam. They were only required to enter into agreements and pay Jizyah in exchange for the social services enjoyed by them. The whole deal was on the basis of fairplay and equity as laid down by Islam.[462]

One would say here that this assertion in modern day Nigeria cannot pass for the truth. Calling on the Moslems to live after the example of their founder, Mohammed, he gave a vivid example of Mohammed in his peace loving mission. It was a case of his patience and forbearance in the midst of provocation by the people of Makkah who feared that Mohammed and his followers were to attack them. He wrote,

> As if to try the patience of the Prophet (S.A.W), some people from Makkah went out when it was dark to throw stones at the Muslims' tents. About fifty Muslim soldiers were sent to capture and bring them to the Prophet for judgement. They had no reason for their action and they were accordingly found guilty. Contrary to the expectation, the Prophet (A.S.W) did not prescribe any punishment for them. Instead, he forgave them and allowed them to go back to Makkah freely.[463]

It is true that he did not punish them, but in a situation like this, one would not have expected him to punish them knowing very well what calamities awaited them as foreigners or visitors with limited man power. However, the amount of insult which Mohammed was alleged to have patiently accepted for the sake of peace is unquantifiable. But it later paid off as many Makkans in admiration of his attitude converted to Islam. So, despite all odds, the Prophet remained resolute to convincing the Makkans and all the Arabs that his ultimate aim was to establish peace. It was on this ground that he sent emissaries to Makkans. It eventually resulted in the two sides signing a treaty, or memorandum of understanding, agreeing on certain terms that were however in favour of the Makkans.

---

[462] Ibid, p. 75.
[463] Ibid, p. 77.

His guiding principle for allowing the Makkans upper hand was the fact that what one does not achieve by force he can achieve by peace. The Moslems were therefore enraged that they could not perform their 'Umrah before returning to Makkah. It was also declared illegal for the Makkans to convert to Islam or join in the Medinah without an express permission of their guardians whereas the Moslems have the free will to revert to their former religion.[464] Attesting to the efficacy of the method applied by Mohammed, coupled with the ten years peace treaty during which the Muslims devoted their times to preaching, many people converted to Islam.

The essence of the above narrations is to make it clear to Nigerian Moslems that they stand to gain if they follow the path of peace than the part of violence in trying to convert people to Islam,[465] or to Islamise Nigeria. It is also to advise them to avoid unnecessary and instigative stories which are capable of inciting hatred between Moslems and the adherents of other religions. Such provocative formulations could lead to conflicts and irreparable damages in body and soul. Accordingly, one reads in Qur'an, "O ye who believe! If an unrighteous person brings you any news, ascertain (the correctness of the report) fully, lest you harm a people in ignorance, and then become repentant for what you have done."[466] It is in full support of this clarion call that the Sultan of Sokoto, Alhaji Mohammed Sa'ad Abubakar III, accused both Christians and Moslems of having lived below expectations, since their attitudes contribute immensely in dragging the nation back to inglorious days of religious crises.[467]

The Sultan, by virtue of his office as the President General of Nigerian Supreme Council for Islamic Affairs (NSCIA) and as the co-President of the Nigeria Interreligious Council (NIREC) made this statement in Owerri, Imo state during a second quarterly general meeting of the Nigeria Inter-religious Council. According to him, the issue of, "peace and stability of the nation and mutual co-existence of Nigerian citizens should be matters that are not negotiable."[468] The only panacea for peace is the coming together of different religious groups to a round table discussion in order to sincerely find a lasting solution to the existing problems. He entrusted this task to the members of NIREC so as to convince doubting Nigerians that the formation of NIREC is not an effort in futility. He pointed out that the goal of this noble group

---

[464] Ibid.

[465] Ibid, p. 78.

[466] The Holy Qur'an, Surah, 49:6.

[467] Okafor, V., "Sultan accuses religious leaders of fuelling crises" in: *Sun Newspaper*, Wed, July 14, 2010.

[468] Ibid.

would be achieved only with hard work, perseverance and sacrifice. He maintained that days are gone when religious leaders made wilful, unguarded, and un-provocative (sic) statements.[469] Obvious that such provocative statements could arise from ignorance and lack of proper education, the JNI (Jama'atu Nasril Islam) wasted no time in condemning in strong words, the few Moslems- who discourage their Moslem brothers from undertaking western education- as "misguided people". They called upon the Moslems not to hearken to such erroneous call, advising them to make sincere efforts to ensure that they are properly educated in both Islamic education and in western education.[470]

There is therefore the need to emphasize here that any nation whose educational system is weak is in deep coma or is half dead. If it offers no variety of educational possibilities to her citizens, such a nation is a living-dead exuding stinking odour that no amount of scent sprayed on it could deodorize. It therefore needs a total overhauling. It is no mistake to state that education is the bedrock of any progressive and dynamic nation or institution. It is certainly on the basis of this assertion that JNI warned its member States to participate fully in western education to avoid the possibility of eradication of the Islamic hold and importance among the tribes that make up the Nigerian nation. This lack of proper education leads to a misinterpretation of some Qur'anic citations or Islamic teachings by some educated Moslems to their selfish gains. This remains a strong force in causing unrest and disharmony.

A typical misinterpretation of the Qur'an is exemplified below. If a territory is conquered by Moslems, the inhabitants of the captured territory have three options awaiting them:

(i). the reception of Islam in which case the conquered become enfranchised citizens of the Moslem State;

(ii). the payment of poll tax (jizyah) by which the unbelievers obtain protection and become dhimmis (people of agreement);

(iii). death by the sword to those who would not pay the poll tax.[471] It is on the basis of the third option that some Shiite Moslems see some texts

[469] Ibid.

[470] Part of the Communique of Jama'atu Nasril Islam after their meeting on June 18, 2009 in Kaduna with the theme, "Constitution Amendment: Northern elders warn Lawmakers". cf. also Ismail Omipidan in, www.sunnewsonline.com

[471] Opeloye, M. O., "The Qur'anic Guidelines on Inter-religious Relations: An Overview" in: Olupona, J.K., (ed.), *Religion and Peace in Multi-faith Nigeria*, Obafemi Awolowo University, 1992, p. 83.

of Qur'an as a strong foundation and direct call to Jihad. They however tabled some conditions that must exist before Jihad is embarked upon:

(i). when the armies of Islam are led by the rightful Imam.

(ii). when arms and ammunitions of war and experienced warriors are ready.

(iii). when it is against the enemies of God

(iv). when he who makes war is in possession of his reason.

(v) . when he has secured the permission of his parents and has sufficient money to meet the expenses of his journey.[472]

The misinterpretation of the following Qur'anic verses serve as justification for the Shiites to embark on islamic holy war or Jihad:

"2:190-193. Fight in the cause of God those who fight you; but do not transgress limits...slay them wherever you catch them and turn them out from where they have turned you out and oppression are worse than slaughter; but fight them not at the sacred Mosque unless they first fight you there, but if they fight you slay them. And fight them on until there is no more tumult for oppression....

2:217. They ask thee concerning fighting in the prohibited month. Say: Fighting therein is a grave offence; but graver is it in the sight of God to prevent access to the sacred mosque and drive out its members. Tumult and oppression are worse than slaughter.

2:246. How could we refuse to fight in the cause of God seeing that we were turned out of our homes and our families...?

4:76. Those who believe fight in the cause of God and those who reject faith fight in the cause of Evil. So fight Ye against the friends of Satan: feeble indeed is the turning of Satan.

8:39. And fight them until there is no more tumult or oppression and there prevail justice and faith in God altogether and everywhere. But if they cease, verily God see (sic) all that they do.

9:5. But when the forbidden months are past, then fight and slay the pagans wherever you find them and seize them, beleaguer them and lie in wait for them in every stratagem (of war). But if they repent and establish regular prayers and practice regular charity then open the way for them...

9:13-14. Will you not fight people who violated their oaths, plotted to expel the apostle and took the aggressive by being the first to assault you? Do you fear them? Nay, it is God whom you should fear. Fight them and God will punish them by your hands cover them with shame.

---

[472] Ibid.

9:29. Fight those who believe not in God nor (sic) the last day nor hold that forbidden which has been forbidden by God and His apostle, nor acknowledge the religion of truth (even if they are) of the people of the book until they pay the jizyah with willing submission and feel themselves subdued.
9:123. O you who believe, fight the unbelievers who gird you about and let them find firmness in you and know that God is with those who fear Him."[473]

Simply put, the above long citations from the Qur'an when critically viewed do not give a faithful Moslem the mandate to engage in Jihad at the least provocation. They do not oblige the Moslems to fight the idolaters except in self defence or the defence of God. They are permitted to fight simply to ward off aggression and in self-preservation.[474] Opeloye went further to explain that even when the fight against idolaters is permitted, it refers to a particular group of idolaters that has violated an agreement rather than all the idolaters of the world. He remarked,

> Commenting on the next verse (verse 5 of chapter 9) which enjoins the Muslims to slay the idolaters wherever they are found, M.M. Ali opines that in view of the clear exception given in verse 4 the idolaters intended are the idolatrous tribes of Arabia assembled at the pilgrimage who had made treaties with the Muslims but later violated them and not all the idolaters of the world. This is a plausible interpretation in view of the principle of religious tolerance enshrined in Qur'an.[475]

Situating the above in the Nigerian situation, Opeloye reiterated the opinion of the Sultan of Sokoto on the way to peaceful co-existence in Nigeria. He emphasized,

> Proselytization should be pursued with caution. It should be done without offending the adherents of the other religions....Recent experiences in this country have shown that religious disturbances have often emanated from the provoking manner of proselytization. If the doctrines enshrined in their religions had been observed without recourse to abuses, sarcasm and mockery, provocation of the adherents of the other religion would have been reduced to the barest minimum....[476]

[473] Ibid, p. 85.
[474] Ibid.
[475] Ibid, p. 86.
[476] Ibid, p. 89.

In an interview granted the Daily Independent (Lagos, 1.07.2010), Khaleefah Rahman called for peace in the nation. He criticized all Moslems and Christians who do not live out their religious duty to maintain peace. Part of this duty is to obey the constituted authority who calls the populace to godly act. Replying to the question of what roles the Moslems have played in the Nigerian society as the country approaches its 50th Independence anniversary, he said,

> Allah says follow Allah, and the prophet and then your leader. Please note that Allah did not make exception as to the kind of leaders we should obey – Muslims or Christians. It was a general statement, made to ensure peace and orderliness in the society. By this statement Allah means we must obey our leaders, regardless of their religion or background...For instance, October 1 has been declared as a public holiday to mark the Independence Day. Muslims are obliged to stay at home and join in prayers for the socio-economic and political development of our fatherland....Then as a contribution to the memorable day, we Muslims can also organise special prayer for the country.[477]

As it is clear that many of the elected office holders are not true to their campaign promises, he left no body in doubt that even some of his elected fellow Moslems have failed when it comes to their leadership qualities as behoves a Moslem. He remarked, "Our leaders, especially those who are Moslems, are not behaving according to the tenet of Islam. Their attitude to the people and the trust entrusted upon them run foul of what Islam prescribes."[478] He narrated the story of Umar (the second caliph of Islam) to enhance his argument and thereby pointed out to the elected leaders how exemplary and selfless they should be. According to the story, Umar who was in his house with a lighted candle was busy writing something of interest to his community when a committee of Moslems visited him. He wanted to know if the reason for their visit concerned him or the entire community he is leading. When he found out that it concerned him as an individual, he unlit the candle and changed the writing materials that he was using replacing them with his personal materials. When they were through with their discussions, he again changed all the writing materials bringing back the ones he was using before they arrived. Perplexed, they required explanation of what

[477] Khaleefah, R., Interview granted the Independent Newspaper, cf. www.dailyindependent.ngr.com

[478] Ibid.

he did. He explained that before their arrival, he was drafting proposals for the community with the materials bought for him by the community for his work as their leader. But when they arrived and were to discuss an issue pertaining to him as an individual, he had to use the candle and writing materials he purchased with his own money. And this is exactly why Umar is referred to as the just caliph[479]

This example is simply a masterpiece which I believe will help the social, economic, political and religious well being of Nigerians if our elected leaders could emulate and toe it. It teaches diligent and just administration of personal and public properties. Such a situation is always chaotic and can lead to destruction of lives and hard earned properties. The misappropriation of public funds can be disgusting and can lead to civil unrest if known to the public. A clear demarcation between personal and public properties by the leaders will always do Nigeria a lot of good. Unfortunately, our leaders are busy competing on who will steal the highest amount from the public treasury entrusted to them. If they try to imbibe the spirit of service for which they are elected, surely many unemployed citizens will get job thereby avoid the incessant clashes, religious or political, that bedevil our dear country. He did not stop with the elected officers. For him, Islam is a religion of peace and should be seen as such. Islam brings peace, tranquillity and harmony. You can't possibly call yourself a Moslem when your neighbour is afraid of you. Moslem should be a source of blessing and mercy to human race. Critics may say anything - and correctly so because of what some people calling themselves Muslims do. Violence has no place in Islam. He agreed that the prophet fought wars. However, his wars were only defensive rather than aggressive. Following this claim, it is therefore totally out of Islamic precincts for anybody to pose unnecessary threat to his neighbours or the entire human race. It could only be described as quite puzzling for anybody to wake up one morning and to think that the next and best thing to do is to kill his neighbours. In Islam all humans are one and they are brothers. Muslims are brothers to their fellow Moslems and to anybody at all. It is believed in Islam that those killing fellow human beings have ulterior selfish motives. This attitude is said to negate the teachings of the Qur'an and the Holy Prophet known for his peaceful life style. He pointed out that history is full of instances of people who waged violent wars against the Prophet who in return urged calm and peace, and taught patience. He won millions of souls through his good character. Following this he called on the Moslems to be very careful about what we do or preach. The best attitude to life for the Moslems

[479] Ibid.

should be to follow the teachings of the Holy Book and emulate the Prophet.[480]

As a backing to the above statement, Shehu Usman Muhammad, a research and education officer of the National Mosque Management Board, Abuja and a top Aide of the Imam of the National Mosque, made a more explicit statement outlining reasons why Muslims and Christians should live in peace. His opinion shows the place of honour that Christians enjoy in Islam being followers of Christ, a respectable Prophet in Islam. Abusing or fighting Christians will tantamount to fighting the Prophet, Jesus Christ. He argued,

> You can't be a Muslim except if you believe the whole thing from Adam to the last Prophet including Jesus. That's why it is ignorance for any Muslim to abuse Jesus. You find out that those who don't understand their religion are the ones that will abuse Jesus Christ. If a Christian abuse (sic) Islam and a Muslim abuses Jesus in return, it shows the level of ignorance of the person. If you are a Muslim and you believe in the Qur'an and you open your mouth to abuse Jesus, then you are no more a Muslim and you are not of Islam.[481]

The topic of the article where he took this stand is in itself, offensive- "Peace in Nigeria is dependent on Christians stopping their bias against Islam". It is curled from one of his statements in the course of an interview he granted on 13th June 2010. It is however not my intention here to go into arguments as to who is biased about the other, Christians or Moslems or even Traditional Religionists. Suffice it to say that I am satisfied with the above quotation that can motivate both Christians and Moslems to accept one another as fellow Nigerians and live in peace. This intention was clearly spelt out by Muhammad, S. U. He said,

> There is this general belief against which I want to appeal to everyone in and out of Nigeria that it is better for all of us not to live with hatred and not to live with predetermined intention against anything that has to do with Islam. Whether we like it or not, it is God Almighty that created us, Muslims and non-Muslims, to live together. If He had wished that everybody in Nigeria should be Christian, nobody can change it. If, in the other

---

480 Ibid.

481 Muhammad, S. U., "Peace in Nigeria is dependent on Christians stopping their bias against Islam" cf. www.weekend-sundaycompass.ngr.com

way, He had wished that everybody in Nigeria should be Muslim, nobody can change it. All He just needed to do was say Kum, fayakum (that is, 'be and so it is). So, if He had wished to make all of us idol worshippers, nobody can change it. If then we know this, why the hatred by one religious group against the other? Nigeria is a cosmopolitan society where we have Christians, Muslims and people of other faiths, not to talk of the ethnic groups that exist herein. Therefore it is better for us to learn now to live together because, whether we like it or not, no one can wipe out the other. The Christians can never wipe out the Muslims neither can the Muslims wipe out the Christians in Nigeria. Nobody, mark my word, can do so. Only let us all learn to live together.[482]

In his article, 'Why Nigerians must resist religious sentiments' Muhammad Ajah on 18th May, 2010, in an attempt to show how disgusting the religious disparity in Nigeria has devastated the good wishes of some peace loving Nigerians, submitted the following, "Both Islam and Christianity are not original religion of Nigerians. But as God has made it so, man can better understand and come to Him through a path that He has carefully made for man."[483] In the case of Nigeria, this path that God has made for us is to live in peace where every citizen will feel at home in any part of this country and participate actively in the activities of the region where he or she resides as long as he or she meets all the constitutional requirements. Ajah emphasized, "Let an indigenous Christian in Adamawa, Kaduna or Kebbi live and be given the opportunity to display his God-given talent. In the same way, let an indigenous Muslim in Imo, Rivers or Bayelsa be given the political opportunity to serve in any field of human endeavour even in government house. What prevents an indigenous Muslim from being a Commissioner in Ebonyi, Cross-River or Anambra? What prevents a Muslim from the east from being a Minister or Special Adviser to President? What prevents an indigenous Christian from being a governor or deputy in Bauchi, for instance?"[484] The search for peaceful co-existence will be enhanced if this prayer point of the Sultan of Sokoto, the highest Moslem head in Nigeria, is given a chance both by Christians, Muslims and Adherents of Traditional Religion. It was a statement following some unfortunate and divisive remarks by some disgruntled elements and enemies of progress after Governor Sambo was made the

---

482 Ibid.
483 Ajah, M., Why Nigerians must resist religious sentiments, cf. www.thenigerianvoice.ngr.com
484 Ibid.

vice president. Following this, his deputy, Mr. Patrick Yakowa, who is a Christian, was to take over the mantle of governorship in the State.

Hearing such unfavourable remarks would push any peace loving Nigeria to join Ajah in presenting his prayer points to God. According to him, "I pray for a country where a Christian will be the happiest, most contented man going about his daily life under a Muslim ruler, and vice versa. I also pray that the type of hate-killing going on in Plateau should be totally reversed and all live, love and embrace one another as brothers and sisters created by God."[485] Continuing he called on Nigerians to play politics of inclusion rather than politics of exclusion and sectionalism if our dear country must progress. To achieve that he advised that, "We must all learn to live with our neighbours, whoever the Almighty chooses for us. Then and only then will our country develop and prosper. We must understand ourselves and co-exist peacefully. Nigerians must continue to build on understanding and we should not allow the devil to come between us."[486]

It is of interest that the Moslem youths could open a youth centre in Calabar, which serves as the Second Unity Conference for the South-South, South-East Moslem Ummah and in areas known to be heavily populated by Christians. Declaring open this Youth Development Centre, the vice president, Mohammed Namadi Sambo represented by Dr. Sheik Hanmed Abdala maintained that the reign of religious tolerance among Nigerians will help the nation achieve its place among the comity of nations. He opined that rights and unity when upheld will be a good medium for peace, enabling Nigerians to live and work anywhere in Nigeria. He noted that the efforts of the Cross River State Government in ensuring peace and unity among the people and his good will in providing social amenities for the upliftement of the people is worthy of emulation.[487]

On the same occasion, the Sultan of Sokoto, speaking as a special guest of honour, expressed his conviction that the Community and Youth Development (CYD) will work for everlasting peace in Nigeria, calling for understanding between Christians and Moslems to ensure peaceful co-existence. He went on to plead that nobody should manipulate jobless youths in the name of Religion and stressed that if Muslims and Christians hold fast unto their religious teachings, there will be no riot or conflicts among them.[488] Speaking in Sokoto, at the closing ceremony of the 24th National Quranic

[485] Ibid.
[486] Ibid.
[487] Cf. "Vice President Sambo sues for Peaceful Co-existence" cf. www.crossriverstate.gov.ng
[488] Ibid.

Competition held at the Sultan Maccido Institute of Quranic Studies, the Sultan of Sokoto hammered on the importance of religious tolerance among Muslims and Christians. For him, that is the only way the nation can move forward for better. He further assured all that he will not relent in ensuring peaceful co-existence between the adherents of the two religions. He added: "Religion of Islam is all about peace and we must desist from actions capable of tarnishing its image. We, as leaders, must continue to build mutual understanding and cooperation between the two religious adherents."[489]

Concurring with this stand, the second republic President, Alhaji Shehu Shagari, aware of the fact that Islam hates violence, challenged Moslem Ummah to seek knowledge and better understanding of the Holy Quran.[490] In Abeokuta, Ogun State capital, at the commissioning of the Multi-billion Naira Egba-Agura Central Mosque where he was invited as a guest of honour, Sultan made it clear that, "We cannot truly face the challenges of building a purposeful society without imbibing the ethos of religious harmony and mutual co-existence."[491] After the Jos crises, moved by his desire for peace in Nigeria, the Sultan was on his knees with hands raised above in prayers as he sued for peace. He asked the Almighty to take to account the perpetrators of the crisis and lay bare their nefarious plans and frustrate their designs. He also stressed that the building of unity and understanding also presupposes the breaking down of any artificial barriers
we may erect to cause division[492] As a gesture to show his serious intent on ensuring peace, he saw to it that a Christian Bishop, Archbishop Bishop Josiah Idowu Fearon was invited to present a paper during the national executive council meeting of the Nigerian Supreme Council for Islamic Affairs. The paper titled, 'Islam in the eyes of a Christian' was followed by questions and answers.[493] From June 15-17 2010, the African Union Inter-Faith Dialogue Forum was held in Abuja. The Forum which was the first of its kind offered the Sultan another opportunity to express his burning desire for peace and harmony among the Nigerian citizenry. In an address entitled, 'Sustaining Peace, Security, Religious Harmony through Partnership' he had this to say,

---

[489] Ozoemena, J., "Sultan Preaches religious Tolerance" May 17, 2010,
cf. www.nigeriancompass.ng
[490] Ibid.
[491].Ozoemena, J., "The Sultan: A phenomenon in religious harmony" July 18, 2010,
cf. www.nigeriancompass.ng
[492] Ibid.
[493] Ibid.

It is with profound gratitude to Allah (SWT) that I stand before you today to welcome you most warmly to this august forum and to deliver my remarks. We must, first and foremost, express our deep appreciation to the African Union (AU), and the chairperson of the AU of the African Union Commission, His Excellency Mr. San Ping as well as the African Council of Religious Leaders... for organizing this timely and strategic meeting. The task of advancing Justice, Peace, Security and Development in Africa is a primary responsibility which rests on the shoulders of all stakeholders of the African Union Project. Religious leaders must serve as effective partners to this continental undertaking, to engender religious harmony and tolerance and to work hand-in-hand with other stakeholders for the realisation of its grand objectives. Secondly, as the President General of the Nigerian Supreme Council for Islamic Affairs (NSCIA) and co-chairman of the Nigerian Inter-Religious Council (NIREC), we would like to avail ourselves of this opportunity to register our utmost thanks to both the African Union (AU) and the African Council of Religious Leaders for choosing Abuja, as the venue for this premier AU-Interfaith Dialogue Forum. Nigeria, with a population of about 150million, spread over 200 ethnic groups and professing a variety of religious persuasions, remains a pivotal state on the continent. It is therefore our ardent hope that the holding of this forum in this blessed country would provide you with a unique opportunity to appreciate the successes we have recorded in engendering peace and religious harmony among our diverse people, the challenges we are facing and the giant strides we have made in recent years in addressing these challenges.[494]

The Sultan condemned the attitudes of some leaders who see their posts as a means of sowing the seed of sectarianism, bias and disunity. He maintained that these leaders are happiest when they succeed in sowing seeds of disunity as a sure mean to their political importance. He called on such leaders to toe the path of honour that guarantees selfless and genuine service to the populace. It was therefore worrisome to witness, in some parts of the continent, the brazen exploitation of Religion and the manipulation of religious sentiments, to achieve nefarious goals and interests that are patently injurious to nation-building and regional integration. Many of our major crises begin as ordinary grievances that are badly mismanaged by those in

[494] Abubakar, M. S., "Sustaining Peace, Security Religious Harmony Through Partnership" ; An Address presented to African Union at the 1st African Union Inter-Faith Dialogue Forum held in Abuja, June 15-17, 2010.

authority. It is unfortunate that some of us view leadership as a license to pursue sectional interests and make life a real misery to the rest of the population. Still others would not hesitate to foment hatred and animosity among our diverse religious communities, with the singular objective of causing conflict and remaining as perpetual arbiters of a divided people. Where religious differences are usually super-imposed on visible societal cleavages including those of ethnicity and race, these leaders would use any card at their disposal as long as it created the enabling environment for them to attain power and remain in power. We must begin to view leadership as the greatest responsibility that Allah places on His servants and it is a trust which these servants must guard with all seriousness.[495]

The Sultan reminded the religious leaders of the importance of sincerity and openness in their task of institutionalising peace in their communities. He mentioned in particular the importance of inter-faith dialogue for any Nation or State that wishes to make any meaningful progress. He was of the view that religious leaders must develop an effective framework for the pursuit of inter-faith dialogue and the realization of peaceful co-existence within their communities. Religious leaders must be honest and sincere and be genuinely interested in bringing peace, reconciliation and development to their people. It is equally important to develop effective networks and strong partnerships to withstand the pessimism of some of their colleagues and the attacks of their detractors who work tirelessly to erode the very bases of their collective existence. The religious leaders must, above all, realise that the search for peace and reconciliation is not a peripheral engagement but the commitment of a life-time. Peaceful co-existence amongst Nigerians should not be a matter of chance. It must be a deliberate and concerted policy for which religious leaders must work in effective partnership with political leaders and other stakeholders to ensure its realisation and sustenance.[496]Emphasizing that the promotion of the common values shared by Christians and Muslims and the respect of these values will go a long way in fostering peace and respect between the duo, he concluded that, "...it is the promotion of the common values we share that would bring us ever closer and help us evolve a society where these values are respected. It is also the promotion of these common values which would help us overcome our differences and resolve disputes and misunderstandings within our peoples and between our diverse communities which are bound to arise from time to time".[497] From all that we

[495] Ibid.
[496] Ibid.
[497] Ibid.

have seen in this chapter, it does seem that Islam is against violence. However, the unanswered question is whether the Moslems themselves are faithful to these teachings.

5.3. African Traditional Religion (ATR)

The importance of peace in ATR is undeniable. This reflects in the names the adherents bear or answer. Taking Nigeria as a case study and sampling some common names especially from the south east part of the country will confirm the claim that ATR upholds peace. Such names include: Udokamma (Peace is preferable); Udodi (Peace reigns); Udoamaka (Peace is cheriched); Udoora (Universal peace). These are just a few of them. Peace in ATR is more of action than words. And we know that action speaks louder than words. It is more demonstrated than explained or told. Its empirical nature makes it seen any where it is. Even one's facial expression tells if he has peace within him or is disturbed. Mbiti was of the opinion that Peace action happens in many levels of life including but not restricted to the following: Peace and reconciliation in person-to-person relations, in the family, in the neighbourhood, in the community and among peoples and tribes that may have disputes or fight with one another. Even if death results in the course of this fighting or quarrelling, Peace is not taken for granted. Religion provides for ways of bringing about reconciliation and peace, where and when such fights ensue.[498]

The Yoruba[499]covenant ritual, which covers wide range of human relations and interactions including marriages, agreements, settling of disputes etc, further proves that peace in Africa is better demonstrated. According to Prof. Idowu as quoted by Mbiti,

> In the ethical system of the Yoruba, covenant plays an important role. In fact, the whole of person-to-person, and divinity-to-person, relations have their basis largely in covenants. The covenant between person and person is usually a parity covenant in that it is 'reciprocal – that is, both parties bind themselves to each other by bilateral obligations.' It appears that, originally, the Yoruba made this kind of covenant before the tutelary di-

[498] Mbiti, J. S., "Peace and Reconciliation in African Religion and Christianity" in: *Dialogue and Alliance*, Vol. 7, no.1, Spring/Summer 1993, p. 22.
[499] Yoruba is one of the three major tribes of Nigeria. Others are Hausa and Igbo.

> vinity of the Earth, and hence the generic name for covenants – Imul′e which means literally, 'Drinking the Earth together' or 'Drinking together from the Earth'. The ritual, in general, is as follows: A shallow hole is dug in the ground; water is poured into it, and kola-nut split and cast into the water. Two people who are entering the covenant kneel face to face with the hole in between them. Then one says, 'O Earth...come and preside as we make this covenant: if I should break the covenant, may I be carried away by the Earth (may I disappear from the face of the Earth).' Then he stoops down and sips some water from the hole, at the same time picking up and eating a piece of the cola-nut. The second person does exactly the same and the covenant is thus concluded. But although the generic name for the covenant is thus suggestive of a particular ritual, covenant-making actually takes various forms: it may be done before any of the divinities, but especially before Ogun. Besides these definitely ritualistic forms of covenant-making, it is believed that to be trusted by a friend, to be bosom friends, to eat together, or to be received hospitably as a guest, is to enter into a covenant which involves moral obligations. A covenant between two parties means, negatively, that they must think or do no evil against each other's body or estate, and positively, that they must cooperate in active good deeds towards each other in every way.[500]

The essence of this long quotation is to bring out the importance attached to peace in ATR. Peace rules where there is love. Love in this case means that no one should harbour evil intentions for his or her neighbour. Instead, neighbours should try to outdo the other in charity and goodness.

5.4. Conclusion

It is consoling to find out that peace has place of pride in both Islam and African Traditional Religion. Inasmuch as I do not propose the type of covenant as is enumerated in ATR, it is consoling to find out that the adherents of the two religions (Islam and ATR) can help in moving the nation forward. The result of this chapter makes it clear that these two religions are not as bad as people paint them. However, selfishness and lack of knowledge have led some of their leaders and adherents to misinterpret and misapply their tenets either for political gains or for religious importance. It is my belief that Nigeria will be a wonderful, enviable country if those selfish, misguided groups join hands with every other Nigerian to spread the good news of

[500] Ibid, p. 25.

peace and tolerance. To achieve this, education of the youth is very essential especially to let them reject any political inducement from any quarter in the name of religion.

CHAPTER SIX

AREAS OF COLLABORATION BETWEEN CHRISTIANITY, ISLAM AND AFRICAN TRADITIONAL RELIGION IN A FUTURE NIGERIA

6. Introduction

We have so far seen some of the high and low tension areas between religions in Nigeria. It is therefore my intention here to pose the question as Riße Günter did for Europe. He asked, "How will Christians and Muslims live together in a future Europe?"[501]Taking note of the political, religious and cultural impact of Christianity, Islam and African Traditional Religions in Nigeria, one has no other option than to face the reality by asking oneself, 'Quo Vadis'? How will the adherents of Christianity, Islam and African Traditional Religions live together in a future Nigeria? This question which has become so necessary, if not long overdue, considering the insensitive and animalistic riots that now and then crop up, could be seen in the same light as the one considered by the Vatican II Council Fathers that motivated them to challenge their members to take the lead in peace initiative:

> The Church... urges her sons to enter with prudence and charity into discussion and collaboration with members of other religions. Let Christians, while witnessing to their own faith and way of life, acknowledge, preserve and encourage the spiritual and moral truths found among non-Christians, also their social life and culture.[502]

The above declaration of the Council Fathers could be described in a positive way as an 'unquenchable' fire that has reshaped and continues to purify the thoughts of the universe. Its resonance has continued to be felt right from the time of its declaration till today. It has brought relative peace to suspicious minds. It is my humble opinion that life in a world that knows no peace is not worth living just like it is very true that a country that has no peace is a failed country heading to annihilation. Peace therefore is a necessary and an essential ingredient for emancipation and growth of any nation

---

[501] Riße, G., „Christen und Muslime, Baustelle Europa erschließen und gestalten“ in: Delgado, M. u. Waldenfels, H. (Hg.), *Evangelium und Kultur, Begegnungen und Brüche*, Festschrift für Michael Sievernich SJ, Fribourg, Academic Press, 2010, p. 455.

[502] Nostra Aetate (NA), no. 2.

that is or seems to be on the track to bottomless sea of tribal, political, religious, social and economic irredentism. It is tenable that the colonial masters who mapped out the country (Nigeria) in 1914 made it hardly governable by the way they left Nigeria. As Idowu pointed out,

> The British came and created Protectorates, the Southern and the Northern. These two were fused together for the convenience of our colonial masters in 1914 and the country Nigeria was born! Despite the fact that the territory presently known as Nigeria was occupied by diverse groups and nationalities (and the colonial powers were aware of this fact), no effort was made to encourage the country to become united. The system of government in North, which was based on the Shari'a, was retained for the North. A separate system of government was adopted in the South, without any modifications in either the South or the North. From the outset, therefore, Nigeria had two systems of government with two sets of values, and a rather confused system in the middle of the country where the people were predominantly pagan and subjected to the rule of the District Heads appointed by the Emirs with the Shari'a as their instrument of justice![503]

But we must urgently take our destiny into our hands. It is our common responsibility and challenge. The British came to Nigeria and worked for their good. Nigerians cannot afford to remain everlasting complainants, holding their jaws in the hand bemoaning what the White men did to them whereas Nigerians in the name of different religious groups are now doing worse damage to themselves. Nigerians must now arise and shine and prove the British wrong by working together as one nation with one destiny to give a democratic peace a chance. Failure and inability to do so (after 50 years of Independence) will be a shame to Nigerians. Knowledge of the implication and importance of the cause we are obliged to fight for is necessary for our time.

---

[503] Idowu, F. J., "Religious Conflicts in Nigeria" in: *Current Dialogue*, published by MWI, Band 23, November 30 1992, p. 9.

6.1. Importance of Peaceful Co-existence

Cognizant of the importance of peace in the world, the leaders[504] of thought- religious and political- gather at times to deliberate on the way forward. It is also for the same peace that many peace-loving minds speak out and participate in the fight against terrorism against humanity in any form it is perceived. This is why we have so many regional, national and international organisations being put together in pursuance of peaceful co-existence. This coming together is mostly termed a 'SUMMIT'. Today it is G-8, tomorrow it is UNO and next morrow it is G-12 or G-34. The most essential thing about these summits is that they have the same aim: Peace in the world-*Pacem in Terris,* which has to do with social, political, religious/spiritual and economic wellbeing of man. Such an important summit which was held in Mosco, (Russia) in 2006 was termed 'The world summit of religious leaders'. This summit therefore touches the very topic of this work. In this summit a generally accepted key note was that the preservation of human life as a gift of God is holy duty of all religious and political authorities.[505] It went on to stress that terrorism and extremism of all sorts and also any attempt to give them a religious undertone will be vehemently fought against. The meaning of dialogue will be underlined; in this case it will be understood as referring to dialogue with the unbelievers and with all structures of the civil societies. According to the Summit, since the beginning of the history, religion had played a key role in the development of thoughts, of cultures, of ethics and of the societal order. In today's society, the importance of faith is increasing. For this reason, religion must be a strong foundation for peace and co-operation between different cultures. It is her duty to build a world order which will unite democracy and respect for the moral convictions, the living style, national and religious traditions. In religious questions, no one in any way may be forced against his religious conviction.[506]

When such far reaching decisions were taken in Moscow for peace among religions and States, it becomes all the more urgent for us in Nigeria. The deliberations on the possibility of peaceful co-existence of the three major religions in Nigeria in the future, if not guided by sincere openness

---

[504] Kirkpatrick, E. M. (ed.), Chambers 20th Century Dictionary, W & R Chambers, Edinburg, 1983. This Dictionary described a Leader as one who leads or goes first: a Chief: --- the head of a party, expedition, etc.
[505] „Gipfel der großen Religionen, Schluss Erklärung" Mosco, Russia, 2006.
[506] Ibid.

from the leaders of these religious groups as demanded by the Council Fathers, will not bear the desired fruit. Some attempts have really been made in the past but failed for the lack of openness and sincere commitment. It is on this note that I find the address delivered by Pope John Paul II to the various representatives of the World Conference on Religion and Peace during the 6th World Assembly in Rome on November 3, 1994 very necessary. For him, "...religious leaders must clearly show that they are pledged to the promotion of peace precisely because of their religious belief."[507] This clarion call by the Holy Father is not miles away from the stand of the Document of the 2nd Vatican Council in Nostra Aetate, 3, advising both Muslims and Christians to pursue a common goal that will safeguard and foster social justice, moral values, peace and freedom.[508]

Following this call and the ones before it, some meetings have been undertaken. It would however not be an exaggeration if one says that some of the meetings turned out simply to be for political expediency for one or both of the sides of the purported partners in dialogue. Notwithstanding, in some of the gatherings, far reaching meaningful theological, ethical and spiritual matters were deliberated upon and some soul consoling agreements were reached, if not for the whole communities, at least for the participants. But for such meetings to be fruitful, openness has to be the watch word whereby the participants will be ready to learn some contents of the faith of the other participants. Accordingly, Thomas rightly emphasized,

> What is needed in both Christian and Muslim countries, and most appropriately in academic institutions, are programmes dedicated to this open form of learning. Its ambitiousness lies not in the satisfaction of arriving at a logically persuasive solution to the problem of a plurality of religious traditions, but in the awareness of gradually coming to appreciate why believers hold what they do and why they engage in it. It is a long business, and it is open to misunderstanding on all sides....What is important from the start is that a respectful, agnostic inquisitiveness will help suppress any hasty judgements made by Christians, (ATR) or Muslims

[507] John Paul II, Address delivered during the 6th World Conference on Religion and Peace, Rome, November 3, 1994, in: *L'Osservatore Romano*, weekly English ed. November 16, 1994, p. 2).
[508] Nostra Aetate (NA), no. 3.

against one another, and resist over-simplified criticisms and condemnations of the other.[509]

This view is in tandem with what Arinze said in his discussion about the place of mutual understanding and growth as it affects peace which comes as a result of dialogue. He stressed the importance of Intereligious dialogue which helps each participant to grow in his own faith when he encounters another of a different religious persuasion and confronts his faith with that of the other. Truth is often better reached, further studied, deepened, appreciated, understood and lived when met by other views. Also, such encounters can purify and deepen one's own faith. Apart from the positive value for individuals in dialogue, there is also mutual enrichment between religions in dialogue. In interreligious dialogue, Christianity can contribute to other religious evaluation, inspiration and universality. Christianity has helped some religions to shed some of their unworthy beliefs or practices. Christianity really holds the view and continues to say that God is our Father, and we are all brothers and sisters. We should hold hands together, work together, build our nations together, move forward together. Through dialogue, Christianity also receives contributions from non-Christian religions. These religions bring with them the cultural settings in which they exist. And the Church is happy to receive these gifts of the various peoples and cultures, and moves on to purify, consolidate and elevate them.[510]

From the above citation, it is clear that encounter with people of other faiths make one richer in knowledge and experience. It helps on behave more maturely in accepting opinions of others who that contradict his.

6.2. Call to dialogue and its consequent fears

To achieve this basic aim of understanding every religion on its merit, some common grounds have to be worked out where these religious groups can meet one another and work under the same umbrella. It is a place where a Muslim can speak and the Christians and ATR will listen and vice versa. Since every individual is a dialogical being, able to dialogue not only with

---

[509] Thomas, D., "The Past and Future in Christian-Muslim Relations" in: *Islam and Christian-Muslim Relation*, Thomas, D, et. al. (eds.), CSIC, Birmingham, U.K, Vol. 18, No.1, January 2007, p. 41, (Bracket- mine).

[510] Arinze, F., *Church in Dialogue, Walking with Others*, San Francesco, Ignatius Press, 1990, p. 167. cf. also John Paul II, in: *L'Osservatore Romano*, Italian ed., December 22, 1984.

his God but also with his fellow human beings, efforts should be made to pursue peaceful coexistence through dialogue. In an open letter of invitation to dialogue sent by some learned Islamic scholars to Pope Benedict XVI and respected representatives of the Christian faith in the whole world, with the title, ' a common word between us and you' these Moslems claimed that Mohammed had for a long time directed such a call to Jews and Christians thus, "Speak: O people of the Scripture, come here to a (same) common word between us and you, so that we can serve only Allah and nothing beside him and that no one from us will take the other as Lord outside Allah. And when they have missed their way, they should say: We confess that we have sinned (against him)."[511] In line with what has been the basis for the search for peace among religions, the letter mentioned love of God and neighbor as the moving force behind them.

Many Christian groups reacted differently to this letter. Pope Benedict accepted the letter with joy stressing that the topic tallied with his encyclical, 'God is Love.' He expressed his wish for peace in the world but prophetically stressed that this common word must be made without each group forgetting their basic beliefs. Another group of Christians, under the leadership of Prof. Harold Attridge in University of Yale made their reply. This is a group of radical theologians and some of the evangelical communities. They joyfully accepted the invitation and went extra miles in asking for forgiveness of the offences committed by Christians against their Muslim neighbours, mentioning Crusades and the 'war on Terror' in Islamic countries as examples.[512] Another group by name, 'Barnabas Fund' which is an organization that dedicates itself to the support of all Christians who are suffering in Muslim countries, warned against the acceptance of this letter. For them, this common word is a mild form of Da'wa, being a call on the unbelievers to convert to Islam and to submit oneself to him. Another criticism came from a Muslim from Jordan. For him, the relations between Muslims and Christians have suffered in the past few years through a series of gruesome destructions in New York, Madrid and London where innocent people were killed in the name of Islam. He requested that those who wrote this invitation should explain whether they were done really in the name of Islam or not. If not in the name of Islam, they should clarify it.[513]

---

[511] Beyerhaus, P. J. und Beck, H. W., „Friedliches Miteinander von Christen und Muslimen?“ in: *Kirche heute*, 16Jahrgang, 1/2009, Monatszeitschrift für die katholische Kirche im deutschen Sprachraum. p.19. cf. also Surah, 3:64.

[512] Ibid.

[513] Ibid, p. 19-20.

Because of the length of the letter from the 138 learned Muslims and the wish to understand it better, the International Christian Network set up a committee of Islamic experts to assess the letter taking into account the criticism from the Banarbas Fund group. This group released a far reaching result. For them, the meaning of the word love in Islam is different from its meaning in Christianity. It means submission to the Islamic divinity and the acceptance of Qur'an as well as establishment of Shari'a as the State law. On no account can we as Christians accept such a demand without denying our Lord and Saviour. This call to common word is therefore not a call to peaceful, tolerant living between Muslims and biblical Christians or an expression of a respect for the faith of those who take Jesus as the Son of God and Saviour. They therefore criticized the stand of those of the University of Yale.[514] With this mutual suspicion reigning within Christians and Muslims and of course ATR folks, it becomes ad rem to raise these questions: What actually is dialogue and could one still hope for a successful mutual dialogue?

6.3. Dialogue

On the side of Christians, dialogue means the exercise of meeting people with an outstretched hand of human fellowship and of brotherliness.[515]Dialogue and meeting must be understood as service for peace on the highest level of commitment under the dictation of the Christian duty, so that Muslims in our land could live out their faith accordingly. But the same condition must also be accordingly granted the Christians in countries with Muslim majority without limitation. Dialogue is of course not a one way traffic street. [516] Dialogue is a method through which the Church and the world meet. Since after the encyclical *Ecclesiam Suam*, which Pope Paul VI announced on August 6, 1964, dialogue has become the method for the meeting of the church and the world of today. Three dialogue fields have been made known: the dialogue with the people of good will, even with atheists, above all, with what has to do with man and with what can support peace in the world (ES 36-39). The dialogue with the believers of other religions (ES40), so that with them we support the general needs in the realm of religious freedom, of human brotherliness, of culture, of social wellbeing and the civil order. In the third

---

[514] Ibid, p. 20.
[515] Riße, G., „Islamisch-christlicher Dialog, Aus christlicher Sicht“ in: Eicher, P. (Hg.); Neues Handbuch Theologischer Grundbegriffe, Band 2, München, Kösel-Verlag, 2005,243-250.
[516] Ibid.

field, it has to do with the ecumenical dialogue with the separated christen brethren (ES41).[517]It has to be clearly stated that respect for human dignity and of course the dialogue partner is a sure way for a successful dialogue.

6.3.1. Dialogue and dialogue partners

The above citation gives a clue to who should be our dialogue partners. But to be more direct, the Council Fathers made mention of possible partners in dialogue. The possibility of dialoguing with these partners is as a result of some common beliefs and values they share with the Church. They possess some truths which can enlighten all men. The Council Fathers maintained that even to the present day, there is found among different peoples a certain awareness of a hidden power, which lies behind the course of nature and the events of human life. At times there is present even a recognition of a supreme being, or still more of a Father. This awareness and recognition result in a way of life that is imbued with a deep religious sense. The religions which are found in more advanced civilizations endeavour by way of well-defined concepts and exact language to answer these questions.[518] The declaration went on to mention Hinduism and Buddhism specifically and finally concluded:

> The Catholic Church rejects nothing of what is true and holy in these religions. She has a high regard for the manner of life and conduct, the precepts and doctrines which, although differing in many ways from her own teaching, nevertheless often reflect a ray of that truth which enlightens all men. Yet she proclaims and is in duty bound to proclaim without fail, Christ who is the way, the truth and the life (Jn. 1:6). In him, in whom God reconciled all things to himself (2 Cor. 5:18-19), men find the fullness of their religious life.[519]

Islam is particularly singled out. The Council Fathers stated that Islam has a place of honor among the Christians because of their worship of the one, living and subsistent, merciful God; in order words, because of their monotheistic faith. They pointed out that,

---

[517] Risse, G,. Anwalt in der Begegnung der Religionen. Dokumente und Äußerungen der katholischen Kirche, in: Hauptabteilung Schule/Hochschule des Erzbischöflichen Generalvikariates Köln (Hg.), Das Eigene stärken – Das Andere verstehen. Dokumentation der Pädagogischen Woche 2007, Köln, 2008, 93-107.

[518] Nostra Aetate (NA), no. 2.

[519] Ibid.

> The Church has also a high regard for the Muslims. They worship God, who is one, living and subsistent, merciful and almighty the creator of heaven and earth, who has also spoken to men. They strive to submit themselves without reserve to the hidden decress (sic) of God, just as Abraham submitted himself to God's plan, to whose faith Muslims eagerly link their own. Although not acknowledging him as God, they venerate Jesus as a Prophet, his virgin Mother they also honor, and even at times devoutly invoke. Further, they await the day of judgment and the reward of God following the resurrection of the dead. For this reason, they highly esteem an upright life and worship of God, especially by way of prayer, alms-deeds and fasting.[520]

Lumen Gentium, though talking about those to be saved or those who are to receive divine light said, "Nor shall divine providence deny the assistance necessary for salvation to those who, without any fault of theirs, have not yet arrived at an explicit knowledge of God, and not without grace, strive to lead a good life."[521]Since dialogue could be tempting for those who do not have proper knowledge of their faith, it could lead to one losing his/her own faith. It could also lead to misunderstanding when one engages in it without maturity. It is therefore advisable that only those who are well grounded in their faith could attempt it if a meaningful result is to be achieved. On the part of a Catholic, it has to be born in mind that dialogue should not diminish the seriousness of the task of proclaiming Christ as the undeniable, authentic means of salvation (Jn.14:5-6).[522] It is based on this that Günter Riße, in order to avoid making dialogue a hide and seek game, clarified the caliber of persons that should be involved in a dialogue of this magnitude. He was of the view that, only one who has a mature Christian faith that is based on conviction is qualified for a genuine interreligious dialogue. Only those Christians, who are deeply immersed in the mystery of Christ and are happy in their own religious communities, could enter into Interreligious dialogue without unnecessary risk and with the hope of a positive result.[523] His submission is completely in consonance with the view held by Cardinal Arinze in his comparison between Evangelization and interreligious dialogue. Aware that the advancement in technology has made the meeting of peoples of different cultures and religions a must, he maintained that a catholic who

---

[520] Nostra Aetate (NA), no. 3
[521] Lumen Gentium (LG), no. 16
[522] Jn. 14:5-6.
[523] Riße, G., op.cit. p. 3

should speak for the Church must be one who has enough knowledge of what his Church is all about and is still in union with her. He was of the view that the Catholic who meets people of other religious convictions needs to have a clear Catholic identity. It means that Dialogue is not an apostolate that should be entrusted to problem children in the Church. A country should choose as its ambassador one of its best citizens, not one who contests his country's constitution or who has forgotten the name of the president of his country! It is a mistake for a Christian engaged in interreligious dialogue to try to hide or to set aside for a moment his religious identity. A serious Moslem, Hindu, Buddhist or other dialogue partner does not want to destroy or neutralize us from the religious point of view, as a condition for dialogue. Indeed, if he succeeds, there would be nobody left with whom to dialogue. Arinze testified from his eighteen years experience in the Pontifical Council for Interreligious Dialogue that sincere dialogue partners want to meet their interlocutors as they are. Dialogue, if it is to be fruitful, presupposes sincerity, openness and readiness to give and to receive.[524]

The needed maturity in ones religion becomes all the more desirable when we consider that religion has much to do with cultures. So, for real peace through dialogue, it must be undertaken by those who are well grounded in the culture of their different religions. The place of religion and culture as essential ingredients of peace can never be underestimated. These two are intimately united in the realization of peace on earth. This is born out of the constant movement of peoples in the modern world in search of greener pasture. Unequivocally, this movement has resulted in the creation of multicultural and multi-religious societies. In order that these conglomerated people understand one another and maintain a relatively peaceful co-existence, dialogue becomes the only reasonable, thinkable avenue in such a mixed society as Nigeria.[525] The importance and weight of this appeal is undeniable so much so that Pope Benedict XVI repeated it in the same year while addressing the representatives of Islamic lands and all Christians and Muslims alike. He remarked,

> The interreligious and intercultural dialogue is necessary in order to build up together the world of peace and brotherliness which all people of good

[524] Arinze, F., "Interreligious Dialogue and Evangelization" in: *Pro Dialogue*, Bulletin 127-128, 2008/1-2.

[525] Pontifical Council for Interreligious Dialogue: Resources for Peace In Traditional Religions; Acts of The Colloquium, with Introduction by Denis, C. Isizoh, Rome, January 12-15, 2005, Vatican City 2006, p. 5.

will so much desire. Regarding this, our contemporaries expect from us an eloquent witness in order to show everybody the worth of religious dimension of being. Also Christians and Muslims in faithfulness to the teachings of their very own religious tradition must learn to work together as it has already happened in different common experiences; that is necessary in order to protect oneself from any form of intolerance and oppose any manifestation of force.[526]

This dialogue would be possible if, despite our differences, we recognise the need to respect each other´s conviction. In 1981 Jean Jadot appealed to Moslems during the feast of the breaking of the Fast, thus, "Conscious of our differences, let us work together with mutual respect for each other´s convictions, rejecting the prejudices that are at the source of so many tensions, so that we can build a world of justice and mercy, in which man can give glory to God the Creator." [527] Pope John Paul II calling on the Catholics to dialogue maintained that such dialoguing with Religions has positive effects in expansion. For an effective fruitful dialoguing however, charity should start at home as the Pope told the Church in Africa in his Post-Synodal Exhortation. In this Exhortation the Pope declared that Openness to dialogue is the Christian's attitude inside the community as well as with other believers and with men and women of good will. The real Dialogue should start first of all within the family of the Church at all levels. Suggested levels are: between Bishops, Episcopal Conferences or Hierarchical Assemblies and the Apostolic See, between Conferences or Episcopal Assemblies of the different nations of the same continent and those of other continents. United to Jesus Christ by their witness in Africa, Catholics are invited to develop an ecumenical dialogue with all other baptized brothers and sisters of other Christian denominations, in order that the unity for which Christ prayed may be achieved, and in order that their service to the peoples of the Continent may make the Gospel more credible in the eyes of those who are searching for God.[528]

---

[526] Benedikt XVI., Ansprache an die Botschafter musslimischer Länder und Vertreter von muslimischen Gemeinden in Italien, Saal der Schweizer, Castelgandolfo, September 25, 2006, copyright 2006 –Libreria Editrice Vaticana, in: www.vatican.de.

[527] Pontifical Council for Interreligious Dialogue, in: *MEETING IN FRIENDSHIP, Message to Muslims for the End of Ramadan* 1967-2002, Vatican City, 2003, p. 33.

[528] Post-Synodal Apostolic Exhortation, "Ecclesia in Africa" of the Holy Father J. P. II to the Bishops, Priests and deacons, Men and Women Religious and all the Lay Faithful on the Church in Africa and its Evangelization Mission towards the Year 2000, cf. www.vatican.va.

Such dialogue can be conducted through initiatives such as ecumenical translations of the Bible, theological study of various dimensions of the Christian faith or by bearing common evangelical witness to justice, peace and respect for human dignity. For this purpose care will be taken to set up national and diocesan commissions for ecumenism.[529] He went outside the circle of Christianity to emphasize the need for dialogue with the Muslims thus: "Commitment to dialogue must also embrace all Muslims of good will. Christians cannot forget that many Muslims try to imitate the faith of Abraham and to live the demands of the Decalogue."[530] This Message made it clear that the Living God, Creator of heaven and earth and the Lord of history, is the Father of the one great human family to which we all belong. We should therefore bear witness to this Living God through our respect for the values and religious traditions of each person, working together for human progress and development at all levels. Far from wishing to be the one in whose name a person would kill other people, he requires believers to join together in the service of life in justice and peace.[531] The Pope also gave a very positive consideration to the dialogue with ATR. According to him,

> A serene and prudent dialogue with African Traditional Religion will be able on one hand, to protect Catholics from the negative influences which condition the way of life of many of them and on the other hand, to foster the assimilation of the positive values such as belief in a Supreme Being who is Eternal, Creator, Provident and Just Judge, value which are readily harmonized with the content of the faith. They can even be seen as a preparation for the Gospel, because they contain precious *semina verbi* which can lead, as already happened in the past, a great number of the people open to the fullness of revelation in Jesus Christ through the proclamation of the Gospel.[532]

This Papal call of attention to the necessity of dialogue among these religions should not be seen as being over stressed. With particular reference to Christianity and ATR, Aylward opined that it is more so a divine plan that dialogue should be undertaken. He held that the Dialogue between Christianity and ATR is without doubt God's Ordinance and part of God´s Plan. If it

---

[529] Ibid, (It must be made clear that this particular statement is directed only to relationship with other Christian denominations in the spirit of Ecumenism. But its principles when applied to non-Christians will still serve a good purpose).
[530] Ibid, no. 66.
[531] Ibid.
[532] Ibid, no. 67.

were not, the missionary expansion of Christianity within Africa would not have taken place. The very presence of the Church in Africa demands dialogue for its own health and growth, for the dialogue with ATR may have consequences for the future shape of the Christian Church of which we now have no inkling.[533]

The Catholic Church also regards Moslems as partners in dialogue. However, some Qur'anic texts seem to encourage otherwise. An example is the verse which Ndiokwere cited: "Oh you who believe take not the Jews and Christians for friends. They are friends to one-another, he among you who taketh them for friend is one of them. Believers do not make friends with anyone rather than your own people (Moslems). They deserve nothing but ruin. Their hatred is clear from what they say but violence is the hatred which their breasts conceal."[534] Reflecting on this verse, Ndiokwere wonders if dialoguing with Moslems will ever be meaningful and effective without the other religions submitting to the dictates and beliefs of Islam. Although this call by the Qur'an is not always hearkened to by some serious minded Moslems who actually aspire for and are on the side of peaceful co-existence, some Moslem countries remain glued to it to the extent that members of other non-Islamic religions suffer untold hardships where Moslems are in the majority. They are not allowed to practice their faith in such countries. It was due to such an attitude that Pope John Paul II, himself a champion of peaceful co-existence and dialogue had to cry out,

> I cannot remain silent about the disturbing situation experienced by Christians living in certain countries where Islam is the majority religion. Expressions of their spiritual distress constantly reach me; often deprived of places of worship, made the object of suspicion, prevented from organizing religious education or charitable activities in accordance with their faith, they have the painful feelings of being second-class citizens. I am convinced that the great traditions of Islam, such as welcoming strangers, fidelity in friendship, patience in the face of adversity, the importance given to faith in God are principles which ought to enable unacceptable sectarian attitudes to be overcome.[535]

---

[533] Aylward, S., *African Christian Theology*, London, Geofrey Chapman, 1975, p. 36.

[534] Ndiokwere, N. I., *The African Church Today and Tomorrow, Prospects and Challenges*, Vol.1, Onitsha, Nigeria, Effective Key Publishers Limited, 1994, p. 78. cf. also Surah, 3:118.

[535] John Paul II, Address to the Diplomatic Corps (13 Jan. 1990), in*: L'Osservatore Romano*, Weekly Edition in English, 29th Jan. 1990, p. 3.

He expressed his earnest hope that if Moslem believers nowadays rightly find in countries of Christian tradition the facilities needed for satisfying the demands of their religion, then Christians will similarly be able to benefit from a comparable treatment in all countries of Islamic tradition. Religious freedom should therefore not be limited to simple tolerance. It is a civil and social reality matched by specific right enabling believers and their communities to witness without fear to their faith in God and live out all the demands of that faith.[536]Inasmuch as we have seen some unfavourable statements in Qur'an that seem to militate against dialogue, the following lines in Qur'an are encouraging: "O ye who believe! Obey Allah, and obey the messenger and those of you who are in authority, and if ye have a dispute concerning any matter, refer it to Allah and the messenger if ye are (in truth) believers in Allah and the last Day. That is better and more seemly in the end."[537] I see this as a call not to take laws into ones hands, rather, to sue for peace as it is found in the Christian Bible that God will come in the fullness of time and will pay everyone according to his deeds (Revelation 22:12). One may possibly argue that this phrase, 'O ye who believe!' may be referring to a case where both Moslems are concerned, but the next admonition further clarifies the fear of uncertainty that may be surrounding it, "And revile not those whom they call upon beside Allah, lest they, out of spite, revile in (their) ignorance. Thus, unto every people have we caused their doing seem fair..."[538]

This verse is a reference to the need for the religions to respect each other. Interaction is necessary if this call to respect must be achieved. For Abdu- Raheem, "It is in this light that one looks forward to a time when seminars, symposia, public lectures and workshops will be organised to provide avenues for the various religious groups to discuss matters affecting them individually and collectively. It is by so doing that they will move closer to each other and learn to accommodate one another."[539] This stand as a way of finding peace is welcomed even in ATR. It is the view of the Catholic Church that,

> The traditional African is adept at negotiation. No dispute or rancour is so ingrained that talking and arriving at a compromise cannot settle it. This

[536] Ibid.
[537] Abdu-Raheem, M. A., "Islamic Concept of Tolerance and the Task before the Nigerian Muslim" in: *Religion and Peace in Multi-faith Nigeri*a, (ed.) J. K. Olupona, Nigeria, Obafemi Awolowo University, 1992, p. 79. cf. also, 4, 59.
[538] Surah, 6:108.
[539] Abdu-Raheem, op. cit. p. 79-80.

> seems to be an imperative given the inevitability of conflict. But its imperative tone underlines the fact that no matter how deep a conflict is; the natural state of existence should be a peaceful one...There is more wickedness in refusing to reconcile than in fighting. In negotiating the focal points of quarrel is brought to light and effort is made to douse the situation of conflict by give and take. It is as though the cake that people are struggling over is split so that each person takes a part.[540]

If the Catholic Church appreciates the fact that the traditional African who is an adherent of ATR is adept in negotiation, it becomes essential to engage this traditional African in dialogue. Who knows why ATR has refused to die despite all negative attacks on it. The extent of attraction that ATR has for the present day African man, even those in the Church need to be addressed. Udobata stressed that despite the tremendous influence of the impact of Christianity, public morality and sense of responsibility in public and private establishments have not equally matched the external profession of faith. The death of the traditional religion does not seem to be in sight, despite the previous iconoclastic attack on it by some missionaries and colonial government officials. Many who belong to one Church or the other secretly and even openly patronize the traditional religion. The religious situation therefore, is acephalous. Specifically he said that a century and half years after planting Christianity, we are still battling with one form of idolatry or the other in the Churches. Some prominent Church members still patronize the oracles, diviners and medicine men in times of stress and need. Some belong to secret cults and seek power and protection through other means.[541] This situation is enough reason to enter into dialogue in the spirit of Inculturation. Dopamu, P. Ade spoke here glowingly in favour of ATR which he thinks is peaceful in approach and may be the reason for the recent fleet of Christians and Muslims back to it. He argued,

> The relations between Afrel and other religions are not basically competitive, for competition brings division. The traditional religion does not attempt to convert the whole world to its own view of ultimate reality, though it welcomes all who seek solace, security, protection and spiritual satisfaction under its umbrella. In this regard, Afrel is self-contained. It

---

[540] Pontifical Council for Interr dialogue: With Introduction by Isizoh Denis. p. 86-87.

[541] Udobata R. O., "Encounter of Christianity with African Religiosity: A Critical Review of Evidence from Eastern Nigeria" in: *Journal of Religion and Theology*, Vol. 1, No.1, Owerri-Nigeria, Omega Communications, 1993, p. 34

> does not borrow anything from Islam and Christianity in order to function and minister to the business of daily living. But it regards Christianity and Islam as counterparts with some similarities so far as considerations such as those regarding belief in the Supreme Being, moral values, life after death, and human relationships, are concerned...it does not provoke other religions through derogatory utterances, particularistic slogans and extirpative tendencies, which are characteristic of other religions. Provocation breads intolerance, and intolerance nurtures division to maturity.[542]

Are the Christians and Muslims really not self-contented? This accusation is so weighty that the two religions of the Book' have to go back to the drawing board and engage the African traditional religion in dialogue for effective relationship. Since ATR is dialogue ready, the basic term here will be finding a way most suited for inculturation. For Onunwa Udobata,

> The new task ahead in the first instance is how to 'reconvert' those in the Church who are encapsulated already in a society that is tremendously going materialistic and second, the outreach to win more souls for Christ. Furthermore, the theological and hermeneutical problems raised by converts to Christianity through objections to certain religious principles and rules like polygamy, witchcraft, evil spirit, demon possession, charms, etc. need to be tackled in a most meaningful and relevant way to the African world view. This is the main soul of inculturation and contextualization in theology. African values should be re-examined in the light of their meaning, persistence and function.[543]

Udobata saw the need not to destroy ATR as was done by the early Missionaries. For him, it would be better to adapt the content of ATR since it has soaked the life and attitude of the Africans. He mentioned Bishop Shanahan as one who saw the need for dialogue with ATR and called for its transformation rather than destruction. He said, "Bishop J. Shanahan who understood that the traditional religion defined and underpinned all facets of experience and life did not hesitate to state that what the traditional religion needs was transformation not destruction."[544] To achieve this, the Nigerian or African

---

[542] Dopamu, P. A., "Religious Tolerance & Peaceful Co-existence: The case of African Religion in Nigeria" in: James, G., (ed.), *Dialogue & Alliance,* A Journal of the International Religious Foundation, Inc, winter 1988-89, Vol. 2, No.4, p. 61-62.
[543] Udobata, R. O., op.cit. p. 39.
[544] Ibid.

Church should try through her indigenous theologians to adapt the message of Christ to the cultures it met. For Udobata,

> The task of committed indigenous West African theologians and Church men would be to seek new ways of making "African Conversion" to Christianity real, meaningful, functional, contextual and purposeful. This could be done first by understanding the traditional world view which is responsible for the people's perception of the universe. With a clearer understanding, the biblical teaching can be made relevant to the people. The Bible is not an abstract philosophy but a living Word of God which must be relevant to people's cosmological perception. Often the problem is that some of the theologians are intellectually sound but "spiritually" weak and cannot effect any change on the life of the people. Some honest Christians are on the other hand, weak in theology. The Igbo explain the problem with an adage of regret – 'Mma nwere isi adighi nko, nke di nko enweghi isi.[545]

Insofar as some part of the assertion by Dopamu may be true, we should not take it hook, line and sinker. It is however important to note from all the assertions and counter assertions by individuals either defending their religion or castigating that of the other, that we have basically established the need and how important it is for us to follow the path of dialogue. Believe it or leave it, from the discussion so far, and without sounding pessimistic, it needs to be stated that the three major religions have come to stay. As each continues to claim uniqueness and orthodoxy, they need to learn to accept each other so as to co-exist peacefully. Peaceful co-existence between the three religions, achievable through dialogue, will contribute seriously, as said before, to overall peace in Nigeria.

6.3.2. The Decalogue and Dialogue

The need for dialogue has gone so far that the Catholic Church has taken it to what I may call the 'next level'. It is a level of concretisation. It was with unbiased confirmation that Pope Benedict XVI in Rome in November 2008 drummed it into the ears of the Catholic and Muslim audience that the love of God and of neighbour is the heart of Islam and Christianity and that they should therefore make it their duty to engage themselves in their interreligious meeting on what will be for the enthronement of human dignity and

[545] Ibid.

human rights.[546]The simple act of calling the Muslims and Catholics alone to such discussion forum speaks volumes. Surely at the end of the discussion they made their commitment to the protection of the minority in the areas where a particular religion is in the majority. This decision stems from the call made by the Pope pointing to the need for the recognition of human dignity. All are supposed to work together in the support of authentic respect for the dignity of human person and the human rights, not minding the differences in theologies and in anthropological points of view. There are numerous areas where Islam and Christianity could work together in support of the moral values which are part of our common heritage. Only when we try to recognise the central status of the human person and the dignity of every man, to respect and defend life (which is for Christians and Moslems God's gift and therefore holy) can we find a common ground for the building up of a brotherly world, in which disturbances and differences will be peacefully avoided and the destructive power of ideologies neutralised.[547]

Since this was the first meeting of this kind, Cardinal Tauran was appointed to coordinate such forum meetings in the future. The Pope expressed his wish for the next step to lead to a possible attempt in harmonising the Ten Commandments with their near possible Islamic interpretation in the texts in Qur'an which could serve as a basis to form a common foundation. Qur'an contains texts which have some similarities with the Ten Commandment.[548] Although there are some similarities, they may be very different in application. It is for this reason that Prof. Riße Günter took the challenge to undertake descriptively a work that will lay the foundation for this project. Surely the basic intention here is to find points of discussion in the future meeting of the two religions. I will therefore consider some of the texts put forward with reference to the book of Exodus and the Surahs, 7, 6 and 17.

6.3.3. The Ten Commandments in Qur'an

The Exodus of the Israelites through the sea was mentioned in Surah 7, 138: "And we brought the Children of Israel across the sea." This act of delivering the Israelites from Pharaoh is too consequential. Its consequence was the opportunity created for Moses to meet God on the mountain where the tablet was given. Surah 7,142-154 as compiled and ordered by Günter

[546] Riße, G., „In ihrer Niederschrift ist Führung und Barmherzigkeit" ...(Sure 7, 154)- Spurensuche: Die „Zehn Gebote" Gottes im Koran. p. 1.
[547] Ibid.
[548] Ibid.

Riße gives the account of events that followed the bringing of the Children of Israel across the sea.[549]
(142) "And when We did appoint for Moses thirty nights, and added to them ten, and he completed the whole time appointed by his Lord of forty nights; and Moses said unto his brother Aaron: "Take my place among the people. Do right, and follow not the way of mischief-makers!"
(143) And when Moses came to Our appointment and his Lord spoken unto him, he said: "My Lord! Show me Thyself, that I may gaze upon Thee!" He said: Thou wilt not see Me, but gaze upon the mountain! If it stand still in its place, then thou wilt see me. "And when his Lord revealed (His) glory to the mountain He sent it crashing down And Moses fell down senseless. And when he woke he said: Glory unto Thee! I turn unto Thee repentant, and I am the first of (true) believers."
(144) He said: "O Moses! I have preferred thee above mankind by My messages and by My speaking (unto thee). So hold that which I have given thee, and be among the thankful!"
(145) And We wrote for him, upon the tablets, the lesson to be drawn from all things and the explanation of all things, then (bade him): "Hold it fast; and command thy people (saying): Take the better (course made clear) therein. I shall show thee the abode of evil-livers."("). As Moses was with the Lord, the Qur'an went on in Surah 7, 148 to describe how the Israelites used their "ornaments to make a calf" for themselves. And it happened how it was supposed to have happened:
(Surah 7, 150) And when Moses returned unto his people, angry and grieved, he said: "Evil is that (course) which ye took after I had left you. Would ye hasten on the judgement of your Lord? And he cast down the tablets..."
(Surah 7, 154) Then, when the "anger of Moses abated, he took up the tablets, and in their inscription there was guidance and mercy for all those who fear their Lord."
What we have tried to establish in Surah 7 is the confirmation that Moses actually met the Lord on the mountain where he received the tablets coupled with the behaviour of the Israelites as Moses was on the mountain with the Lord. It did not tell us what were written on the tablet. The contents of the tablet were made known in Surah 6, 151-153 and Surah17, 22-39. A simple but critical look at the two would reveal that Surah 17 had more information than Surah 6. It is on this ground that Surah 6 is regarded as most recent resume of Surah 17.[550]After all is said and done, it is not my wish here to put

[549] Ibid, p. 2.
[550] Ibid.

down the whole content of the two Surahs. Suffice it here to give a rough arrangement of Surahs 6 and 17 in comparison with the Book of Exodus as given in The New Jerusalem Bible.
Exodus 20: 2-17: I am Jahweh, your God who brought you out of Egypt, where you lived as slaves.

1. You shall have no other gods to rival me
2. You shall not misuse the name of Yahweh your God
3. Remember the Sabbath day and keep it holy
4. Honour your father and your mother
5. You shall not kill
6. You shall not commit adultery
7. You shall not steal
8. You shall not give false evidence against your neighbour
9. You shall not set your heart on your neighbour's spouse
10. You shall not set your heart on your neighbour's possessions.[551]

Surah 17, 22-39: We gave unto Moses the Scripture, and We appointed it a guidance for the Children of Israel..." (17, 2).

1. Set not up with Allah any other god...
2. The Lord had decreed...that you show kindness to parents
3. Squander not (thy wealth) in wantonness...
4. Slay not your children, fearing a fall of poverty
5. And come not near unto adultery
6. And slay not the life which Allah hath forbidden...
7. Come not near the wealth of the orphan...
8. Fill the measure when ye measure, and weigh with the right balance
9. Follow not that whereof thou hast no knowledge!
10. And walk not in the earth exultant...

Surah 6, 151-153: "Say: Come, I will recite unto you that which your Lord hath made a sacred duty for you:

1. That ye ascribe nothing as partner unto Him
2. That ye do good to parents

---

[551] Ibid, p. 4, For English translation, cf. The New Jerusalem Bible, Standard Edition, London, Darton, Longman & Todd Ltd, 1985.

3. That ye slay not your children
4. That ye draw not nigh to lewd things whether open or concealed
5. That ye slay not the life which the Allah hath made sacred
6. And approach not the wealth of the orphan
7. Give full measure and full weight in justice
8. And if ye give your word, do justice thereunto
9. And fulfil the covenant of Allah
10. That ye happily may remember."[552]

Having seen the arrangement, it becomes clearer that these texts contain similar messages and rules of life but their numerical arrangements differ. However what is important here is that we have been able to establish, following the example of Riße Günter, that the Decalogue could possibly provide a common area and basis for dialogue. In the light of all these attempts and successes on the global field, suffice it here to ask how far the issue of dialogue has been taken seriously in Nigeria and what it has contributed towards peaceful co-existence among the citizenry.

6.4. Dialogues between Religions in Nigeria and their Successes

6.4.1. Nigerian Association for the Study of Religions (NASR)

Several attempts have been made to settle conflicts in Nigeria. According to Udobata, "The first major attempt for a real inter-faith encounter was the formation in 1975 of the Nigerian Association for the Study of Religions. This organization encourages academic study and teaching of religions, and provides a unique forum for frank and meaningful dialogue on interreligious issues for mutual understanding and cooperation among Christians in particular, and humanity in general."[553] This was a good step as the group dedicated itself to the good of the nation with the intention of constructively bringing about peace. Udobata further explained that,

> For the purpose of achieving these objectives, the Association organizes annual conferences and publishes books and journals. The...book of the Association published in 1984 is Religion, Peace and Unity in Nigeria...The book examined the various factors that led to religious intoler-

[552] Ibid, p. 4, For English translation, cf. The Glorious Qur'an, Text and Explanatory Translation by Muhammad M. Pickthall, Islamic Publications Bureau, Lagos, Abuja et. al.
[553] Udobata, R. O., op.cit. p. 60.

ance and crises in Nigeria, the means of averting tensions and fostering unity. Speaking from the perspectives of the three principal religions practiced in Nigeria, the contributors feel that it is necessary to emphasize those things that can bring us together rather than those that divide us.[554]

Another attempt that was made before NASR functioned, not as an association but, only on the pages of paper. It was in 1974 when a journal captioned, 'Nigerian Dialogue,' that devoted itself to the issues of relations between Christians and non-Christian religions, was created. University of Nigeria Nsukka happened to be the birthplace of the journal that could not be transformed into an Association.[555] In 1978, another attempt was made within the four walls of University of Ilorin by the Department of Religions. It was an indirect effort made by organizing a seminar with every hope that it was ripe for religious leaders and adherents in Nigeria to come together in the open and speak unanimously against the ills of the society. At least, the seminar put something on record. According to Udobata, "The Seminar holds the view that considering the natural admixture of religious faiths within individual families which, nevertheless, live happily together in the country, Nigeria is in a very good position to offer to the world at large laudable religious tolerance which is so much universally lacking today. It is, therefore, recommended that Nigerians, both the government and the public, should utilize this golden opportunity to the benefit of the world."[556]

After all these have failed, we now turn our attention to an Association that seems to have stood the taste of time and is making inroads into the lives of Nigerians- religious, political economic and otherwise. The association is named 'Nigeria Inter-Religious Council.'

6.4.2. Nigeria Inter-Religious Council (NIREC)

It is comprised of 50 Nigerians made up of 25 Christians and 25 Muslims. It is a voluntary organization that concerns itself with peace among the two major religions in Nigeria. This Council is not financially dependent on the government for its operations and activities. It is however open to any wilful donation from the government. As reported on its website,

[554] Ibid, p. 61.
[555] Ibid.
[556] Ibid.

> The establishment of NIREC as a Council was occasioned by the incessant ethno-religious crises which punctuated the socio-political landscape of Nigeria as a Country. NIREC, also known as the Council, is a permanent and an independent body established to provide religious leaders and traditional rulers with a variable forum to promote greater interaction and understanding among the leadership and their followers as well as lay foundations for sustainable peace and religious harmony in Nigeria...(was) Supported and encouraged by President Olusegun Obasanjo, who saw the body as a wonderful project emanating from the leadership of both major faiths...[557]

The formation of this association has been hotly contested. Some claimed that it was formed by the government of President Obasanjo. But the citations from the association itself clearly put the record right as it stated that,

> The representatives of the two principal religions in Nigeria, Christianity and Islam, voluntarily decided by themselves, in a joint meeting to form an association on the 11th day of September 1999. The association was inaugurated on the 29th day of September, 1999 and herein after referred to as NIREC. The association passionately conscious of the respective divine revelations and the dictates of THE CREATOR, determined within the content of the two religions, to forge inter-religious harmony and concern, having firmly and solemnly resolved within the confines of the Constitution of the Federal Republic of Nigeria, to live in unity, harmony and peace, for the welfare, security and prosperity of the people of the nation.[558]

My effort in 2009 to know more about NIREC led me to the venue of their meeting that lasted from 16th-18th August. After the meeting, my effort to meet the Secretary met brick walls. Fortunately I was granted audience by the Co-chairman of the Association, His Grace Archbishop J Onaiyekan who had time to answer my questions, throwing more lights on their functions and objectives as given in their website. For the purpose of this dissertation, I hereby outline some of the objectives and success story of the association.

---

557 NIREC, "History of NIREC" cf. http://nirecng.org/history.html

558 Nigeria Inter-religious Council, 3rd quarter general meeting in Port Harcourt, Rivers State, South-South zone on August 16th – 18th, 2009, p. 10

6.4.2.1. Objectives and Functions of NIREC

Among others, NIREC has the following as its objectives and functions:

> To honestly and sincerely endeavour by themselves and through them, their followership, to understand the true teachings of the two religions-Christianity and Islam – including their peculiarities and personal mannerisms through dialogue, discussions, work-shops, seminars, conferences, pamphleteering -etc.
> To create a permanent and sustainable channel of communication and interaction thereby promoting dialogue between Christians and Muslims in Nigeria so that the members of both faiths may have mutual understanding of each other's religious position, co-existence among all the people of Nigeria irrespective of their religious or ethnic affiliations.
> To promote and include moral. Ethical (sic), social and cultural values of the two faiths for the rebirth and rebuilding of a better society.
> To provide a forum for mutual co-operation and promotion of the welfare of all citizens in the nation;
> To create for and channels for the peaceful resolution of any friction or misunderstanding that may arise from time to time.
> To serve as an avenue for articulating cordial relationship amongst the various religious groups and between them and the government;
> To assist the Federal, State, and Local Governments of Nigeria and the Populace by emphasizing and accentuating the positive roles religion should play in nation building and development;
> To serve as a forum to achieve national goals, economic growth, national unity and promotion of political stability;
> To consider and make recommendations to the Federal and other levels of Government on matters that may assist in fostering integral and spiritual development of Nigerians;
> To make recommendations on such other matters as the Federal and other levels of Government may from time to time refer to the Council.
> To network with organizations of similar aims at home and internationally for the furtherance of the objectives of the Council.[559]

The Association has actually done much and is still doing more. Their meetings which normally held in Abuja is now being rotated within the six geo-political zones of Nigeria. With this new trend, they intend to create

[559] Ibid.

awareness and make other people feel their existence. They listed their achievements with little explanations to include among others[560]:

(i) Intervention during Religious crises- The Co-Chairmen of NIREC on December 2007 had to visit a scene of religious crisis in Bauchi State of Nigeria to address adherents of both faiths on the essence of religious tolerance and peaceful coexistence. They were able by their visit to reinstall sanity and order in the community. This act has been unprecedented in the history of religious crisis in Nigeria...
(ii) A new dawn in Christians/Muslims Relations- In Shendam, Plateau State, a Reverend Father, on noticing that a mosque was to be torched by some hoodlums risked his life to stop the arsonists during which the attackers inflicted matched cuts on him. Also in a similar gesture, a group of Muslims, on noticing that a church building was on fire rushed there to stop the fire out break before the Christian community got to the scene.
(iii) Public lectures and Communiqués at zonal meetings- Addresses of the Cochairmen (sic), paper presentations and communiqués released at the end of every zonal meetings of the Council have always contained messages that provide answers to religious questions in Nigeria. Most Nigerians have found better understanding and guidance on religious tolerance and peaceful coexistence courtesy of these lectures and seminars.
(iv) Forum for Communication and Dialogue- NIREC has created a permanent and sustainable channel of communication and interaction between Christians and Muslims in Nigeria today for mutual understanding of each other's religious position and co-existence among Nigerians, irrespective of their religious or ethnic affiliations.
(v) Nigerian Youth Summit- NIREC organized a summit in Minna, Niger State Capital where 250 Muslims and Christians (sic) youths all over Nigeria participated. This great and unprecedented event was prepared with a view to fostering better understanding among them.
(vi) Call for Equity and Fairness- The Co-chairman of NIREC, the Sultan of Sokoto, on hearing that Nigerian government funded some Islamic projects in the North of the country without (sic) iota of any biasness (sic) encouraged and supported the leadership of Christianity to balance the issue by requesting for the same sum of money from the federal govern-

[560] Ibid.

ment for execution of Christian projects as well. Situations of this nature can only be made possible through NIREC.
(vii) Implementation of Inter-faith Projects- NIREC has gone beyond conflict resolution to corporate ventures on issues that are of common interest to both religions. Recently, NIREC inaugurated Nigeria Interfaith Action Association against Malaria (NIFAAM) in Abuja to rid Nigeria of mosquitoes. Similarly, the Council supports and participates in campaigns against HIV Aids.

I still deem it necessary to present some of their recent Communiqués and resolutions issued after their plenary meetings. The contents of these Communiqués, I believe, will go a long way in providing an insight into this Association's love for the citizens of this nation and her efforts to help build a nation where peace and harmony will reign among the populace, religion or ethnicity notwithstanding.

6.4.2.2. NIREC'S Contributions towards Peace

In 2008 in Enugu, NIREC after a meeting resolved in a communiqué to:

1. "Sustain and step-up efforts of the leadership of the Council aimed at reducing inter-religious tensions; fostering and promoting inter-religious cooperation for the common good of the people of Nigeria;
2. Admonish all religious leaders to jointly champion the cause of truth, honesty, accountability, fear of God and justice and ensure that our followers in all walks of life embody these virtues and put them into practice;
3. Call on the Federal Government to strengthen and vigorously pursue its anti-corruption campaign in various sectors;
4. Call on Governments at all levels to invest more in education and the proper upbringing of children and promotion of moral rejuvenation through religious education;
5. Urge the Government to create enabling environment in order to check the high rate of youth restiveness and to protect lives and property;
7. Call for the establishment of NIREC Clubs that will promote interaction and co-operation between Christians and Muslims at the Secondary Schools and tertiary institutions in Nigeria as a way of promoting and entrenching religious understanding and mutual respect;
8. Note the plight of Nigerian Pensioners and call on Federal and State Governments to urgently address the matter;

9. Note the efforts being made through the National Assembly to discourage indecent dressing in Nigeria;
10. Commend the Federal Government for establishing the Electoral Reform Panel as this would assist in identifying the flaws in the electoral process and the Council resolved to send a memorandum to the committee..."[561]

Also in 2008, NIREC aware that peace is a process of ensuring and sustaining justice, fairness and equity in any given society, did not hold back their support for peace and security which are bedrocks of development in any country, Nigeria inclusive. Noting that the sources of conflicts are multidimensional and mostly socio-economic and political in nature, the meeting condemned the elites who surely get involved in inciting and fomenting social unrest aimed at achieving political and their selfish goals. Their resolutions are, to:

1. "Call on Government at various levels to grant compensation to victims of religious disturbances to enable them mitigate the effects of human and material losses caused by unwholesome activities of a few misguided elements.
2. Caution reckless religious preachers who conduct inciting sermons without regard to the feelings of others and therefore fan the embers of religious misunderstanding and disturbances.
3. Urge adherents of the two religions to adopt dialogue as an effective means of promoting understanding and peaceful co existence among the people.
4. Affirm our commitment to the pursuance of practical actions towards the resolutions of conflicts arising from interactions of peoples in a multi ethnic religious society so that the impact of the Council would be felt by all.
5. Call on Governments, groups and all Nigerians, particularly the faith-based Organisations to build a systematic platform for peace and religious harmony in Nigeria through the promotion of socio-economic justice, transparency and good governance.
6. Call on the media to abide by the ethics of their profession which promotes social responsibility and demands factual and accurate reporting of events.

[561] NIREC, Communiqué by NIREC at its 1st Quarter Meeting held at Protea Hotel, Enugu, February 17th-20th, 2008.

7. Urge Nigerians living in various parts of the country to be sensitive to the culture and religion of the people of the host community as a step to ensuring peaceful co existence.
8. Call for moral conversion of Muslims and Christians and urge them to tackle the pervasive corruption in the country by taking their religious values seriously and living by them.
9. Call on faith-based Organisations to educate their members on the tenets and injunctions of their religion...."[562]

In her meeting of 2009 in Jos, the Council resolved to:

1. "Use religion as an instrument for social harmony, growth and recipe for a stronger and united Nigeria.
2. Be totally committed to the cause of promoting peace, justice and fair play without fear or favour.
3. Call on Governments at all levels to carry out specific activities aimed at promoting peace in their domains.
4. Urge the Federal and State Governments of Nigeria to create and sustain the requisite environment for the actualization of the fundamental rights of all Nigerians to live, work and practice their trade or profession in any part of Nigeria without the fear of any molestation or expulsion without the due process of law...."[563] I have left many of the resolutions of the 2009 meeting since they are just a repetition of the past resolutions. The Association, NIREC has given us wonderful tips in their different communiqués, but the problem is that many people are illiterate and cannot understand the importance of these communiqués or may never even hear of or read them. In a situation like this educating the unlettered becomes very essential and surely the only option. Taking cognisance of the fact that the poor masses that are usually used by the politicians to inflame the embers of disunity are illiterates and cannot read, the leaders of the different religions should be made to use these Communiqué on a particular Sunday or Prayer day as their homily. In this case, the meeting should pick a Week in the month within which all religions should read out the communiqué in all their places of worship.

[562] NIREC, Communiqué after its Quarterly Meeting held at Murtala Muhammed Library, Kano City, November 13th, 2008.
[563] NIREC, Communiqué after its 1st Quarterly Meeting held at the Conference Hall Station Hotel, Jos, Plateau State, May 18th-20th, 2009.

6.5. Healing of the Past (Reconciliations) for Peace

If Nigeria must experience peace, the warring attitude of the religious groups in an attempt to convert the adherents of the other religious group needs to be discouraged. Terminating the acrimonious relationship may not be enough. It deserves a visible sign not to fall back to a situation that will antagonize others. It needs open confession and apology to one another. None of the three largest religious groups in Nigeria should claim to have not offended anyone. The three religions have inclinations to war. As Mbon remarked,

> Those familiar with ... Islam, and Christianity know that despite their preaching of peace, much of their history has often been marred by periods of war. In African Traditional Religions, too, gods of war are galore. For instance, the Yoruba of Nigeria have Ogun as their god of war who possesses all iron and steel, materials from which instruments of war and destruction can be made. Other African ethnic localities also have their own gods and goddesses of war and peace.[564]

This is enough reason for every religion in Nigeria to make an examination of conscience for the sake of peace which guarantees happy and long life. This is in line with Traditional African world view which sees peace as fundamental for happy and fulfilled life, and in a special way, for general progress in the human society. The quest for this peace makes reconciliation and forgiveness necessary. There is a realization that if peace is to reign, human beings must engage one another in mutual attempt to make peace a reality. Forgiveness and reconciliation is viewed not only as beneficial to one party in a dispute, but to all concerned, and in fact to the whole community. The Yoruba say that if we do not forget yesterday's quarrels, we will not have somebody to play with tomorrow (Ti a ka ba gbage oro). It means that forbearance is an element in the effort towards peace. One may not insist on all his points if he is to gain peaceful relationship with his neighbours. The Igbo of Nigeria say that malu ghalu bu uto (knowing and forbearing is the meaning of friendship).[565]

---

[564] Mbon, F. M., "Possibilities for Peace in a Multi-Faith World" in: *Dialogue &Alliance* (Phan, P. C, ed.): A Journal of the International Religious Foundation, Spring/Summer 1993, Vol.7-No.1 p.6.

[565] Pontifical Council for Interreligious Dialogue, with Introd. by Isizoh, D., p. 585-86.

It is with the above sayings and citations that one will see the wisdom in what His Holiness, Pope John Paul II did in Assisi on March 12, 2000. He prayed all the Religions for forgiveness, apologising for the mistakes of the Catholic Church. The apology rendered by the Pope, as reported by the International Theological Commission, was very exemplary. He called on all the world religious groups to go back to their memory lane and search out their mistakes and then apologise. As a good commander of a battalion, he did not just sit down to marshal the order but he himself gave an example of what he expected others to do. He did this in the spirit of Our Lord Jesus Christ who washed the feet of his disciples, thereby setting them an example. He pleaded:

> As the successor of Peter, I ask that in this year of mercy, the Church, strong in the holiness which she receives from her Lord, should kneel before God and implore forgiveness for the past and present sins of her sons and daughters... Today, the First Sunday of Lent, seemed to me the right occasion for the Church, gathered spiritually around the Successor of Peter, to implore divine forgiveness for the sins of all believers. Let us forgive and ask forgiveness![566]

Emphasizing that this *Mea culpa* should not be undertaken with a hope of a reward from anybody but with a sincere heart ready to begin anew, the Pope said, "Let them do so without seeking anything in return, but strengthened only by 'the love of God which has been poured into our hearts' (Rom 5:5)."[567] The reason why the Pope undertook this line of action is not far-fetched. He explained that this Church, which embraces her sons and daughters of the past and of the present, in a real and profound communion, is the sole mother of grace who takes upon herself also the weight of past faults in order to purify memory and to live the renewal of heart and life according to the will of the Lord. The Church is able to do this insofar as Christ Jesus, whose Mystical Body extended through history she is, has taken upon himself once and for all the sins of the world.[568] It was on record that this single act of the Pope gave the search for peace in the world a new direction and meaning. In line with this assertion, the Theological Commission appealed to

---

[566] International Theological Commission: *Memory and Reconciliation: The Church and the Faults of the Past*, Dec. 1999 and Homily of John Paul II Mass for the Day of Pardon, March 12, 2000, Pauline Books &Media, Boston, 2000, p. 84-85, cf. Incarnationis Mysterium, 11

[567] Ibid, p. 11.

[568] Ibid, p. 13.

history and maintained that there have been no precedents in the entire history of the Church for requests for forgiveness by the Magisterium for past wrongs. Councils and papal decrees applied sanctions, to be sure, to abuses of which clerics and laymen were found guilty, and many pastors sincerely strove to correct them. However, the occasions when ecclesiastical authorities (Pope, bishops, or councils) have openly acknowledged the faults or abuses which they themselves were guilty of, have been quite rare. One famous example is furnished by the reforming Pope Adrian VI who acknowledged publicly in a message to the Diet of Nurremberg of November 25, 1522, the abominations, the abuses and the lies of which the Roman court of his time was guilty, deep-rooted and extensive sickness, extending from the top to the members. He, Adrian VI deplored the faults of his times, precisely those of his immediate predecessor Leo X and his curia, without, however, adding a request for pardon. It will be necessary to wait until Paul VI to find a Pope express a request for pardon addressed as much to God as to a group of contemporaries. In his address at the opening of the second session of the Second Vatican Council, the Pope asked who may have felt offended by us (the Catholic Church), and declared himself ready for his part to pardon offences received. In the view of Paul VI, both the request for and offer of pardon concerned solely the sin of the division between Christians and presupposed reciprocity.[569]

It was in the same spirit of request for pardon that Vatican Council Fathers expressly requested for pardon. They wrote: "Thus, in humble prayer, we beg pardon of God and of our separated brethren, just as we forgive them that offend us."[570] They mentioned some grey areas for which pardon is needed. According to them, "We cannot but deplore certain attitudes (not unknown among Christians) deriving from a shortsighted view of the rightful autonomy of science; they have occasioned conflict and controversy and have misled many into opposing faith and science."[571]Another area where the Church may necessarily ask for forgiveness is her shrouding some truths in secrecy. This failure on the part of Christians may have contributed to the emergence of atheism. The Vatican Fathers stated that, "...atheism, taken as a whole, is not present in the minds of man from the start...It springs from various causes, among which must be included a critical reaction against religions and, in some places, against the Christian religion in particular.

569 Ibid, p. 16-17.
570 Unitatis Redintegratio, (UR), no. 7.
571 Gaudium et Spes, (GS), no. 36.

Believers can thus have more than a little to do with the rise of atheism. To the extent that they are careless about their instruction in the faith, or present its teaching falsely, or even fail in their religious, moral, or social life, they must be said to conceal rather than to reveal the true nature of God and of religion."[572] The Council did not hesitate in pointing out the mistakes of the Church for her involvement in enflaming the embers of hatred and persecution. The Council declared, "Remembering, then, her common heritage with the Jews and moved not by any political consideration, but solely by the religious motivation of Christian charity, she deplores all hatreds, persecutions, displays of anti-Semitism levelled at any time or from any source against the Jews."[573] All these areas where the Church openly accepted some culpable responsibility ended with requests for pardon being directed to God and our separated brethren. The Church's historical turning point of the attempts at asking for forgiveness for her sins and those of her sons and daughters was reached with John Paul II - A Pope known and always remembered for his charismatic love. Pope John Paul II did not only renew expressions of regret for the sorrowful memories that mark the history of the divisions among Christians, as Paul VI and the Second Vatican Council had done, he also extended a request for forgiveness to a multitude of historical events in which the Church or individual groups of Christians were implicated in different respects. In the Apostolic Letter Tertio Millennio Adveniente, he expressed the hope that the Jubilee of 2000 might be the occasion for a purification of the memory of the Church from all forms of counter-witness and scandal which have occurred in the course of the past millennium.[574]

He explained that the Church is invited to become more fully conscious of the sinfulness of her children and she acknowledges as her own her sinful sons and daughters" and encourages them to purify[575] themselves, through repentance, of past errors and instances of infidelity, inconsistency and slowness to act. The responsibility of Christians for the evils of our time is likewise noted, although the accent falls particularly on the Church of today with

---

[572] Ibid, no. 19.

[573] Nostra Aetate, (NA), no. 4.

[574] International Theological Commission, op. cit. p. 19-20.

[575] Cardinal Ratzinger Joseph (now the Pope), was the Chairman of the International Theological Commission that compiled and published the book, 'Memory and Reconciliation: The Church and the Faults of the Past' So, to avoid misinterpretation or misrepresentation of the word, "Purify" as the Pope John Paul II used it, explain further what the Pope meant by the purification of Memory: The Church of Today cannot serve as a tribunal to judge the Church of the past...But we can seek to ′do′ the truth—that is, we cannot deny the faults of the past – while at the same time we will not adopt a stance of false humility, and acknowledge errors which have not been demonstrated historically."Cf. http://www.churchinhistory.org/purifying-memory

past faults. Some of the faults, such as the separation of Christians or the methods of violence and intolerance used in the past to evangelize, are explicitly mentioned.[576] This gave some adherents of ATR the impetus to demand for immediate and unalloyed forgiveness from the Church. For traditional religion, the Christians should apologise for their great offences. As part of the offences they wrongly quoted a statement in the Novel, 'Things Fall Apart' written by a literary icon, Chinua Achebe. In this novel, Obierika, a titled man, in answer to a question put to him by exiled Okonkwo regarding their peoples' loss of the power to fight, said, "How do you think we can fight when our brothers have turned against us? The white man is very clever. He came quietly and peaceably with his religion. We were amused at his foolishness and allowed him to stay. Now he has won our brothers, and our clan no longer act like one. He has put knife on the things that held us together and we have fallen apart."[577] Although their claim is clearly out of order, they insisted that the Church used force even amidst her show of attitudinal quietude, peace and meekness. Obierika actually is talking about the calm and diplomacy used by the white missionary. The Missionary was not violent and intolerant. However, such misrepresentation helps us see reasons with some faithful Catholics who feared that this request for forgiveness could jeopardise the holiness of the Church. Some even seemed fade-up with the Church. According to the International Theological Commission, "...some of the faithful are disconcerted and their loyalty to the Church seems shaken. Some wonder how they can hand on a love for the Church to younger generations if this same Church is imputed with crimes and faults. Others observe that the recognition of faults is for the most part one sided and is exploited by the Church detractors, who are satisfied to see the Church confirm the prejudices they had of her."[578]Happily, these new dimensions introduced by the Pope, "have been understood in many circles as signs of the Church's vitality and authenticity, such that they strengthen her credibility. It is right, moreover, that the Church contribute (sic) to changing false and unacceptable images of herself, especially in those areas in which, whether through ignorance or bad faith, some sectors of opinion like to identify her with obscurantism and intolerance."[579]

---

[576] Ibid, p. 20-21.
[577] Achebe, C., *Things Fall Apart*, London, Heinemann Educational Books, 1958, p. viii.
[578] International Theological Commission, op. cit. p. 23.
[579] Ibid.

Approximately a month after Pope John Paul II rendered this barrier-breaking apology on behalf of the Catholic Church for her past mistakes, he wrote a letter to all Heads of States and Government putting them on the track of events that took place in Assisi with the unequivocal commitment to peace made by those who participated. He wrote,

> I observe that those who took part in the Assisi meeting were more than ever motivated by a common conviction: Humanity must choose between love and hatred. All of them, feeling that they belong to one and the same human family, were able to express their aspiration through these ten points, convinced that if hatred destroys, love, on the contrary, builds up. The ten points, tagged "A Decalogue for Peace", are:
> 1. We commit ourselves to proclaiming our firm conviction that violence and terrorism are incompatible with the authentic spirit of religion, and, as we condemn every recourse to violence and war in the name of God or of religion, we commit ourselves to doing everything possible to eliminate the root cause of terrorism.
> 2. We commit ourselves to educating people to mutual respect and esteem, in order to help bring about a peaceful and fraternal coexistence between people of different ethnic groups, cultures and religions.
> 3. We commit ourselves to fostering the culture of dialogue, so that there will be an increase of understanding and mutual trust between individuals and among peoples, for these are the premises of authentic peace.
> 4. We commit ourselves to defending the right of everyone to live a decent life in accordance with his own cultural identity, and to form freely a family of his own.
> 5. We commit ourselves to frank and patient dialogue, refusing to consider our differences as an insurmountable barrier, but recognizing instead that to encounter the diversity of others can become an opportunity for greater reciprocal understanding.
> 6. We commit ourselves to forgiving one another for past and present errors and prejudices, and to supporting one another in a common effort both to overcome selfishness and arrogance, hatred and violence, and to learn from the past that peace without justice is no true peace.
> 7. We commit ourselves to taking the side of the poor and the helpless, to speak out for those who have no voice, and to working effectively to change these situations, out of the conviction that no one can be happy alone.

8. We commit ourselves to taking up the cry of those who refuse to be resigned to violence and evil, and we desire to make every effort to offer the men and women of our time real hope for justice and peace.
9. We commit ourselves to encouraging all efforts to promote friendship between peoples, for we are convinced that, in the absence of solidarity and understanding between peoples, technological progress exposes the world to a growing risk of destruction and death.
10. We commit ourselves to urging leaders of nations to make every effort to create and consolidate, on the national and international levels, a world of solidarity and peace based on justice.[580]

The positive effect of this hard, dangerous but sincere and rewarding step taken by the Pope wasted no time in rearing its admirable head. This claim is supported by the report of the Commission which stated: "The requests for pardon formulated by the Pope have also given rise to positive emulation both inside and outside the Church. Heads of state or government, private and public associations, religious communities are today asking forgiveness for episodes or historical periods marked by injustices. This practice is far from just an exercise in rhetoric, and for this reason, some hesitate to do so, calculating the attendant costs – among which are those in legal plane – of an acknowledgment of past wrongs."[581] In sincere admiration for what the Pope did, Thomas, D. advised that Christians and Moslems should accept that both religions are not all perfect since each of them had some elements of violence so as to make amends. He urged, "It is important for the followers of both faiths to admit this fact, to know about the long shared experience of condemnation and warfare between them and to seek to find realistic ways forward in a future where they must encounter each other with increasing intimacy."[582] It is for this typical situation that Carey unequivocally said that, "There is much to apologize for."[583] Cardinal Arinze gave his total support to

---

[580] Cf. Address of Bishop Joseph D. Bagobiri in 2002 to open the Study session of IRDC-AECAWA in Accra-Ghana with the theme, "Religion, Violence and Peace in West Africa" published in: *Notizen aus der Weltkirche*, in Missio Korrespondenz, Bibliothek/Doku MISSIO/MWI, März 6, 2008, p. 42-43, cf. also Gioia, F., (ed.), Interreligious Dialogue: The Official Teaching of the Catholic Church from the Second Vatican Council to John Paul II (1963-2005), 1230*, p. 949.

[581] International Theological Commission, *Memory and Reconciliation: The Church and the Faults of the Past*, p. 23

[582] Thomas, D., op.cit. Vol.18, No.1, p. 33.

[583] Archbishop Carey of Canterbury, in: "Documentation: The Challenges Facing Christian-Muslim Dialogue" being a paper presented on October 4, at Al-Azhar University Egypt reported in: *Islam and Christian-Muslim Relations*, Vol. 7, No. 1, 1996, p. 95.

this urgent call to forgiveness stating the need for all to say their 'Mea Culpa.'[584] He pointed out that,

> We have to ask each other's pardon. We have to be willing to give the other a chance and listen, not only to their explanation, self-defence or justification but also to what is deepest in their hearts but is most difficult to express. We have to admit the possibility of a change of heart in ourselves and in others; we must acknowledge that none of us is determined or enslaved by our personal or social past. The negative attitudes which we communally inherit do not bind us forever. They can be overcome, where there are the will and reason to do so. There is more. Sometimes we need to take part in the giving and receiving of symbolic acts of admission of guilt and desire for reconciliation...We must be aware that people and groups are different. My way of coming to reconciliation and building trust might not be the way of some other nation, religion, race or cultural group. I must be ready to learn the gestures and symbols of trust of others so that I can recognise them when they are offered. I must accept that the actions and procedures of peace which are normal and mutual for me could be unfamiliar, meaningless or even threatening to others. We all have so much to learn about each other for trust to find a strong and lasting foundation.[585]

As some people go on arguing for and against this good intention of the Pope, the Pontiff saw his action as part of the fulfilment of the Church's stand as role model for peace in the world. He defended his action sealing with it the mouths of some doubting Thomases. He maintained that,

> The request for forgiveness...primarily concerns the life of the Church, her mission of proclaiming salvation, her witness to Christ, her commitment to unity, in a word, the consistency which should distinguish Christian life. But the light and strength of the Gospel, by which the Church lives, also have the capacity, in a certain sense, to overflow as illumination and support for the decisions and actions of civil society, with full respect for their autonomy....On the threshold of the third millennium, we

---

[584] Mea Culpa is a part of the Latin prayer, "Confiteor Deo Omnipotenti" which is a prayer through which Catholics show remorse and ask God for forgiveness of their sins. In English it means, I confess to Almighty God, cf. Ordo Misssae, (Oder of Mass) by CBECS, Nigeria, 1973, p. 158.

[585] Arinze, F., op. cit. p. 303-304.

may rightly hope that political leaders and peoples, especially those involved in tragic conflicts fuelled by hatred and the memory of often ancient wounds, will be guided by the spirit of forgiveness and reconciliation exemplified by the Church and will make every effort to solve their differences through open and honest dialogue.[586]

In spite of the call by the Pope for healing of the past and for dialogue, many leaders in Nigerian, both in educational institutions and in the government do not seem to be interested in peaceful co-existence, dialogue and healing of the past. Here we refer to the attitude of a Provost of a college of Legal studies in Yola (Nigeria) as reported in The Guardian Newspaper of Thursday, October 23, 2008 by Emmanuel Ande. According to the report, thirteen final-year Christian students of the College of Legal studies, Yola were suspended for alleged hugging and wearing a necklace that has a symbol of a cross. Out of this number, three were initially suspended for one semester on the order of the College Provost, Musa Yahaya Nuhu for the alleged hugging. Nine other Christian students were summarily expelled by the provost because they peacefully protested before the State House of Assembly. The hugging was simply the normal joyful routine by students, male and female, who came out of the exam hall excited with the outcome of the exam. The provost claimed he spotted them. He called them to his office handing them out one-semester suspension as punishment, despite pleas by students and the fellowship of Christian students.[587]

What I find strange is the offence committed by these students for expressing joy over hope- hope over a seemingly successful examination pending the grading by the professors. The mature approach taken by these peace-loving students by taking the case to the Adamawa State House of Assembly and various law enforcement agencies, instead of sending a sincere message to the partisan provost, sent his head revolving and fuming. Although the provost seemed to have accepted the intervention of these concerned citizens, he kept his bitterness within him looking for an opportune time to strike again. As the case was thought to have been settled, the provost withheld the results of these students and went further to expel them, declaring that for him as a Moslem, it was wrong for a man and woman to hug each other. He adamantly, stubbornly and with an unfortunate, unintelligent, unrepentant

[586] Ibid, p. 80, cf. also the foot notes of the same book from p. 27-31 for biblical citations in support of the pleas for forgiveness.

[587] Ande, E., "Provost suspends students over cross necklace" in: *Guardian Newspaper*, October 23, 2008.

arrogance declared to the pressmen that he had the power to hire and fire, urging whoever felt aggrieved to go to court and stating without equivocation his readiness to resign rather than allow the students go against his religion.[588] It is strange when such situations arise signalling that National Institutions could be appropriated for religious politics by whoever is place in charge of them.

6.6. Mary as a Bridge-builder or boundary-crosser

That there are yawning gaps between religions asking to be filled up is not uncommon and is not questionable. These gaps are simply check-points where one has to clear oneself before crossing to the other side. It is a barrier that cannot be manoeuvred. It is such a barrier that no single corrupt Nigerian Politician could buy with laundered money. You cannot jump over it or avoid it if you must enter the other side. Even if you want to enter through another means, this boundary is their waiting for you. But Mary, the Mother of Jesus stands at both sides of this boundary to help all cross peacefully. Günter Riße, had no problem confirming the truth that there are borders. One has to think here of the customs' stand with their barriers and borderlines. Borderlines serve as clear delimitation, as the clear demarcation of a checkpoint. Arrival at the border demands and challenges even the attitude of the existing borderline. Here one asks the question: Do I stop at or do I cross the border lying before me? Those crossing the border must always decide anew and know at the same time about their risky travel. In that case they roll between the worlds, between inside and outside, and between foreign and known, between past and future. To open and to shift the borders belong at the same time to our daily life as man. In the border-crosser appears lastly a spiritual basic concept, which makes it at all possible to accept and recognize borders. Border-crossers are in interreligious dialogue imperative. Particularly acceptable to me are the "Border-crossers", whose religious history crosses religious-borders to connect men of different religions. In this case as regards Islam are Abraham and Maria particularly to be mentioned. Abraham is in the Bible and Quran the model of Trust in God, the fundamental example of all believers. The "trusted one of God", as Quran refers to Abraham (Surah 4, 125), is seen as the prototype of faith who heard and accepted the

[588] Ibid.

word of God, but in different ways has become the contact-point of the three monotheistic religions Judaism, Christianity and Islam.[589]

Having seen that Abraham in the old Testament had a connective function to the world religions as mentioned above, it is not my intention here to go into details x-raying his roles as connector of religions. It is my humble intention to look at an all important figure in the New Testament history that could serve as a wonderful link or bridge-builder in the bid to bring the major religions of Nigeria together-especially Christianity and Islam. This link, bridge or border-crosser could be seen in the mother of Jesus- Mary whose faith-account in the Holy Bible and Quran could bring Christians and Moslems closer to one another and indirectly the members of ATR. Mary, who with her special place of honour in the Christian and Moslem world, who call upon her in this scattered world, can lead people to God.[590]

To this effect, I wish to observe what happened in Germany on November 22, 2009 at exactly 11.55. Mr. Schäuble Wolfgang, (at the said time the internal minister in Germany) ended his speech before hundreds of listeners who gathered during the honouring of His highness King of Jordan. The occasion which I watched live on Television was well attended by different religious groups. Speeches dealing with the possibility of Christians and Moslems living together in Germany were delivered by eminent people. What I found interesting after his speech was entertainment of the audience with a piece of beautiful, melodious song in honour of the mother of God titled 'Ave Maria'. It may not be a direct emphasis on the place of Mary in the two religions. However, the indirect connection is not to be wished away. The Spirit moves wherever it wills. This situation however goes to buttress the point made by Arinze in his goodwill message to Moslems in 1988 during their Ramadan feast. He wrote: "Among the true believers who have been animated by the Spirit of God and who have lived in accord with the obedience of Abraham, we would like to make special mention of Mary, the Mother of Jesus, whom both Christians and Muslims – without according her the same role and title – honour as a model for believers."[591]With this assertion from Arinze, we now turn to consider the place of Virgin Mary in Qur'an and in Islamic Tradition.

---

[589] Riße, G., „Maria- Grenzgängerin im Gottes-Glauben von Christen und Muslimen" in: George, A/Krämer, K. (Hg), *Gott denken und bezeugen*, Festschrift für Kardinal Walter Kasper zum 75.Geburtstag. Freiburg, Verlag Herder, 2008, p. 630-631.

[590] Ibid, p. 631.

[591] Arinze, F., "Good will message to Muslims on the feast of Ramadan" in: *Meeting in Friendship*, 1967-2002, Vatican City, 2003, p. 44.

6.6.1. Virgin Mary in Qur'an and in Islamic Tradition

That Mary occupies a considerable place in Islamic faith is unquestionable. According to Riße,

> Mary is the only woman who was called by name in Quran. This already shows a distinct person of Mary. The virgin birth of Mary, her stay in the temple as well as her childhood and the birth of Jesus were completely narrated. The Surah 19 contains her name. Mary was chosen by God (Surah 3, 42), she was dedicated to God by her mother (Surah 3,35) and like in Christianity Quran confesses that Jesus was born of the virgin Mary (Surah 19, 20 and 3, 47). ...In a special way, it is in Mary, who is truly just and devout (Surah 5,75) that the work of God can be seen. Mary as a woman who is ready to believe, is presented as an example to the believers who humbly seek God (Surah 66,12; 3,43). Nothing describes better the Arabic word Muslim than that of somebody who submits himself totally to the will of God. For the fact that Mary has done that, she is the sign, example and model for all the faithful.[592]

The statement accredited to Mohammed in the Islamic Tradition gives clear indication as to the high esteem in which the Moslems hold Mary, the virgin mother of Jesus Christ. In the statement, Mohammed declared that he stands next to Jesus, the son of Mary both in life and in the next world.[593] In this case, the founder of Islam himself has given a strong testimony that Mary belongs to those chosen by God. As a woman who is lifted from among women, Mary is lifted above all other women especially the mothers. Even if there is no special Marian cult in Islam, the honouring of Mary plays a very important role in the piety and the Islamic fundamental faith. In this case one thinks only on the "House of virgin in Ephesus" in Turkey. Describing this House of Virgin in Ephesus and its importance, Riße explained,

> Many Muslims go to the house of the Virgin Mary when they have much to worry about, for instance, because of incurable sickness, unemployment and lack of marriage. They present their worries and wishes to the Virgin Mary and expect her to plead for them before God. From their perspective, the great Creator will not turn down the request of such a believer whom he so much loves, and that is why prayers in such places are

---

[592] Riße, G., op.cit. p. 632.
[593] Ibid.

fulfilled when they are said with sincere and unshakable faith....Mary is surely one of God's beloved believers who he cannot refuse anything.[594]

Their love for the Mother of God is so high that some of them join their Christian counterparts in visiting a well known Marian shrine. Riße reports that this Christian Marian-pilgrimage centre is the 'Sanctuary of our loving woman of Africa in Algiers' which is almost exclusively visited by the Muslims who consider this place as one of the most important places in the city. Just like in all the other pilgrimage centres in the whole world, the Moslems do come to this place with their worries and wishes. In many Moslem families, their daughters take their names after the Virgin Mary.[595]This epic honour to Mary and supplication to her by these two great religions holds hope and can serve as a point of convergence for them. It is very interesting to hear the stand of one of the hard-line theologians on the Virgin Mary. This strict theologian is Ibn Hanbal (855 Rip). In one of the Traditions that he handed down, Mary was depicted as one of the best four women to have ever lived and her elevated position remains still underlined in the holy biographies. In the biographies, it was said that God, on the judgement day will allow the people to enter into Paradise and calls, "O men!" Mary will be the first being to enter because she is higher than all other human beings, Men and Women alike.[596]

It is very clear in Islamic tradition that Jesus and Mary were depicted as the only human beings who were not touched by the devil at birth. The strict thinker Ibn Hazm (1064 Rip) went to the extent of saying that Maria was clothed with the dignity of a prophet. This stand was however contested and denied by most theologians.[597] But Mary played a very important role in the Islamic mystical tradition. Riße reported that Mary is regarded as the symbol of earth, Bloom and water full of blessings, and often and on the Poets, using figures from the Qur'an teach that her total submission to the word of God, the complete humility and silent acceptance of her fate has become for humanity a source of blessing. Mary is the symbol fur the people, similar to the Christian tradition where she is 'Mother Virgin Queen'.[598]

---

[594] Ibid.
[595] Ibid.
[596] Ibid, p. 633.
[597] Ibid.
[598] Ibid.

6.6.2. Mary - Mother and Virgin?

The virgin birth of Mary was not questioned in Islam. Her attitude and question concerning the message of God's messenger 'the Angel' made this assertion unambiguous. Being a virgin, she took the message of God's messenger as being impossible and asked out of fear, how it could come to pass. In the gospel of St. Luke, we read, "How can that happen since I know no man?" (Lk. 1: 34.). In Surah 19, 20 the question is, "How shall I bear a baby when no man (human being) has touched me and I am not a prostitute?" Also in Surah 3, 47a the question is, "Lord! How can I bear a child where no man (human being) has yet touched me?" To Mary's question, the Angel answered in Qur'an with an authoritative word of God. For God, it is a decided issue. Being the decision and wish of God, Mary submitted herself to this divine will. That Mary did not argue against the decision of God is found in the gospel of Luke (1: 38), "I am the Handmaid of the Lord, be it done to me according to your words." Even if this response of Mary in New Testament is not made explicit in the Qur'an, it is clearly implicit in the text. Mary submitted herself and accepted with fear of God what she was told. With this the Qur'an testified without doubts to Mary's virgin conception.[599]

Unfortunately however, the way Mohammed reported the virgin birth of Jesus by Mary was filled with suspicion. This suspicion has its reasons. The report stated, "As Mary was pregnant, she withdrew herself and went to a distant place."[600] The reason behind this verse whose content is hardly understood is probably hidden in the statement from the apocryphal gospel of James. The apocryphal gospel stated that after Mary's pregnancy had become clear, Mary was forced to drink the 'water of proof' as an oath of innocence. This oath mentioned in the book of Numbers (5:11-31) states that according to Israel's tradition, when a woman is unfaithful to her husband, she would be brought to the priest. The priest would pour holy water in an earthen jar and put dust gotten from the floor of the dwelling in the water. He would place the woman before the Yahweh. In his own hands the priest will hold the water of bitterness and cursing.[601] As stated in the book of Numbers,

> The priest will then put the woman on oath. He will say to her: If it is not true that a man has slept with you, that you have gone astray and made

---

[599] Riße, G., "Gott ist Christus, der Sohn der Maria" Eine Studie zum Christusbild im Koran, Bonn, Verlag N. M. Borengäser, 1989, p. 176-177

[600] Surah 19, 22.

[601] Riße, G., op.cit. p. 180, cf. also Num. 5:11-17.

yourself unclean while under your husband's authority, may this water of bitterness and cursing do you no harm. But if it is true that you have gone astray while under your husband's authority, that you have made yourself unclean and that a man other than your husband has slept with you... Here the priest will impose an imprecatory oath on the woman. He will say to her...May Yahweh make you the object of your people's execration and curse, by making your sexual organs shrivel and your belly swell! May this water of cursing entering your bowels, make your belly swell and your sexual organs shrivel! To which the woman will reply: Amen! Amen! Having written these curses on a scroll and washed them off in the water of bitterness, the priest will make the woman drink the water of bitterness and cursing...[602]

The report from the apocryphal gospel of James had it that Mary was sent to the desert after she had taken the water of proof, the proof of which we have mentioned in the Qur'anic birth story of Jesus. (Surah 19, 22). The apocryphal gospel further states that as the date of birth came nearer, Mary was filled with fear and fright that she shouted, "How I wish I had earlier died and been forgotten!" (Surah19, 23). This Mary's cry of fear does not in any way call the wonderful conception into doubt, and it is also no disputation of God's deed on her. Mary has surely submitted herself to the will of God. This call from Mary is also not out of fear of the imminent pangs of birth. Mary was afraid that the birth of her promised son will be an object of discussion in the society which would consequently result to her son's and her exclusion from the society. But the miracle happened. In response to her cry, Mary received an answer from an unknown He- speaker[603]who called to her from below: 'Do not be sad'."[604]

Attempts have been made by many authors to clarify who this speaker was. Since it is not my intention here to go into exegetical analysis of different contributors, suffix it to call to mind the stand of a renowned writer, R. Paret as given by Riße Günter. The interpretation of Paret is more acceptable. For him, it is verisimilitude that Mohammed was influenced in his birth story of Jesus by the Pseudo-gospel of Mathew. He narrated the story of flight of Joseph and Mary with the child Jesus to Egypt. On their way, they rested under a palm-tree. Under this palm-tree, Mary became very hungry and thirs-

---

602 Num. 5:19-24ff cf. also Riße, G., Ibid. p. 180-181.
603 Ibid, p. 181.
604 Ibid, p. 181. also, Surah 19, 24.

ty.[605] According to the pseudo-gospel, "There, the child Jesus who with joyful expression was sitting on his mother's laps spoke to the palm: Tree bend your branches and refresh my mother with your fruits. Soon in obedience to this call the palm lowered her topmost to the feet of the blessed Mary and they gathered from her all the fruits on which they freshed/feasted."[606]Again the child said, "Include waterwheel under your roots which is hidden under the sand and let water flow that we shall quench our thirst from it. She (the palm- G.R.) lifted herself immediately and a complete clear, fresh and totally light water-source began to bubble on her root."[607] The probability that the unknown speaker in verse 23 was the child Jesus was confirmed in the other following verses 24-33. Till the end of the birth story in verse 33, the child Jesus was the only person active and speaking.[608] In order to shut the mouths and thoughts of the doubting Thomases, Qur'an made it clear in Surah 19, 30f where Jesus through the words he directed to the people made a self revelation of his nature. "He said: 'I am the servant of God. He has given me the Scripture and made me a prophet. (31) And he has made it, no matter where I am, that (the gift of) blessings is to be bestowed on me, and it will be ordered that prayer (be offered) and almsgiving be (given) to me, as long as I live'."[609] As I said before that it was not my intention to go into exegetical analysis, what is important here is that the He-Speaker that asked the Virgin not to be sad, was the child Jesus. Mary was not to be sad because the administration of the Oath of truth on her was unnecessary as she truly conceived under the influence of the Holy Spirit.

6.6.3. Mary as Peacemaker between Religions

The recognition of the biblical Mary as border-crosser is not a concept that started today. The history of Christianity impressively emphasized that Mary, as the prototype of faith is a link between the two testaments.[610]Mary is a key figure in Christianity and –even if very late- in contemporary Judaism, where with the finding of Jesus among his Jewish people, his mother Mary was also mentioned not just as a Jewish woman but interestingly an exemplary mother .She was spotted again by the Jewish people as rooted in

605 Ibid, p. 182.
606 Ibid.
607 Ibid.
608 Ibid.
609 Ibid, p. 183.
610 Riße, G., Grenzgängerin, p. 633, cf. also Söll, G., „Mariologie" in: *Handbuch der Dogmengeschichte*, Band: III, Faszikel 4, Freiburg 1978, p. 34ff., u. p. 63ff.

the culture of her people.[611] Bringing back to consciousness the place of Mary in Qur'an and her place of honour in Islamic tradition shows preferably that Mary, the mother of Jesus as border-crosser is honoured by Christians and Moslems. With her life she shows the people of good will that what should stand in the middle point of the life of every human being should be basically the readiness, always and everywhere, to do the will of God.[612] Part of the task of doing the will of God is to contribute in making the future of the world peaceful and therefore habitable.

6.7. Education

One thing that rightly comes to mind when a particular religion is mentioned is that it is meant for peace. Any religion that teaches violence has got so many question marks. It is therefore not out of place to join Mbom in expressing the view that, every religion teaches its adherents to be loving, kind, truthful, just, honest, humble, disciplined, tolerant, harmless, hardworking, altruistic and selfless toward their neighbours, even neighbours who do not share their religious convictions. Such teaching is usually predicated on the fact of our common humanity and, in the theistic traditions, on our common ancestry in the fatherhood of God, the Supreme Creator or, in non-monotheistic traditions, on the recognition of the supreme power of some Ultimate Reality.[613] Despite this glowing tribute to religions in general, clear evidences abound where religion has been used to rock havoc in communities and towns. Why should such unfortunate and unhealthy situation arise? According to Onaiyekan,

> Experience shows that prejudice and ignorance of one another are among the chief obstacles to a peaceful coexistence of Christians and Muslims. A deepened knowledge of our own religion is as important as the adequate knowledge about the religion of our partners. Knowledge comes through information. In addition to a better presence in the mass media (e.g. parish bulletin, diocesan newspaper, radio, TV and internet) and various forms of adult education, catechesis and school education constitute the main instrument for fostering Christian identity and for providing the necessary knowledge of Muslim and Islam. The Church has to strive, wherever possible, for an adequate education in mutual respect, espe-

---

[611] Ibid. cf. also Schalom Ben-Chorin, Mutter Mirjam, Maria in Jüdischer Sicht, München,1982.
[612] Ibid, p. 634.
[613] Mbon, F. M., op.cit. p. 13.

cially when Christian and Muslim children attend the school. For this adequate teaching material should be provided.[614]

Adequate teaching materials do not just mean books and other writing or reading and teaching materials. Its scope covers also the teachers. In his homily during the beatification ceremony of Cardinal John Henry Newman, Pope Benedict said,

> What better goal could teachers of religion set themselves than Blessed John Henry's famous appeal, for an intelligent, well-instructed laity: "I want a laity, not arrogant, not rash in speech, not disputatious, but men who know their religion, who enter into it, who know just where they stand, who know what they hold and what they do not, who know their creed so well that they can give an account of it, who know so much history that they can defend it.[615]

According to Rimmel, "Religion should lead humankind to the love of God and of neighbour : "Anyone who says, I love God, and hates his brother, is a liar, since a man who does not love the brother that he can see cannot love God, whom he has never seen" (cf. 1 Jn 4:20). Therefore, violence in the name of God goes against the very essence of religion and shows lack of understanding of one's own religion. It simply reduces God to our human level of jealousy, quarrel and hatred."[616]If those to lead the education of the masses on the need for respect for one another's religion are broad minded people, not fanatics or extremists, who instead of trying to bring peace fan the embers of religious bigotry, surely the adherents of every religion under their leadership would be inspired to love their neighbours. They are to be those who will teach the joy and love of living peacefully with people of other religions without compromising their own faith. A teaching that will make the people see reason in living together with other fellow human beings that will stand them out as people who love God in their fellow creatures. It is a thing of joy that our universities, as they are today, are principally secular. It is my candid opinion that the introduction of religious studies in all higher institutions of learning and making it a compulsory subject will not be a mistake.

---

[614] Onaiyekan, J. (Introd.), "Christians and Muslims- Partners in Dialogue" in: *Stimmen der Weltkirche* Nr. 38, p. 33.
[615] Rimmel, T. M. et. al (eds.), op. cit. p. 7.
[616] Ibid, p. 28.

It will be amazing if such undertaken is also extended to our secondary schools. In this case, I do not mean the moral instruction that is already introduced. It is a religious study that has to be handled by corresponding experts. When I mean experts, I intend to suggest that a real Moslem who knows the authentic Islamic teachings should be employed to teach the Islamic religion in a Catholic or Christian school in the case of secondary schools just as a Christian will be employed in a secondary school in the North to teach about Christian religion. It will give the students the opportunity to know really what these religions believe and practice rather than the negative statements made about these religions in their Churches or Mosques. Care needs to be taken to see that those who may be appointed to take up such teaching positions must be people who have basic knowledge of the tenets of other religions which will place them on a better platform to give balanced answers to any question that the students may raise. This will help students ask questions where possible for a proper clarification concerning what they might have been told in their churches or mosques.

However, the question that may arise is, what and what will actually be taught? On the issue of what should be taught, I suggest that the government should set up a committee of the leaders of different religions or their representatives with some government representatives. This committee should sit down and with all possible good intention for peace find out areas that will be included in the curriculum of studies – be it social, economic, ethical/religious. Getting such a group formed through NIREC would not be a bad idea. After the formulation of the curriculum, it will be made available to every school. It should no more be left only for the students of religion. I am very much aware that many of our senior seminaries are already doing this following the call made on them to show respect to other religions including ATR for the sake of peace. Pope John Paul II urged, "The adherents of African traditional religion should therefore be treated with great respect and esteem, and all inaccurate and disrespectful language should be avoided. For this purpose, suitable courses in African traditional religion should be given in houses of formation for priests and religious."[617]This treatment may not be easy if we do not know why the other believes and practices what he holds to heart. This is why it is for me, very necessary to educate all on the need to try to learn and appreciate the other.

[617] Ecclesia in Africa, No. 67.

6.8. Cooperation between Government and Religions

A critical peep into the world of politics and political history shows that no government has been hundred percent successful. In other words, there are good and bad sides of every government. To maintain a relative peace and orderliness, the advocacy pendulum falls in the direction of democracy as the best option that can guarantee checks and balances. Even the worldly envied United States of America has not had it so easy. European countries have not also had it easy. It has been a gradual progress to the promise land. In Nigeria, inasmuch as one regrets to observe that after 50 years of independence, we have nothing to show for it, we still have hope. There is no denying the fact that the military has contributed immensely to the sorry state of the nation. We should not continue to dwell simply on the rot that they laid on our heads. We must try to move forward now that there seems to be a green light on the end of the tunnel. Seen now as a democratic country, the Nigerian government must try to be seen as a serious co-operator and partner with all stake holders that are considered advantageous to the country. One such example is the co-operation with the religions in the country. In this case, the Nigerian "governments should encourage religious groups to perform their social and religious functions to promote societal harmony. As much as possible, governments should respect their constitutional provisions of freedom of religious expression and practice for their citizenry (where such constitutional provisions are applicable), and refrain from unnecessary control of, and intervention in, religious activities, except, of course, where such activities threaten the peace and stability of the society."[618]

Right form its independence, the Nigerian government is known to be a secular state. This secular nature should be cautiously upheld but not without some relaxation. When I talk of relaxation, I mean that the government should not pretend to have come from the moon. The Nigerian government should show itself to be Nigerian enough. In this case, the fact that Nigerians are a religious people, would make it funny if government enacts laws that are considered irreligious. A typical example would be a situation where the State's National Assembly members try to institutionalise abortion. To do that would be setting itself in a war part with these religions who price the respect for human life so highly. A situation of that nature was reported sometime in southern Nigeria. For the first time, we saw the Catholic Bishops leading the faithful of their region on a protest march to the government

[618] Mbon, F. M., op.cit. p. 8

house to deliver the important message about the sacredness of human life from conception to natural death. As Machado emphasized,

> The life of every human being is sacred... The dignity of the person and defence of the rights which that dignity confers must represent the goal of every social endeavour and of every effort to bring it to fruition. This message is conveyed to us unmistakably by the quiet but clear voice of conscience. It is a message which must be heeded and communicated to others: should it ever cease to find an echo in people's hearts, the world would be exposed to the darkest of a new barbarism. Only through recognition of the centrality of the person can common basis for understanding be found, one which enables us to move beyond cultural conflicts and which neutralises the disruptive power of ideologies.[619]

Instead of making such laws, the government should try to partner with these religions in the education and good upbringing of the youths. A partnership with the religions in setting up places where the members of these religions could recreate themselves would be a big plus for the government. Fully aware that every Nigerian belongs directly or indirectly at least to any of these three major religions, it behoves the government to make people-oriented policies (social, economic political) that will benefit the masses. It will favour the government to take note of Tonsor's stand who maintained that politics without religion is not visible for religion serves as the source of the basic paradigms of order in human societies. The historic past has known no completely irreligious or secular societies. It will not be surprising to discover under a careful investigation the religious inherent colouration of those political orders which today pride themselves on their secularity.[620] This assertion of Tonsor needs no contradiction.

The constant prophetic call of Pope Benedict XVI on the European governments to return to the European root is enough evidence. It is on this ground that religion should see itself as a co-worker, endeavouring to build a befitting society for the societal good. They should help the government fight the evil menace in the society and speak out to tell the government without

---

[619] Machado, F. A., "Witnesses of Hope in an Ecumenical and Interreligious Milieu" (quoted Pope Benedict XVI) in: *Pro Dialogo, Pontificum Consilium Pro Dialogo Inter Religiones*, Bulletin 125, 2007, p. 161.

[620] Tonsor, S., "Religion in Contemporary Politics" in: Howard, J. A. (ed.), *Belief, Faith and Reason*, Belfast, Christian Journals Ltd., 1991, p. 49.

fear or favour that it is deviating. By this I mean that religious groups should raise constructive criticisms on the government that is losing its bearing thereby playing prophetic and redemptive role. The religious leaders should see themselves as "voices of the voiceless" as the Catholic Bishops have called themselves. The suffering of their flock should move them to tell the government plainly that the citizenry are suffering. This is exactly what God did for his people Israel as the suffered in Egypt. God declared, "I have indeed seen the misery of my people in Egypt. I have heard them crying for help on account of their taskmasters. Yes, I am well aware of their sufferings. And I have come down to rescue them...."[621] A delay or failure to act would lead to impatience on the part of the citizenry which could culminate in their taking laws into their hands. Surely the final result would be unrest, violent protestation and destruction of public peace.

It will be a woeful failure for instance if the religious groups keep quiet when the citizenry are suffering and dying. Hunger is a very big enemy of progress and productivity. Therefore, even when the government seems to delay, these religious leaders must try to take up some challenges. They must therefore listen to the call to help the hungry as Jesus challenged his disciples: "Give them something to eat yourselves."[622] Giving them something to eat must not be interpreted to mean just food but any basic means to succeed in life. There should be no politicking about this basic duty. The religious groups should not compromise their role on the altar of religious politics. Moses spoke out and condemned the societal evil as ordered by God. Since the religious groups in Nigeria claim to speak for the Supreme Being, they should speak out, in season and out of season, listened to or neglected. It is very important to affirm that the liberation of the populace from socio-economic poverty is totally in line with the unmitigated Good News proclaimed by Jesus Christ.[623] Even as the religious groups undertake this prophetic and missionary role, they must not lose sight of the need to do them within the ambient of the just legal order of our county Nigeria. So they must refrain from undertaking some moves that might endanger or jeopardise the efforts of the government and its good economic policies and programmes.

---

[621] Ex. 3: 7-8a.

[622] Mk. 6:37.

[623] Barreiro, A. J., *Basic Ecclesial communities: The Evangelization of the Poor*, New York, 1992, p. 28.

6.9. Conclusion

As a Nigerian, my heart bleeds always when I hear of violent killings and loss of innocent lives. Sometimes, this barbaric, irresponsible und insensible wastage of innocent lives occurs due to some inhuman policies and programmes of either the central or the state government. At times, they allegedly occur due to hate and violent instigative preaching of some insensitive religious leaders. This is why I have dedicated this chapter to finding possible solutions. If "he/she" who is presently reading this chapter sincerely opens himself/herself to the truths contained here and follows the recommendations in conjunction with the contents of the next chapter, 'evaluation and conclusion', Nigeria, despite her religious plurality, will be a nation to beat in the realm of peaceful co-existence. You are capable of effecting some changes.

CHAPTER SEVEN

EVALUATION AND CONCLUSION

7.1. Evaluation

This research work aimed from its beginning at presenting the chaotic situation in Nigeria and searching for the possibility of Nigerians living together in peace. The place of religion, her importance and contributions to fostering violence and peace among the citizenry of the multi-cultural and multi-religious groups of Nigeria were not neglected. In trying to get an answer to this topic, we have looked in the direction of the three major religions in Nigeria. We saw some areas of conflicts and problems facing the realisation of peaceful co-existence. Contributions of some important religious groups and personnel were also examined to see how they tried to help disunite or hold Nigeria in being. Some viable solutions were also brought forward.

Unfortunately the question as to whether religion helps in fostering peace or peaceful co-existence in Nigeria in particular or in any nation in general as well as in the nation building, which is our concern in this work, got a thumb-downing answer from many Nigerians. These negative answers are consequent on their negative experiences associated with religion. Among them we name a respected Nigerian human rights activist and literary icon Wole Soyinka. He responded unambiguously in the negative:

> Religion is one enemy of potential nationhood that requires, not just a separate address of its own, but a full week, even a month of seminars, lectures, expositions, artistic events, films and documentaries – but all of a frank, even brutally frank nature, since the intervention of religion in nation being has been of the most savage, unconscionable, and increasingly intolerant kind. No other word for it but butchery, waste and devastation. (We cannot continue pretending that, as long as any one religion aspires to dictatorship in secular matters, we can call ourselves a nation. A theocratic order is anathema to nation-being, since it implicates exclusion, not inclusion). Only the secular order embraces all...Any religious following can evoke parallel but opposing sets of protocols, citing the authority of some unseen and unknowable god in realms that have no perceptible contact with the actual. Religion must therefore submit to com-

munity, to nation, otherwise co-existence becomes impossible and the human entity reverts to a state of brutishness.[624]

It is regrettable that religion has become really a source of worry and, to peace loving Nigerians a nightmare. A very deep scrutiny of the Nigerian problems has however shown that religion is not always the problem. It is more or less the manipulation of the less informed and uneducated but brainwashed religious bigots who are tied to iron pillars waiting execution by hunger under the watchful eye of big-belly politicians that more often than not wear the religious outfit to implicate religion and implode the nation. We cannot however deny out-rightly what Soyinka has said just as we cannot because of that subscribe totally to his opinion. His call if well interpreted could translate to a call for secularism where religion could be swallowed and manipulated by the same political do-no-goods. Secularism is a worst enemy of a nation building since it removes the element of the inner voice and submits to externalism. This inner voice no doubts could however be abused by some politicians who hide under religious piety to foment crises. Continuing Soyinka argued that, "insincerity, indeed hypocritical, double-talk and matching conduct of a handful of individuals, their abuse of the trust of the people"[625] are unarguably the bane of nation building that has continued to put Nigerians on a war part.

However, I must observe that in trying to solve the problem emanating from religious riots, we don´t need to subject religion to the whims and caprices of the nation, rather, religion and the State should work harmoniously towards a nation building. This could be achieved if we borrow a leaf from Soyinka calling for seminars, lectures, workshops, expositions which will be undertaken with tolerance, patience even if it lasts for months or years. All this boils down to the idea of dialogue which Catholic Church has been championing. Soyinka was right in making it unambiguously clear that the problem of Nigeria not attaining peace and nationhood is latent in insincerity on the part of our political figureheads/leaders. It is however not to be denied that some religious leaders make statements that are inimical and antithetic to peace. To curb this, we should heed the strong and wise call by the former President of the Christian Association of Nigeria, Most Rev. Dr. John Onaiyekan and the Sultan of Sokoto, Alhaji Sa´ad Abubakar. Both of them called on the government to enact laws that would help prosecute religious leaders

---

[624] Soyinka, W., as reported by Akinrefon, D & Kumolu, C., "Religion threatens Nigeria's nationhood" in: *Vanquard Newspaper*, March 4, 2009, cf. also www.vanguardngr.com
[625] Ibid.

who support violence by preaching riot-inciting messages to their adherents. They were also unified in maintaining that the ostracism and isolation of such hate and violence-prone religious leaders would serve as deterrent to others who may be inking towards violent religious incitement through their preaching.[626] Both made this call while delivering papers to the participants of the Senior Executive Course 31 of the National Institute for Policy and Strategic Studies, Kuru near Jos. While Onaiyekan spoke on 'The Role of Traditional and Religious Institutions in the Achievement of Good Governance and Sustainable National Development,' the Sultan spoke on 'The Responsibilities of Leadership in National Development.'

It must however be made clear that the problem of non-peaceful co-existence due to religious manipulation is surely not only a Nigerian problem. The majority of African countries are regrettably affected. This is why the delegation of African Bishops to the 6th meeting of the African and German Bishops held in Akosombo, Ghana painfully observed that, "...in many countries of Africa, religion has become a source of constant friction, great tension, bitter rivalry, conflicts, violence and discrimination and in some cases open war against one another."[627] But this communiqué by the African bishops is an embodiment of truth when one takes Nigerian case into consideration. That is why I have undertaken in this work the search for the roots of the Nigerian religious problems in order to suggest ways that can lead to peaceful co-existence.

The way out does not in any way lie in Nigerians becoming completely Muslims, Christians or adherents of ATR. Primarily, it is important that we retrain our mind-set and consciences which have been so negatively formed that they are more dangerous than even the visible weapons of mass destruction. This mind-set-retraining will involve disabusing our minds of the belief that peace will reign only when Nigeria becomes either totally Islamic or Christian. Nigeria as it is today constituted will hardly ever be totally so. For that reason, it pays that we, despite the multiplicity of religion, strive to live in peace with one another in the spirit of give and take. According to Arinze,

> When we say peace, we think of tranquillity, order, calm, security, and normalcy, but also of development, of justice and of respect for the rights

---

[626] Punch Newspaper, March 5, 2009, cf. www.punchontheweb.com

[627] Sekretariat der Deutschen Bischofskonferenz, (Hg.), „Christians and Muslims- Partners in Dialogue" in: *Stimmen der Weltkirche* Nr. 38, VI. Deutsch-Afrikanisches Bischofstreffen in Akosombo, Ghana, October 11 – 15, 2004, p. 27. March 5, 2009, cf. www.punchontheweb.com

[627] Sekretariat der Deutschen Bischofskonferenz, (Hg.), „Christians and Muslims- Partners in Dialogue" in: *Stimmen der Weltkirche* Nr. 38, VI. Deutsch-Afrikanisches Bischofstreffen

of others. And when we think of lack of peace, our mind goes to disturbance, disorder, insecurity, abnormal conditions violence and war, but also to underdevelopment, oppression, injustice and violation of rights....War does not lie primarily in armaments or missiles, but in the human heart. The human conscience, convictions, system of thought to which one is bound and also the passions which influence one, are the origins of war or peace. It is in his conscience or heart that man is sensitive to the absolute values of goodness, justice, brotherhood and peace. It is also in the depths of his heart that he can reject the appeals of these absolutes.[628]

Apart from retraining our mind-set, I have no fears of contradiction in stating that tribalism is another cankerworm that has continued unabatedly to eat deep into the fabrics of peace thereby making peaceful living in Nigeria, at least for now, a mere wishful thinking. This tribal or racial inclination of Nigerians is linked with the popular saying in Igbo language, IMA MMADU abbreviated as IM or IMA ONYE MA MMADU- IMM.[629]It is therefore very important that the political class or the haves should for the sake of peace do the right things. When contracts are awarded based on qualification, the effect will be a great job done. According to Pope John Paul II in his message on the World day of peace, termed 'From a new heart, Peace is born',

> Over and above ideological systems properly so-called, the passions that disturb the human heart and incline it to war were also many kinds. People can allow themselves to be carried away by a sense of racial supremacy and by hatred of others for this reason, or by jealousy, envy of the land and resources of others, or in a general way, by the desire for power,

---

[628] Arinze, F., "The Contribution of the Various Religions to the Building of Peace" in: *Secretariatus pro non Christianis Bulletin*, 1986-87 Nr. 61-66, p. 241.

[629] IM refers to a situation where one helps or supports another because he is known to the other or for the simple fact that they are from the same tribe or race or even from the same section of the country. In extended sense, it can happen between those who belong to the same political party. In the case of political IM, contracts are given not based on qualification but based on relationships. It can be awarded as a reward to a political big weight who sponsored A or B to get a political office. The consequences of such contracts are not obscure. A contract given under such a condition will never be done or if at all done, it will be half-hazardously done. The final recipients of such a shabby work are the poor innocent citizens who continue to languish in silent hopelessness and powerlessness as they pluck the bitter fruit of corruption sown by 'the shameless haves'. Awareness of such ill-treatment mostly breeds mutual hostilities that can last for a long period of time.

by pride, by a desire to extend their control over other peoples whom they despise.[630]

Nigerians are not intellectual dwarfs or dullards. They know when contract is awarded to the rightful person and when it is given simply based on racial or political affiliation termed IM or when the appointment is purely made on merit. A typical example of a meritorious appointment was that of Prof. Jega as the INEC Chairman in 2010. The president was highly praised since many knew him as one who will excellently execute the Job without fear or favour. If he negatively rewrites his track of good records simply because of election, he will bear the burden of self-image destruction all alone. Nigerians have passion for good things. It needs the courage of a fearless sincere person or group to make things move the right way or demand that things be done as it should. When the citizenry suffer real or imagined injustice for long, it could lead to frustration. Their burning passion for justice could lead them to taking a violent step. Surely, this will lead to anarchy and disorder and peaceful co-existence will suffer a heavy blow. This violent step may be directed against the government, but eventually, it is the common, innocent ones who bear the effect. It is for this that the Pope further said that, "... passions are often born of the real frustrations of individuals and peoples when others have refused to guarantee their existence or the sharing of wealth. Injustice is already a great vice in the heart of the exploiter. But passions are sometimes fed deliberately. It is difficult for wars to start if the people on both sides do not have powerful feelings of mutual hostility or if they are not convinced that the claims of their opponents threaten their vital interests."[631] This is therefore a call to justice which is essential for peace. In recognition of the effect of injustice as opposed to Justice in a nation building, the Bishops of Ghana let their mouths loose, admonishing their countrymen and –women. They admonished them to seek Justice and Peace in their daily lives and to be actively involved, especially in their families, in education IN and FOR Justice. They admonished them to give to everybody with whom they come in daily contact, common witness to justice. They maintained that Bribery and Corruption, favouritism and nepotism, extortion and intimidation, lying and intrigues have become so common in Ghana that they are almost taken for granted, and their inherent injustice is overlooked. But the gravity of the danger they pose both to the

---

[630] John Paul II, "From a new heart, Peace is born" being Message for the Celebration of the World Day of Peace, January 1, 1984, cf. http://www.vatican.va

[631] Ibid.

national peace and prosperity, and to the dignity of the human person, is not thereby minimized. They denounced these vices and drew the attention of the citizenry to their malice.[632] The exact picture of Ghana painted by this statement of the Bishops is not far away from the Nigerian situation which if not drastically fought will spell doom for the country. This clarion call tallies with the Igbo proverb, 'Egbe belu ugo belu, nke siri ibeya ebena, nku kwaa ya', (Let both the kite and eagle perch. Whichever says the other should not perch, let its wing break) which literally means, 'live-and-let-live' should be taken to be a high-plus point to ATR.[633] The essence of this explanation is to show the essence of justice in the three religions. A popular traditional Yoruba song says, "Be just do good, Be just do good. It is the just that the divinities support."[634] It will be overlabouring the obvious to list the numerous pages of the Holy Bible and Qur'an awash with citations on Justice. For the benefit of doubt, suffice it to mention just but a few: Ex.15:2; Prov.29:7; Matt.6.1; Lk.6:20-26; Qur'an 14, 58; 16, 90. Since the three major religions in Nigeria all speak of Justice which is a fast root to peace, it will be very welcomed if they cooperate in a more visible way.

That this work has dwelt more on Christianity and Islam should be seen from the point of view of their great number of followers. But the bitter truth for ATR is that when Christianity and Islam find peace among themselves, peace will surely rule in Nigeria taking their numerical strength into consideration. An article in *Kirche heute* confirms this assertion maintaining that this write-up is with the conviction that Muslims and Christians together make up more than half (55%) of the world population and inferred/concludes from that this penetrating thesis: Without peace between this two religious communities, there will be no true peace in the world. The future of the world depends on peace between Muslims and Christians."[635] This is not to down-play the presence of ATR but to maintain the obvious. This is clear even in the world arena. Onaiyekan John, a Catholic Archbishop was even surprised to learn that in the whole world, Nigeria stands as the

---

[632] Ghana Bishops Conference: A Collection of Communiqués, Memoranda and Pastoral letters, compiled by the Department of Social Communications of the National Catholic Secretariat, St. Francis Press, Takoradi- Ghana, 1999, p. 11.

[633] The suitability of this proverb is today hotly contested. It is seen to be against the New Testament teaching of Christ calling us to turn the other cheek. On this ground, it has been re-baptized to have a divine face. In this case, the last part 'Nku kwaa ya' (let its wing break), is replaced with, 'ya gosi ya ebe oga ebe' (the other should be shown where to perch).

[634] Owolalu, J. O., "Religion and social Justice" A paper read at the Religious Studies Conference, Ibadan University, February 3, 1981.

[635] cf. Friedliches Miteinander von Christen und Muslimen, in: *Kirche heute*, Aufbruch der Kirche in eine neue Zeit, 16 Jahrgang 1/2009, p. 19.

country with the greatest number of Muslims and Christians living together as a country, thanks to His Grace Archbishop Henri Teensier, who brought this to his knowledge.[636] Despite the fact that ATR has lost a lot of its followers to Christianity and Islam, it is necessary to carry them along. It must be made clear that no religion should be seen as a toothless bulldog simply because the group refuses to join in the destruction of places of worship of other religious groups. Mbon adviced:

> The religions of the world must be willing, both at the official and individual levels, to change their particularist claims, such as the claim to be the only path to humankind's spiritual and socio-cultural salvation. They should be willing to concede that each of them has a role to play in the process of human emancipation. Such a change of attitude, if achieved, will aid not only the process of dialogue and a cordial working relationship among them, but will also reduce considerably, if not eliminate completely, the rivalry and hostility that now characterize their attitudes toward each other as they struggle to win converts.[637]

This should not be interpreted as a call to all religions to come and worship under the same roof. It rather encourages all religious groups to maintain their tenets but come together to fight a common cause that will ensure peace despite our doctrinal differences. The unifying role of religion should be pursued in matters that can help inspire peaceful co-existence. Since the three religions teach the basic truth that every human being is a creature of God, it baffles to see that they don't accept one another as being from the same God/Allah/Supreme Being. Accordingly to Onwu, "The acknowledgement of God as creator is not only necessary in acknowledging our creatureliness, dependence and independence but also makes us open to other and aspire to the ideal in the fear of God and love of men. If religion has any unifying role in human society, it must be from this common perspective."[638]

The coming together for peace by these religions will be helpful if they take it as their duty to fight for the inculcation of moral rectitude and principles in the public life. In this realm we have to turn attention to the contribution made by one time Bishop of Nakuru Diocese but now Archbishop of

[636] Onaiyekan, J., The Shari'a in Nigeria: Issues and Perspectives (Paper delivered at the National Seminar on Shari'a, organized by the Jama'atu Nasril Islam, Kaduna, February 12, 2000, p. 3.
[637] Mbom, F. M., op.cit. p. 7.
[638] Onwu, N., "Religion and National Unity in Nigeria: Problems and Prospects" in *The Nigerian Journal of Social Studies*, Vol.III, (October1986), p. 37.

Nairobi in Kenya, Right Rev. Raphael S. Ndingi Mwana Nzeki. Known for his strong statements on social and public life as it concerns freedom and Justice, he advised Africans and indirectly Nigerians on how best they can find a lasting peace. For him, "If we are to bring lasting peace in Africa, (Nigeria) and indeed it is our grave obligation, we must bring moral awareness to public life. The fact is that public life cannot by-pass ethical criteria. Peace is achieved first of all on the terrain of human values, values that are lived and transmitted by citizens and by people. Whenever, the moral fibre of a nation begins to wear away, the worst is to be feared."[639] In an attempt to inculcate moral rectitude in the public life and avoid the possibility of moral decadence, I suggested that the populace be adequately informed and educated. This is to be done through proper instructive education. The place of education in nation building which involves peaceful association and dialogue is not to be doubted. But, if the truth has to be said without equivocation, let it be heard that some Moslem countries are not living up to expectation on this issue of getting their religious members informed concerning the need for respect towards non-Moslems in the countries where Moslems are majority. This is exactly why the Pope in Ecclesia in Africa, No.66 calling for reciprocity on the side of Moslems said,

> Particular care will therefore be taken so that Islamic –Christian dialogue respects on both sides the principle of religious freedom with all that this involves, also including external and public manifestations of faith. Christians and Muslims are called to commit themselves to promoting a dialogue free from the risks of false irenicism or militant fundamentalism, and to raising their voices against unfair policies and practices, as well as against the lack of reciprocity in matters of religious freedom.[640]

In line with the above statement, Benedict XVI recalling part of the words he addressed to the United Nations General Assembly in 2008 opined that there are many areas of the world today in which forms of restrictions and limitations to religious freedom persist. Such areas include both where communities of believers are a minority and where communities of believers are not a minority. They include also where more sophisticated forms of discrimination and marginalisation exist both on the cultural level and in the spheres of public activity. In those areas he described the situation as incon-

[639] Nzeki, R. S., "Peace in Africa" in: *Welt Kirche*, Nr. 3/1990), by Common Service of Adveniat, Misereor and Missio (AMM), Munich, 1990, p. 75.
[640] Ecclesia in Africa, No. 66.

ceivable where the believers have to suppress a part of themselves – their faith – in order to be active citizens. It should never be necessary to deny God in order to enjoy one's rights. The rights associated with religion are all the more in need of protection if they are considered to clash with a prevailing secular ideology or with majority religious positions of an exclusive nature.[641] In order to reduce this to its barest minimum, the Government should see to it that laws are made which will help uphold peace initiatives in union with the different religions. European countries should serve as good examples for Nigeria despite the awareness of differences in social and political settings. As Pope Benedict XIV remarked,

> In Africa and Europe Christians and Muslims live in different social and political settings. Experience shows that relations between Christians and Muslims can be guaranteed and enhanced by a legal framework that includes the rule of law, equal citizenship, human rights in the political, economic and cultural fields, religious freedom, good governance and the promotion of justice and peace. Rule of law means a constitutional order characterized by legitimating government through free elections, control of government by independent judiciary and by the absence of discrimination as to ethnicity, language and /or religion. That is why the Church, in line with the teaching of Vatican II, advocates a secular state order. A secular order does not mean an anti-or non-religious order, but rather one that provides the best conditions for all believers to practice their respective religion freely, a precondition for the harmonious and respectful living together of Christians, Muslims and others.[642]

It is however necessary to note that the freedom of religion meant here is not a license for any religion in Nigeria to try to implement its religious tenets to the detriment of the lot of other citizens. This would constitute a breach to public- and civic order. It is for this reason that Pope Benedict warned,

> Any legal provisions which are derived from religious traditions and teachings of only one religion, as for instance the prescriptions of the sharia, understood as a religio-political law, are incompatible with this understanding of civic order. However, to strive for a legislation in confor-

---

[641] Benedict XVI, "Religious Freedom, The Path to Peace" July 13, 2010 being the Theme chosen for the 2011 World Day of Peace, in: *Vatican Information Service, (VIS).*
[642] Ibid, p. 32.

mity with the ethical values lying at the bottom of the sharia does not undermine the bases of a just and pluralist order. There is nothing wrong in expecting Muslims to accept that religious demands derived from Islamic law can only be enforced within the legal framework of a democratic secular state. Legal framework in this context implies constitutional guarantees of civic rights and fundamental values that cannot be altered even by majority vote. As Christians we work for a state that gives consideration to religions as well as promotes values and ideals emanating from them. In all her actions in the field of politics, of the media and of academics, and especially, wherever Christian-Muslim relations are involved, the Church stands for this concept of civic order.[643]

Equality of all citizens and of all religions before the law of any land is a strong and sure guarantee for peaceful co-existence. A state is legitimated when it is able to act as a provider of necessary public goods and more importantly when it takes no sides but remains a neutral arbiter that guarantees the security of all sections of the society. Unfortunately, when the State is generally perceived as being particularistic, promoting the interest of one group, it loses its legitimacy, and indeed its authority. Consequent upon this, governments, political and civic leaders must create a political order that guarantees fairness, equity and justice for all. This includes non-adoption of a State religion (either for a whole country or a part of it), ensuring that every person is entitled to freedom of thought, freedom of conscience and freedom of religion.[644] Going to specifics, I dare to mention a European country like Germany where different religions live peacefully together. Indicating the importance of religious freedom and its successful application in Germany, Robert Zöllitsch, the President of German Catholic Bishops Conference addressing Nigerians explained that Germany is in his history and culture influenced by Christianity. Nearly three third (2/3) of the population are Christians. But Germany from political and legal point of view is not a Christian land. In 1919, a clear differentiation between the state and the church, as well as state and religion in Germany were made but not strictly separated from one another. They co-operate for the good of the people who are both citizens of the state as well as members of a church or of one of another religious organization. In the centre of this co-operation is the religious freedom. Already the preamble of the General Declaration of Human Right of the United Nations of December, 10, 1948 stressed that, the highest

---

[643] Ibid, p. 33.
[644] Ibid, p. 29.

desire of Man is that of a world in which the people should enjoy the freedom of speech and religion. The guarantee of comprehensive application of religious freedom belongs in Germany therefore to the basis of state rules. Germany is a land that is influenced by Christianity, Christian principles and worthily attached to it but is neutral in matters of religious confession. It has therefore to see to it that all his citizens, not minding their religious confession could profess and practice their faith. The presence of Islam in Germany will be seen in public life especially through (the building of) Mosques. A Mosque shows a realization of religious freedom. Its building is hence in line with the German rule of law of basic right of religious freedom protected.[645] From this example given by Zöllitsch, Nigerians should and must imbibe the spirit of brotherliness and good example of living together. This must be done in such a way that religious and ethnic boundaries must be crossed both by politicians and religious leaders. It is a task that Nigerians will carry out on their own if they must continue to exist.

For this to be a dream come true, the convocation of National Constitutional Conference (N.C.C) would be of great help, where every constituency will be represented for a round table conference. This will guarantee a bright future for Nigeria and her citizens. We should not wait or expect international bodies to come and do it for us. Allowing external (foreign) bodies to influence the peace process will tantamount to self-imposed Neo-colonialism. According to Michael Gregory, "If Nigeria should have a future, the politicians and religious leaders of the country must understand that they must find the solutions to the problems in the country itself. This can only happen over and above religious and ethnic barriers."[646]Typical example already in Nigeria which is worthy of emulation is the popular good relationship that exists between Archbishop of Jos diocese, Ignatius Kaigama and Alhaji Haruna Abdulahi, the Emir of Wase. These two have become household names in Germany. This popularity gained ground after the visit of the President of the German Bishops and the president of Missio to Nigeria. They were highly marketed to the German Media as the epicenter of peaceful co-existence in Nigeria. It also has its base on the decision of the two never to allow the riots in their areas of control to escalate. Even when it happened

[645] Zöllitsch, R., Ansprache anlässlich einer Begegnung mit S.E., Erzbischof Ignatius Kaigama und Seiner königlichen Hoheit Alhaji Abdullahi Haruna Maikano, Emir von Wase, September 3, 2009 in Jos, in: Missionswissenschaftliches Institut Missio e.V.

[646] Gregory, M., „Nigeria braucht Zusammenarbeit seiner Religionen und Völker" in: *Die Tagespost*, Germany, Januar 9, 2010

in the past, they had worked together to bring the situation under control. Giving credence to this assertion, after the violence of Jos in 2008, Archbishop Kaigama said, "At the centre of the crises, many thought that this wave would separate us now. But we were brought closer."[647] Speaking on the same issue, the Emir explained what has always been his message to his people, "I tell those who allow themselves to be politically manipulated: "The basis of Islam is peace. If one behaves differently, one distances himself from the basis of his faith. And that makes one an unbeliever."[648] The example of these two tally with the notion that the faithful of the two religions can help to a large extent to install peace among Nigerians. Accordingly Ehusani wrote,

> Thus, in a country like Nigeria, devastated by many years of dictatorship, with an economy that has been ruined by corruption, greed and graft, yes, a country that is today crying for moral rearmament or ethical revolution, a coalition of moral and spiritual forces among Christians and Muslims can play a pivotal role in the emergence of an accountable leadership and a corrupt-free nation, since the individual and social morality of the majority of our people is often determined by their religious beliefs and practices. Nigerian society needs the moral persuasion of Christianity and Islam in the project of raising a more honest, transparent and accountable leadership, and a more law abiding, disciplined and productive population. A number of well-known religious leaders in Nigeria can help in many ways to strengthen the organs of civil society. With so much religiosity in Nigeria, religious leaders of both persuasions, especially when they act together, could indeed be the rallying point and the catalyst for the emergence of a new Nigeria of social transformation and peaceful coexistence....[649]

This could only be possible if the three major religious groups in Nigeria adhere sincerely to their different good moral and social teachings. Living in accordance with the tenets of their morally correct teachings can protect humanity from the self-destruction that will otherwise arise. Christianity and Islam shall enhance social integration taking into consideration that both

[647] Kappel, J., „Der Emir und der Erzbischof" in: Kirche+Leben, Oktober 18, 2009, p. 8
[648] Ibid.
[649] Ehusani, G., "Case Study of Nigeria" in: *Human Rights, Opportunities for Christian-Islamic Co-operation in upholding human rights and establishing civil societies*- Conference in closed session 11/3/2002 – 14/3/2002, Berlin, p. 93.

religions give men and women a sense of meaning. Enhancement of wholesome existence for individuals and peace for society belong to the task they can successfully embark upon since they teach people that the meaning of human life is beyond humanity. They are capable of promoting justice and equity in society, following their admonishing that people should not do to others what they would not want others to do to themselves. Surely, Christianity and Islam in collaboration have the potentiality of promoting solidarity among the various segments of society, since they teach their adherents to be charitable towards those in need, and to be their brother/sister's keeper.[650]

Despite the better understanding existing between Christianity and Islam, ATR should be incorporated in this search for peace through dialogue. It is a not to be doubted that ATR prepared the way for these two religions with the largest followership in Nigeria. According to Isizoh, "It is well known that the early Christian missionaries in sub-Saharan Africa from the onset did not promote dialogue (as understood today) with followers of other religions. With reference to African Traditional Religion, the adherents were in most cases open to other religious expressions. Christians found them potential members and were, therefore, not interested in engaging them in normal dialogue (as already defined in many documents by the (PCID). Early efforts to know African Traditional Religion were mainly geared towards its elimination or displacement, or adaptation of aspects of it. The main focus of interest was the conversion of adherents of ATR."[651]

However, it would not be out of place if inculturation be sought by these religions with ATR. Inculturation will help the different religions to appreciate the good values in our traditional religion and so pave way for peaceful co-existence. Some clear examples have already taken place. Certain things that used to be considered an abomination are now praised by the Church. Some of the instruments that were abhorred, tabooed and termed devilish are now being used in the Church to the joy of all. It is in connection to this that Wells wrote, "It was a serious sign of real conversion to Christianity to tear the skin of the drum. The idea behind this action was sequel to the traditional belief connecting the beating of the drum and the call to the ancestors. A traditional healer connects with the ancestors through the sound of the drum. The attention and presence of the ancestral spirits are sought through the

[650] Ibid, p. 192.
[651] Isizoh, D. C., "Forty Years of Dialogue with Religions in Sub-Sahara Africa and withTraditional Religions in the World (A Report)" in: *Pro Dialogo, Plenary Assembly,* May 14-19, 2004, Pontificum Consilium Pro Dialogo Inter Religiones, Bulletin 116-117 2004/2-3, p. 205.

sound and rhythmic noise (music) emanating from the drum. This sound restores the lost and distorted equilibrium and brings healing equaling the physiotherapeutic healing of the western medicine."[652] The use of drums has now won a place of pride in the Christian tradition. It is no more a taboo but now employed even in liturgical celebrations. Because of its symbolic application, in some African countries, drums are now being used during consecration at Eucharistic celebrations not only to create a conducive atmosphere of worship but also to acknowledge the divine presence after the words of consecration have been pronounced. This is real adaptation.

It must be said loud and clear that no level of co-operation between the leaders of different religions, and no degree of inculturation and education will bring peace in Nigeria without a corresponding effort on the part of government to provide the citizens with enabling environment. Government must put smiles on the faces of Nigerians by making them feel and enjoy the fruits of democratic dispensation. The time of promises of a bright future that cannot be fulfilled is now a thing of the past and outmoded. The reality on ground now is that many Nigerians are poor and hungry and their daily bread is not guaranteed. This poverty level is the root of so many atrocities that we experience in Nigeria including the unfortunate absence of peaceful co-existence. Hunger does untold underground havoc. A hungry man sees trouble even where there is peace. A hungry man can see a devil where an angel may be. A hungry man acts before knowing the reason for his actions. In fact, a real hungry man is senseless. When he is senseless, surely he can kill for the sake of money for food. The many thieves we have in Nigeria are hungry men. For him, life is meaningless and could be ended at any time. Surely most of the riots and violence we witness in Nigeria is due to hunger and injustice and not religion. Violence which disturbs the peace of the nation is 'tap-rooted' in hunger and poverty. Therefore, the government must, as a matter of urgency, evolve economic policies that will put smiles on the faces of the Nigerians. If this happens, the number of hungry citizens who are bought over to foment troubles during electioneering campaigns with a bag of rice or a piece of cloth will be reduced to the barest minimum if not totally. I refuse to call them hooligans or thugs as many would like to label them. Instead, I call them hungry men and women who are eager by all means to get something to survive. After all, the politicians buying them and sending them to cause havoc are more culpable. They are the real hooligans and thugs who specialize in milking the nation dry. From what they have

[652] Wells, R. E., *An Introduction to the Music of the Basotho*, Morija, 1994, p. 238.

stolen, they now buy this hungry Nigerians to cause commotion using religion as a cover up. This use of religion creates tension and unrest in the country as many Nigerians attach much importance to their religion.

As we pointed out the menace of poverty in the destabilization of the decorum of any country, we deem it necessary to call the Nigerian authority to work towards economic advancement of its population. Completely aware of the horror effect that poverty can bring a country Germany organized campaign against poverty and made it pivotal in her parliamentary decisions.[653] This wise decisive step changed the lives of her citizens. There is no doubt that it is the duty of the government of any land to see to the good of her citizens. The moment the government makes her commitment towards the good of the electorate felt in her principle of governance, the electorate will surely reply with good will. This has to start with the government making it a point of duty to organize a credible election in the country. Once those who are aspiring to political offices in the land are the rightful people and not those who will give more bribes to the office of the INEC in order to be selected, there begins indirectly our economic emancipation and poverty alleviation. It is so because those who are elected through fair and free election will see it as a challenge to proof those who elected them right by providing them with the promised democratic gains. I deem it unnecessary to mention all the areas that government, whether Federal or State, should pay attention in order to carry the electorate along with her. It is known to all even the politicians themselves who mention them during their political campaigns. A simple fulfillment of 2/3 of their campaign promises is already a move in the right direction. Promising heaven only to turn around to bring poverty on the electorate is a grade one crime against humanity. Such failures when addressed, investigated and punished by subsequent governments will bring unimaginable result that will increase the lots of the population and empower them economically. In this case, the salaries of the workers will be increased and commitment to official duties will bounce back. When people take their duties seriously, economy will grow and more industries will be built to accommodate greater number of those who cause havoc in the society because of unemployment. If one has nothing to eat, and has no hope of a visible sign of an end to his poor situation in view, how does such a person cope with life? For him, government policies on ethics and moral may be a waste of time. Surely such a person will be ready to do anything to sur-

[653] Beschluss des Bundestages vom 2. März, 19887, bekräftigt am 20 Juni 1988, vgl. Drucksache 1989 11/6137.

vive, or to keep the body and soul in motion.[654]It is my unwavering opinion that the moment government tackles the issue of election malpractice and poverty, Nigerians will surely co-operate with one another in peace. To come out of this impoverished situation, a dialogue that is not just based on openness on religious level but as well on political level will help put so many wrongs aright. This coming together according Pope John XXIII should be a union from which countless blessings can flow. He said,

> Nevertheless, we are hopeful that, by establishing contact with one another and by a policy of negotiation, nations will come to a better recognition of the natural ties that bind them together as men. We are hopeful, too, that they will come to a fairer realization of one of the cardinal duties deriving from our common nature: namely, that love, not fear, must dominate the relationships between individuals and between nations. It is principally characteristic of love that it draws men together in all sorts of ways, sincerely united in the bonds of mind and matter; and this is a union from which countless blessings can flow.[655]

Although this citation is meant for the globe, its application in Nigeria will still bear the desired fruit. It will be a forum where all stake holders in Nigeria political as well as religious, will come to a round table conference and chart a new path for Nigeria. As said before, National Conference is a laudable option. If undertaken with a sincere open mind and readiness to do the will of God, National Conference will surely pave a way to success for Nigeria. The openness and humble submission of Mary, the virgin mother of Jesus to the will and word of God through the Angel can serve as a good example of the type of openness and humility we need for a dialogue. Having seen that both Christians and Muslims are of the same opinion that Jesus is the son of Mary and conceived without original sin, I see it as a meeting point where the two can discuss on how to live in peace- taking her as a model of humility. This is a basis for achieving peace as Riße put it: In order to ensure peace among the religions, we are called to direct our attention to Mary, the Mother of Jesus. More importantly than ever, we need this woman, the border crosser, who -as an exemplary believer in God- can unite people from different religions, spiritualities and cultures – with very personal identity – in the basic concept of a tolerant, respectful and peaceful co-

---

[654] Yuzon,L, A., Mission in the Context of Endemic Poverty: Papers of a Consultation on Mission in the Context of Poverty and in Situations of Affluence, Singapore 1983.

[655] John XXIII, *Pacem in Terris*, Encyclical Letter Establishing Universal Peace in Truth, Justice, Charity, and Liberty, April 11, 1963.

existence.[656]Every religion in the bid to foster unity must be ready to drop some aspects of its religious practices that would not destroy her basic tenets. The Catholic Church has done it before and continues to do it for the sake of peace. Without such attitude, dialogue may never be possible. As Riße acknowledged, The church believes in it that the spirit of Jesus Christ, in a way which God alone knows, is also effectively present outside the visible boundaries of the church and in those who without their fault do not know Jesus Christ, but in their way do the will of God as they recognize him in their consciences, have through the grace of Christ, who died for all, the possibility to receive the everlasting salvation. This thought calls for a deeper knowledge in a theology of the non-Christian religions. Christianity respects and appreciates all that is good, true and noble in other religions. At the same time, Christianity wants through a prophetic criticism to purify those areas, where their Essence has been misplaced and up-turned, where they distort the image of God and suppress the human dignity, and to bring the true and good which they contain, and which has been purified in Christ to the fulfillment which can surpass their own abilities.[657]

A Khoury pointed out that "dialogue demands a decisive openness of the spirit and a great readiness of the heart. Whoever seeks dialogue must be ready to go out of himself, to move out from the usual certainty of one's tradition in other to meet the other. The spontaneous exhibition of Feeling of mistrust towards the foreigner, which destroys the normal and threatens to question the oriented Norms of the practical life must be tamed/controlled and overcome."[658] It does not mean that one has to deny his belief. It calls however for strong conviction in one's faith as well as pursuing this dialogue in a sincere way, in which case one tries to see the stand of the other with charity. Khoury threw his weight behind this statement when he declared that:

> Dialogue lives at the same time on the dynamism of the most serious Faithfulness to one's faith and to one's religion. This faithfulness is not a blind stand on all, what in any form belongs to the tradition. In other way round, he does not allow that one throws away easily the substance of one's tradition and what informs the identity of one's religion... Dialogue, therefore does not mean the renunciation of the truth and the condemna-

[656] Riße, G., Maria-Grenzgängerin, p. 638.

[657] Ibid, p. 639, quoting Cardinal Kasper, W.

[658] Khoury, A. T., „Wahrheit und Dialog“ in: *Kirche heute*, 17Jahrgang, 4/2010, Aufbruch der Kirche in eine neue Zeit, p. 20.

tion of the truth of the represented teaching but contrary on the faithfulness to the recognized truth of one's faith, and actually of the two sides. The dialoguing partners owe themselves the duty, to inform one another and their religious groups on what their faith lives and on what their religious spiritual live feeds...[659]

We must try to avoid a situation where one partner sees dialogue as a means of pushing for the indirect destruction of the other partner's article of faith. In the year 2006 in Germany for instance, the worldly acclaimed apostle of Unity among Christians Cardinal Walter Kasper could not hold himself following the decision of the parliament that Crosses should be removed from public places. This action or decision according to them was meant to be a way of showing that one religion is not superior to the other. But it was seen in Catholic circle as a direct attack on the very basis on which Christianity stands. Speaking about this decision concerning the Crosses in public places, Kasper a champion of dialogue, cried out as he reinstated the importance of Cross in Europe. In a clear reference to the Cross he said,

> It is Europe's symbolic identity. To take the cross down, to restrict it in a private room or to hide it is the same as surrender and denial of our culture as well as our religion. With that, we will not harvest respect but scorn from people of other faiths. Could anyone imagine a land with Muslim majority which will renounce the symbol of the half moon or could the Christians in such countries hope of success if they would complain that their night peace are being disturbed by the call of the Muezzin? Or would the Muslims among us in the future give up building a Mosque simply because a native or a group of natives kicks against it?...Tolerance means respect and attention for others conviction, not renunciation of one's conviction...Surely the Muslims do not believe that Jesus is the son of God but they have great respect for him as prophet. Even the Qur'an knows about the Christmas story (including the virgin birth). Why then should of all, our Nursery schools do away with telling our children the Christmas stories and letting them see it clearly through the presentation of cribs? Such type of tolerance itself leads to absurdity.[660]

---

[659] Ibid. p. 21.

[660] Kasper, W., "Wir werden Verachtung ernten"in: *Kirche heute*, Aufbruch der Kirche in eine neue Zeit, 12/2009, 16.Jahrgang, p. 13.

From the statement made by Walter Kasper, it is easy to find that this action was taken without dialogue. And if so, government failed in her responsibility to carry every one along. Such a situation should be discouraged in Nigeria. It is an indirect wrong jihad of the sword and does not justify the end, which is forceful conversion. Surely, no bad deed, no matter the good intention with which it was done, could be justified. The end does not justify the means.[661] Instead, 'JIHAD' should be recommended. I mean Jihad against oneself. Jihad as mentioned here is one of the types mentioned in many places in Qur'an in which case the true fighter, Mudschahid, is the one who fights himself if he wants to defeat mistakes and sins in order to come nearer to God. Jihad should therefore be seen as a personal struggle and effort on the way to God. Representatives of a group set on reforming Islam are pleading unanimously for the Jihad to be carried out as a duty for justice, and peace, as a struggle for economic development against poverty and suppression and this should be done only by means of peace. Example is to lead with the power of conviction. One should start to work on oneself in order to live the Islamic life in its fullness; that is the aim that will help to reach it, i.e. reaching God. It will be wonderful when other Moslems should address to themselves the question asked by the President of the central Council of the Moslems in Germany, Nadeem Elyas. He said, "We Muslims must critically ask ourselves the question, why should such violence in the name of our religion come presently among us and in some other countries. We must not lead such a Jihad."[662]

This question from Nadeem should be repeated in Nigeria. In Nigeria, it should no more be directed only to Moslems but to the members of the three major religions in the country. Why must the name of Nigeria be always on the air for different categories of conflicts? We must try to imitate some people who have done humanity proud by devoting their time for the course of Justice and have become symbols of peace. According to Ehusani we should imitate St. Francis of Assisi who was one such symbol of peace at the height of the crusades and jihads of the 12th century. He was acknowledged as a "man of God" by Muslims and Christians because of his commitment to peace and universal brotherhood in the midst of the deafening drums of war. Also Mahatma Ghandi lived as a Hindu. But with his radical non-violent ideology he made innumerable disciples among Christian and Muslim clerics

---

[661] Cf. Artikel 4, „Der sittliche Charakter der Menschlichen Handlung, Nr.1759, in: *Katechismus der Katholischen Kirche*, München, Oldenbourg Verlag, 1993, p. 469.
[662] Riße, G., Der Islam, Religion der Gewalt oder des Friedens? p. 24-25.

alike. One such disciple was the black civil rights leader, the Rev. Martin Luther King Jr., who has today been proclaimed as a frontline American hero. Mother Teresa of Calcutta was a Catholic nun. But her commitment to peace and upholding human dignity was acknowledged and acclaimed by Buddhists and Hindus and Christians and Muslims alike. In our day Pope John Paul II has successfully established a reputation as an agent of peace even in the minds of those who are hostile to the Catholic faith.[663]

To achieve the required peace in Nigeria, I call all to take to heart the four pillars of peace given in Pacem in Terris as summarized by Cardinal Arinze. These pillars are, "truth, justice, freedom and love. Truth comes from God. Every person has the right to receive objective information. Justice promotes impartiality towards individuals, protects weak people and proclaims that might is not right. Freedom is characteristic of man. The human person should enjoy freedom of religion, opinion and movement. And he should use his freedom with a high sense of civic responsibility. Fraternal love comes from recognition of our solidarity as a human family under God."[664] When a day like this comes, I will be the happiest man on earth just as I know that many will lay claim to being happier than myself as every religion lays claim to being the authentic one. Could such a day ever come when the Catholic Bishops' Conference of Nigerian will speak like their Ghanaian counterparts, "Fortunately, Our country Ghana (Nigeria) has been blessed with a good number of political parties, of parliamentary and presidential candidates from which we are being asked to choose those to be entrusted with the government of this country for the next four years."[665] The joy will be great because it is not a hidden mater that most of those who offer themselves for elective posts are not after the good of the electorate. The good ones who have the wellbeing of the populace at heart are not allowed to emerge from the party primaries. The party leaders try always not to elect but to select their likes who will water their pockets after they have been foisted on the people- by their fruits you shall know them. I am talking of a day when we shall be our brother's keeper. It is a situation where a Moslem will help settle a dispute trying to blow a Christian community in his neighbor or a Christian helps to quell a squabble between two Moslem faith-based com-

---

[663] Ehusani, G., op.cit. p. 9.
[664] Arinze. F., *Church in Dialogue Walking with Others*, San Francisco, Ignatius Press, 1990, p. 199.
[665] Ghana Catholic Bishops, Pastoral Letter of the Catholic Bishops of Ghana for the Election Period 1996, in: *Ghana Bishops speak* St, Francis Press, Takoradi- Ghana, 1999, 285. (Bracket mine).

munities in his area. A typical reference point for us could be the situation when, the rift over the 1975 patriarchal constitution in the Methodist Church of Nigeria (Christian Church) threatened to throw the town o Alocha, near Umuahia into chaos in 1977. The report narrated how the adherents of African Traditional Religion met in the town and intervened in the rift to save what seemed to be developing into open clashes. This religions group took their "juju" to the church premises and performed a cleansing ceremony. Relying on the powers of the traditional instrument known as "Ofo", they went round the town with the instrument and invoked the powers of their dead ancestors to rise against any indigene that foments trouble as a result of the religious disagreement. Marching from one community to the other, they invoked God for divine guidance on their people so that the rift would not tear the town asunder.[666]

This interreligious co-operation could be seen in the spirit of Karl Rahner's theory of anonymous Christianity through the grace of Christ. With this theory, Karl Rahner made case for non-baptised people who according to him have implicit faith in Jesus Christ but do not belong to the visible Church.[667]Through this theological standpoint on the universal salvation brought us by Jesus, he gives grounds for hope of salvation to all people of good will because, God "wants everyone to be saved and reach full knowledge of the truth. For there is only one God, and there is only one Mediator between God and humanity, himself a human being, Christ Jesus, who offered himself as a ransom for all."[668] He also gives impetus to the struggle to bring all together as people of the same creator, God, who unfortunately is not sought by all from the same perspective. His thought surely influenced some aspects of the Second Vatican Council when the council declared their readiness to go into dialogue with different religions and cultures. Unfortunately, this good intentional argument of Karl Rahner supported by the Catholic Church would hardly be accepted by our Moslem brothers. However, I have put it down here not considering how every other religion will see it, but to point out that such understanding will make for peaceful co-existence if all religious groups accept this teaching.

---

666 Adegbola, E. A. A. (ed.), op.cit. p. 204, cf. also *Daily Times*, Lagos, December 28, 1977.
667 Rahner, K., *Schriften zur Theologie (SzTh)* V, Einsiedeln/Zürich/Köln, 1962/1968, p. 155.
668 1Tim. 2:4-5.

7.2. Conclusion

Having come thus far, it has become clear that peaceful co-existence has for long eluded Nigerian citizenry. Improper political amalgamation of Nigeria and the unfortunate consequent indirect rule have not helped the populace. But these situations are what could be mastered and rightly ordered to the joy and glory of Nigerians. Unfortunately greed and insincerity have denied us the chances we could have utilized to foster peace among us. Peace here does not refer to absence of war but also does not exclude it. Peace here refers to knowledge. I am of the opinion that, Knowledge is peace. Knowledge is power. Knowledge is strength and Knowledge gives courage to act rationally. Nigeria will know peace and live together in peace if the populace have the required and proper information about what is and why things are how they are. This will dismiss unnecessary suspicion and wrongful accusation. As the Fathers of the Vatican Council pointed out,

> Peace is more than absence of war: it cannot be reduced to the maintenance of a balance of power between opposing forces nor does it arise out of despotic dominion, but it is appropriately called 'the effect of righteousness'. It is the fruit of that ordering for things with which the divine founder has invested human society and which must be actualised by man thirsting after an ever more perfect reign of justice.[669]

Without Justice in Nigeria as is inscribed in our Constitution, peace will continue to be limited to a platonic wishful thinking. Our politicians must as a matter of urgency stop the appeal to religion in political matters- I mean religious politics which if not well handled, may lead Nigeria to religious war. On this note I wish to refer to a statement by Samuel Huntington. In 1996, he wrote a book entitled "Clash of Civilization" which Henry Kissinger described as one of the most important publications since the end of the cold war.[670] Huntington was of the view that the cause of war in 19th century was the idea of nationality and in 20th century it was the struggle over ideologies. He envisaged that the cause of war in 21st century might be the clash of cultures. He numerated the cultures involved as: Western, Orthodox, Islamic, Chinese-Confucius, Buddhism, Hinduism, Japanese, Latin-American

[669] Gaudium et Spes (GS), no. 78.

[670] Gerl-Falkovitz, H. B., "Gottes Platz in der Seele ist zu einer Leerstelle geworden" (Günter de Bruyen) in: Riße, G/Kathke C. A (Hg.), *Diaspora: Zeugnis von Christen für Christen*, 150 Jahre Bonifatiuswerk der deutchen Katholiken, Paderborn, Bonifatius Verlag, 1999, p. 499.

and African cultures.[671] His work suffered much criticism as lacking merit especially where five of these mentioned cultures were named in connection with their religious background. Hanna-Barbara Gerl-Falkovitz maintained that despite the fact that this book left much to be desired, it underscored the importance and influence that religion and religious politics in 21st Century which is already being discussed worldwide. Therefore, in such international discussions, according to Hanna-Barbara, religion shows its importance for the future politics and ethics of the "One World".[672]

If we consider many of the Terrorist attacks we experience these days, it becomes clearer that religion has been used to foment them knowing fully well the importance of religion. The many wars here and there may be economically or politically induced but at the end of it, it is redirected in the direction of religion. Nigeria is not an exception. The many riots and violence that have bedevilled the country Nigeria in the most recent yester years may have been economic, political, or ethnic. But what the common man knows is that it is either the Moslem North against the Christian South or vice versa. I am therefore convinced that Nigerians can live in peace together when religious politics is led to rest and sincere dialogue is pursued. But if not, we must be sure that the next war in Nigeria, GOD FORBID, will surely be religious war. The effect of global import of religion is already felt everywhere in the world and leads now to international co-operation among the people of the same religion worldwide. Because of the possibility of the destruction of the world peace, the German Bishops Conference has shown itself always disposed to engage the national and international Islamic groups in dialogue. It does not debar them from forming a strong alliance with their likes in other parts of the world to make sure that they are not suppressed. In his comment on the efforts of the German Bishops, Riße Günter wrote,

> There are dialogue and conflicts with Islam in our land as it is worldwide. That is why the Church in Germany is connected with the local Churches, which have their own different practical experiences with Islam. In numerous meetings, the German Bishops stay connected with the Bishops of their sister Churches in Africa, Asia and the Near East. The German Bishops Conference will also...move the initiative, 'Solidarity with the

[671] Ibid.
[672] Ibid.

persecuted and the oppressed Christians.' The work-guide will direct its attention towards the Holy Land, Egypt and Iraq.[673]

Therefore we must work for the enthronement of real democracy in which case every Nigerian, no matter where he is or may live, and no matter his religion, will enjoy his citizenship by being protected by the constitution of the land. Nigerians will surely live in Peace with one another when the government ensures that everyone or every group receives what is due to him or them as are wonderfully and unambiguously enshrined in the law of the land. In the Constitution we read, "Accordingly, national integration shall be actively encouraged, whilst discrimination on the grounds of place of origin, sex, religion, status, ethnic or linguistic association or ties shall be prohibited"[674] The unfortunate neglect of this constitutional rights of the citizenry has contributed in no small measure to the troubles in Nigeria. Following that, the constitution proscribed sectarianism which has continued to bedevil the country. In the constitution, we read, "The State shall foster a feeling of belonging and of involvement among the various peoples of the Federation, to the end that loyalty to the nation shall override sectional loyalty."[675]

On the side of economic objectives, the constitution orders the government to, within the context of the ideals and objectives for which provisions are made, "(a) harness the resources of the nation and promote national prosperity and an efficient, a dynamic and self-reliant economy; (b) control the national economy in such manner as to secure the maximum welfare, freedom and happiness of every citizen on the basis of social justice and equality of status and opportunity."[676] It went on to clearly state that the social order of Nigeria is based on the principles and ideals of Freedom, Equality and Justice.[677] In the same vein, the social order as is meant in our constitution implies that, "(a) every citizen shall have equality of rights, obligations and opportunities before the law; (b) the sanctity of human person shall be recognized and human dignity shall be maintained and enhanced; (c) governmental actions shall be human; (d) exploitation of human or natural resources in any form whatsoever for reasons, other than the good of the community, shall be prevented; and (e) the independent, impartiality and integrity of courts of

---

673 Riße, G., „Wegweisung: Muslime in Deutschland – Dokumente der Deutschen Bischofskonferenz zur Begenung" in: *Zeitschrift für Missionswissenschaft und Religionswissenschaft, (ZMR)* Heft 3-4, 91 Jahrgang 2007, EOS Verlag, p.199.
674 *1999 Constitution of the Federal Republic of Nigeria*, Chpt.11, Section 15, No. 2, p. 31.
675 Ibid, no. 4, p. 32.
676 Ibid, Section 16, no. 1, a & b, p. 32.
677 Ibid, Section. 17, no. 1.

law, and easy accessibility thereto shall be secured and maintained."[678]I believe that all the above unfortunate situations persist in Nigeria simply because the citizens do not know their rights and even those who know them are deep rooted in corruption. These citations from our constitution are good but only if they are implemented. For instance, the constitution talked of equality of human rights. It is clear that this equality is only for the haves and the political class. Opposed to the issue of the sanctity of human person, we hear on daily basis of dead bodies lying on the streets, either politically killed or killed for charm to win elections or make money. Stipulating that government actions should be human, the real experience is that of gross acts of man's inhumanity to man. Our constitution forbids the misuse and exploitation of human resources, but daily trillions of Naira are being laundered and siphoned out of the country by politicians and their cronies. How many have been prevented except if the politician involved is in the opposition camp. Even when they are prevented, where are the recovered money kept? The constitution priced the independence and impartiality of the courts of law high. But the question is, 'do we mean the catch and carry courts of law where the highest bidder or 'most benevolent briber' wins the case?

It is on this ground that I recommend that the Nigerian constitution be included in the Nigerian University curriculum where every undergraduate must study it at least as one of the introductory courses, with exams thereafter. Even the constitution stressed the importance of education. It stated in 18-(1), that, Government shall direct its policy towards ensuring that there are equal and adequate educational opportunities at all levels...(3) Government shall strive to eradicate illiteracy..."[679] It is regrettable that after fifty years of independence, Nigeria is still trying to find a suitable form of education to adopt. Strikes re-occur due to improper funding of the schools. I must say that as teachers are being poorly paid for the wonderful services they render to the nation, the politicians smile monthly to the banks with millions of naira- 'Monkey de work, baboon de chop' is a popular pidgin English adage. The government must therefore live up to expectations by finding the best salary scale for the professors and teachers and provide State governments who have private universities with enough fund for their maintenance.

It is not totally out of track if the citizenry from time to time put up a little resistance through reasonable and peaceful demonstration to press home their disgust with inhuman governmental policies. This is however recommendable only as the last resort after all reasonable dialogues may have

[678] Ibid, no. 2 a-e, p. 34.
[679] Ibid. Sect.18, no. 1-3. p.35.

failed. Another good step that would give authentic hope for peaceful co-existence will be when the leaders of different religions, coming under one umbrella, NIREC for instance, and trying to pursue a common cause- peace and of course with sincerity and with one voice, speak for the poor and the voiceless as well as the voiceless poor. This is why the Nigerian Bishops' Conference referred to themselves as 'Voice of Voiceless' due to their bold and non-partisan criticisms which they normally make public after their quarterly meetings. This is actually what all the major religions in Nigeria should be for the citizenry. This could be achieved when they help educate their members in such a way that the people being educated will find the seriousness with which they embark on such a project. They can as well try to undertake common projects where the members of those religions could come together to exchange ideas on their beliefs. As I mentioned the good works being done by NIREC, it must be regrettably pointed out that NIREC, as it is presently hierarchically constituted lacks the credit of being the best example of an association to fight for co-existence. It is a case of having two captains in a ship. NIREC has always maintained a Moslem Co-President in the person of the Sultan and a Christian Co-President in the person of who-ever is the President of Christian Association of Nigeria. It is either that the Nigerian Politics of Christian/Moslem dichotomy has crept in or that the members lack intrinsic trust of leaving the leadership in the hand of a section. It could also be a fight over supremacy. In this case, it might be an unaccept-able slap on the face for the Moslems to see the Sultan being under the authority of a Christian religious leader. The same could be said of a Christian leader being under a Moslem religious head. NIREC must clarify the reason for this double-pack Chairmanship.

Finally, peace or peaceful co-existence will continue to elude Nigeria:

(a) If all the religious leaders and the government (State or Federal) fail to lead by example which is the reason for their being elected. In reference to this task of the leaders, Pope Leo XIII declaraed in his well celebrated encyclical, *Rerum Novarum*: "State must not absorb the individual or the family...rulers should anxiously safeguard the community and all its parts...because both philosophy and the Gospel agree in laying down that the subject of the administration of the State should be not the advantage of the ruler, but the benefits of those over whom he rules"[680];

[680] Leo XIII, Rerum novarum, (RN), no. 28.

(b) If the government fails to fulfil its obligations by instituting justice and respect for every human being;
(c) If our politicians do not desist from the misappropriation of religious sentiments of the less informed and the unemployed for their political gains;
(d) If the citizenry are not able to control their greed and passion for materialism in which case some sell their consciences (even those who should know) and make themselves cheap articles for the roaring and ready-to-devour political leopards and lions.

Peace is possible in Nigeria if the above "IFS" are taken care of and will be achieved gradually and of course with dialogue as a tool for enlightenment. When this is done, Nigeria will honourably retain her pride of place as the giant of Africa – a title which is gradually passing her by. It is on this ground that I conclude this work with the assertion as given by the Council Fathers with the words in brackets being inserted by myself:

> Peace cannot be obtained on earth (in Nigeria) unless the welfare of man (Nigerians) is safeguarded and people (Nigerians) freely and trustingly share with one another the riches of their minds and their talents. A firm determination to respect the dignity of the other men (Nigerians) and other peoples (with their religions) along with the deliberate practice of fraternal love are absolutely necessary for the achievement of peace.[681]

[681] Gaudium et Spes, (GS), no. 78. (Brackets mine).

BIBLIOGRAPHY

Sacred Scriptures

The New Jerusalem Bible, Standard Edition, London, Darton, Longman & Todd Ltd, 1985.
The Glorious Qur'an, Text and Explanatory Translation by Muhammad M. Pickthall, Islamic Publications Bureau, Lagos, Abuja.

Conciliar Documents

Dignitatis Humanae, Declaration on Religious Liberty, December 7, 1965.
Gaudium et Spes, The Pastoral Constitution on the Church in the Modern World, December 7, 1965.
Nostra Aetate, The Declaration on the Relation of the Church to Non-Christian Religions, October 28, 1965.
Unitatis Redintegratio, Decree on Ecumenism, November 21, 1964.

Papal, Magisterial Documents and Publications

Benedikt XVI, Ansprache an die Botschafter muslimischer Länder und Vertreter von muslimischen Gemeinden in Italien, Saal der Schweizer, Castelgandolfo, September 25, 2006, copyright 2006 –Libreria Editrice Vaticana, cf. www.vatican.de

Benedict XVI, "Freedom, The Path to Peace" being the theme chosen for the 2011 World Day of Peace, cf. visnews_en@mlists.vatican.va, July 13, 2010.

John XXIII, Encyclical "*Pacem in terries*" of April 11, 1963, no. 31 in: O'Brien, J. D/Shannon, T. A. (eds.), Catholic Social Thought – The Documentary Heritage, Encyclical letter on establishing Universal Peace in Truth, Justice, Charity and Liberty, Maryknoll, NY, Orbis Books, 1992.

John XXIII, *Pacem in Terris*, Encyclical Letter Establishing Universal Peace in Truth, Justice, Charity, and Liberty, April 11, 1963 http://www.vatican.va

John Paul II, Encyclical "*Sollicitudo rei socialis*" of Dec. 30, 1987, no. 44, in: Walsh, M/Davies, B. (eds.), Proclaiming Justice and Peace – Papal Documents from Rerum Novarum through Centesimus Annus, Encyclical letter on Social Concern of
John Paul II, Twenty-Third Pub. Connecticut, 1991.

John Paul II, Address delivered during the 6th World Conference on Religion and Peace in Rome on November 3, 1994, in: *L'Osservatore Romano*, weekly English ed., 16 Nov.1994.

John Paul II, Address to the Diplomatic Corps (January13, 1990), in: *L'Osservatore Romano*, Weekly Edition in English, 29th Jan. 1990.

John Paul II, "Africa Exult in all your sons and daughters who have believed in Christ's resurrection"! Nr. 3 in: *Observatore Romano*, weekly Ed. in English, April, 13, 1994.

John Paul II, "Ecclesia in Africa" being Post-Synodal Apostolic Exhortation of the Holy Father to the Bishops, Priests and deacons, Men and Women Religious and all the Lay Faithful on the Church in Africa and its Evangelization Mission Towards the Year 2000.

John Paul II, "From a new heart, Peace is born", being Message for the Celebration of the World Day of Peace, Jan. 1, 1984, cf. http://www.vatican.va.

John Paul II, Homilies and Addresses in Nigeria: Address to Christian families, no.1, 1982.

Leo XIII, Encyclical "*Rerum novarum*" no. 28 of May 15, 1891, cf. Walsh, M/Davies, B. (eds.), Proclaiming Justice and Peace – Papal Documents from Rerum Novarum through Centesimus Annus, Encyclical letter on Social Concern of John Paul II, Twenty-Third Pub. Connecticut, 1991.

Gioia, F. (ed.), *Interreligious Dialogue, The Official Teaching of the Catholic Church from the Second Vatican Council to John Paul II* (1963-2005), Boston, Pauline Books & Media, 2006.

Episcopal Documents, Publications and Addresses

Arinze, F. A., *Church in Dialogue - Walking with other Believers*, San Francisco, Ignatius Press, 1990.

Arinze, F. A., Good will message to Muslims on the feast of Ramadan, in: *Meeting in Friendship*, 1967-2002, Roma, Vatican City, 2003.

Arinze, F. A., "Interreligious Dialogue and Evangelization" in: *Pro Dialogue*, Bulletin 127-128, 2008/1-2.

Arinze, F. A., "Interreligious dialogue: Problems, prospects and possibilities" being a Paper presented at the Celebration of 150th Anniversary of Nashville Diocese, USA on 19th March, 1987.

Arinze, F. A., "Pastoral Attention to African Traditional Religion" in: *Bulletin* XXIII/2:102-06, Rome, 1988.

Arinze, F. A., Sacrifice in Ibo Religion, Ibadan, University Press, 1970.

Arinze, F. A., "The Contribution of the Various Religions to the Building of Peace" in: *Secretariatus pro non Christianis,* Bulletin, Nr. 61-66, 1986-87.

Cardinal Tauran, J. L., "Religion carry a Message of Peace and Reconciliation" in: VIS 081113.

Ezeanya, S. N., "God, Spirits and the Spirit world" in: K.A. Dickson and P. Ellingworth (eds.), Biblical Revelation and African Beliefs, Maryknoll, NY, Orbis Books, 1969.

Ezeanya, S. N., The method of Adaptation in the Evangelisation of the Igbo-speaking People of Southern Nigeria, Rome, Pontifical Urbaniana University Press, 1956.

AECAWA, "Christianity and Islam in dialogue" being Communiqué, Resolutions and Recommendations after its Fourth plenary assembly, Lagos, October, 20-27, 1986.

Bagobiri, J. D., Opening Address for the 2002 Study session of IRDC-AECAWA in Accra-Ghana with the theme, "Religion, Violence and Peace in West Africa" in: *Notizen aus der Weltkirche*, by Missio Korrespondenz, Bibliothek/Doku MISSIO/MWI März 6. 2008.

AECAWA, "Inter-Religious Dialogue and Nation-Building in the 21st Century West Africa" Communiqué issued by AECAWA Inter-religious Dialogue Commission at the end of the 2000 Annual Study Session/Workshop held at the Pastoral Institute, Ibadan, Nigeria 3rd – 6th October, 2000.

AECAWA, "Offer Forgiveness and Receive Peace : A Challenge to Multi-religious Society" Communiqué issued at the end of its annual study/workshop held in Social Centre, Kaduna, 10th -14th Nov. 2003 and published in: Islamochristiana, Maurice Borrmans, (ed.), PONTIFICIO ISTITUTIO DI STUDI ARABI E D'ISLAMISTICA, Rome.

CBCN, "The Nation is in Jeopardy" in: *Catholic Life*, Easter Edition, 1987, Lagos, Toklast Enterprises.

CBCN, "The Bible: the Word of God for our Times" Communiqué issued at the end of its First Plenary Meeting at the Generalate of the Eucharistic Heart of Jesus Sisters, Ikeja-Lagos, March, 10th-14th, 1987.

CBCN, "The Jubilee and National Reconciliation" being Communiqué issued at the End of its First Plenary Meeting for the year 2000, held at St. Leo's Catholic Church, Ikeja, March 13th-18th, cf. also Leader Newspaper, Vol. XL II No. 6 on April 2, 2002.

CBCN, "Let us live and work together in peace and harmony" being Communiqué issued at the end of its Second Plenary Meeting at the Catholic Social Centre, Kaduna, September 11th-15th, 2000.

Catholic Secretariat, Statement by the Catholic Bishops' Conference of Nigeria, September 10th, 2001.

CBCN, "Hope for a Better Nigeria" Communiqué issued at The End of The Second Plenary Meeting at The Assumpta Pastoral Centre, Owerri, September 1st - 6th, 2003 titled 'Hope for a Better Nigeria'.

CBCN, "Mission to Serve" being Communiqué issued at the End of its Second Plenary Meeting held at Pope John Paul II Pastoral Centre, Makurdi, September 13th-17th, 2004.

CBCN, "The Church in Nigeria, Family of God on Mission" being a Pastoral Exhortation of the Catholic Bishops' Conference of Nigeria to the Clergy, Religious and Lay Faithful on the First National Congress, Enugu: CIDJAP, 2004. cf. also Ani, I., in: *Forum Mission*, Jahrbuch Band 1/2005.

CBCN, "The Church in Nigeria: Keeping Hope alive" being a Communiqué after its 1st Plenary Meeting held at Divine Love Retreat and Conference Centre, Abuja, March, 6th-11th, 2006.

CBCN, "To Restore all things in Christ" being Communiqué at the end of its First Plenary Meeting at Divine Love Retreat and Conference Centre, Abuja, February 11th-16th, 2008.

CBCN, Ibadan Ecclesiastical Province, A communiqué issued at the end of two day meeting at Pastoral Institute, Ibadan, January 18th to 19th 2010.

Ghana Bishops Conference: A Collection of Communiqués, Memoranda and Pastoral letters, compiled by the Department of Social Communications of the National Catholic Secretariat, Takoradi, St. Francis Press, 1999.

Ghana Bishops Conference: "Ghana Bishops speak" being a Pastoral Letter of the Catholic Bishops of Ghana for the Election Period 1996, Takoradi, St, Francis Press, 1999.

Kasper, W., "Wir werden Verachtung ernten" in: *Kirche heute*, Aufbruch der Kirche in eine neue Zeit, 12/2009, 16. Jahrgang.

Katechismus der Katholischen Kirche, Artikel 4, „Der sittliche Charakter der Menschlichen Handlung" Nr.1759, München, Oldenbourg Verlag, 1993.

Onaiyekan, J. (Introd.), „Christians and Muslims- Partners in Dialogue" in: *Stimmen der Weltkirche* Nr.38, VI. Deutsch-Afrikanisches Bischofstreffen in Akosombo, 11– 15. Oktober 2004.

Schineller, P. (ed.), *The Voice of the Voiceless:* Pastoral Letters and Communiques of the Catholic Bishops' Conference of Nigeria 1960-2002, Ibadan, Daily Graphics Nigeria Ltd, 2002.

Zollitsch, R., „Religionsfreiheit als Menschenrecht" Ansprache anlässlich einer Begegnung mit Erzbischof Ignatius Kaigama und Alhaji

Abdullahi Haruna Maikano, Emir von Wase, am September 3, 2009 in Jos, cf. *Missionswissenschaftliches Institut Missio e.V.*

Other Books

Kirkpatrick, E. M. (ed.), Chambers 20th Century Dictionary, Edingurg, W & R Chambers, 1983.

Abdu-Raheem, M. A., Islamic Concept of Tolerance and the Task Before the Nigerian Muslim in: Olupona, J. K., (ed.), *Religion and Peace in Multi-faith Nigeria*, Nigeria, Obafemi Awolowo University, 1992.

Abdul-Rauf, M., *Islam: Faith and Devotion*, Lagos, Islamic Publications Bureau, 1982.

Abdul, M. O., *Islam as a Religion*, Lagos, Islamic Publications Bureau, 1982.

Achebe, C., *Things Fall Apart*, London, Ibadan, Nairobi, Heinemann Educational Books, 1976.

Adegbola, E. A. A., Traditional Religion in West Africa, Ibadan, Daystar Press.

Awolalu, J. O, & Dopamu, P., *West African Traditional Religion*, Ibadan, Onibonoje Press & Books Industries, 1979.

Aylward, S., *African Christian Theology*, London, Geofrey Chapman, 1975.

Barreiro, A. J., *Basic Ecclesial communities: The Evangelisation of the Poor*, New York, 1992.

Boer, J. H., Christianity and Islam under Colonialism in Northern Nigeria, Abuja, Beacon Communications Ltd, 1988.

Bujo Be´ne´zet, *The Ethical Dimension of Community*, Nairobi, 1998.

Butzkamm, A., "Im Namen Alllahs, des Allbarmherzigen" Eine kleine Einführung in den Islam, Paderborn, Bonifatius GmbH Druck, 2002.

Carey, G., in 'Documentation: The Challenges Facing Christian-Muslim Dialogue' being a lecture given on October 4, at Al-Azhar University Egypt reported in: *Islam and Christian-Muslim Relations*, Vol.7, No. 1, 1996.

CBECS, *Ordo Misssae (The Order of Mass*), Nigeria, 1973.

Clarke, P. B., *West Africa and Christianity*, London, Edward Arnold, 1982.

Crowther, M., The story of Nigeria, London, Faber and Faber, 1978.

Dopamu, P. A., "Religious Tolerance & Peaceful Co-existence: The case of African Religion in Nigeria" in: James. G. (ed.), *Dialogue & Alliance*, A Journal of the International Religious Foundation, Inc, winter 1988-89, Vol. 2, No.4.

Dudley, B., *Instability and Political Order*, Ibadan, University Press, 1973.

Ekwunife, A. N. O., *Politics and Religious Intolerance, the Nigerian Experience*, Enugu, Spiritan Publications, 1992.

Elger, R. (Hg.), *Kleines Islam-Lexikon, Geschichte. Alltag . Kultur* Band 383, Deutschland, BPB.

Eneh, J. O., *The Sharia and Islamic philosophy: The Nigerian Experience*, Enugu, Snaap Press Ltd, 2001.

Federal Ministry of Information, "Proceedings of the Constituent Assembly" Official Report, Vol.1, Lagos, 1978

Gerl-Falkovitz, H. B., „Gottes Platz in der Seele ist zu einer Leerstelle geworden" in: Riße, G./Kathke, C. A. (Hg.), *Diaspora: Zeugnis von Christen für Christen*, 150 Jahre Bonifatiuswerk der deutschen Katholiken, Paderborn, Bonifatius Verlag, 1999.

Hastings, A., *The Church in Africa 1450-1950*, Oxford, Clarendon Press, 1994.

Hirshfield, C., The Diplomacy of Partition: Britain, France and the Creation of Nigeria, 1890-1898 (Studies in Contemporary History, vol. 2), The Hague, Martinus Nijhoff, 1979.

Idowu, E. B., African Traditional Religion: A Definition, London, SCM Press, 1973.

Idowu, E. B., Oludumare: God in Yoruba Belief, London, Longmans,1962, p. 54ff.

Ikenga-Metuh, E., African Religions in Western Conceptual Schemes, Ibadan, 1985.

Ikenga-Metuh, E., The Gods in Retreat, Continuity and Change in African Religions, Enugu, F. D. P, 1986.

International Theological Commission: *Memory and Reconciliation: The Church and the Faults of the Past*, Dec. 1999 and *Homily of John Paul II Mass for the Day of Pardon*, March, 12 2000, Boston, Pauline Books &Media, 2000. cf. Incarnationis Mysterium.

J. D., A History of the West Africa, London: Cambridge University Press, 1969.

Jomier, J., *How to Understand Islam*, London, Butler & Tanner Ltd., 1989.

Jordon, J., Bishop Shanahan of Southern Nigeria, Dublin, Clonmore & Reynolds, 1948.

Kenny, J., "Christian-Muslim Relations in Nigeria", in: *Islamochristiana*, Rome, 1986.

Khadduri, M., *War And Peace in the Law of Islam*, London, John Hopkins Press, 1952.

Kirkpatrick, E. M. (ed.), Chambers 20th Century Dictionary, Edingurg, W & R Chambers, 1983.

Kukah, M. H., "Christian-Muslim Relations in Sub-Saharan Africa: Problems and Prospects", in: *Islam and Christian-Muslim Relations*. Vol.18, No. 2, April 2007.

Kukah, M. H., *Religion, Politics and Power in Northern Nigeria*, Ibadan, Spectrum Books Ltd, 2003.

Makozi, A. O. & Ojo, G. J. A. (eds.), *The History of the Catholic Church in Nigeria*, Nigeria, Macmillan Nigeria, 1982.

Mbiti, J. S., *African Religions and Philosophy*, 2nd ed., London, Heinemann, 1990.

Mbukanma, J. O., *Preaching & Crisis of Faith*, Ibadan, Newborne Enterprises, Dec. 2001.

Muzrui, A. A., *The Africans: A Triple heritage*, Toronto, Little, Brown & Company, 1986.

Ndiokwere, N. I., *The African Church Today and Tomorrow: Prospects and Challenges*, Vol. 1, Onitsha, Effective Key Publishers Limited, 1994.

Nigeria: 1999 Constitution of the Federal Republic of Nigeria with Fundamental Rights (Enforcedment Procedure) Rules 2009.

Nwankwor, C., Unpublished tabulation of Nigeria Population by Dr. Nwankwor, C. of Nnamdi Azikiwe University and Catholic Institute for Development, Justice and Peace, Enugu based on 2006 Census.

Nwobi, S. O., *Sharia Law in Nigeria: What a Christian must know*, Nigeria, Totan Publishers Ltd., 2000.

Nwosu, V. A., *The Catholic Church in Onitsha, People, Places and Events*, EPL, Onitsha, 1985.

Nyamiti, C., Christ as our Ancestor, Gweru, 1984, p.107 in: Ezekwonna, F. C., *African Communitarian Ethic: The basis for the Moral Conscience and Autonomy of the Individual*, Bern, Peter Lang AG, 2005.

Obadiegwu, M., *The Catholic Church in Aguleri: A Centinary of Aguleri Parish* 1891-1991, Onitsha, Veritas Press, 1991.

Oborji, F. A., *In Dialogue with African Traditional Religion, Studies in Interreligious Dialogue* 10/1: pp.57-76, 2000.

Oborji, F. A., *Towards a Christian theology of African Religion, Issues of Interpretation and Mission*, Kenya, AMECEA Gaba Publications, 2005.

Okolo, B. C., *Towards Decolonizing the Church* (An African Liberation Theology), Onitsha, Tabansi Press Ltd, 1975.

Okolo, B. C., *To all Igbo Catholics- In their quest for understanding their Faith*, Obosi-Nigeria, Pacific College Press, 1985.

Olupona, J. K. (ed.), *Religion and Peace in Multi-Faith Nigeria*, Ibadan, Obafemi Awolowo University, 1992.

Onwubiko, K. B. C., *History of West Africa*, Bk.1, Nigeria, A.E.P. 1961.

Onwubiko, A. O., *The Church in Mission in the Light of Ecclesia in Africa*, Kenya, Pauline Publications Africa, 2001.

Opeloye, M. O., "The Socio-Political Factor in the Christian-Muslim Conflict in Nigeria" in: *Islam and Christian-Muslim Relations*, Vol. 9, No. 2, 1998.

Owhonda, J., *Nigeria: A Nation of Many Peoples*. New Jersey: Dillon Press, 1998.

Parrinder, E. G., *African Traditional Religion*, 3rd Ed. London, Sheldon Press, 1974.

Parrinder, E.G., *African Traditional Religion*, 3rd Ed. London, Sheldon Press, reprint, 1976.

P.C.I.D., with introd. by Isizoh, D. C., *Resources for Peace in Traditional Religions; Acts of The Colloquium*, Rome, January 12-15, 2005, Vatican City 2006.

P.C.I.D., *Meeting in Friendship, Message to Muslims for the End of Ramadan* 1967-2002, Rome, Vatican City, April, 2003.

Rahner, K., *Schriften zur Theologie (SzTh)* V, Einsiedeln/Zürich/Köln, 1962/1968.

Rashid, M., "Political Dynamism of Islam in Nigeria" in: *Islamic Studies,* February 26, 1987.

Riße, G., *Gott ist Christus, der Sohn der Maria' Eine Studie zum Christusbild im Koran*, Bonn, Verlag N. M. Borengässer, 1989.

Robinson, D., *Muslim Societies in African History*, UK, Cambridge University Press, 2004.

Schwachulla, W., (red.), *Der Brockhaus in einem Band*, Leipzig, F. A. Brockhaus, GmbH, 1998.

Stride, G. T. & Ifeka, C, *Peoples and Empires of West Africa 1000-1800*, London, Thomas Nelson Ltd., 1971.

Suleiman, K., "Judiciary Under the Draft Constitution" in: *Suleiman Kumo & Abubakar Aliyu (eds.): Issues in the Nigerian Draft Constitution*: Report of the Conference on Issues in the Draft Constitution , Zaria, A.B.U, 21-24 March, 1977.

Suleiman, K., *The Organisation and Procedure of Sharia Courts in Northern Nigeria*, London, SOAS, 1972.

Sundkler, B. & Steed, C. (ed.), *A History of the Church in Africa*, Cambridge, Cambridge University Press, 2000.

Tasie, G. O. M., "Christian Awakening in West Africa, 1914-18, A Study in the Significance of Native Agency" in Kalu, O. U., *The History of Christianity in West Africa*, London, Longman, 19980.

Thomas, D., "The Past and the Future in Christian-Muslim Relations" in: Thomas, D. (ed. et al.), *Islam and Christian-Muslim Relations*, Birmingham, CSIC Vol.18, No.1, 33-42, January 2007.

Tonsor, S., "Religion in Contemporary Politics" in: Howard, J. A. (ed.), *Belief, Faith and Reason*, Belfast, Christian Journals Ltd., 1991.

Troll, C. W., *Muslims Ask, Christians Answer*, India, Anand Press, 2005.

Uchendu, V. C., *The Igbo of South-East Nigeria*, NY, London, Holt, Rinehardt and Winston, 1965.

Vellguth, K. (Hsg.), *Missionarisch Kirchen sein, Erfahrungen und Visionen*. Freiburg, Herder, 2002.

Welch, A. T., „Islam" in: Hinnels, J. R., (ed.). *A Handbook of living Religions*, New York, Penguin Books, 1991reprint; Ist published in 1984; cf. also http://www.Adherents.com: Religions by location.

Wells, R, E., *An Introduction to the Music of the Basotho*, Morija, 1994.

Yusuf, H. B., "Managing Muslim–Christian Conflicts in Northern Nigeria: A Case Study of Kaduna State", in: *Islam and Christian – Muslim Relations*, Vol. 18. No.2, April 2007, USA, Taylor & Francis Group.

Zebiri, K., "Muslim Anti-Secularist Discourse in the Context of Muslim-Christian Relations" in: Esposito, J. L., et al. (eds.), *Islam and Christian-Muslim Relations*, Vol. 9, No.1, USA, Taylor & Francis Ltd, 1998.

Articles: Magazines and Newspapers

Abashiya, C., "Sharia Debate" in: *New Nigerian*, March 27, 1977.

Abubakar, M. S., "Sustaining Peace, Security Religious Harmony Through Partnership"; An Address presented to African Union at the Ist African Union Inter-Faith Dialogue Forum' held in Abuja from 15-17June, 2010.

Adinuba, D., "Reaction to Sharia Case" in: *Guardian Newspaper*, March 27, 2000.

Al-Hajj, C.F.M.A., "A Seventeenth Century Chronicle on the Origins and Missionary Activities of the Wangarawa", in: *Kano Chronicles*, 1:4 (1968).

Anaba, I., Akoni, O. et.al, "Police uncover Boko Haram arms depot in Bauchi" in: *Vangurd newspaper*, August 3, 2009.

Ande, E., "Provost suspends students over cross necklace" in: *Guardian Newspaper*, October 23, 2008.

Asemota, A., "35 Islamist militants nabbed in Katsina... 2 found dead" in: *Daily Sun*, July 31, 2009.

Awolalu, J, O., "Sin and its removal in African Traditional Religion," in: *Journal of the American Academy of Religion*, 44/2 (1976).
Ayandele, E. A., "The Collapse of 'Pagandom' in Igboland" in: *Journal of Historical Society of Nigeria,* (Vol. II, No. 1, Dec. 1973).
Ayyuba, Z. T., "OIC Debate" in: *Sunday Sketch,* Feb, 1986.
Beier, U., "The Egungun Cult" in: *Nigeria Magazine*, No. 51, 1956.
Beschluss des Bundestages vom 2.März 19887, bekräftigt am 20 Juni 1988, vgl. Drucksache 1989 11/6137.
Beyerhaus, P. J. und Beck, H., „Friedliches Miteinander von Christen und Muslimen?" in: *Kirche heute*, Monatszeitschrift für die katholische Kirche im deutschen Sprachraum, 16 Jahrgang, 1/2009.
Duniya, F., "The Challenges of Religious Intolerance in the Third Republic" in: *The Nigerian Journal of Theology*, No.1. (June 1993).
Duniya, F., "The Zango Kataf Crisis In Retrospect of Minority Culture in Northern Nigeria" Bulletin of Ecumenical Theology, Violence and State Security, 7: 1-2, 1995.
Duruji, A. C., "Ofo Na Ogu In Igbo Traditional Religion: The Meeting Point Of Christianity And Igbo Ancestral Religion" in: '*Religion in a World of Change: African Ancestral Religion, Islam and Christianity*' Okere, T. I. (ed.), on the occasion of an 'International Symposium, Owerri, 8th-12th Oct. 2002.
Ebuziem, C. E., "Religious Tension in Nigeria Today: A Call for Depolarization" in: *Nigeria World*, January 2, 2008.
Ehusani, G., "Case Study of Nigeria" in: *Human Rights, Opportunities for Christian-Islamic Co-operation in upholding human rights and establishing civil societies*- Conference in closed session 11/3/2002 – 14/3/2002, Berlin.
Ekpunobi, C., "Religious violence looms in Kano, As non-Muslims petition Yar'Adua over Hisbah" in: *Daily Champion*, June 29, 2009.
Elger, R., „Islam" in: Eicher, P. (Hg.), *Neues Handbuch Theologischer Grundbegriffe*, Band 2, München, Kösel-Verlag, 2005.
Enwerem, M. I., A Dangerous Awakening, The Politicization of Religion in Nigeria. First published in *IFRA/Institut Francais de Recherche en Afrique/French Institute for Research in Africa*, Nigeria, University of Ibadan, 1995.
Eyoboka, S. et. al., "Sallah: Jonathan, Mark, others tasks Muslims on peace" in: *Vanguard News paper*, November 16, 2010.
Fafunwa, A. B., 'Educational Backwardness of the North: A colonial Phenomenon' in: *New Nigerian*, July 4, 1974.

Greene, S. E., "Religion, History and the Supreme Gods of Africa: A Contribution to the Debate" in: *Journal of Religion in Africa* XXVI/2: 1996.

Gregory, M., „Nigeria braucht die Zusammenarbeit seiner Religionen und Völker" in: *Die Tagespost*, Jan. 9, 2010.

Human Rights Group, "The Report of the Findings of the Human Rights Group on the implications of Sharia law for non-Muslims in Zamfara State" in *Guardian Newspape*r, Wed., March 27, 2000

Idowu, F. J., "Religious Conflicts in Nigeria" in: *Current Dialogue*, Aachen, MWI, Band 23, Nov.30 1992.

Ikenga-Metu, E., "Two Decades of Religious Conflicts in Nigeria: A Recipe for Peace" in: *Bulletin of Ecumenical Theology, on Power, Authority, and Leadership: Africa and Christian*. 6/1: (1994).

Isizoh, D. C., "Forty Years of Dialogue with Religions in Sub-Sahara Africa and with Traditional Religions in the World" (A Report), in: *Pro Dialogo, Plenary Assembly 14-19 May 2004*, Pontificum Consilium Pro Dialogo Inter Religiones, Bulletin 116-117 2004/2-3.

Jama'atu Nasril Islam, "Constitution Amendment: Northern elders warn Lawmakers" being Communique after their meeting in Kaduna, June 18th 2009.

Kaigama, I., "Death Toll in Jos Rises to 350" as reported by Okocha, C. et. al., in: *Thisday Newspaper*, November 30, 2008.

Kappel, J., „Der Emir und der Erzbischof" in: *Kirche+Leben*, Oktober 18, 2009.

Khoury, T. A., „Wahrheit und Dialog" in: *Kirche heute*, 17Jahrgang, 4/2010, Aufbruch der Kirche in eine neue Zeit.

Kilete, M., "Military in Control" in: *Daily Sun*, July 31, 2009.

Kößmeier, N., „Leben auf dem Pulverfass" in: *Herder Korrespondenz 63*, 11/2009.

Kukah, M. H., Boko Haram: "Some reflections on causes and effects", in: Dr. Otmar Oehring (ed.), *Human Rights,* Aachen, Pontifical Mission Society, Human rights office, 2009.

Laleye, D., "Sharia: VC bans hugging of female students" in: *Tribune Newspaper* October 27, 2010

Lawanti, K., "Boko Haram and the Culpability of the Northern Elite" in: *Daily Trust*, August 3.

Mbiti, J. S., "Peace and Reconciliation in African Religion and Christianity" in: *Dialogue & Alliance*, Vol. 7, No.1, Spring/Summer 1993.

Mbon, F. M., "Possibilities For Peace in a Multi-Faith World" in: *Dialogue &Alliance*, A Journal of the International Religious Foundation, Spring/Summer 1993, Vol.7- No.1.

Miles, W., "Muslim Ethno-politics and Presidential Elections in Nigeria" in: *Journal of Muslim Minority Affairs*, Vol. 20, No. 2, 2000.
NIREC, Communiqué after its 1st Quarter 2008 Meeting at Protea Hotel, Enugu from February 17th-20th, 2008.
NIREC, Communiqué after its 1st Quarter Meeting held at Murtala Mohammed Library, Kano City, November 13th 2008.
NIREC, Communiqué after its 1st Quarter Meeting held at the Conference Hall Station Hotel, Jos, Plateau State, May18th -20th 2009.
NIREC, Communiqué after its 3rd quarter general meeting in Port Harcourt, Rivers State, South-South zone on 16th – 18th August, 2009.
Nyiam, T., "Sharia Problem" in: *Sunday Punch*, March 1, 2000.
Nzeki, R. S., Contribution to the discussion on "Peace in Africa" in: *Welt Kirche*, Nr.3/1990), Published by common service of Adveniat, Misereor and Missio (AMM), Munich, 1990.
Obemeata, J., "OIC Debate" in: *Independent news paper*, February 23, 1986.
Okeke, V., "In what areas has the dialogue across religions been successful in that it has not engendered the kind of tolerance that would douse inter-religious conflicts?" Interview granted in *The Guardian Newspaper*, Sunday, June 21, 2009.
Ola, T., Revealed! "How they killed our Father "– Mohammed Yusuf's family in: *Saturday Sun*, August 8, 2009.
Olanrewaju, T., "Islamist militant leader, Mohammed Yusuf, flees" in: Daily Sun newspaper, Friday, July 3, 2009.
Onaiyekan, J., "Expressing his opinion concerning the Sharia Problem" in: *The Punch*, March 8, 2000.
Onaiyekan, J., "The Shari'a in Nigeria: Issues and Perspectives" (Paper delivered at the National Seminar on Shari'a, organized by the Jama'atu Nasril Islam, Kaduna, February 12, 2000.
Onotu, J. J., "Muslim Master Plan and Method" (Anim. Seminar Paper, published by Anim. Diocesan Priests Asso.), 1988.
Oritsejafor, A., "Bauchi crisis: Stem religious violence or"...Oritsejafor warns "FG, Slams Senator Yerima" reported by Osewele, B., in: *Daily Sun Newspaper*, March 2, 2009.
Owolalu, J. O., "Religion and social Justice" being A paper read at the Religious Studies Conference, Ibadan University, February 3, 1981.
Report of the Civil Liberties Organisation, in: *Guardian Newspaper*, Thursday, March 2, 2000.
Rimmel, T. M et.al (Hg.), „Papst zum Religionsunterricht“ in: *Kirche heute* 10 /2010, Monatszeitschrift für die katholische Kirche im deutschen Sprachraum, 17. Jahrgang Oktober 2010.

Riße, G., „Anwalt in der Begegnung der Religionen- Dokumente und Äußerungen der katholischen Kirche“ in: Hauptabteilung Schule/Hochschule des Erzbischöflichen Generalvikariates Köln (Hg.), *Das Eigene stärken – Das Andere verstehen.* Dokumentation der Pädagogischen Woche 2007, Köln 2008.

Riße, G., „Christen und Muslime, Baustelle Europa erschließen und gestalten“ in: Delgado, M. u. Waldenfels, H. (Hg.), *Evangelium und Kultur, Begegnungen und Brüche,* Festschrift für Michael Sievernich SJ, Fribourg, Academic Press, 2010.

Riße, G., „Der Islam – Religion der Gewalt oder Religion des Friedens?“ in: *Lebendiges Zeugnis*, 58. Jahrgang, Heft 1, Paderborn, Bonifatius GmbH, März 2003.

Riße, G., „In ihrer Niederschrift ist Führung und Barmherzigkeit“ (Sure 7, 154)- Spurensuche: Die „Zehn Gebote“ Gottes im Koran.

Riße, G., „Islamisch-christlicher Dialog, Aus christlicher Sicht“ in: Eicher, P. (Hg.), *Neues Handbuch Theologischer Grundbegriffe*, Band 2, München, Kösel-Verlag, 2005,243-250.

Riße, G., „Maria- Grenzgängerin im Gottes-Glauben von Christen und Muslimen“ in: George, A/Krämer, K. (Hg.), *Gott denken und bezeugen,* Festschrift für Kardinal Walter Kasper zum 75. Geburtstag, Freiburg, Verlag Herder, 2008.

Riße, G., „Wegweisung: Muslime in Deutschland“ – Dokumente der Deutschen Bischofskonferenz zur Begegnung, in: *Zeitschrift für Missionswissenschaft und Religionswissenschaft,* (ZMR) Heft 3-4, 91 Jahrgang 2007, EOS Verlag.

Shani, M. B., “Sharia Debate” in: *New Nigerian*, September 15, 1977.

Shiklam, J., Sharia: Northern Christians slam Kano government in: *Daily Champions Newspapers*, Tuesd, August 07, 2007.

Sem Onwu, N., “Religion and National Unity in Nigeria: Problems and Prospects” The Nigerian Journal of Social Studies, Vol. III, Oct.1986, Cf. also an article on ‘Shari’a’ organized by the Jama’atu Nasril Islam, Kaduna on 12 Feb, 2000.

Soyinka, W., as reported by Akinrefon, D & Kumolu, C., “Religion threatens Nigeria’s nationhood” in: *Vanquard Newspaper*, March 4, 2009.

Ubaka, C. O., Sharia in Nigeria: Its Implications for Non-Muslims, (a paper presented at the 29th Convocation Ceremony of Bigard Memorial Seminary Enugu on the 10th of March 2000).

Udobata R. O., “Encounter of Christianity with African Religiosity: A Critical Review of Evidence from Eastern Nigeria” in: *Journal of Religion*

and Theology, Vol. 1, No.1, Owerri- Nigeria, Omega Communications, 1993.
U.S Missions in Nigeria, "Religious Violence in Nigeria" cf. *International Religious Freedom Report* 2004'
Vatican Information Service (VIS), „Gipfel der Religionen, Schluss Erlärung" July 5, 2006.
Vellguth, K., „Wenn Religion als Vorwand dient, Unruhen in Nigeria haben vielfältige Ursachen" in: *Heilung und Heil*, 3/2009.
Vellguth, K., „Armut und Religionskonflikt in Nigeria" in: *Stimmen der Zeit*, Heft 10, Oktober 2009.
Yuzon, L, A., "Mission in the Context of Endemic Poverty": Papers of a Consultation on Mission in the Context of Poverty and in Situations of Affluence, Singapore, 1983
Zikirullhi, M., "Reaction against Sharia Imposition" in: *Guardian Newspaper*, September 12, 2000.

Internet

Abdul, M. G., "Re-Shiites Sunnis Clash Again in Sokoto...3killed"cf. www.islamicmovement.org.
Adinoyi, S., "Nigeria: Jos- House Burnings Escalate" January 10, 2011 cf. http/www.thisdaylive.com
AFP, "Nigeria: Scores injured in Sunni-Shia violence" cf. http://www.joomla.org
Ajah, M., why Nigerians must resist religious sentiments, cf. www.thenigerianvoice.ngr.com
Aymer, E., "Nigeria: Clash of Religions 1996" cf. hppt://www.yale.ed/inforum/nigeria
Free Encyclopedia Wikipedia, "Roman Catholicism in Nigeria" cf. htpp://en.wikipedia.org/wiki
Free Encyclopedia Wikipedia, "Shi'a – Sunni relations" cf. http//en.wikipedia.org/wiki
Gambrell, J., "Shoot-to-kill orders issued in Nigeria after riot" January 18, 2011 cf. http/www.wtop.com
Jones, G. W., Karin, S.M., "Islam, the State and Population" cf. http://book.google.de)
Khaleefah, R., Interview granted daily Independent News Paper on "what roles the Muslims have played in Nigerian society as the country approaches 50th Independent Anniversary" cf. www.dailyindependent.ngr.com

Muhammad, S. U., "Peace in Nigeria is dependent on Christians stopping their bias against Islam" cf. www.weekend-sundaycompass.ngr.com
NIREC, 'HISTORY OF NIREC' cf. http://nirecng.org/history.html
Onwuamanam, J., "Sultan, Onaiyekan call for law against religious incitement" Jos, March 5, 2009 cf. www.punchontheweb.com
Ozoemena, J., "Sultan Preaches religious Tolerance" May 17, 2010, cf. www.nigeriancompass.ng
Pike, J., "Nigeria Christian / Muslim Conflict" cf. http://www.göobalsecurity.org
Ratzinger, J., "The Purification of Memory" as compiled by the Secretary of UNITAS, cf. http://www.churchinhistory.org/purifying-memory
"RoP Burns Govt't Building in Nigeria" cf. http://rcm-images.amazon.com. (source: IRIN) June 6, 2005.
"Roman Catholicism in Nigeria:" cf. http://en.wikipedia.org/wiki/Roman_Catholicism_in_Nigeria
Umar, F. & Shirbon, E., "African Crises" http://www.reuters.com/article/africaCrisis

ABBREVIATIONS

A.B.U:	Ahmadu Bello University
AECAWA:	Association of Episcopal Conferences of Anglophone West
Afrel:	African Religion
AMM:	Adveniat, Misereor and Missio
Anim:	Anambra and Imo
ATR:	African Traditional Religion.
CA:	Constituent Assembly
CAN:	Christian Association of Nigeria
CBCN:	Catholic Bishops' Conference of Nigeria
CBECS:	Catholic Bishops of East Central States of Nigeria
CC:	Constitutional Conference.
CDC:	Constitution Drafting Committee
CPC:	Congress for Progressive Change
CYD:	Community and Youth Development
DDI:	Director Defence of Information
DH:	Dignitatis Humanae
DHQ:	Defence Head Quarters
GS:	Gaudium et Spes
ICSA:	Interim Common Service Agency
IRDC:	Inter-Religious Dialogue Commission
JNI:	Jamaata Nasril Islam
LG:	Lumen Gentium
MWI:	Missionswissenschaftliches Institut
NA:	Nostra Aetate
NASR:	Nigerian Association for the Study of Religions
NCA:	Northern Christian Association
NIREC:	Nigeria Interreligious Council
NOSCEF:	Northern States Christian Elders Forum
OIC:	Organization of the Islamic Conference
PCID:	Pontifical Council For Interreligious Dialogue
PMS:	Pontifical Mission Society
RoP:	Religion of Peace
SCIA:	Supreme Council for Islamic Affairs
SzTh:	Schriften zur Theologie
UR:	Unitatis Redintegratio
VIS:	Vatican Information Service
ZMR:	Zeitschrift für Missionswissenschaft und Religionswissenschaft

EOS-VERLAG ▪ THEOLOGISCHE REIHE

Band 90
Markus Höbel
Was kommt nach dem Drinnen?
Gefangenenseelsorge und Strafvollzug
zwischen Restriktion und Resozialisierung
220 Seiten, € 28,00, ISBN 978-3-8306-7367-5

Band 91
Shaoxian Jia
Konfuzianische Christologie
Das Jesusbild in der Zeitschrift
Zhenli yu shengming (Wahrheit und Leben)
468 Seiten, € 29,80, ISBN 978-3-8306-7440-5

Band 92
Markus Schrom
Die Kirche als Gebetsgemeinschaft
Überlegungen zum Verhältnis von Kirche und Gebet in der Liturgie
auf dem Hintergrund der Texte des Zweiten Vatikanischen Konzils
402 Seiten, € 29,80, ISBN 978-3-8306-7452-8

Band 93
Edith Olk
Die Barmherzigkeit Gottes als zentrale Quelle des christlichen Lebens
Eine theologische Würdigung der Lehre von Papst Johannes Paul II.
468 Seiten, € 34,95, ISBN 978-3-8306-7476-4

Band 94
Hyacinth Nwankwor
Religious Freedom, the Bed-rock of National Unity in Nigeria
286 Seiten, € 24,95, ISBN 978-3-8306-7514-3

EOS Verlag Sankt Ottilien
www.eos-verlag.de | mail@eos-verlag.de